D1539799

THE UNITED STATES CONGRESS

THE UNITED STATES CONGRESS

Edited by Dennis Hale

Transaction Books
New Brunswick (U.S.A.) and London (U.K.)

Transaction Edition 1983.
© 1982 by the Trustees of Boston College
Chestnut Hill, Massachusetts.

Library of Congress Catalog Number: 83-7992
ISBN: 0-87855-939-6 (paper)
Printed in the United States of America
Library of Congress Cataloging in Publication Data

Thomas P. O'Neill, Jr., Symposium on the U.S. Congress
   (1981 : Boston College)
   The United States Congress.

  Reprint. Originally published: Chestnut Hill,
Mass. : Boston College, c1982.
   Includes bibliographical references.
   1. United States. Congress—Congresses.   I. Hale,
Dennis.   II. Boston College.   III. Title.
JK1041.T48 1981   328.73   83-7992
ISBN 0-87855-939-6 (pbk.)

PREFACE

Boston College, in 1981, established the Thomas P. O'Neill, Jr., Chair in American Politics in honor of the Speaker of the United States House of Representatives, an alumnus of the university. The first holder of the O'Neill Chair was Prof. Samuel Beer, who joined the Department of Political Science in January 1982.

Prior to appointing the first O'Neill Chair, the university's political science department organized a symposium on the United States Congress as a way of marking the creation of this endowment. The Symposium was held in January 1981, and this volume is a substantial reproduction of the papers and responses delivered at that time.

Speaker O'Neill graduated from Boston College in 1936 and received an honorary doctor of laws degree from the university in 1973. In 1936, he was elected to the Massachusetts House, where he served until 1952. Named speaker of that body at the age of 36, he was the youngest ever to hold that position.

He was first elected to the Congress in 1952 and has ever since represented the Eighth Massachusetts District, which includes Cambridge, the city of his birth. He became Speaker in 1977.

The citation accompanying his Boston College honorary degree refers to him as a man who "knows no South, no East or West, no North, and is a lasting hurrah whose patriotism is the tranquil and steady dedication of a lifetime." The Speaker's commitment to education is illustrated by advice he once gave to a group of Boston College students: "In all your endeavors, use not only your minds, which have been educated for inquiry and thought, but also your hearts, which have been trained for compassion and understanding. These are the resources of intellect and sensitivity that your education has developed in you."

This Symposium volume is offered in that spirit of rigorous examination and humanistic concern, which characterizes both the Speaker's career and the purpose of the Chair established in his honor.

ACKNOWLEDGMENTS

Many hands made this book possible. First, there were those who organized the O'Neill symposium, without which there would have been nothing for me to edit and proofread. Acknowledgment must go immediately to my colleagues in the Department of Political Science, and especially to the committee which planned the event: David Manwaring, Department Chairman; Robert Scigliano; Gary Brazier; Kay Schlozman; and Marc Landy.

We came up with the ideas; those ideas would not have gotten very far were it not for the expert planning of the Office of Development Programs and Events, and in particular the very able work of its then director, Mary Lou Duddy. University President, Father J. Donald Monan, S.J., lent us the resources of his office whenever called upon. University Vice President Margaret Dwyer was especially helpful in smoothing the way toward the eventual publication of this volume. Extraordinary assistance was given me in that task by the Word Processing Office (Fred Mills, Director), and especially by Joanne Brennan, Lisa Fegley-Schmidt, and Cheryl Simcoe. I want to thank them for their diligence and their patience.

Finally, I am grateful to the participants at the symposium, who responded to my editorial suggestions and did their level best to meet my manuscript deadlines.

NOTES ON CONTRIBUTORS

Professor Joel D. Aberbach of Michigan graduated from Cornell and received graduate degrees from Harvard, Ohio State, and Yale. His *Politicians and Bureaucrats* will be published by Harvard. He has been a guest scholar at the Brookings Institution.

Professor Herbert B. Asher of Ohio State is the author of *Presidential Elections in American Politics* and co-editor of the *American Journal of Political Science*. His degrees came from Bucknell and Michigan.

Professor Joseph M. Bessette of Catholic University is an alumnus of Boston College, where he held a University Presidential Scholarship, and Chicago. He is the author of *The Presidency in the Consititutional Order*.

The Honorable Edward P. Boland has represented the Second Massachusetts District in Congress since 1952. A contemporary of Speaker O'Neill at Boston College, he has received an honorary degree from the university.

The Honorable John Brademas, a Phi Beta Kappa graduate of Harvard and a Rhodes Scholar, represented the Third Indiana District from 1958 to 1980. He is an honorary Fellow of Oxford, where he received his doctorate, and a member of the American Academy of Arts and Sciences. In 1981 he was appointed president of New York University.

Professor David W. Brady of Rice is the current chairman of the Standing Committee on Congressional Election Research at the Center for Political Studies at Michigan. His writing has focused on Congress and public policy.

Dr. Joan Claybrook worked for Ralph Nader's Public Interest Research Group and Congress Watch, a citizen-interest group, before she was named by President Carter to head the National Highway Traffic Safety Administration, a post which she held until 1981.

Richard P. Conlon, prior to becoming director of the Democratic Study Group, was a newspaper reporter, press secretary to then Sen. Walter Mondale, and a Fellow at Harvard's John F. Kennedy Institute of Politics.

The Honorable Silvio O. Conte, a Boston College Law School graduate, has been elected twelve times to represent the First Massachusetts District, which includes his native Pittsfield. The university has awarded him an honorary degree.

Elizabeth Drew, a Phi Beta Kappa graduate of Wellesley College, is a regular contributor to the *New Yorker* and publishes frequently in the *Atlantic* and the *New York Times Magazine.* Since 1973, she has been a commentator for Post-Newsweek television stations. She is the author of *Washington Journal: The Events of 1973-74, American Journal: The Events of 1976,* and *Senator.*

The Honorable Robert F. Drinan, S.J., a graduate of Boston College and former dean of its Law School, was the United States Representative from the Fourth Massachusetts District for five consecutive terms. He served as chairman of the House Judiciary Committee. He is currently a member of the faculty of Georgetown University Law School.

Professor Richard F. Fenno, Jr., of Rochester graduated Phi Beta Kappa from Amherst and received his doctorate at Harvard. Among his books are *The President's Cabinet, Federal Aid to Education and National Politics,* and *Home Style: House Members in Their Districts,* the last winning a Woodrow Wilson Foundation Award. He is a member of the American Academy of Arts and Sciences.

Professor Morris P. Fiorina of the California Institute of Technology is the author of *Congress: Keystone of the Washington Establishment.* A Phi Beta Kappa graduate of Allegheny College, he received his doctorate at Rochester. He has been a Herbert H. Lehman Fellow.

The Honorable Robert N. Giaimo represented the Third Connecticut District in Congress from 1958 until his retirement in 1980. He was chairman of the House Committee on the Budget and a member of the Select Committee on Congressional Operations.

Professor Dennis Hale of Boston College is the editor of this symposium volume. He is a graduate of Oberlin College and received his doctorate at the City University of New York. He is currently researching a book on Proposition 2½.

Kenneth W. Hunter is responsible at the General Accounting Office for improvements in program and policy reporting to Congress and in that legislature's acquisition and use of information. He is a lecturer at George Washington University.

Professor Dennis S. Ippolito, chairman of the political science department at Emory, wrote *The Congressional Spending Power* and *The Budget and National Politics*. A graduate of Adelphi, he received his doctorate at Virginia.

Professor Gary C. Jacobson of California graduated from Stanford and received his doctorate at Yale. *Money in Congressional Elections, American Parties in Decline,* and *Congressional Elections* are among his published works.

Professor Arthur Maass of Harvard, a former Guggenheim and Fulbright Fellow, graduated from Johns Hopkins and received his doctorate at Harvard. His publications include *Muddy Waters: The Army Engineers and the Nation's Rivers, Design of Water-Resource Systems,* and *The Desert Shall Rejoice.*

Dr. Michael Malbin has been conducting research on congressional matters at the American Enterprise Institute for Public Policy Research, where he is a Resident Scholar, since 1977. His books include *Parties, Interest Groups and Campaign Finance Laws.* He has taught at Catholic University.

Martin F. Nolan, a Boston College alumnus, was a member of a *Boston Globe* reporting team that won a Pulitzer Gold Medal. A former Duke and Harvard Fellow, he was *Globe* Washington bureau chief for eleven years until he became editorial page editor in 1981.

Professor Leroy N. Rieselbach of Indiana, a Harvard alumnus, received his advanced degrees at Yale. He wrote *Congressional Politics, Congressional Reform in the Seventies,* and *The Roots of Isolationism,* and is a member of the editorial board of *Policy Studies Journal.*

Dr. Alice M. Rivlin is the first director of the Congressional Budget Office. A former Senior Fellow at the Brookings Institution, she has served as assistant secretary of HEW. She is the author of *Systematic Thinking For Social Action*.

Steven V. Roberts, a Harvard graduate, was the *New York Times* bureau chief in Los Angeles and Athens, before joining the *Times* Washington bureau in 1977. He covered the 1980 presidential campaign. His book, *Eureka*, is about California.

Professor Francis E. Rourke of Johns Hopkins previously taught at Yale and California. He is the author of *Secrecy and Publicity*, *Dilemmas of Democracy* and *Bureaucracy and Foreign Policy*. He is a member of the editorial board of *Administration and Society*.

Professor Robert Scigliano, an alumnus of UCLA who earned his doctorate at Chicago, is coauthor of *Technical Assistance in Vietnam* and author of *The Courts*. He taught at Michigan State and the State University of New York before joining the Boston College faculty.

Professor Carole J. Uhlaner, of the University of California (Irvine), received graduate degrees from Stanford and Harvard, and an undergraduate degree from Radcliffe. Her research and publications focus on comparative political behavior, models of collective decision making, and Canadian politics.

The Honorable Charles A. Vanik, first elected to Congress in 1954 from the Twenty-First Ohio District, represented the Twenty-Second District from 1968 until his retirement in 1980. He was the chairman of the House Ways and Means Committee, and a member of the House Subcommittee on Trade and the Ways and Means Subcommittee on Health. He is a graduate of Adelbert College and the Western Reserve School of Law.

Dr. Paul Weaver taught at Harvard prior to joining *Fortune* in 1974. He has also served as economic communications planning director at Ford Motor Company, and is co-author of *The Americans: 1976*. A Cornell graduate, he received his doctorate at Harvard.

Dr. Thomas R. Wolanin is a graduate of Oberlin and received advanced degrees at Harvard. He currently holds a Spencer Fellowship from the National Academy of Education. His books include *Presidential Advisory Commissions: Truman to Nixon*. Since 1981 he has been executive assistant to the president of New York University.

Professor Peter Woll of Brandeis is an alumnus of Haverford and Cornell, where he received his doctorate. He is a consultant to the U. S. Civil Service Commission, Bureau of Training, and co-author of *America's Political Systems: Urban, State and Local*.

CONTENTS

Part IV: Budget and Fiscal Policy

Part V: Reforming Congressional Procedures

Part VI: Congress and Foreign Policy

Part VII: Congress and the Agencies

Part VIII: Financing Congressional Elections

Part IX: Second Plenary Session

INTRODUCTION

I.

It is a remarkable and curious fact that in a century which has seen such abundant political change, one important political fact has scarcely changed at all: our dissatisfaction with the U. S. Congress. In 1885, Woodrow Wilson published *Congressional Government*, the first of a long list of academic and popular works which indict the Congress for everything from dishonesty to incompetence. It will be useful to recall here some of the things Wilson said in that book, because they put what is said in *this* book into historical perspective, and raise some interesting questions about the legislative process and our attitudes toward it.

One thing, of course, *has* changed. We can no longer say, as Wilson did, that American government is congressional government. The president is now the center of the constitutional order, a development Wilson earnestly hoped for but did not feel bold enough to predict in 1885. *Congressional Government* was written against a backdrop of weak presidents: Johnson, Grant, and Hayes. (Wilson's record of presidents does not extend as far back as Lincoln.) The election of Grover Cleveland in 1884 must have suggested to Wilson the idiosyncratic nature of the presidency, whose powers could ebb and flow with the personality of the incumbent, but *Congressional Government* emphasizes the institutional weakness of the office. The customary two-term limit; the dependence of cabinet secretaries on the Standing Committees; the shortage of presidential candidates with real administrative experience; and above all the insignificance of parties—all of these conspired to make the presidency incapable of providing the nation with the leadership it desperately needed. (Wilson's first ambition was to become a United States Senator from Virginia.)

To an extent, therefore, American government was congressional government by default. Power flowed to Washington in ever increasing amounts after the Civil War; once there, it had nowhere to go but through the channels dug by the Standing Committees. What was the result?

Immediately we hear a familiar refrain: congressional government is bad government. And this is so only partly because of the caliber of men elected to Congress. It is mostly the *structure* of the institution and the general conditions of American public life that cause the Congress to govern badly.

That structure, and those conditions, render the Congress incapable of concerted action and strong leadership.

The House of Representatives is especially chaotic: ". . . its complicated forms and diversified structure confuse the vision, and conceal the system which underlies its composition."[1] The public is especially mystified by the Congress, but no more so than the new member, who must serve a long and humiliating apprenticeship before he can even understand what is going on around him. True power in Congress waits even longer.

When the public looks at Congress, it sees a swarm of activity, but no order. Order there is, to be sure, hidden within the maze of rules and customs which deliver power to the chairmen of the Standing Committees. But the public does not see these men. They do their work in the relative obscurity of the committee chamber, behind closed doors. The one leader the public does see, the Speaker of the House, is too constrained by his need for collegial support from the committee chairmen to be a true leader. His is not a "formative and imperative power in legislation. . . ." He "sits too still in his chair, and is too evidently not on the floor of the body over which he presides. . . ."

In truth, the House has "as many leaders as there are subjects of legislation. . . ." The committee chairmen, however, do not constitute a body with a single will. They are a "disintegrate ministry. . . . They do not consult and concur in the adoption of homogeneous and mutually helpful measures; there is no thought of acting in concert. Each committee goes its own way at its own pace."

Wilson finds this arrangement unsatisfactory for reasons that contemporary students of Congress will recognize. Congress cannot draft consistent and comprehensive legislation; it cannot provide a public forum for a debate on the nation's problems; it cannot educate the public about those problems; it provides no great prizes of leadership sufficient to attract the best men into Congress; it can harass, but not direct, the bureaucracy; it cannot comprehend the nation's financial affairs; its procedures are liable to corruption by "special pleaders"; and there is nowhere in the system a sense of responsibility or accountability.

What student of Congress has not encountered arguments like the following?

---

1. All quotations from Wilson are from *Congressional Government: A Study in American Politics* (Cleveland, Ohio: The World Publishing Co., Meridian Books, 1956 [1885]).

1) *On congressional law making.* Because of the way Congress is organized—with imperious committees representing both the majority and minority parties, each committee following its own (bipartisan) policy—legislation is designed to be "neutral and inoffensive," dressed "to the liking of all factions." No consistent set of policies can come out of the Congress, because it has no center of authority that can hold it to a single course: "Power is nowhere concentrated; it is rather deliberately and of set policy scattered amongst many small chiefs. It is divided up, as it were, into forty-seven seigniories, in each of which a Standing Committee is the court-baron and its chairman lord-proprietor."

2) *On congressional debate.* Congressmen have lost even the habit of debate, Wilson observes. The idea that a problem can be clarified by public discussion never even occurs to most members. Everything about Congress—even the architecture of the House, with its great airy spaces—discourages the give and take of oratory.

One reason is the press of time. Congress has its finger in everything, it has too much to do, and it cannot afford to give most subjects more than fleeting attention. The "theater of debate" therefore shifts to the committee chambers. But debates in committee have a special flavor, Wilson believes. Most committee work is done in secret; a committee's debate can never educate the public, which is given a bill without having a chance to learn the reasons which prompted Congress to adopt it. Even members not on a committee may be unaware of the reasons for a given piece of legislation. They have accepted a division of labor in which each committee rules its own province. What goes on there is nobody's business but its own.

3) *On public support.* A related complaint is that what the public cannot see, it cannot understand or learn from, and therefore will have no reason to support. The Congress is very busy—no other legislature is so single-mindedly devoted to law making, in Wilson's estimation—but its business has no effect on the public. Carried out behind the closed doors of the committee, restricted to a narrow spectrum of policy, committee debates "have about them none of the searching, illuminating character of the higher order of parliamentary debate." Congressional debate becomes nothing more than a "joust between antagonistic interests, not a contest of principle."

Wilson returns to this point again and again: the Congress is not exciting enough to draw the American public from its private concerns; it is not dramatic; it is scarcely even interesting. Its deliberations are prosaic; its procedures are confusing; its reasoning is hidden; its leaders are invisible.

Why should the public pay any attention to the Congress? It doesn't. So the Congress drifts dangerously from its mooring in public sentiment, and American government begins to lose its popular support.

This is one of the reasons, Wilson believes, for the public's hostility to the Congress. He quotes Green on British public opinion during the reign of George III, and finds ominous parallels to the United States: ". . . the bulk of the English people found itself powerless to control the course of English government. . . ." The government became divorced from "that general mass of national sentiment on which a government can alone safely ground itself." The public, "stripped of the feeling of responsibility which the consciousness of power carries with it," grew "ignorant and indifferent to the general progress of the age, but at the same time . . . hostile to Government because it was Government. . . . For the first and last time . . . Parliament was unpopular, and its opponents secure of popularity."

4) *On the absence of leaders in Congress.* Another reason for the public's indifference to Congress is the absence there of great and exciting contests between prominent national politicians. "To know Gladstone is to know Parliament"—but no similar personification of authority, principle, and institution can be found in the United States. The reason, of course, is the lack of "responsible parties" in the United States, another of Wilson's prophetic themes. Great, organized, responsible parties are useful for many reasons, not the least of which is that they offer tempting prizes for the most capable politicians, and great drama to grab the public and hold its attention. "Leadership and authority over a great ruling party is a prize to attract great competitors, and is in a free government the only prize that will attract great competitors."

In Congress, the only visible leader is the Speaker of the House. But great as his powers are—and, depending on the Speaker's personality, Wilson finds them potentially "autocratic"—they do not approximate the leadership Wilson is looking for. The Speaker's powers are procedural and not concerned with policy or contests over principle. They are directed inward, toward the members, rather than outward, toward the public. They fail to create a legislative officer who is also a leader of national opinion, capable of going to the country, raising enthusiasm, educating the public, helping to shape popular majorities, and above all drawing the public into the great drama of politics. (This is a shrewd observation. Consider how few presidential aspirants have been Speakers of the House, despite the fact that the Speaker is invariably one of the most skilled and experienced politicians in Washington.)

5) *On congressional oversight of administration.* As early as 1885, if Wilson's testimony can be credited, the federal bureaucracy was beginning to evade the control of the legislature. Then, as now, congressional oversight of administrators was problematic: the Congress could not direct the agencies, but neither would it consent to a total surrender of its creatures to presidential direction. The result was a completely unsatisfactory compromise between presidential and congressional control: the Congress could not rule, but it could harass. It could meddle in the "details" of administration, making life difficult for cabinet secretaries and career civil servants, investigating, prying, criticizing, and heaping annoyance upon humiliation.

This is a strikingly modern complaint. It was the committee system, Wilson found, that gave oversight its petty and despotic character. Tucked away in the committee room, beyond the public's notice, unrestrained by either party program or party leadership, powerful members were able to badger administrators into concessions and compromises that were trivial individually but in aggregate presented a major obstacle to the sound administration of the public's business. (Here, certainly, is the "cozy triangle" in its earliest form.) But such harassment brought no real control. Congressional oversight, "limited and defective," can "disturb, but it cannot often fathom, the waters of the sea in which the bigger fish of the civil service swim and feed. . . ." Cabinet secretaries are not brought to heel, but only driven to find more cunning stratagems for evading Congress. Some members find this satisfactory: their limited goals are served by the petty despotism of the committee room. But the public loses, by losing its voice in the administration of the nation's business.

6) *Congress and public finance.* A partial exception to the rule, public finance is the one subject which Congress does debate, and in which it does not blindly accept the dictates of the Standing Committees. Wilson is even willing to go so far as to acknowledge that "the supervision exercised by Congress over expenditures is more thorough than that which is exercised by the Commons in England." High praise indeed! Eight separate committees in the House audit the spending of executive departments; "upon all fiscal questions Congress acts with considerable deliberation and care." Indeed, finance is the only subject which can command the attention of the entire House at once: rules allow reports of the Ways and Means and Appropriations Committees to interrupt any other business and receive the full attention of the entire body.

But then, as now, the federal budget presented the Congress with unusual problems. In the late nineteenth century, however, the problem was surpluses rather than deficits. In 1870, Congress moved to gain control of over $174 million lying fallow in the executive branch, the accumulating residue of unspent appropriations. Even in such flush circumstances, public finance strained the Congress's oversight abilities. It was getting increasingly difficult for committees to penetrate the details of executive spending. Was money being spent as authorized? What was the reason for this or that estimate of need? How *much* money was being spent? Then, as now, a symbiotic relationship existed between committees and "their" departments which encouraged increased appropriations on an automatic yearly basis. The Committee on Rivers and Harbors did a brisk business.

Meanwhile, the tariff continued to pile up huge surpluses in the federal treasury. This puzzled Wilson. In England, he noted, a budget surplus would be an embarrassment serious enough to topple a government. In the United States, by contrast, surpluses were a matter of indifference, because the major purpose of revenue measures (chiefly the tariff) was not budgetary but economic: i.e., the tariff was written to protect domestic industries, not to raise a predetermined amount of money to satisfy the needs of the government. Wilson found this a failing, without noticing that the very different economic requirements of Britain and the United States would necessarily lead to very different budgetary processes. There is more to budgets than simple accounting.

7) *On corruption.* No mention of the tariff would be complete without mentioning corruption, one of the tariff's chief by-products. The army of "special pleaders" that descended on the nation's capital to influence legislation—the tariff being the chief object of their concern—found a congenial atmosphere in the fragmented, leaderless Congress. Public support for Congress was damaged in proportion. The "special pleaders" can influence the Congress, Wilson concludes, because each committee conducts its business in secret, but also because their deliberations are so narrow in focus, and so specialized in their appeal, that nobody but the special interests have any reason to follow them. Corruption flourishes best where nothing of dramatic importance takes place, and where legislators can be despotic in a narrow sphere: "It is ever the little foxes that spoil the grapes."

8) *On accountability and responsible parties.* Embracing all that has gone before is Wilson's central organizing theme: there is no way for the Con-

gress to be held accountable because Congress has no leaders. Indeed, this is the chief failing of American politics, and its source is the Constitution itself. Wilson quotes Bagehot's wonderful description of our inherited constitutional disability (American politicians sound like "trustees carrying out a misdrawn will") and adds his own very powerful indictment: "I know of few things harder to state clearly and within reasonable compass than just how the nation keeps control of policy in spite of these hide-and-seek vagaries of authority. Indeed, it is doubtful if it does keep control. . . . This, plainly put, is the practical result of the piecing of authority, the cutting of it up into small bits, which is contrived in our constitutional system."

Wilson's solution—responsible party government—is well known and oft repeated. Responsible parties with recognized leaders would fill the gaps created by the division and separation of powers. It would prevent Congress from evading its collective responsibility; it would prevent cabinet secretaries from passing the buck to Congress; it would prevent individual congressmen from putting the blame on committees, and committees from putting the blame on cabinet secretaries. "If there is one principle clearer than another, it is this: . . . *somebody must be trusted*, . . . *Power and strict accountability for its use* are the essential constitutents of good government."

II.

"Responsible party government," Sam Beer observed recently, "is an idea that dies hard." For nearly one hundred years, that idea has provided the standard by which most academic observers have judged the United States Congress. But is there another way of seeing Congress, a different vantage point which might yield different standards of judgment?

So dominated has our discussion been by this single standard that it is necessary to go outside the American context for a second opinion. What does the perspective of comparative politics have to offer? Another way of putting this is to ask what the role of the legislature has been, historically, and what it has become in most modern states.

The historical question has a simple answer. The original function of the legislature was to form a barrier to tyranny. In his essay, "On the Evolution of Forms of Government," Bertrand de Jouvenel notes that the legislature grew to its eighteenth-century form only after a long struggle to limit the royal prerogative. As the royal administration in the sixteenth and seventeenth centuries was developing "its capacity to serve the nation, it was indispensable to find practical devices precluding the royal authority from arbitrary practices." These "devices" were of two types, both of which contributed to the creation of the eighteenth-century legislature: the judicial veto (common in France) and the parliament representing the Nobles and the Commons (as in England).[2]

It was never the function of either of these devices to govern. The Parlement sitting in Paris merely "registered" or "rejected" royal edicts, and when its members performed their function of rejecting a royal proposal they did so with the "utmost politeness," forever urging that "it was out of respect for the King who can do no wrong that they could not let through a measure unsuitable to the royal character." The British Parliament had a somewhat broader function: to counsel the monarch whenever his policy required information on conditions in the country, on the needs of his people, and on the state of public opinion.[3] Parliament provided the "sense of touch" to complement the monarch's "sense of vision."

This was the earliest meaning of representation. Through the people represented in the legislature, the King could be steered down the path of prudence (a function performed much earlier by the Church). He could be stopped when he went too far—when he overreached his authority, when he trampled on "immemorial custom," when he violated the rights of individual subjects, when his plans proved destructive to his kingdom's prosperity, or when his schemes were foolish or ill-prepared. The legislature existed to shape, to channel, to obstruct, and to inform: but not to rule. The best barrier to arbitrary power, according to English jurists, was presented by a body whose members had no hope of assuming that power themselves.

This is representation in two senses: the parliament represented the people before the king, but it also represented the king before the people.

---

2. Bertrand de Jouvenel, "On the Evolution of Forms of Government," in *Futuribles: Studies in Conjecture*, ed. Bertrand de Jouvenel (Geneva: Droz, 1963), pp. 65-119.

3. An excerpt from the king's "Summons of Representatives of Shires and Towns to Parliament" in the year 1295 gives a flavor of this early function of the legislature: "The king to the sheriff of Northamptonshire. Since we intend to have a consultation and meeting with the earls, barons, and other principal men of our kingdom with regard to providing remedies against the dangers which are in these days threatening the same kingdom; and on that account have commanded them to be with us on the Lord's day next after the feast of St. Martin . . . to consider, ordain, and do as may be necessary for the avoidance of these dangers. . . we strictly require you to cause two knights, . . . two citizens . . . and two burgesses . . . to be elected without delay . . ." (From *The Medieval World: 300-1300*, ed. Norman F. Cantor [New York: Macmillan, 1963], p. 301).

The legislature turned its face first toward the monarch, counselling or rejecting, as prudence dictated; then it turned toward the people, explaining the king's policy, defending it, urging its support, helping the public to understand. For this task the legislator needed to be the sort of person (a "Notable," as de Jouvenel calls him) who could secure a hearing among his constituents, commanding respect on his own, with or without royal favor.

In its origins, therefore, the independent legislature complemented the independent executive, very much the arrangement contemplated by the authors of the U.S. Constitution. By keeping legislative and executive offices separate, the Constitution intended to erect an obstacle to the tyranny of the chief magistrate: a problem that had dominated the thinking of jurists ever since the late Middle Ages. In this respect, at least, the Constitution is a pre-modern document—The Framers' "science of politics" notwithstanding. As Wilson sensed (to his frustration) the Framers succeeded admirably: their work has hindered the growth in the United States of what is now the most common form of contemporary democracy, the parliamentary team exercising full executive power, supported by a majority in the legislature. From the eighteenth century onwards, the independent executive retreated from European politics, to be replaced by unitary governments in which legislative and executive powers were in the same hands; the independent executive has survived only in the United States. For that reason, the independent legislature has survived here as well, virtually the only nation in which it *has* survived, and the only nation among the major powers.

We are led then to an extraordinary paradox: we have a form of government whose antecedents lie in the thirteenth century, which makes us almost as old-fashioned as Saudi Arabia. (De Jouvenel traces our ancestry even farther back in time: ". . . to me, seeing an American Senator is the way to understanding a Roman Senator.") The king and parliament: we are like the British after all, only not the way the British are, but the way they once were. The presidency has long since escaped the institutional weakness Wilson found in 1885. (Wilson would have foreseen this even then, had he not been too much of a Democrat, and too much of a Southerner, to see Lincoln as anything but an "abnormal" president.) It is not fanciful to say that the presidency is our equivalent of the monarchy; it is the simple truth. The anti-Federalists caught on to this right away, after only a quick reading of the Constitution. To the extent that Alexander Hamilton had anything to do with shaping the office, this is what it was intended to be. The legislature, accordingly, was shaped to perform the traditional tasks of limiting, counselling, even obstructing (where necessary) an office of potentially royal scope.

No wonder progressives despair of American government! When they accuse it of being "medieval" or "archaic" they are more right than they know. And by and large, progressives have joined Woodrow Wilson in urging upon the United States an adaptation of the responsible party government model that has become the modern democratic norm, and which makes of the two formerly contesting powers one unitary power, one single "center of command." The virtues of this model appeal to the contemporary mind, which believes that modern problems are so complex that only a single-minded sovereign can cut through them to quick and decisive solutions. The independent legislature is obviously a poor candidate for this role. Congress is inevitably and unreformably many wills. Modern government, it is argued, cannot tolerate the luxury of legislation shaped to please a hundred factions and as many interests. The legislature is inefficient; it takes too long to respond to current events; its response, when it finally comes, is more often than not incoherent.

The executive, by contrast, can act quickly and decisively—which is why even eighteenth-century commentators gave the executive control over foreign policy. Is this office dangerous? Wilson was willing to admit as much, but was also prepared to make the gamble: "You must confide without suspicion in your chief clerk, giving him the power to ruin you, because you thereby furnish him with a motive for serving you."

This is the modern logic, and it is hard to argue with it. So all governments, including our own, move inexorably in the direction of the Principate (to borrow once more from de Jouvenel): the government of a single will. Here is what the Principate sounds like: "I ask the Congress to take this action by the first of October. Inaction on your part by that date will leave me with an inescapable responsibility to the people of this country. . . . In the event that the Congress should fail to act, and act adequately, I shall accept the responsibility, and I will act. . . . This I will do. The President has the powers, under the Constitution and under Congressional acts, to take measures necessary to avert a disaster. . . . I have given the most thoughtful consideration to meeting this issue without further reference to the Congress. . . . The American people can be sure that I will use my powers with a full sense of my responsibility to the Constitution and to my country. . . . I shall not hesitate. . . ." It does not matter very much that this is Franklin Roosevelt speaking, or that he is speaking about the Price

Control Act of 1942, a wartime measure. It is the voice of the modern executive, at any time, on nearly any subject, and in any nation.[4]

One set of modern conditions requires decisiveness, and thus the subordination of the legislature. Another set of conditions has the same result: more and more of what modern governments do has nothing directly to do with law making. In the essay cited above, de Jouvenel recalled the mood of his contemporaries during the 1920's, when it was hoped that government could be fashioned to achieve full employment, economic growth, and social security. "Of all the objectives we had in mind, only one, social security, could be achieved *by means of law*, and even then the measure of its implementation must depend upon the general progress of the economy. Full employment and economic growth were objectives which could not be achieved by the promulgation of once-for-all edicts but only by the ceaseless *adjustment of policy* to their attainment." This constant adjustment is more naturally the work of executives—or, rather, of civil servants working on behalf of the executive. To the extent that the executive cannot realistically be tied down by routines proscribed by the legislature, to that extent the legislature is devalued.

So the legislature becomes an assembly of backbenchers, waiting their turn at a ministerial post, which alone can confer on them any real power. Seats on the backbench are not eagerly sought by the most "notable" members of society, and the legislature therefore begins to lose its credibility among the public. The real authority of the nation becomes personified in the chief magistrate, a modern Prince who comes to embody the nation, even in democratic countries, in ways undreampt of by medieval kings. Behind this "divus Caesar" (de Jouvenel again) the routine business of the nation is conducted by "an invisible and informal Senate"—the bureaucracy. This informal senate even has its own "talking-over places" where civil servants are in contact with "respresentatives" of "constituencies more real in our day than local constituencies; union leaders, farmers' leaders, business leaders." But the real power remains with the Prince, who rules not *with* the legislature but against it, circumventing it where necessary by direct mass media appeals to the public.

This, then, is one portrait of modern government, as compelling as it is disturbing. Where does the Congress of the United States fit into this picture?

---

4. Quoted in *Congress: Its Contemporary Role,* by Ernest Griffith (New York: New York University Press, 1961), p. 11.

III.

No one familiar with the United States Congress would describe it as an idle collection of backbenchers, awaiting their turn in the executive branch. Alone among the legislatures of the world (as de Jouvenel appreciated) the Congress is not "led" by the executive. In his contribution to this volume, former Representative Charles Vanik claims that "there is nothing in the world like a United States congressman." From the perspective of comparative politics, it would seem that he is right.

That the Congress has not gone the way—not entirely, at any rate—of other modern legislatures is due to the very qualities of the Congress that are most often criticized. The Congress is *obstructive*, it is *truculent*. For these reasons, it is also the only modern legislature that has not been reduced to utter subservience and triviality. That much is clear from the papers in this volume, which portray a legislative institution that is deeply involved in nearly every phase of public policy; that has fashioned a budgetary mechanism more deliberative than many people—including many congressmen—ever thought possible; that has resources of information nearly equal to those of the administrative branch, and on occasion superior; that has abundant (perhaps even excessive) staff; and that has made its will, fragmented though it may be, felt at a thousand points. The Congress has also been favored with the loyal service of men and women of more than average intelligence and decency. The Speaker is only one among many members of Congress who fit very well de Jouvenel's definition of a "Notable." In fact, the generally supportive tone of the papers presented here is in marked contrast to the critical tone that has been the norm for several decades in scholarly discussions of the Congress. It may be a sign that we are coming to have a more mature appreciation of what a legislature is supposed to do, or to be.

From this point of view, the problem with the Congress can be tentatively reformulated. The problem is not that the Congress fails to be like the president—decisive, single-minded, and efficient—but that it may no longer be capable of serving its medieval function of providing the bridge between the people and the monarch.

What evidence do the papers presented here bring to this question? The evidence is mixed, as is the evidence of our recent history. Let me take the historical evidence first.

Consider, for example, the Watergate saga and the current dispute over the federal budget.

It was often said after President Nixon's resignation that the event proved that the system "worked," but it was not often noted in precisely what sense. Retrospective analysis has generally focused on the bribery and corruption implied by the huge campaign funds accumulated by the Nixon camp. This was how Congress interpreted events, once the impeachment question was settled, as the campaign finance reform legislation attests. But it was not larceny which made the Nixon White House unusual; it was the mad schemes concocted there for trampling on the law. And the Congress reacted just as it was intended to react: gravely and judiciously putting an end not only to the schemes but to the man responsible for hatching them. At no time has the medieval quality of American government been more visible than it was during the Watergate hearings.

The budget crisis is still unfolding and it is impossible to say how it will end, but this much is clear: the president, his claims to the contrary notwithstanding, has not been able to have his way, in the manner of Franklin Roosevelt of the Hundred Days, with a supine legislature. His budget proposals of last year were changed in important respects, and they received extraordinary scrutiny and publicity. No citizen who paid even the slightest attention to the news reports of the debate in Congress could fail to understand, at least in a general way, what was contained in the president's budget, or what that budget implied. In 1982, the drama is even sharper. In addition to changing specific portions of the budget, the Congress is moving (slowly, to be sure) toward the creation of its own bipartisan, bicameral alternative to the budget submitted by the president, as Mr. Reagan proves to be increasingly stubborn and unrealistic. Is it stretching the evidence too far to see in this sequence of events an echo of the Parlement in Paris, rejecting a royal edict as "unsuitable to the royal character"?

What does this symposium volume tell us about the traditional functions of the legislature?

1) Congress continues to resist the fate modern history has prepared for legislatures. Listen to Charles Vanik dismissing members of Parliament as so many "puppets" and hear a voice that has been stilled everywhere else in the world. Congress has not preserved its independence without some cost, of course: its increased staff has proved difficult to manage, and its tendency toward specialization has probably gone as far as it ought to. But here, as elsewhere, the benefits need to be calculated along with the costs.

2) The budgetary process, despite its evident drawbacks, suggests that the Congress is still able to scrutinize the executive's spending plans with a

great deal of care. In this respect, it remains far in advance of other legislatures.

3) If the Congress can still stand up to the executive, what of its other
function, that of counselling the people? Here the evidence is not just
mixed, but disturbing. The most ominous discussions in this volume are of
changes in the political environment outside of Congress: in the "conditions of public life" that Wilson referred to. Some of these changes are: the
further decline of parties; the fragmentation of the electorate into a hundred
warring camps, as petty in their goals as they are puny in size; the decline in
the number of communities coherent enough to *be* represented in Congress; the fact that congressional districts seldom coincide with the communities that do exist (an unfortunate by-product of *Baker* v. *Carr*); a strange
and disturbing selfishness infecting more and more voters; the evolving
rules governing (or misgoverning) campaign finance, which appear to give
extraordinary power to fanatics of one kind or another; the trend toward
early, voluntary retirement from Congress; the "fear" which grips more
and more congressmen as they confront their constituents. These trends
make it harder for the member to know his district, feel at home in it, and
talk honestly to the voters back home about the nation's problems. "Know
your district" was once a simple but reliable rule in American politics. That
is apparently no longer the case, as John Brademas testifies so eloquently.
All congressmen complain about the increasing difficulty of holding public
office, and more importantly, many complain that their relationship with
the voters has gone sour for some reason. No legislator placed in such a
position can hope to lead his constituents, or even learn from them.

Congressmen adapt to these conditions in various ways, as the symposium participants discuss. They "posture and grandstand"; they harass
administrators; they become errand runners for constituents. They become
specialists in narrower fields of policy. They lurch about, trying to find
some way of making contact with unreachable constituents. And, true,
they sometimes obstruct simply for the sake of obstructing. Meanwhile,
their ratings in the polls continue to decline.

Is it possible that the public is disappointed in the Congress because it has
been taught to have the wrong expectations of a legislative institution? Has
the public, like the majority of the academic community, come to think of
the Congress as a second-rate president? Certainly, the public's well-
known tendency to criticize the Congress but reelect individual congressmen suggests some fundamental ambivalence at work. At any rate, it is

clear (as it was to Wilson) that the Congress is not a substitute for a good president, any more than the medieval parliament was a substitute for a good king. Like our ancestors, we must endure bad kings; governing will never become a science, and neither will the selection of rulers. But even a good president is no substitute for a healthy Congress. What we need to think about is how, under presidents good, bad, and indifferent, the Congress can perform the ancient and honorable tasks of a legislature, without at the same time becoming so obstructive that it goes the way of its predecessors.

The art of ruling takes many forms. The life of the Speaker—a man who, despite his evident qualities, is on nobody's list of presidential possibilities—suggests very clearly that one form of that art is irreducibly legislative. And having read and proofread the papers in this volume many times, one image stands out more than any other: it is the image of Silvio Conte travelling around his district in Massachusetts with his movie projector and home-made films of the foreign aid program, trying to persuade "his people" that the program was worthy of their support. That is the authentic legislative art. The United States Congress is the last place where that art can still be practiced by masters. All the more reason to understand, and to nourish, its uniqueness and even its eccentricity.

Dennis Hale
Boston College
April, 1982

PART I:
IS CONGRESS A
DELIBERATIVE BODY?

IS CONGRESS A DELIBERATIVE BODY?

Joseph M. Bessette
Department of Politics
Catholic University

Before this decade is over the American people will celebrate the two-hundredth birthday of the world's oldest continuing republican form of government. The most visible manifestation of that government, both to its own citizens and to those of other nations, is not the Congress, the subject of this conference, but the presidency. Whatever the relative importance of the Congress and the presidency to the nature and direction of American public policy, the perception has steadily grown throughout this century that the president is the leader of the government, that the president and his appointees have more power for good or ill than the members of the House and Senate, and that consequently presidential elections matter more than congressional elections. Given the strength of this perception, Americans are often surprised to discover that the Constitution of 1787 placed Congress first and the presidency second.

However much the contemporary Congress operates in the shadow of the presidency, there is one respect in which it is unrivaled not only by the presidency but by any other political institution in the United States. Congress can claim the dubious distinction of being our most denigrated political institution. Although I haven't actually investigated this systematically, I think it is fair to say that more critical commentary has been written about Congress during this century than about the presidency, the Supreme Court, the state governors, or even the state legislatures—perhaps more than all these others put together.

The chief critics of Congress have come from the three estates present at this conference: academia, journalism, and politics. Political scientists of a generation ago regularly attacked Congress for its archaic procedures, conservative bias, and lack of competent staff. Journalists have a long tradition of exposing the seamy underside of the legislative process, whether in Congress or the state legislatures, especially the backroom deals, the power of well-financed interests, or the "wheeling and dealing" of the greedy or ambitious. Even congressmen themselves, whom we might expect to be ardent supporters of the institution, have been among its most vociferous critics. Book titles like *House Out of Order* and *Congress: The Sapless Branch* give some of the flavor of the dissatisfaction felt by many who have served in our national legislature. It is hardly surprising, then, that the public has come to embrace a largely negative opinion about Congress, something that the sex and bribery scandals of recent years have only exacerbated.

Congress, of course, has held no monopoly on critical commentary during the past several decades. We are all familiar, for example, with the scathing attacks on the "imperial presidency." In two important respects, however, criticism of Congress has differed from that of the presidency. One is its remarkable persistence. Americans seem to be forever dissatisfied with Congress but only occasionally dissatisfied with the presidency. The other difference, which is related to the first, is that most criticism of Congress is not informed by any clear articulation of what a good or effective Congress would look like and how it would operate. There is no generally accepted standard of an ideal Congress against which we can measure the functioning of the contemporary institution. Consequently most criticism of Congress is ad hoc, timebound, or the mere reflection of the particular ideological dispositions of the critic. In the case of the presidency, on the other hand, there is widespread, if not unanimous, agreement among political scientists, journalists, and those in public life that Franklin Roosevelt embodied the presidency at its best. In his command of his office, his vigorous efforts to meet the twin crises of depression and war, and his inspirational leadership of the American people, Roosevelt stands for many as the model of the ideal president. Even President Reagan, whose politics could not be much further from FDR's, is a professed admirer of Roosevelt, especially of Roosevelt's success as a popular leader.

What, however, has all this to do with the announced subject of this panel: "Is Congress a deliberative body?" Simply this: I contend that much of our dissatisfaction with the American Congress, whether as academic observers, journalists, members of the institution itself, or simply interested citizens, stems from the belief that Congress is *not* the truly deliberative institution it was designed to be and that effective modern democracy requires. Yet the issue is rarely, if ever, articulated in this way. Instead we complain that Congress functions too slowly or too fast, that it gives too much power to committee chairmen or too little, that it is understaffed or overstaffed, that it is too responsive to outside interests or not sufficiently attentive to their needs, that it has delegated away its constitutional responsibilities or that it oversteps its bounds by interfering with the functions properly belonging to the executive branch. But all of these particular complaints, on one side or the other, point us back to a single set of concerns. Is Congress a truly deliberative institution? If not, why not? And what can be done to enhance its deliberative character?

What is sorely lacking in the perennial debates about our national legislature is a clear understanding of just what it means to be a deliberative institution. For those of us with a serious professional interest in the nature, functioning, and well-being of Congress, this kind of consideration should be at the center of our attention. Unfortunately, for many decades it has been no closer than the periphery. The organizers of this conference are to be commended for placing this issue at the forefront of our reflections. I believe it is no exaggeration to say that we will get the kind of Congress this nation deserves only when we have a much firmer grasp of this central issue.

What, then, does it mean to describe a legislative body as a deliberative institution? What *is* deliberation, how are we to recognize it, and how does it differ from nondeliberative activities or processes? Most simply, a deliberative institution is one in which the members reason together about the problems facing the community and seek to promote what they judge to be good public policy. In the United States Congress, then, deliberation is a process of reasoning on the merits of public policy. It includes activities like the investigation and identification of social needs, the evaluation of ongoing programs, the formulation of legislative remedies, and the consideration of alternative proposals. Deliberation requires that legislators make decisions with an openness to the facts, arguments, and proposals brought to their attention and with a general willingness to learn from their colleagues and others.

So defined, deliberation may take a variety of forms. It may range from private reflection in the quiet of a study to an emotionally charged debate on the floor of the House or Senate. It may take place through open and public discussion set forth in an official record or through private exchanges with staff, lobbyists, or executive branch officials. It may involve a thorough and careful review of the relevant facts and issues, as might be expected in the most hard-working committees, or only a superficial and casual consideration, as is often said to happen with much floor voting in Congress.

Whatever form it takes, however, deliberation necessarily involves three basic elements: information, arguments, and persuasion. Deliberation must begin with the serious consideration of pertinent substantive information on policy issues. Information alone, however, is not enough to determine appropriate courses of action. It is necessary also to connect mere facts with desirable goals. This is the function of arguments. In a body like Congress numerous disagreements will arise over public policy alternatives. Opponents will advance a variety of reasons to justify their respective positions. These arguments and reasons will constitute a necessary element of the deliberative process. Finally, information and arguments must have some real persuasive effect. They must actually influence the outcome of the decision-making process. This is clearest when a congressman actually changes his mind on a policy question as a result of his consideration of the relevant information and arguments. Often, however, a congressman may have no initial preferences on an issue, or at best only broad dispositions. If the serious consideration of information and arguments induces a congressman in this condition to make a firm decision or take a specific position on a legislative matter, this would also constitute persuasion. Indeed, this more subtle kind of persuasion is probably more common in Congress than actual changes of mind.

How well, then, does Congress measure up to this standard? How seriously do congressmen seek to promote good public policy? How open are they to instruction from their colleagues and others? We know that Congress is awash with information on virtually every conceivable subject, but does the enormous effort devoted to generating and distributing information substantially affect the formulation of public policy? Similarly, the legislative process is replete with arguments at every stage, for and against controversial measures, but does anyone really listen to these arguments? Do they actually influence opinion within Congress? Anyone who has studied, observed, or worked within Congress knows that on the surface Congress gives the appearance of being a deliberative institution. The real question is whether that surface deliberation is simply window dressing that disguises the true underlying forces, or whether it reflects a genuine reasoned effort to promote good public policy.

My simple answer to this question is that Congress is a much more deliberative institution than is generally recognized, but much less deliberative than it ought to be. Moreover, changes that have taken place within Congress during the past several decades have, on the whole, had a deleterious effect on deliberation within Congress and threaten serious long-term consequences for the institution.

Perhaps the principal reason why Congress has a reputation for being other than a deliberative institution is because floor debates in the House and Senate generally bear so few visible characteristics of collective reasoning on the issues facing the nation. It is one of the frequent surprises and great disappointments of tourists to Capitol Hill to sit in the gallery of the largely empty House or Senate chambers and observe a succession of members reading speeches into the *Record*. Even those few members who *are* present don't seem to listen to the "debate." It is a mistake, however, to take the nature of floor debate as the key consideration; for usually it is only a brief final stage in a much longer and more complex legislative process. By the time an important bill reaches the floor there is little new to be said; the relevant information and arguments have already been digested by the interested parties; opinions have largely been formed. If true deliberation exists, it would likely be concentrated in the earlier stages of the process.

In a format such as this I cannot actually prove that Congress is a more deliberative institution than usually thought, but I can report on some of the findings of my own research—research which includes both original investigation of policy making in Congress and careful analysis of the extensive secondary literature, including more than thirty case studies of the legislative process. The following results bear directly on our subject.

1) Deliberation can begin as early as the drafting of legislative proposals when a small group of individuals (e.g., congressmen, staff, interest-group representatives, and executive branch officials) work to fashion a legislative remedy to some commonly perceived social or political problem.

2) Committee hearings on important bills are rarely a mere pro forma exercise. More so than is usually recognized, committee members demonstrate an interest in and openness to what can be learned in this forum. At most hearings on important issues the two sides of the controversy are well aired; questioning of witnesses is often highly detailed and contributes to a clarification of the issues at hand.

3) A committee's influence within the full House or Senate is determined in part by how thoroughly and competently it carries out its legislative responsibilities. A reputation for deliberativeness enhances a committee's standing within the full body and makes it more likely that the parent chamber will follow its lead.

4) One of the principal ways in which representatives of both the executive branch and outside interests seek to influence Congress is by persuad-

ing congressmen of the merits of their proposals. Central to this effort is the generation and presentation of supportive facts and arguments.

5) One way for an individual representative or senator to accrue influence within his body is to become a substantive expert on a particular set of legislative issues. Knowledge is convertible into power.

6) Much deliberation within Congress takes place within informal or semiformal groupings of like-minded congressmen: e.g., party caucuses on committees, state or regional delegations, or ideological groups. Although the two sides in a legislative controversy may not persuade each other, each may arrive at its particular position through a deliberative process.

7) Throughout Congress's consideration of an important public issue the major actors in the legislative process manifest a keen interest in the facts and arguments supporting their position. Simultaneously, they seek to undermine their opponents' case while responding to criticisms from the other side. In a word, something like a genuine debate evolves on most controversial proposals.

If these statements are largely accurate, then one must conclude that the conventional wisdom vastly underestimates the force of reason in congressional decision making. We have been even more cynical toward Congress than it deserves. By focusing on the "wheeling and dealing," the pursuit of ambition, and the play of power within Congress, we have overlooked— and therefore do not well understand—the deliberative character of the institution.

It would be silly, of course, to suggest that nondeliberative forces or activities are absent from Congress, that all that matters in the institution is the reasoned analysis of the merits of legislative proposals. We know, on the contrary, that congressmen sometimes vote for bills not on their merits but as part of a prearranged logroll with one or more colleagues, that those in positions of power can influence votes by activating obligations or threatening sanctions, and that the personal political ambitions of legislators can incline them to focus their energies on public relations activities at the expense of their legislative responsibilities. Indeed, as I will shortly argue, these nondeliberative forces and activities have become even more prominent in recent years.

In one respect Congress seems to have become *more* deliberative. Contemporary congressmen are a much more opinionated lot than their forebears of a generation ago. They have more ideas on more different issues, and they are less willing to defer to the judgment of colleagues with more institutional authority, seniority, or substantive experience. One could say that although the number of congressmen has remained fixed, the number of deliberators on important legislative matters has increased dramatically. This has opened up the deliberative process to a greater variety of information and arguments and made it more likely that all sides of an issue will be heard before formal action is taken. This proliferation of opinion, however, has generated or paralleled structural changes that are more a threat to deliberation than an aid.

These changes include the increase in the number and power of subcommittees in Congress, the opening up of committee markup sessions and conference committees to public scrutiny, the televising of committee hearings and floor debate in the House, the vast increase in recorded voting in both chambers, the increase in allotments for personal staff and district travel, and the weakening in the Senate of informal norms of conduct promoting specialization, a period of apprenticeship for new senators, and devotion to legislative work. The avowed purpose of these changes was to make Congress more democratic, more open to public scrutiny, and more responsive to the desires (legislative or otherwise) of constituents. Although these goals may have been achieved, they have not come without some costs for the deliberative process in Congress.

One effect of these changes has been to increase the opportunities, incentives, and rewards for nondeliberative behavior, specifically for the kind of public self-promotion that serves a legislator's electoral ambitions but does not contribute to serious reasoning about public policy. In a deliberative legislative body the members meet together in committees and the full body in order to educate and learn from one another. It is more and more the case in the U.S. Congress that these forums have become platforms for members to reach outside audiences, in order to impress their constituents or develop statewide or national reputations. Posturing and grandstanding are replacing serious discussion and argument.

The relatively small size and greater prestige of the Senate compared to the House has provided its members with more public visibility and opportunity for developing a reputation outside of the body itself. A generation ago it was widely recognized within the Senate that the unregulated pursuit of private ambition would promote neither the well-being of the institution nor responsible public policy. Senators, it was thought, must be given an *incentive* to deliberate. Their personal interest must be connected to their constitutional responsibility to study policy matters seriously, to pay close attention to the details of proposed legislation, and to reason about the public interest with their colleagues. The problem is that there are few, if any, external rewards for devotion to legislative work and responsible lawmaking. Consequently, the practice in the Senate was to maximize the *internal* rewards for responsible behavior, rewards like positions on prestigious committees, leadership posts, and the informal authority that comes from the respect of one's colleagues. Some senators, especially those with presidential ambitions, still chose to play to an outside audience, but they did so with the knowledge that this route would not lead to power within the institution.

In the House of Representatives the relatively large size has denied most of its members the opportunity to use their positions to foster national reputations. Nonetheless, representatives too have ambitions, including reelection and, for many, the desire to move up to statewide office. As in the Senate, there may be little direct connection between the activities that promote these ambitions and those that foster a deliberative legislative process. In recent years this problem has been exacerbated by changes that have raised a large fraction of the House membership from the relative obscurity that previously accompanied service in the House. Fully one-half of the Democrats in the Ninety-Sixth Congress chaired at least one subcommittee. Because radio and television broadcast of committee and subcommittee sessions is now permitted, there has been a vast expansion of the audiences for controversial issues. In the House, as in the Senate, there still exist incentives for deliberative behavior—traditionally, for example, seats on the prestigious Rules, Appropriations, and Ways and Means Committees were reserved for hard-working and responsible legislators—but these incentives will have little effect if representatives come to believe that more is to be gained by public self-promotion.

There is, moreover, another way in which the changes of recent years have jeopardized deliberation within Congress. Congressmen are now much more accountable for their actions. There is less they can do in secret. Nearly all committee markup sessions and conference committee meetings are now open to public scrutiny. Votes within committees must be recorded in ways not required a decade ago. The institution of the recorded teller vote on the House floor has reduced the likelihood that important decisions will be made without a record of each congressman's vote. Largely overlooked, however, in this drive for accountability has been the effect on deliberation. Reasoning on the merits of public policy is not the same thing as registering constituent opinion at each stage of the legislative process. Deliberation requires both some measure of independent judgment by the legislator and a degree of flexibility in the decision-making process that allows for evolving opinion and changes of mind. This is particularly difficult if the public is looking over the legislator's shoulder at each step in the process.

The government-in-the-sunshine movement may have had its greatest effect on deliberation in the committee markup stage. When these sessions were secret, congressmen were not strictly accountable for their opinions and actions on the details of a legislative proposal. They had little reason to fear offending a powerful constituency or interest group if they failed to back their requests in every respect. Now these same groups are actually present during the line-by-line reworking of the bill. They can monitor the congressman's actions on every vital point. It is hard to imagine how any truly deliberative process—of openness to information and argument, of reasoned give and take, and of education on the substance of policy—can occur in such an environment.

Those who created the American political system were highly sensitive to the importance of interest and ambition in governing the conduct of political leaders. They knew that it was not enough simply to seek out the virtuous and wise for high office and encourage them to do a good job. Although some officeholders might have a genuine desire to serve the public, many others would seek first monetary gain, personal power, or reputation. Consequently, the Framers sought through their carefully contrived institutions to make it in the interest of the officeholder to do what public-spiritedness and patriotism otherwise demanded.

The same task faces us now. It is not enough to complain that Congress fails to meet our expectations. It is not enough to argue that all would be well if only we elected more responsible and dedicated public servants to the institution. Congress will become more deliberative when the opportunities, incentives, and rewards for serious reasoning about public policy are increased and the attractiveness of nondeliberative activities is reduced. Determining what developments or changes will contribute to this end requires at a minimum a clear understanding of the nature, importance, and requirements of deliberation in a legislative institution.

CONGRESS IS DELIBERATIVE: COMPARED TO WHAT?

Hon. Charles A. Vanik
Member, United States House of Representatives, 1954-1980

I'll probably prove to you very satisfactorily and completely that Congress is not a deliberative body. But I think it's fitting and necessary we define the terms of discussion. *Deliberative*, according to my Webster, means "assembled or organized for deliberation or debate." Now Congress is certainly that. For twenty-six years of my life in the Congress, I can bear full witness that the Congress is well organized for deliberation and debate. The rules for the conduct of business in the Congress are so highly developed that they have become the pattern and the model for the conduct of business in every kind of organized group in every community of America. The Congress of the United States is certainly a deliberative body. The question is, compared to what? It certainly is more deliberative than the potato, which can neither think nor exercise any reflex action.

There's a great division in the United States over whether the American people desire reflex action from the Congress—requesting their will be done—rather than deliberate action—reflecting the legislator's thought. Most constituents say: "I don't give a darn about what you think." In the election just completed, I would suggest that the electorate opted for reflex action. They demanded certain things without deliberate consideration. They demanded an instant relief from the burdens of inflation. They demanded instant relief from the burdens of taxation. They demanded smaller governments at home and a more aggressive government abroad. They demanded more action and less deliberation. I think that was the mandate. If there were a national poll conducted on the subject, I believe most Americans would express the opinion that the Congress should react to these demands.

There have been other times like the present. In Franklin Roosevelt's New Deal, Congress was called upon to provide reflex action demanded by a strong and zealous president, extending all the way up far beyond the House, and the ethereal Senate, all the way to the United States Supreme Court. There was no time for any deal except the New Deal. There was no time for a legislative body that deliberated. In a time when domestic recovery was interwoven with a menacing world war, the deliberative powers of the Congress atrophied to perhaps their lowest level in our history.

When we look at the United States Congress as a deliberative body, we must consider other legislative systems. The parliamentary system gives legislative bodies not only the power to legislate, but also the power to determine the nation's leadership. In America, under our concept of separation of powers, we often find our country choosing a president who is at considerable variance with Congress. During the Truman years there was a Republican Congress. In the Eisenhower-Nixon years, there was a Democratic Congress. At the present time we have a Republican Senate with a symbolic Democratic House, and for all practical purposes the president has a good working majority in both houses for his economic and tax programs. (One of the reasons I left the Congress is because I felt that I was completely out of tune—and I sensed this in January—with the decisions I thought America would be making in November.) So we cannot really compare the American Congress with the British Parliament, or the French Chamber of Deputies, or the Japanese Diet, or the German Bundestag, or the Israeli Knesset. The separation of powers doctrine separates and diffuses political responsibility, and also diffuses bureaucratic responsibility, which very often operates completely apart from both the executive and the legislative branches. Today we would not find ourselves in the regulatory morass that we're in if we were operating under a parliamentary system. The demand for greater efficiency and accountability may drive America to that option. Although the parliamentary systems of other countries provide, as the professor would say, eloquent and florescent debate, there is more reflex action than reflective action behind the debate. In those systems, the parliamentary representatives are substantially instructed and directed by party policy to talk as freely as they will. But when it comes to the ultimate vote, they are wired. They are wired for action by the party mandate. The parliamentary debate is, for all practical purposes, a puppet show, manipulated by party headquarters.

There is nothing in the world like the United States Congress. (And absolutely nothing in the universe like the United States Senate.) Although both are elected through a party process in either the Democratic party or the Republican party, all semblance of responsibility to party policy ends at the election gate. The party platform commitments are simply a false label for the policies contained. In most states, under the primary laws, the candidate pledges to support the principles of either the national Democratic party or the national Republican party. But only rarely has anyone suffered any discipline for his failure to live up to that oath. We did have some cases—Representative Abernathy in 1978, and John Bell Williams. But in the twenty-six years of my experience, I had practically no relationship with the Democratic National Committee. That was the president's little plaything. And on many occasions, I was disturbed that the national chairman should even endeavor to offer national party positions. In 1974, I served on the O'Hara Commission, but twice in thirteen elections, the Democratic National Committee donated $500 to my campaign for reelection. And during those twenty-six years, I received baskets and bushels of political and policy material, but most of the time the national committee was asking something *from* me, rather than providing *for* me.

For all practical purposes, we have in the United States 537 political parties. One is the national Democratic party, one is the national Republican party, and then there are 535 free and independent political parties headed by each representative and each senator. The staff of each congressman is usually the largest staff available for political use in each congressional district or, in the senators' case, in each state. These political organizations are artfully designed—not to deliberate, but to protect the tenure of the incumbent. In addition to the public purse, which supports these parties, they seek auxiliary support. Last year there was about $200 million of it, as far as I've been able to count. There must have been a great deal more. So in a very real sense, the American congressman, supported by his own party, with public subsidies of staff and free use of the mails to support his positions, can be more flexible, can be more deliberate, he has more freedom from party discipline, than any of his parliamentary peers. And I believe that most Americans, and certainly most congressmen, would agree that they like it this way.

The crucible of legislation, however, has to face up to tighter and much more difficult tolerances. In the parliamentary system, legislation is the process of blending three or four different approaches that are provided by minority parties into a majority position. But in the American process, it's a lot more difficult. The process does not operate with simple blending. It requires a huge legislative osterizer to develop various viewpoints into a majority position—which is not a blend, but only what remains after individual viewpoints have been crushed and broken into a majority emulsion. Now it's for this reason that the final product has to be expanded by either legislative history or by bureaucratic regulation.

"Legislative history"—oh, you read a lot about it in the academic volumes. But it's an insider's science, which can subvert or distort the words of a law. "Legislative intent" is often created when there are only three or four members in the chamber. And one member asks a prearranged question, to which the respondent—the chairman or the subcommittee chairman—has a prearranged answer. These answers could be at complete variance with the original legislation. In this procedure, it is possible, or example, to be excluded from the regulatory aim of a bill, or even to be included in the benefit of a public appropriation or subsidy. Now the advantage of this kind of a public change—it's all done in open daylight—is that it can be privately inspired and publicly enacted. In a public chamber, when the roar of the crowd has passed, when the sound has been turned down, and the kleig lights have been turned off, it is an extremely useful tool. I do not know the extent of the use of legislative history in parliamentary systems, but I think we ought to look at it, because I have an idea that it really was an import.

Now under the unique American process, the legislator can be deliberate and thoughtful, but these are privileges which must be compressed out of the legislator's time. This privilege comes after and in the time that remains after what I'm going to list now, these essential functions.

1) Political action. Meetings with political groups, community groups, special-interest groups, the League of Women Voters, the Democratic or Republican parties in each county, city, town, village, or precinct. Special-interest groups, for or against abortion, busing, gun control. Now this is a primary service, since it provides security, defensive watch, and survival. You don't have a chance to do anything in the Congress if you don't survive. You can't do anything at all. So survival is first. You've got to understand that.

2) General service to the constituent community, relationships with federal agencies on behalf of community needs, community planning, industrial expansion and protection, preserving or extending job bases, getting the fair share of public spending—you know, cut the budget but get your hometown every darn dollar you can squeeze out of Washington.

3) Service to constituents. Helping individuals, corporations, passport and visa service (oh, that's very important). Casework. Social security, black lung disability cases, health plan controversies—everybody's having problems with their health plans.

4) Committee work—this is official now. Hearings. Preparation of questions and policy discussions. Meetings with lobbyists and affected constituents. This takes ten or twenty hours per week. Then you have the problem of staff administration. You've got to monitor eighteen or nineteen employees. She's working harder than he is, and so forth, and all those controversies, disputes. One of my colleagues said the other day that we all walk in minefields, you know. I have a colleague who, if he had been in the bureaucracy, the government would have accepted liability. He interviewed a girl for a job and then he wrote her a letter: "You have all the qualifications but I want a man for that job." He paid $100,000 out of his own pocket for that. And $100,000 in legal fees. I have a colleague who got a letter from a school board in his area: Does a certain bus company have a violations record? So he just sent the letter over to the Interstate Commerce Commission and they came back and said: Oh yes, the bus company has a violations record. So he sent it back to this hometown school board, and he got sued by the company for $3 million in loss of profit. Well, he's got $13,000 of his own money in that. A congressman runs a small business, one of the smallest businesses in America. And you've got liability! A congressman sends a staff person to deliver a press release over to another building and he can be sued if there's an accident. The victim can sue the person that drives the car on his insurance, or he can sue the congressman, under the doctrine of master and servant. There's no insurance he can buy for that. It's one of the reasons I got out. (Laughter) And I think that a cause of action might lie with your constituents for being derelict in your duty—voting the wrong way. Failing to be deliberate! Cause of action. (Laughter) Damages not limited to $60,500 salary!

5) Press time. Conferences with newspeople, media representatives. Preparation of press releases. Most of what we do, we've got to prepare press releases. No one will know you're here! You've got to let them know.

6) And you have office time with constituents and visitors and contributors. Now who do you spend more time with? (Laughter) And you've got pictures and discussions with students. You run up the Capitol steps, you're all out of breath, you don't even know where they are—sometimes you mention the wrong school. "Glad to see the children here from Chestnut Hill"—and they're from some other place. (Laughter) Then you've got luncheons and receptions with organized groups. That's the real bonanza part of this. Every group that comes to Washington has at least one constit-

uent that you've got to see. You go through ten or twelve hours a week with a bad food hazard.

7) And then you have travel time. The bureaucrat gets paid for his travel time. Well, the congressman just lumps that in. The travel time to your home district. Committee meetings, your oversight responsibilities. Once in a while you might take a junket—two weeks here and there. There's nothing better than a congressional junket, let me tell you. I want to defend those. (Laughter) I'm going to write a book, professor. *Travels with My Uncle. . .Sam.*

8) And then you have time in your district offices—meetings with constituents, in the offices and the other places of assembly. This is important, because you have to know how the system is working. And only in this process do you find out. Only by the case study, sitting down with a person that's had trouble with the bureaucracy, can you really determine whether or not the law has operated right, or whether it's operating wrong.

9) Then, of course, way down low on the list is set-aside time for family and personal life. Well, not much left.

Now after all of the aforesaid, there may be time for deliberation on the national issues which confront the Congress. Now it could be readily seen that a congressman has little time left for this very, very important function. In many situations, he follows the leader on voting issues. You know, you vote with others whom you trust and whom you feel have had time for deliberation, and whose views are generally in line with yours. Sometimes you stagger into the room, you don't even know what they're voting on. How did George vote? Okay. It used to be a lot more difficult when they didn't have the votes put on the monitors. Now you can just look up there and decide how to vote. The deliberative time is such time as is required to see how someone else voted. (Laughter) You sort of have to match that up with other people from your area. You don't really find very many people coming from the same area voting at great discrepancy with each other. You know: "Let's see, how did that one go? Oh, yes." And then they cast that vote.

Now I'd say about two-thirds of the average member's votes are follow-the-leader votes. Two-thirds. I don't condemn the system, I think it's alright. Just knowing which leader to follow constitutes deliberation. Some guys are right and some are not. How does the system work? I think it works surprisingly well. Deliberation does not always demand independent judgment. Consistently deciding whom to follow—that's a very important thing. In a few situations, the legislator may vote by hunch, or by instinct. There are some legislators and some committees which never offer a decent proposal. With such situations, a no vote is usually the right vote. And so it becomes quite apparent, under these circumstances, that Congress can't be given a high mark as a deliberative body. But I think that these reasons are indigenous to the constitutional system of the separation of powers.

If it were possible, it would be helpful and desirable to abolish the United States Senate. (Laughter) I'm not kidding about this. I'm serious. And transfer its treaty ratification authority to the House. There's no need in America for a House of Lords. None whatsoever. The Senate provides representation for wide areas of land, fields, lakes, and streams. It represents cattle, deserts, mountains, and just plain open space. It provides distorted power and benefits to areas and places instead of people. The Constitution serves in this way to discriminate against people, giving a few who dwell in the wide open spaces distorted additional power over the many. It has given property a greater protection under the law than is provided to citizens. We must soon conclude that the Senate is an unnecessary appendage to the legislative process, and we ought to have a Constitutional Convention to help straighten that one out. We could streamline the legislative process without losing the principle of separation of powers. In my twenty-six years of legislative work, I would have to report that an inferior product results considerably from the bicameral system. Time and time again, I have seen the House, much more exposed to political challenge, respond with courage and with fervor to adopt a brave new course, only to have the product downgraded and dessimated by provincial and special-interest modifications in the Senate. In today's competitive world, we've been privileged to afford the cost, the inefficiency, and the downright procrastination of our system. But I would say to you that the future may not be as tolerant or as kind. Thank you very much.

Response by Arthur Maass
Frank G. Thomson Professor of Government.
Harvard University

I join Professor Bessette's complaint that much of the persistent criticism of Congress is incoherent, ad hoc, timebound, or a mere reflection of the liberal or conservative disposition of the critic—that we have been more cynical towards Congress than it deserves. By focusing on wheeling and dealing, and the pursuit of ambition by individual members, we have overlooked, and therefore do not well understand, the real character of the institution. I think that is the main point of his presentation. I agree with his concern about the increase in the number and power of subcommittees, the opening of markup sessions and conference committees to the public, and the increase in congressional staff. And I concur with his view that criticisms of Congress and many recent reforms of Congress are misguided because they pay too little attention to the basic question: What is the role of Congress in American government? What does, or perhaps what should Congress do, as distinguished from the executive, or the courts, or other less formal institutions?

Professor Bessette's answer to these questions is that Congress makes or should make good public policy, and that it does this or should do this by deliberation. But this is not quite enough, it seems to me. The executive and the judiciary also make public policy, as Representative Vanik pointed out. And they also deliberate. They too require information, listen to arguments, and are open to persuasion. Now obviously Congress is different in its interests, and in its deliberating. But why is it different, and how is it different? We need, I think, a more detailed specification of what Congress does or should do. Representative Vanik has helped to enlighten us on this by comparing Congress in our system to parliamentary systems, by emphasizing the separation of powers, and by distinguishing the roles of the executive, the bureaucracy, the parties, and the small enterprise that each member has to operate.

Fortunately, we have recently been given important data that should help us to specify further what Congress does. I refer to the data published by the House Commission on Administrative Review, the so-called Obey Commission of 1977. Based on questionnaires and interviews with all members, these data show the several roles that members think the House should play—such as legislation, oversight of administration, constituency service—and the several roles that members think they are *expected* to play, which are not necessarily the same as the roles *they* think they should play. Representative Vanik has given us an excellent list of the roles that he has played as a member. He has mentioned political action, constituency service (including casework), committee work, oversight, staff administration, press work (including news releases), district office work, raising funds to get reelected, and other assignments. We have cumulative data of a similar character—though not as carefully elaborated as the congressman's—for 435 respondents. Further analysis of these and related data should help to establish the basics which Professor Bessette says so rightly must precede any prescriptions for reform.

Indeed, it is a failure to understand the several roles of Congress, especially the distinction between legislation and oversight, on the one hand, and constituency service, on the other, that has led to much of the unjustified criticism of Congress. An example: Some years ago I was giving a seminar on congressional supervision of the executive for middle-level public servants who had been in government for five to ten years and had been given the equivalent of a sabbatical year to reflect on their experience. I said in one presentation that Congress, in enacting every few years a reauthorization of the airport program, had not concerned itself with individual airports, but rather with the broad standards and criteria that should govern federal grants to airports—whether money should be given for reception rooms, as well as control towers, what size cities should be eligible for grants, and so on. A student in the seminar spoke up, saying I was wrong. He was the legislative liaison officer for the airport program in the Federal Aviation Administration. "I'm on the phone all day talking to congressmen," he said, "answering specific questions about specific airports." Well, I made a deal with this student, to see who was right. He would write a paper for which he would read all of the hearings on the authorization and reauthorization of the airport program over the last fifteen years, and all of the annual appropriation hearings on that program. He did that, and he found in several thousand pages only two references to specific airports. In other words, Congress, in authorizing the program and re-authorizing it, did, as I said, concern itself with general standards and criteria. And in appropriating money, the members concerned themselves largely with the same; it was a lump sum appropriation. So why was my student getting all these calls? After the money was appropriated, congressmen would urge the FAA to process applications for airport grants in their constituencies. The point is that there are two different roles involved here. The first role is the legislative role and that is what I was talking about. He was talking about constituency services, although he didn't know that one should distinguish these roles. He hadn't thought in those terms before.

Now all members play both roles. Some give more time and attention to the legislative role, others, to constituency service. Prof. Lewis Dexter pointed this out a great many years ago. Members are clear that there are these two separate roles, and others too. They conduct them through separate institutions. Legislation and oversight are conducted in the members' office, normally by their legislative assistants, and by congressional committees and floor debate. But constituency service is not conducted through legislative committees or floor debate. There's a different set of institutions for constituency service. The congressmen's administrative assistants have direct contacts with the departments and with the departments' legislative liaison officers, like my FAA student. And they have district offices and other apparatus too. It is a failure to understand these distinctions that leads investigative reporters and others to focus on wheeling and dealing when they write about Congress. By focusing only on constituency service and misinterpreting it, they distort Congress, and this quite properly bothers Professor Bessette.

Turning our attention to Congress's role in legislation, Professor Bessette speaks about deliberation in the drafting of legislative proposals. It would be useful, I think, to relate this concern to the work on initiation of legislation by John Johannes, and the even more recent work by John Kingdon and others on agenda setting. Johannes points out that most legislation is initiated in the executive branch, and that there are good reasons for this. The early stages of the legislative process involve a large amount of data accumulation and analysis. There are thousands of employees in the executive branch available for that sort of work. Furthermore, the early stages of the legislative process involve coordination to make sure that related programs proposed by different agencies are consistent. This type of coordination is better performed in a hierarchical organization like the executive, than in a diffuse organization like the Congress. Having made these points, Johannes then develops a model of legislative initiation involving five or six steps, and points out that under certain circumstances Congress can and does perform one or more of these steps. Thus, he develops a full and a rich analysis of the initiation of legislation; and I'm suggesting that Professor Bessette's analysis of deliberation by Congress in the early stages of legislation would be enriched by references to this work and to similar work that is now going on in agenda setting.

Professor Bessette is concerned also about deliberation in committees, and the effects of this deliberation on floor debate and on voting. Here I think his discussion could be elaborated by reference to the recent research and literature on cueing theory—the work of Kingdon, Frans Bax, and others. Let me illustrate with Bax's work, in part because it has not been widely published, unfortunately in my view. Bax points out that because mem-

bers obviously cannot study carefully all issues on which they have to vote, they take cues from certain sources to help them.

There are several possible cues that the congressman can follow. He can take his cue from the House leadership of his party. Or he can take his cue from the president or from lower down in the executive. Or he can take his cue from his constituents' opinions or his perceptions of their opinions. Or he can take his cue from the views of the committees that report the bills. Now Bax tried to examine all of these cues to see which ones congressmen relied on more than others. He found that on most important issues, most of the time, a congressman takes his cue from members of the committees that have reported the bills. How does this work? The member or his legislative assistant may read the committee report and in doing so look especially for dissenting views, if any. Or he may simply watch the tally board to see how committee members vote on the floor. A congressman most frequently takes his cue from senior members of his own party on the committee. They may not be the most senior, for the member may have more respect for someone further down the line. But it is usually a member who has been on the committee for a while, who knows the program, and whose views he respects.

This result has interesting implications for deliberation in Congress, which is Professor Bessette's concern, and for how Congress works, and for the role of party in Congress. Interestingly, it would appear that the role of party in congressional voting is determined very much by how the committees operate. If a committee brings in a unanimous report, then the noncommittee Republicans and the noncommittee Democrats get the same cue. They seek cues from members of their party whom they respect, but they get the same cue. If, on the other hand, the committee brings in a report with a significant split between the members based on party, then noncommittee members of the two parties will get different cues. The expression of partisan differences on the floor of the House may depend more on how the committees perform than on the work of party leaders and leadership groups. This conclusion, I am sure, will be challenged, but it is a very interesting interpretation of how Congress works and one that relates very closely to Professor Bessette's interest. This understanding, then, of the role of committees in the House should be of help in analyzing the House as a deliberative body. Representative Vanik has said very much the same thing, that in many situations members follow a leader. In two-thirds of the votes, approximately, they take cues from someone else, so that deliberation does not demand independent judgment by each member on each issue. And this, he says, is not necessarily inconsistent with Congress being a deliberative body. My point is much the same.

Analysis based on cue theory might also help in resolving the fascinating question that Professor Bessette raises near the end of his paper, the conflicts between accountability on the one hand and deliberation on the other. Thank you.

Response by Peter Woll
Department of Politics, Brandeis University

My remarks will address some broad issues about the role of Congress as a deliberative body. Criticizing Congress is a little bit of a sport in the United States. Public opinion pollsters go around and they ask individuals, "What do you think of our political institutions?" And everybody has been saying in recent years, "Well, since you asked me, our political institutions are rotten." "What do you think of the presidency?" "Well, we have a very low opinion of the president because the presidency hasn't been able to get very much done." "What do you think of Congress?" Congress is rated even lower than the presidency in recent polls. "What do you think of the Supreme Court?" "Well, we have a very low opinion of the Supreme Court as well."

Do citizens really believe what they say to the pollsters? If they do, in my view it's a reflection more on the citizens than it is on the government. The reason people criticize the Congress, the president, and the Supreme Court, is simply because, from their particular perspectives, those institutions are not doing what people think should be

done. Right-to-lifers, for example, criticize the Supreme Court and have the privilege of going to Washington on January 22nd every year, the anniversary of the *Roe* v. *Wade* (1973) decision, and marching around, going through the offices of congressmen and engaging in all sorts of activity critical of the abortion decision and critical of Congress for not taking action to overrule the court.

Congress operates within our pluralistic political system. The extraordinary freedoms that we enjoy allow each and every group in the United States, each and every individual, freely to express their opinions about any matter that they want. These freedoms bubble up in Washington in hundreds of pressure groups expressing particular viewpoints, each and every one demanding that Congress accede to its will, and then rating Congress at a low level when it does not act.

The Congress of the United States is a reflection of our broader political system. We get the Congress that we deserve, and we have the Congress that is the reflection of our nation. It is remarkable that in congressional elections the turnout of voters is extraordinarily low, often less than 50 percent. In primaries the turnout can be as low as 20 percent. And at the same time, the majority of citizens turn right around and criticize the institution. There is an irony there. If the people do not deliberate before choosing Congress, can we expect Congress to be a deliberative body?

Deliberativeness does not necessarily imply a Burkean Congress in which the representatives heed the national interest in making their policy decisions. Nor does it require direct representation of the people. It simply implies that Congress does not act spontaneously. In many respects, at least on important issues, Congress *is* a deliberative body. The nature of Congress is a reflection of our broader political system.

In 1942, a famous British scholar, Sir Ernest Barker, wrote a book which had wide currency at the time entitled *Reflections on Government*. The book was written against the backdrop of Nazi Germany and Fascist Italy and the struggles that were occurring at that time. Barker was attempting to defend not just the British parliamentary system but democracy in general. He suggested that a truly democratic system should be one in which there is "government by discussion." A government by discussion or delib-

eration has to exist at all levels of society. If it does not exist from the bottom up, it's not going to exist from the top down.

The government by discussion written about by Barker included disciplined political parties, and required discussion among the electorate. It was based upon a premise of the rationality of man, a belief in "political man," much in the same way that the liberal economists in the early nineteenth century talked about the rationality of economic man. The United States does not fully reflect a system of government by discussion. But the failure to achieve a government by discussion is not a failure of the Congress, or political leadership. It is a failure that is more widely shared.

Barker argued that a government by discussion was best achieved through a parliamentary system. Representative Vanik commented on the contrast between the parliamentary and the American system. Congress is a bastion of free enterprise and entrepreneurship. Only in Congress, a uniquely American body, can each and every member make a mark. Legislators, particularly those in the majority, have a degree of political power and an opportunity to make an imprint upon public policy that simply does not exist in parliamentary systems.

In the early 1950s the American Political Science Association suggested very seriously that the United States should institute a parliamentary system, which, it argued, was the only way to achieve responsible government. But the fact of the matter is, parliamentary bodies are not more deliberative than Congress. Parliamentary debates may look good on television—for example, in the Canadian Parliament. But the repartee that goes back and forth between the majority party and the opposition is really a drama that often has very little substance in terms of the actual decisions that the parliament is going to make, which are the rubber stamp of the majority party.

The fragmentation of Congress through the committee system and the development of staff does not necessarily imply a lack of deliberation. Congress is attempting to strengthen its deliberative process in a number of important ways, one of which is through the creation of a more integrated and rational budget process. The budget committees are seeking to integrate the budget process and make it far more deliberative than it has been before.

Congress is by far the most interesting body in our national government. It is an exciting and dramatic branch. It is more professional than commonly thought. The presidency has become in many respects an amateurish institution. That amateurishness is becoming particularly acute due to the growth of the primary system and grass-roots democracy. Congress reflects a degree of professionalization and expertise not only in particular subject matter areas but in politics, which is an area of expertise that goes beyond any particular substantive policy concerns. The deliberativeness of Congress will continue to buttress our system of constitutional democracy, one both of representative government and checks and balances.

PART II:
CONGRESSMEN
IN THEIR DISTRICTS

Congressmen and Their Constituents: 1958 and 1978

Morris P. Fiorina
Division of the Humanities and Social Sciences
California Institute of Technology

If a student of congressional elections had dozed off in the library in 1965 and slept until 1981, imagine the surprise in store for him. In 1965 our portrait of congressional elections was dominated by the 1958 representation study carried out by scholars associated with the University of Michigan's Survey Research Center (now Center for Political Studies). The highlights of that study were reported to the discipline at large in two widely reprinted articles by Warren Miller and Donald Stokes, and the complete picture of House elections was to appear in the same authors' eagerly awaited forthcoming book.[1] Though the book remained forthcoming, the portrait arising from the initial installments was the critics' choice until the early 1970s. That portrait had several principal features.

First, and in common with much of the early literature on voting behavior, the portrait violated the prescriptions of popular democratic theory. Information levels among House voters were low, and citizens' perceptions were general, imprecise, and almost devoid of policy or ideological content. Second, House elections appeared to be largely party-line affairs, and the Michigan researchers emphasized that this did not imply an informed choice between responsible parties, but rather the habitual affirmation of apolitical party attachments. Third, fluctuations in House election results arose not from the actions of the candidates, but from fluctuations in turnout and party defection arising from events and calculations associated with the presidential candidates and/or the incumbent president.[2] And fourth, the survey-based portrait conflicted in important ways with that

The research reported in this paper was supported by NSF Grant # SES 8010662. Thanks are due to Bruce Cain and John Ferejohn who commented on an earlier draft of this paper.

1. Warren Miller and Donald Stokes, "Party Government and the Saliency of Congress," *Public Opinion Quarterly* 26 (1962): 531-546; and idem, "Constituency Influence in Congress," *American Political Science Review* 57 (1963): 351-372.

2. Angus Campbell, "Surge and Decline: A Study of Electoral Change," *Public Opinion Quarterly* 24 (1960): 40-62.

described by the House candidates, who evidently were misperceiving the situation.[3]

In 1981 a new portrait of House elections is loose upon the land. This portrait too rests on a CPS election study, though not the 1958 study. In 1978 the first major congressional election study in two decades was carried out, and it has quickly provided the basis for a new portrait of House elections markedly different from the old. This new portrait too has several principal features.[4]

First, and in common with much of the later literature on voting behavior, the new portrait suggests that popular democratic theory is not so empirically inaccurate as previously believed. Information levels in House elections, particularly incumbent-contested elections, are no longer described as dismal. The policy/ideological content of citizen perceptions also appears higher than previously found, though still not exactly widespread. Second, the importance of party attachments appears lower than in 1958. As various studies have shown, the proportion of independent congressional voters has increased, and the loyalty of voters in each partisan category has declined.[5] Third, fluctuations in House results are now attributed principally to the qualities and activities of the individual candidates. In the bold words of one scholar (writing prior to the 1978 study, but strongly supported by its findings):

> The major conclusion of the study reported in this book is that congressional elections are local, not national, events: In deciding how to cast their ballots, voters are primarily influenced not by the president, the national parties, or the state of the economy, but by the local candidates.[6]

Fourth, the new portrait has a closer fit with the perceptions of 1958 House incumbents, and presumably with those of their successors as well.

---

3. The following passage is frequently quoted: "Of our sample of congressmen who were opposed for reelection in 1958, more than four-fifths said the outcome in their districts had been strongly influenced by the electorate's response to their records and personal standing. Indeed, this belief is clear enough to present a notable contradiction: Congressmen feel that their individual legislative actions may have considerable impact on the electorate, yet some simple facts about the representative's salience to his constituents imply that this could hardly be true" (Miller and Stokes, "Constituency Influence").

4. T. Mann and R. Wolfinger, "Candidates and Parties in Congressional Elections," *American Political Science Review* 74 (1980).

5. John A. Ferejohn, "On the Decline of Competition in Congressional Elections," *American Political Science Review* 71 (1977): 166-176.

6. Thomas Mann, *Unsafe at Any Margin* (Washington, D.C.: American Enterprise Institute, 1978), p.1.

Thus, in the short space of a decade and a half, one portrait of House elections has been replaced by a very different one.[7] While such intellectual turnabouts are not unusual in the academic world, it is important to understand, as best we can, the reasons for the change. Intellectual history is not the issue; rather, the issue is one of recalling *why* many scholars felt it was important to do a congressional elections study in 1978. Stated summarily, those reasons were that the 1958 portrait had become increasingly at odds with temporal *changes* and *trends* in House elections. For example, Erikson and Mayhew each noted that congressional incumbents, long rather successful electorally, became even more so during the 1960s.[8] Similarly, Burnham wrote of the increasing "insulation" of House elections, a sharp departure from Stokes's earlier "nationalization" thesis.[9] To explain such electoral change, these authors and others proposed numerous hypotheses, many of which focused on the qualities, activities, and strategies of the individual House candidates, factors which according to the 1958 portrait did not matter. Thus, the natural question arose: How had the 1958 portrait changed? If the influence of party was down, were information levels correspondingly up? Had other variables which affect vote choice changed, or had the manner in which other variables — and party — affect the vote choice changed?

Questions like the preceding provided the motivation for the 1978 study and exerted a major effect on its design. It is at least mildly surprising, then,

7. Note the obvious parallel with the literature on voting in presidential elections. *The American Voter*, a 1950s portrait, has been pushed aside by *The Changing American Voter*, a 1970s portrait. But here too there is considerable disagreement over the amount and nature of real change that has occurred. Some scholars, such as Christopher Achen and David RePass, suggest that a variety of weaknesses in the 1950s survey instruments produced a poor likeness of the electorate as it then existed (Christopher Achen, "Mass Political Attitudes and the Survey Response," *American Political Science Review* 69 [1975]: 1218-1231; David RePass, "Issue Salience and Party Choice," *American Political Science Review* 65 [1971]: 389-400). Other scholars suggest that differences in questionnaire design hopelessly confound the study of temporal change (see the articles, responses, and rejoinders in the May 1978 and February 1979 *American Journal of Political Science*).

8. Robert Erikson, "Malapportionment, Gerrymandering, and Party Fortunes in Congressional Elections," *American Political Science Review* 66 (1972): 1234-1255; David Mayhew, "Congressional Elections: The Case of the Vanishing Marginals," *Polity* 6 (1974): 295-317.

9. Walter D. Burnham, "Insulation and Responsiveness in Congressional Elections," *Political Science Quarterly* 90 (1975): 411-435; Donald Stokes, "Parties and the Nationalization of Electoral Forces," in The *American Party Systems: Stages of Political Development*, eds. William Nisbet Chambers and Walter D. Burnham (New York: Oxford University Press, 1967), pp. 182-202.

to note that since the release of the 1978 study such questions have received little *direct* attention. The 1978 study is a scholarly goldmine which can help us learn a great deal about the parameters of contemporary congressional elections. But 1978 data alone do not and cannot be used to explain the change in aggregate House elections over the past twenty years. That subject demands longitudinal data.

This paper addresses the subject of change in knowledge, perceptions, and voting behavior in congressional elections between 1958 and 1978. The method involves comparing data elicited by "comparable" items in the two SRC/CPS election studies, an admittedly difficult and dangerous enterprise. Even when item wording remains constant over time, changes in the social or political context may change the way in which citizens respond to the item.[10] When item wording varies, as is often the case in what follows, the difficulties and dangers are compounded. And special features of the 1958 study make comparative work still more difficult. None of what follows in this paper is conclusive. Certain comparisons are suggestive, some are not even that. But on the supposition that some information is better than none, I will proceed.

Recent Congressional Elections: What Has Changed

By now, thousands of professors, students, and journalists have seen diagrams such as those in figure 1, which Mayhew first used to illustrate the dramatic increase in the electoral margins of incumbents.[11] Because American political thought places great importance on electoral competition—insecurity supposedly encourages responsiveness and faithful representation—Mayhew's diagrams caused many of his colleagues to sit up and take notice. If the characteristics of House outcomes were changing, something affecting those outcomes must also be changing. The question was what. Were the voters undergoing some sort of behavioral change? Were the candidates doing something different? Was it some combination of the two? Or was it something larger than both?[12]

---

10. Nie, Verba, and Petrocik provide a good illustration with their discussion of the changing meaning of the "size of government" item between 1964 and 1972 (Norman Nie, Sidney Verba, and John Petrocik, *The Changing American Voter*, 2nd ed. [Cambridge, Mass.: Harvard University Press, 1980]).

11. Mayhew, "Congressional Elections."

12. An example of the latter possibility was the suggestion that the increasingly comfortable margins of incumbents were the direct result of an increasing tendency by state legislatures

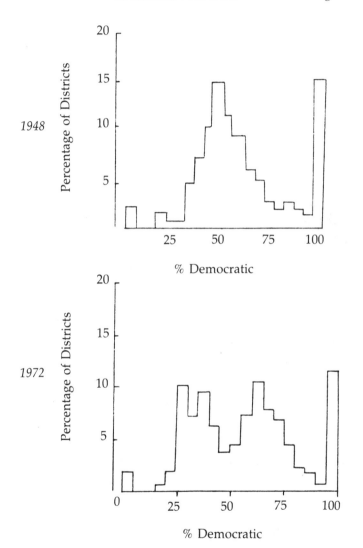

Figure 1:
Distribution of Congressional Vote
in Districts with Incumbents Running

to protect their House incumbents by providing them with districts in which their party held a comfortable registration edge. This suggestion was quickly rejected (Charles Bullock, "Redistricting and Congressional Stability, 1962-1972," *Journal of Politics* 37 [1975]: 569-575; Ferejohn, "On the Decline of Competition").

Only one of the proposed explanations for the increased advantage of incumbency fit reasonably well with the 1958 portrait of congressional voting behavior. This was the "incumbency as voting cue" theory advanced by Erikson, Burnham, and Ferejohn.[13] These authors accepted the prevailing view of House elections as low-information, party-line affairs, but observed that the extent of party identification had declined somewhat, and that the influence of party identification in structuring both presidential and congressional voting had lessened since the 1950s. If an increased number of voters had no party identification, or hesitated to rely on it as much as previously, then they might be casting about for an alternative rule-of-thumb for voting. Because incumbency is easily ascertained, it might serve as a readily available cue for voters no longer reliant on party identification.

The problems with such arguments at first hinged more on their inherent plausibility than on conflicting data. Voting for incumbents seemed like a rather simple-minded way to vote, particularly since explanations for the lessened importance of party identification usually posited an electorate becoming *more* rather than less sophisticated. Moreover, public opinion data showed that citizens were becoming increasingly cynical and distrustful of people in government. How could one square such suggestions with arguments that increasing numbers of citizens were casting more or less automatic votes for incumbents? Very recently, empirical analyses have tended to further undercut the "incumbency as cue" theory. Born has pointed out that the incumbency advantage is not uniform; it varies systematically across House cohorts.[14] If the incumbency advantage were merely a by-product of the decline in party identification, there would be no particular reason to expect anything other than random variation in its extent.

Still, if the decline in party identification is not *the* explanation for the increased incumbency advantage, it might constitute part of a more complicated explanation. In particular, perhaps *some* incumbents (the advantage was not uniform) behave in ways calculated to take advantage of weakened party ties—or even in ways calculated to weaken those ties still further. For one thing, a variety of indicators suggest that incumbents have grown more

---

13. Erikson, "Malapportionment"; Burnham, "Insulation and Responsiveness"; Ferejohn, "On the Decline of Competition."

14. Richard Born, "Generational Replacement and the Growth of Incumbent Reelection Margins in the U.S. House," *American Political Science Review* 73 (1979): 811-817.

solicitous of their constituents over the postwar period. Mayhew notes that congressional use of the frank skyrocketed during the mid-1960s.[15] Authorizations for travel, staff, and offices increased greatly between 1958 and the present.[16] And of course, campaign expenditures have clearly increased, though reliable data are available only for the 1970s.[17] There is little doubt that the availability and use of tangible resources by House incumbents has increased greatly between 1958 and 1978. There are even suggestions that intangible resources increasingly favor incumbents. Payne, for example, speculates that there has been a shift in the old "work horse v. show horse" dichotomy from the former to the latter, and that "show horse" personality types do better in the electoral arena.[18]

Resource allocation theories have in common the presumption that the 1958 portrait of congressional elections no longer holds—indeed, that incumbents, by their behavior, have worked a change in the old portrait. At a minimum, resource allocation theories appear to imply that contemporary voters know more about the incumbent than those of yesteryear. But do they? Only one relevant data series exists.

Table 1, compiled by Ferejohn, contains name recall data for incumbents and challengers over the 1958 to 1974 period.[19] The reader should bear in mind that the 1978 study has confirmed the argument of various researchers that spontaneous name recall demands much more of the citizen than the simple name recognition actually demanded in the voting booth.[20] Thus, we know that the 1958 SRC study and all others using name recall

---

15. Mayhew, "Congressional Elections."

16. Glenn Parker, "Sources of Change in Congressional District Attentiveness," *American Journal of Political Science* 24 (1980): 115-124; Morris P. Fiorina, *Congress—Keystone of the Washington Establishment* (New Haven, Ct.: Yale University Press, 1977).

17. Gary Jacobson, *Money in Congressional Elections* (New Haven, Ct.: Yale University Press, 1980).

18. It is not clear, however, why Payne's argument is not symmetric—that is, those who challenge incumbents should also increasingly tend to be "show horse" types and thus offset the increase on the incumbent side (James Payne, "The Personal Electoral Advantage of House Incumbents, 1936-1976," *American Politics Quarterly* 8 [1980]: 465-482).

19. Ferejohn, "On the Decline of Competition."

20. Alan I. Abramowitz, "Name Familiarity, Reputation, and the Incumbent Effect in a Congressional Election," *Western Political Quarterly* 27 (1975): 668-684; Mann, *Unsafe at Any Margin*. To illustrate, name recognition of House incumbents in 1978 was about 80 percent, whereas their recall figure was about 35 percent. Name recognition of the challengers was about 40 percent, whereas their recall figure was about 11 percent.

underestimate the sheer visibility of congressional candidates. Still, there is no obvious reason why the extent of the underestimate should vary over time. Thus, name recall might provide an accurate assessment of *changes* in candidate visibility, and of differences in visibility between, say, incumbents and challengers. If that assumption is granted, then table 1 poses a problem for resource allocation theories. As shown in the table, while the incumbency advantage grew, the visibility of incumbents remained constant, both in absolute terms and relative to the challenger. This was an exceedingly surprising finding. It seemed to imply that all the incumbent's efforts were for naught — that they fell on deaf ears — a conclusion quite in keeping with the 1958 portrait of the electorate.

Table 1
Name Recall of House Candidates Among Voters,
Contested Races with Incumbents Running: 1958–1974

	Incumbent	Challenger	Difference
1958	58%	38%	20%
1964	63	40	23
1966	56	38	18
1968	64	47	17
1970	55	31	24
1974	60	44	16

In 1977 I suggested one solution to the preceding puzzle. Perhaps incumbents had not made themselves more visible to their constituents, but had changed their image among those to whom they *were* visible. In other words, the sheer amount of information had not changed, but the *content* of the information had.[21] Briefly, I argued that the expanded federal presence had increased the importance of two traditional roles of House members, that of ombudsman for constituents experiencing frustration with bureaucratic decisions, and that of broker between groups seeking a share of federal largesse and the federal agencies which controlled it. Clearly there has been an increase in the casework loads of House offices, and a similar increase in the number of federal programs for which some local group or government might be eligible. If House members increasingly emphasized such activities when dealing with their constituencies, we

---

21. Fiorina, *Keystone of the Washington Establishment*, p. 51.

might observe a substitution of nonpartisan, nonprogrammatic, nonideological perceptions for more partisan, programmatic, and ideological ones. In a nutshell, less controversial information would replace more controversial information in the memories of those having any information at all. Thus, increased support for incumbents would stem from an increase in the positive-negative ratio of constituent information, rather than from an increase in the absolute level of information.

Perhaps the most notable thing about the foregoing argument was the complete lack of evidence bearing on it. The 1978 CPS study has taken care of part of that problem. The latter contains a wealth of items designed to elicit information about the existence and nature of perceptions and evaluations of congressional candidates, especially incumbents. There are the traditional candidate likes/dislikes, thermometers, seven-point scales, items inquiring about the nature of contacts candidates have made with citizens, focused questions about the incumbent's service activities, questions about the relative importance of various activities, and so on. Analyses to date have shown that, indeed, constituent assistance and district service are a major component of incumbents' images, second only to candidate personal qualities, and far ahead of policy, ideology, party, group alliances, or whatever.[22] Moreover, analyses have shown that constituent assistance and district service, actual and reputed, exert a significant influence on congressional voting.[23] The question remains, though, whether 1978 information levels, candidate images, and voting behavior differ from those of previous years. Consideration of that question is the subject of the body of this paper.

Information Levels, 1958 and 1978

In 1958 the SRC carried out an ambitious two-part study. The first consisted of the standard national sample of voting age citizens (n = 1450, weighted to 1822). The second part consisted of an elite survey of candidates whose districts fell in the mass sampling frame. In what follows I will be dealing exclusively with the mass survey.

Table 2 contains some basic comparisons of information levels between 1958 and 1978. It also illustrates several of the problems we will be dealing

---

22. Parker, "Sources of Change."

23. Morris P. Fiorina, "Some Problems in Studying the Effects of Resource Allocation in Congressional Elections," *American Journal of Political Science* 25 (1981): 543-567; Gary Jacobson, "Incumbents and Voters in the 1978 Congressional Elections," *Legislative Studies Quarterly* 6(1981): 183-200.

with throughout the remainder of the paper. The first finding in the table —
and it is a surprising one — is that candidate name recall actually is *lower* in
1978 than in 1958, marginally so for incumbents, greatly so for challengers.
A small part of the explanation for the former lies in the heavy retirement
rates of the mid-1970s. In 1978, 40 percent of House incumbent candidates
had entered the institution since Nixon's resignation; lower aggregate
name recall partly reflects the lowered visibility of relatively junior
incumbents.[24] Less substantive and more unfortunate reasons apparently
underlie the low level of challenger recall. Jacobson has argued that
whether through sheer bad luck or malevolent intervention, the 1978 sample contains both poorer challengers than actually ran, and fewer citizens
favorable to challengers than actually were.[25] Specifically, the sample voters reported casting only 21 percent of their vote for challengers, who
actually garnered about 32 percent.[26] In addition Jacobson points out that
the challengers in the sample spent only four-fifths as much as all challengers, and that politically experienced challengers in the sample (i.e., those
who had held previous elective office) spent only half as much as experienced challengers not in the sample. Thus, the 1978 survey contains reactions from people "extraordinarily hostile to challengers, fond of incumbents, or both," reactions moreover elicited by a poorer group of challengers than actually contested all races.[27] This unfortunate situation means
that information levels, positive/negative evaluation ratios, and so forth,
are all biased downward in the case of challengers.

A second indicator of information levels in the 1958 survey consists of
responses to the item: "Now we're interested in knowing what sorts of
persons people think these candidates are. Have you read or heard anything about Mr. [Name of Republican/Name of Democrat]?" (This question
was asked *after* those who did not recall the candidate's name were provided with the name.) As shown in the table, 1958 incumbents had a

---

24. This explanation does not begin to account for all of the drop between the 1958 and 1978
figures, however. The senior third of incumbents in 1978 had a recall figure of only 37
percent, still noticeably below the 1958 figure.

25. Gary Jacobson, "Congressional Elections, 1978: The Case of the Vanishing Challengers,"
in *Congressional Elections*, ed. Louis Maisel, *Sage Electoral Studies Yearbook* 7 (1981).

26. The well-known tendency for voters to over-report support for the winner (in presidential elections) does not appear to underlie this finding. Jacobson reports that in previous
House elections the reported and actual totals were very close (ibid.). See also the 1958
figures in table 2.

27. Jacobson, "Congressional Elections, 1978," p. 16.

Table 2
Some Basic Facts About Contested Races with Incumbents
Running, 1958 and 1978*

| | *All* | | *Voters Only* | |
	1958	*1978*	*1958*	*1978*
Name recall:				
Incumbent	43.0%	34.4%	56.7%	48.5%
Challenger	25.8	10.9	33.9	16.5
Read or heard about incumbent	37.8	—	49.1	—
Read or heard about challenger	18.5	—	25.1	—
Some contact with incumbent	—	78.9	—	89.4
Some contact with challenger	—	37.3	—	44.0
Know which candidate is incumbent	58.5	66.9	70.8	82.3
Vote for incumbent:				
Sample	—	—	59.8	78.6
Actual	—	—	57.8	66.8

*1958 figures do not include at-large races in Connecticut and New Mexico (which were in addition to district races).

two-to-one edge over their challengers according to the "heard or read" item. The 1978 survey does not include the latter item. The closest item appears to be the contact battery which asks the respondent whether he or she has come into contact with the incumbent and challenger or open seat candidates in any of the following ways: met personally, attended a meeting where the incumbent appeared, talked to a staffer, received mail, read about in newspaper or magazine, heard on radio, or saw on TV. The contact battery appears comparable to the "heard or read" item in that it explicitly mentions most of the ways a citizen might hear or read something about the candidates, but the distribution of responses to the contact battery is greatly different from that of the "heard or read" item. As table 2 shows, the two-to-one informational advantage of incumbents also appears in 1978. But the absolute levels for both incumbents and challengers are much higher than in 1958, twice as high for the whole sample.

The question obviously is whether information levels actually have doubled in the past twenty years, the decline in name recall notwithstanding, or whether the contact battery simply elicits a much higher proportion of positive responses than the "heard or read" item. At first glance the latter possibility seems the more likely. Today's incumbents possess greatly increased resources by which to communicate with their constituents, but their challengers, particularly the weak ones in the 1978 sample, have no obviously greater resource base. On the other hand, doubling the information level for challengers required only a 20 percent absolute increase, whereas doubling the incumbents' level required a 40 percent absolute increase, so perhaps the data *are* consistent with the increased resource advantage incumbents have over challengers. The question merits additional study.

The third indicator of information levels which appears in table 2 is the percent correctly identifying the incumbent *after receiving the names of the candidates*. Nearly identical items appeared in both the 1958 and 1978 surveys, and as table 2 shows, about 10 percent more respondents could correctly identify the incumbent in 1978 than in 1958.[28] But here too we must raise a caution flag. In 1958 respondents were asked to identify the incumbent immediately after receiving the names of the candidates. In 1978, however, a battery of likes/dislikes items intervened. It is certainly plausible that in racking one's brain for things one likes and dislikes about a candidate (up to four of each) one would think of something which would create an association between a name and incumbency. Thus, again, we cannot confidently say whether the simple ability to identify the incumbent has increased over time.

In sum, comparisons of information levels between 1958 and 1978 are inconclusive. Name recall actually suggests a *decline* in information levels, though there are good reasons to discount this suggestion. Two other indicators suggest an increase, but in these cases differences in survey items and question sequencing make one hesitant to have much confidence

---

28. In the 1958 study the House candidates' names were given to the respondent as part of the "know incumbent" item:

> Q. 48. Of course, the names aren't too important, but there were two major candidates, Mr. [name of Democrat] who ran on the Democrat ticket and Mr. [name of Republican] who ran on the Republican ticket. Do you happen to know [if either of these candidates] [if he] is already in Congress?

In the 1978 study, names were provided prior to the likes/dislikes battery, then the "know incumbent" item was asked:

> Q. A21. Do you happen to know if either of these candidates, [the Democratic House candidate] or [the Republican House candidate], was already in the U.S. House of Representatives before the election?

in the resulting figures. Perhaps the most reasonable conclusion is that the comparisons produce no solid support for the proposition that information levels have changed over time. Thus, popular explanations of the enhanced incumbency advantage which point to sheer advertising have little support in the data.

Constituency Relations, 1958 and 1978

The major reasons congressional election researchers have despaired over the 1958 study is the use of various filters in the interview schedule which pare away large segments of the sample. For example, the 1958 study includes items which inquire whether the respondent has had a casework experience, and whether the respondent recalls anything special the incumbent has done for the district. *These items were asked, however, only of those constituents who could correctly identify the incumbent.* Granted, it might seem logical that constituents who could not identify the incumbent would report no recollections of casework or district service, but any experienced analyst of survey data would be wary of such logic.[29] The strategy I have followed is to attempt to construct analogous filters for the 1978 survey, and to compare the responses of the subsamples which pass through the filter in each case. There are two obvious dangers in such a procedure. The first is that the filters fail to correspond and thus do not produce comparable subsamples. The second is that the eliminated subsamples are simply ignored. If there are systematic differences between them, the mode of analysis I have adopted would overlook them. But given that the omitted portion of the 1958 sample has no relevant data whatsoever, I know of no obviously better way to proceed.

In 1958, 88 percent of the sample lived in districts with incumbents running for reelection—exactly the same figure as in the 1978 sample. As reported in table 2, about 10 percent more respondents could identify the incumbent in 1978 than in 1958. Thus, application of the "know incumbent" filter nets a marginally larger proportion of the 1978 sample than of the 1958 sample. Both samples were asked a nearly identical item: "Can you remember anything special [the incumbent] has done for this district or for the people in this district?" In each year two responses were coded and,

---

29. It turns out, however, that in the 1978 study only 2 percent (n = 15) of those who could not identify the incumbent later reported casework experiences. The figure was 4 percent for district service. If the 1958 situation was comparable, failure to ask the items of the whole sample probably led to very little loss of information. I am much less sanguine about the situation with the 1958 open-ended items discussed in the text below.

happily, SRC/CPS used the identical open-ended coding scheme both times. Between the similar filter item and the similar survey item, we have a relatively clean comparison of recollections of district service. Both samples were also asked about casework experiences, but here the items differed. The 1958 sample was asked: "Has he ever helped you or done anything personally for you or your family?" Up to two responses were coded. I defined casework as the category "personal favors and services" and about half the category "information and publicity," omitting respondents in the⁴ latter category who specified receipt of *unsolicited* public relations materials. In 1978 respondents were asked whether they or a family member had ever contacted the incumbent, and if so, whether it was to express an opinion, seek help with a problem, or request information. I defined the latter two categories as casework. Though the 1958 and 1978 items clearly differ, the 1978 items are, if anything, more "difficult." The respondents in 1978 were asked whether they had taken the initiative and contacted the incumbent, whereas the respondents in 1958 were asked only if some contact had ever occurred.

Table 3 contrasts the 1958 and 1978 casework and district service variables. If the 1978 items are granted to be at least as demanding as the 1958 items, it appears that casework experience among constituents has tripled over the two decades. Such an increase has been hypothesized, and certainly it is consistent with the growth in personal staffs and district office operations, and with fragmentary reports of casework loads made by House staffs. From an electoral standpoint, reaching an additional 10 percent of one's constituency in a very personal way could easily account for several percentage points of additional support.

Table 3

Casework Experiences and District Service Recollections
Among Citizens Who Could Correctly Identify the
House Incumbent, 1958 and 1978

| | All | | Voters Only | |
	1958	1978	1958	1978
Personal help	3.5%	9.9%	4.1%	10.8%
Information	1.1	7.7	1.5	9.8
Total casework	4.5	14.9	5.6	17.2
District service?	33.2	29.0	37.2	34.3

The district service variable, on the other hand, produces findings quite contrary to prior expectation. Recollection of special services were *more* widespread in 1958 than in 1978. How can this be, when federal programs have proliferated between 1958 and 1978, and when congressmen have developed credit-claiming to a fine art? The answer emerges when we look at the breakdown of responses to the district service item. These appear in table 4. As shown, the number of responses clearly referring to local problems and projects has risen considerably — by more than 25 percent. Such responses are now far and away the most common, though they were also the modal category in 1958. The only other figure in the table that deserves notice is the virtual disappearance of volunteered *negative* responses to the district service item over the twenty-year period.

Table 4
Nature of District Service Recalled, 1958 and 1978

	1958		1978	
General competence	8%	(32)	7%	(30)
Provides access to government	4	(17)	7	(29)
Communicates with constituents	7	(28)	4	(19)
National legislation, policy	22	(92)	22	(96)
Local problems/pork	30	(127)	42	(183)
Good party member	2	(7)	—	(1)
Group references	14	(59)	15	(64)
Negative comments	5	(22)	1	(4)
Other/miscellaneous	8	(35)	2	(9)
Total comments		(419)		(435)

So, the data suggest an increase in the proportion of constituents who associate their representative with particularistic benefits, either in the very personal sense of casework, or in the somewhat broader sense of localized problems and projects. Though the comparisons are not as clean as we would ideally prefer, they appear considerably less ambiguous than those involving information levels in the preceding section. Some real change appears to have taken place in the area of constituent recollections of particularized benefits.

Before moving on, a final comparison might be of interest. This one concerns the representative's action in the policy sphere, but the connection with the foregoing discussion occurs through the question of who should ultimately control his policy decisions. In both the 1958 and 1978 surveys all respondents were given a version of the classic delegate-trustee distinction:[30]

> Sometimes voters want their U.S. representative to do something the representative disagrees with. When this happens, do you think the representative should do what the voters think best, or should the representative do what he or she thinks best (1978 wording)?[31]

The distributions of responses to this item are most suggestive. Consider table 5. In 1958, a plurality of Americans opted for the trustee pole of the classic dichotomy. By 1978, however, a solid majority of Americans were unwilling to grant their representatives such personal discretion. The shift may well be connected to declining levels of trust and confidence in government officials, a question I will not pursue here. Suffice it to say that in addition to an increased association of House incumbents with particularistic benefits, the data suggest an increased willingness to impose particularistic standards on representatives' policy decisions. The assiduous polling and other means of information-gathering utilized by contemporary representatives may have a very real basis in the attitudes of their constituents.

Table 5
Delegate or Trustee? 1958 and 1978

In case of conflict repre-sentative should follow:	*All*		*Voters Only*	
	1958	*1978*	*1958*	*1978*
District	38.4%	55.4%	42.2%	56.4%
Conscience	45.3	29.8	43.7	29.5
Depends	10.5	11.0	11.9	12.1
Don't know	5.7	3.8	2.2	2.0
n =	1774	2290	1014	1057

30. John C. Wahlke et al., *The Legislative System: Explorations in Legislative Behavior* (New York: John Wiley, 1962).

31. In the less enlightened 1950s the question phrasing was as follows:

> Q. 67. Sometimes when a man is elected to Congress the voters want him to do something he disagrees with. When this happens do you think he should do what the voters think best, or should he do what he thinks best?

Candidate Images, 1958 and 1978

Both the 1958 and 1978 surveys contain open-ended items designed to explore the content of citizen perceptions and evaluations of House candidates. Given that such items permit respondents to describe their attitudes in their own words — and assuming that respondents offer their most central or salient attitudes — open-ended responses are the most suitable form of data for ascertaining the content of candidate images. As one would expect, however, there are various difficulties attendant to the temporal comparisons of open-ended responses. In increasing order of seriousness they are the following: first, the coding categories utilized by SRC/CPS in 1958 and 1978 differ; second, the filter used in the 1958 study does not appear in the 1978 study; third, the format, wording, and sequencing of the open-ended items differ between the two studies.

Coding differences create no insuperable difficulties. In the 1958 study, responses were placed into a 70-category "Congressional Candidate Code." In 1978 the standard party/presidential candidate master code was augmented by a number of categories dealing specifically with congressional matters, yielding a classification with upwards of 500 categories. For the most part (i.e., the most commonly offered responses) it is easy to identify the comparable codes in the two studies. Table 6 contains the codes underlying the broad categories presented in the tables which follow. The reader can examine these and take issue with my judgments or not as the case may be.

Filtering out comparable subsamples from the 1958 and 1978 samples poses a more serious problem. *The open-ended items in 1958 were asked only of respondents who stated that they had "heard or read" something about the candidate.* As mentioned in the discussion of table 2, the "heard or read" item does not appear in the 1978 study. The most comparable item in the latter appears to be the contact battery. Recall, however, that twice as high a proportion of the sample passes through that filter as passes through the "heard or read" filter in 1958. If the items actually are comparable, no problem exists—the 1978 sample is simply better acquainted with the candidates. But if the contact battery is "easier to pass" than the "read or heard" item, we will be examining different subsamples for the two years.

Question wording creates by far the greatest difficulties for a temporal comparison of candidate images. In 1978 respondents were asked the standard battery of likes/dislikes items. Probes elicited up to four positive and four negative responses. In the 1958 study two types of open-ended items appear. The first reads as follows: '

> Now how about Mr. [name of candidate]. Forgetting about his
> party for a moment, do you think of him as being the right sort of
> person to be a congressman, or don't you have any opinion on
> this.

Those offering opinions were then asked the reason for their opinion, with
up to two responses coded. Notice two features of the "right sort" item.
First, party connections are explicitly downplayed, a fact we should bear in
mind when examining the kinds of responses the item elicits. Second, and
more important, the question is asymmetric in that a negative response is
extremely negative—it is tantamount to an assertion that the candidate is
not fit to serve in Congress. In contrast, the likes/dislikes items are quite
symmetric with their almost casual inquiry into "anything in particular"
that the respondent likes or dislikes. Moreover, the probes to the "right
sort" item implicitly ask for up to two positive *or* up to two negative
responses, rather than both, in contrast to the probes for the likes/dislikes
items.

Table 6
Coding Categories Equated in Comparisons of
1958 and 1978 Open-Ended Responses

Category	1958(Note 1)*	1978(Note 7)*
General, good man, bad man	00	201
Record and experience	1-2	211-297
Personal abilities and attributes	3,5,13	301-320
relevant to leadership		397,505
Personal qualities	4,6-9	401-497
Party	10-12	500-504
		506-508
Constituency attentiveness		
Helps with problems	—	321-322
Understand district	15	323-324
Keeps constituents informed	—	325-326
Listens, accessible	14	327-328
Local issues, projects	30-31	329-331
National domestic issues	20-29	900-1009
Foreign policy	40-49	1101-1197
Philosophy, ideology,	32-39	601-697
general approach to		531-536
government		800-897
Group references	50-69	1201-1297
Personal considerations	70-79	—
Other	80-90	701-723

* Notes in back of SSRC code books. Many of the codes listed under note 7
were not utilized in coding the congressional likes/dislikes.

Following the "right sort" item and probes, the respondent was asked a number of questions dealing with the candidate's social class, religion, nationality, group affiliations, issue positions, and whether he or she understood the problems of people like the respondent. Then, in concluding that portion of the interview, the respondent was asked, "Is there anything else about Mr. [name of candidate] that made you want to vote for him" and an analogous item with "against him." Up to two responses were coded for each of the items (according to the same coding scheme previously used). These for/against items are symmetric as are the likes/dislikes, and thus appear to offer a better comparison with the latter than do the "right sort" items.

In sum, the 1958 respondent has the opportunity to give four positive and two negative responses, or vice versa. In contrast, the 1978 respondent has the opportunity to give an equal number (four) of positive and negative responses.[32]

Table 7 shows that the reservations expressed in the preceding two paragraphs may well be justified. Consider the figures for incumbents. The 575 respondents who pass through the "heard or read" filter in 1958 show a 7:1 positive/negative ratio on the "right sort" item, but only a 3:1 ratio on the for/against items. These figures contrast with the 4:1 ratio on the likes/ dislikes items turned in by the 1545 respondents who passed the contact filter in 1978. Similar differences appear for the challengers, though here we face the aforementioned complication that the 1978 group appears to be a ·weaker group than actually contested the elections.

Table 8 provides another view of the overall configuration of the open-ended responses, organized here by number of comments rather than number of respondents. Again we see the expected differences. The "right sort" items elicit disproportionately positive responses.

The upshot of tables 7 and 8 is that it is virtually impossible to compare the overall "positivity" of candidate images between 1958 and 1978. If we added together all the open-ended responses in 1958 we would find that the positivity of candidate images had actually declined, something we might be prepared to believe in the case of challengers, but something that seems

---

32. There is a plausible argument to the effect that this particular asymmetry between the 1958 and 1978 question forms has little empirical import. In 1978 only twenty respondents gave more than two incumbent dislikes and only four gave more than two challenger dislikes. Thus, it is probable that few 1958 respondents were denied the opportunity to make more negative comments thàn they might have wished. Still, the 1958 wording may well have stimulated more positive comments than the 1978 wording.

quite dubious in the case of incumbents. If we adopted the more reasonable strategy of comparing responses to the 1958 for/against items with the 1978 likes/dislikes, we would find that incumbent images appear slightly more positive in 1978. But given the comparability problems I have discussed, and the apparent problems with the 1978 challenger sample, I conclude that it is simply not possible to ascertain whether candidate images are any more or less positive today than in 1958.

Table 7
Evaluations of House Candidates I: 1958 and 1978

Item		Incumbent (n = 575)	Challenger (n = 222)
1958			
Is he right sort?	Yes	75%	49%
	No	10	14
	Don't know	15	37
Anything else?	For	47	34
	Against	15	18
1978			
Anything in particular?		(n = 1545)	(n = 584)
	Like	54	19
	Dislike	14	18

Table 8
Evaluations of House Candidates II: 1958 and 1978

	1958		1978
	Right Sort	*For/Against*	*Likes/Dislikes*
Incumbents			
Positive	90%	79%	84%
Negative	10	11	16
Number of comments	636	468	1755
Challengers			
Positive	77	67	57
Negative	23	33	43
Number of comments	203	157	315

What about the *content* of candidate images? The positivity bias of the 1958 "right sort" question should not prevent us from comparing the nature of positive responses in 1958 with those in 1978, and similarly for negative responses. And in fact, the positive (negative) responses to the "right sort" item are distributed over the coding categories in very much the same manner as the positive (negative) responses to the for/against items. Thus, I combine the two for purposes of this analysis. Table 9 shows that the content of incumbent images has changed in only one major respect between 1958 and 1978—the proportion of comments about the incumbent's attentiveness to constituents and the district has more than doubled. (New categories were added in 1978 to handle the comments on personal assistance and communication/education.) Again, if we believe that incumbents' increasing use of staff, the mail, district offices, etc. has *any* effect, such a change in the distribution of responses is no more than should be expected.

Table 9
Breakdown of Positive Evaluations of Incumbent: 1958 and 1978

Category	*1958*	*1978*
General, good man	11%	7%
Experience and record	20	15
Personal attributes	30	30
Qualities and characteristics relevant to serving	(17)	(4)
Personality	(13)	(26)
Constituency attentiveness	11	25
Helps with problems	—	(6)
Understands district, keeps in touch	(5)	(7)
Keeps constituents informed	—	(7)
Listens, is accessible	(4)	(6)
Local issues, projects	(2)	(2)
Philosophy, ideology, general approach to government	2	7
Domestic issues/policy	3	5
Foreign policy	0+	1
Group references	6	5
Party affiliations/connections	5	1
Personal considerations	8	—
Other	4	4
Number of comments	942	1475

Several minor changes in the distribution of responses also are present. There is perhaps a marginal increase in the policy and ideological content of the 1978 responses, though I have been generous in equating coding categories in the area of philosophy and ideology. Notice too that party-related aspects of the image have virtually disappeared. And given that the "right sort" items in 1958 explicitly asked the respondent to exclude party considerations, the decline in this category is probably greater than shown. Finally, note that the "personal considerations" code for 1958 has no comparable code for 1978.[33] Probably such responses in the latter year were placed in the much more extensive personal-attributes-characteristics-experience codes which existed in 1978. Incidentally, there appears to be a noticeable difference between the two years in the types of personal attributes mentioned by constituents. But I frankly had difficulty distinguishing many of the categories listed. As shown, when all the various personal characteristics and qualities are combined, the proportion in this general category is identical between the two years.

Table 10 contains a breakdown of negative aspects of the incumbent's image. There is not much to discuss here. The increased proportion of negative comments directed at the incumbent's personal attributes is probably an artifact of the more elaborate 1978 coding scheme which absorbed the relatively large "other" category which existed in 1958. All other differences are too small to pay much attention to, though again we see that party connections are fewer in 1978 than in 1958.

And what about the challenger's image? While substantively of great importance, there is little reason to dwell on this question here, for in addition to all the problems previously discussed, we have the additional one of working with a relatively small number of comments. Moreover, given the apparently unrepresentative nature of the 1978 challengers in the sample, the things people say about them might be similarly unrepresentative. But for the sake of completeness, the breakdown of the open-ended evaluations of challengers appears in table 11.

The most notable thing about the comparison of response distributions is the considerably greater focus on personal characteristics by the 1978 respondents. This shift comes at the expense of references to the challenger's experience and record (the weak group of challengers again, or something more?), group references, and party-related references. Such

---

33. The 1958 "personal considerations" category included "friends and neighbors" comments and general "I just like (dislike) him" sentiments.

Table 10
Breakdown of Negative Evaluations of Incumbent: 1958 and 1978

Category	1958	1978
General, bad man	2%	4%
Experience and record	7	10
Personal attributes	25	44
Constituency attentiveness	6	9
Philosophy, ideology, general approach to government	7	12
Domestic issues, policy	9	6
Foreign policy	1	1
Group references	6	6
Party affiliations/connections	11	6
Personal considerations	8	—
Other	19	1
Number of comments	162	280

Table 11
Breakdown of Challenger Evaluations: 1958 and 1978

	Positive		Negative	
Category	1958	1978	1958	1978
General, good person	14%	9%	2%	6%
Experience and record	13	4	13	4
Personal attributes	30	57	45	66
Constituency attentiveness	7	0	2	0
Philosophy/ideology/approach	5	13	3	13
Domestic issues/policy	5	9	3	1
Foreign policy	0+	1	0	0
Group references	11	3	3	1
Party affiliations/connections	10	2	9	4
Personal connections	2	—	9	—
Other	5	3	10	4
Number of comments	262	180	98	135

findings are consistent with arguments that the declining value of a congressional seat, the increasing strength of incumbents, the increasing costs of campaigning, or whatever, have the effect of deterring strong, experienced challengers today who might have entered the lists in earlier days. Or then again, and not incompatible with the preceding hypotheses, local party organizations may no longer perform their function of recruiting and working for credible candidates as well as they did (on average) in the past. The table contains grounds for a wealth of speculation, but as mentioned, it would be imprudent to place much confidence in the comparisons.

In looking back over the tables which describe and summarize the open-ended candidate evaluations, it is easy to understand the emergence of the old portrait of House elections. In my opinion, Miller and Stokes should have given more attention to the possibility of two-step flows and other indirect processes—i.e., the likelihood that many general and/or personal attribute responses had some long-forgotten and/or several-times-removed service or policy basis. In addition, today's scholars would be less likely to discount the political relevance of group- and party-related responses. But despite such caveats it is clear that Miller and Stokes were basically correct. Information levels *were* low, and perceptions of the candidates *were* largely devoid of policy or issue content. In 1958, House elections *were in fact* low-information, party-dominated affairs.

The surprising thing is that the comparable 1978 data give rise to a portrait not much different from the old one. Citizen responses *remain* relatively devoid of policy and/or issue content. Ideology and personal philosophy may be slightly more common (or my coding may be more generous), but they are still small relative to other categories. Twice as large a proportion of the sample reports some contact with the 1978 incumbents as reports having heard or read about the 1958 incumbents, but comparisons of name recall and ability to identify the incumbent in a two-horse race suggest that differences in item wording may underlie the apparent increase.

Actually, much of the impetus for the rapid acceptance of the new portrait of House elections appears to arise from too enthusiastic inference from a single 1978 comparison. As discussed earlier, the later survey contained name *recognition* as well as name *recall* measures, and the latter were found to underestimate the former by perhaps half. Implicitly, some scholars seem to presume that because the 1958 study underestimated name familiarity by half, it underestimated everything by half; but there is little evidence for this presumption. In fact, *in the absence of a compelling argument to the effect that name recall has become a steadily larger underestimate of name recognition, the figures in table 2 suggest that name recognition would have been higher in 1958 than in 1978, had the items been included in the former study.*

The fact is that most of the basis for revising the old portrait comes from items new to the 1978 study. Although few respondents mention policy or ideology in response to the likes/dislikes items, about 40 percent of the sample is willing to offer an opinion of the incumbent's voting record, and a similar percentage places the incumbent on the liberal-conservative scale. But such contrasts raise caution flags. Do they mean that citizens have perceptions of the incumbent's policy positions and ideology, but do not attach sufficient importance to them to mention them in response to the likes/dislikes battery? That suggestion is belied by the large, significant coefficients that voting record and ideological variables achieve in analyses of 1978 voting behavior. Or is it? Perhaps such coefficients indicate that policy and ideological evaluations are rationalized expressions of more general overall evaluations.

In writing the foregoing I am raising questions, not offering conclusions, though I write as one surprised by the comparison of 1958 and 1978 survey results. There is less change in the data than one might plausibly have expected. At best the data show some indication of change in the content of perceptions, but there is no conclusive evidence that a vastly increased proportion of the population has perceptions to report.

Voting Behavior: 1958 and 1978

Changes in information levels and in the content of candidate images obviously may produce changes in voting behavior. The absence of such changes, however, does not preclude change in voting behavior, because variables may rise or decline in behavioral importance even while their values or distributions remain constant. In the preceding pages we have sought (and generally failed) to find dramatic changes in the distribution of variables thought to affect the House voting decision. In this section we seek to ascertain whether those variables do affect House voting decisions, and whether they do so any differently in 1978 than in 1958. All of the methodological difficulties previously discussed come together at this point, but in a cautious spirit let us consider some statistical models of the vote decisions in the two elections.

In this type of analysis comparability of variables is the essence. No problem exists for certain important variables—name recall, party identification, and the party of the incumbent, for example. Other variables, however, require a bit of work. In the analyses to follow I have used the responses to the open-ended items in the two surveys to create a number of dummy variables which attempt to capture similar kinds of evaluations. Thus, the critical step is the equation of codes between the two surveys, a problem discussed in the preceding section. The challenger variables were simple. So few people had any comments to make about the challenger that I reduced all comments to two categories. "Challenger positive evaluation" and "challenger negative evaluation" are dummies which take on a value of 1 if the voter says *anything* positive or negative respectively. The same consideration governed the creation of a single "incumbent negative evaluation" variable. I divided positive evaluations of incumbents into three categories, however. Referring back to table 9, "incumbent constituency attentiveness" is a dummy which takes on a value of 1 if the respondent mentioned anything coded in that category. Similarly, "incumbent policy agreement" is coded 1 for any positive response dealing with policy, ideology, or general philosophy. Finally, "incumbent candidate attributes" is a variable whose value is the total number (i.e., integers from 0 to 4) of positive comments about the incumbent's record and experience, leadership qualities, or personal qualities. It would be desirable to break this category down further, but as I remarked in the preceding section, equation of the codes across the two surveys is the most difficult for this general category. The reader should bear in mind, additionally, that general approval of the incumbent's record and experience, attribution of leadership qualities, and admiration of his personal qualities may all have a basis in policy, constituency work, partisan rationalization, or whatever.

Table 12 presents probit estimates of the 1958 and 1978 vote decisions using the variables just discussed. In each equation, vote for the incumbent—a (0,1) dummy—is the dependent variable. Thus, positive signs indicate that a variable contributes positively to the probability of incumbent support.

In each year a negative evaluation of the incumbent or a positive evaluation of the challenger exerts a major negative influence on the probability of incumbent support. Such evaluations are rare, of course, but clearly important when present. A negative evaluation of the challenger is the largest single influence on the probability of incumbent support in 1958, but the coefficient of this variable falls by two-thirds in 1978. Perhaps this is the peculiarity of the 1978 challenger sample at work again; perhaps not. Name

Table 12
Voting Behavior in House Incumbent-Contested Races, I: 1958 and 1978

	1958	1978
Recall incumbent	1.00*	.72*
Recall challenger	.77*	-1.08*
Party ID: Same as incumbent	1.18*	.92*
Party ID: Opposite incumbent	-1.17*	-.73*
Democratic incumbent	.60*	-.09
Incumbent candidate qualities	.61*	.52*
Incumbent constituency attentiveness	.48	.77*
Incumbent policy agreement	-.33	.75*
Incumbent negative evaluation	-1.69*	-1.36*
Challenger positive evaluation	-1.29*	-1.25*
Challenger negative evaluation	1.89*	.66*
Constant	-.17	-.77*
$\hat{R}^2$	.79	.70
% Correctly predicted	90	86
n	721	755

*p<.01

recall is important in both years, though the magnitudes of the incumbent and challenger coefficients shift. The impact of party identification shows the expected decline between 1958 and 1978, but note that it is still a highly significant influence on the vote. Moreover, remember that 90 percent of the voters have a party identification, whereas far fewer have negative evaluations of the incumbent or any evaluations of the challenger.[34] Another party effect, the Democratic tide running in 1958, shows up in the extra bonus accruing to Democratic incumbents that year. In 1978 no such national force was operative.

The most interesting coefficients are those attached to the several types of incumbent positive evaluations. The variable representing the broad categ-

---

34. Strong, weak, and independent identifiers of the incumbent's party are classified as "same." Strong, weak, and independent identifiers of the other party are classified as "opposite". The suppressed reference category is pure independent.

ory of incumbent candidate qualities appears to have about the same association with the vote in the two surveys. Real differences appear in the other two variables, however. The coefficient of "constituency attentiveness" increases considerably between 1958 and 1978 and goes from insignificant to highly significant at the same time. Of course, the increase in the number of respondents in the category contributes to the increased statistical precision of the coefficient. The equation suggests, however, that not only is incumbent constituency attentiveness more salient to the 1978 electorate than the 1958 electorate (table 9), but that it is more important for their vote as well. Even more interesting are the coefficients of "policy agreement." The coefficient was insignificant and wrong-signed in 1958, but positive and highly significant in 1978. Again, a very small number of respondents composed the variable in 1958, but some real change is likely. For the small proportion of the sample which mentions a policy or ideological matter, perceptions of how the incumbent relates to it are quite important.

Perhaps the most interesting difference between the two equations in table 12 is that the constant term in the 1958 equation is not significantly different from 0, whereas the 1978 constant term is significantly positive. This means that an independent who did not recall either candidate, and offered no open-ended comments, would have voted in 1958 mostly on the basis of the national tide (probability = .43 for a Republican incumbent, .67 for a Democrat). The same individual in 1978 would have voted for the incumbent far more often than not, regardless of party (probability = .75 for a Democratic incumbent, .78 for a Republican). Thus, the 1978 equation apparently does not exhaust the considerations which lead to votes for incumbents. I regret to say, however, that efforts to pursue this question serve mainly to further becloud an already murky picture insofar as candidate visibility is concerned.

Consider table 13. This table differs from table 12 only in that the estimated equations contain an additional dummy variable which takes on a value of 1 if the respondent can correctly identify the incumbent when presented with the candidates' names. As seen, the addition of the "know candidate" variable does absolutely nothing to the 1958 equation. No coefficients change by more than .01 between tables 12 and 13, and the new variable itself is almost literally of zero estimated importance. The story is different in the 1978 equation, however. The "know incumbent" variable is highly significant, and a comparison of the constant terms in the 1978 equations in tables 12 and 13 reveals that addition of the new variable diminishes the importance of the constant, though the latter remains statistically significant and of moderate size. One begins to suspect that name recall captures more of what we mean by candidate visibility in 1958 than in 1978.

Table 13
Voting Behavior in House Incumbent-Contested Races, II: 1958 and 1978

	1958	1978
Know incumbent	.02	.48*
Recall incumbent	-.99*	.64*
Recall challenger	-.77*	-1.07*
Party ID: Same as incumbent	1.17*	.95*
Party ID: Opposite incumbent	-1.18*	-.73*
Democratic incumbent	.60*	-.11*
Incumbent candidate qualities	.61*	-.47*
Incumbent constituency attentiveness	.48	.72*
Incumbent policy agreement	-.33	.72*
Incumbent negative evaluation	-1.69*	-1.45*
Challenger positive evaluation	-1.29*	-1.27*
Challenger negative evaluation	1.89*	.70*
Constant	-.18	.48**
$\hat{R}^2$	.79	.70
% Correctly predicted	90	88
n	721	755

*p<.01
**p<.05

Table 14 adds to such suspicions. The first equation in this table is simply a reproduction of the 1958 equation from table 12. The second equation is the same as the 1978 equation in table 12 except that incumbent name *recognition* is substituted for name recall. The results are rather striking. Incumbent recognition in 1978 behaves as name recall did in 1958. Their coefficients are virtually identical, and the 1978 constant finally fades to insignificance. In a statistical sense the 1978 equation now exhausts the considerations which produce support for incumbents. The second 1978 equation in table 14 contains both recognition and recall variables for incumbents and challengers. As seen, both recall and recognition contribute significantly to incumbent support. Recognition, however, adds little to challenger support after recall is taken into account. We have no comparable equation for 1958, of course, but based on tables 13 and 14 the suspicion would be that recognition measures would not contribute anything significant beyond the effects of recall in that year.

Table 14
Voting Behavior in House Incumbent-Contested Races, III: 1958 and 1978

	1958	*1978*	*1978*
Recall incumbent	1.00*	—	.63*
Recognize incumbent	—	.96*	1.02*
Recall challenger	-.77*	—	-.97*
Recognize challenger	—	-.72*	-.29
Party ID: Same as incumbent	1.18*	.95*	.98
Party ID: Opposite incumbent	-1.17*	-.77*	-.75
Democratic incumbent	.60*	-.08	-.21
Incumbent candidate qualities	.61*	.52*	.46*
Incumbent constituency attentiveness	.48	.85*	.74*
Incumbent policy agreement	-.33	.71*	.73*
Incumbent negative evaluation	-1.69*	-1.30*	-1.45*
Challenger positive evaluation	-1.29*	-1.31*	-1.27
Challenger negative evaluation	1.89*	.64*	.64**
Constant	-.17	.13	.18
$\hat{R}^2$	.79	.69	.71
% Correctly predicted	90	88	87
n	721	755	752

*p<.01
**p<.05

At several points in preceding sections I have remarked that there is no compelling argument to the effect that name recall is any more of an underestimate in 1958 than in 1978. I still know of no compelling argument, but the statistical results in this section suggest that recall was less of an underestimate in 1958 than today. This is only the most tentative of hypotheses, and it is based on a post hoc attempt to account for perplexing statistical results rather than good substantive arguments. Still, the statistical results *are* perplexing unless some temporal difference in the effects of the recall measure is posited. One possibility is that the greatly increased use of the frank and other means of mass communication has created a new group of individuals with only the faintest glimmer of knowledge about the incumbent, a group only slightly above zero on some underlying visibility scale. Possibly the sensitive application of sophisticated scaling techniques might enable us to explore the structure of candidate visibility over time, but this is a matter far beyond the scope of this paper.

Summary, 1958 and 1978

Many pages ago I observed that House voting decisions might have changed in any or all of several ways between 1958 and 1978. First, and most obviously, change in the frequency of occurrence of a variable (e.g., more widespread name recall) would imply a change in the number of people whose decisions that variable could affect. Second, evaluations of candidates (e.g., the ratio of likes to dislikes) might change even while a constant proportion of the electorate reports such evaluations. Third, the *content* of evaluations (e.g., what citizens like and dislike) might vary even while the proportion of citizens holding such evaluations and the ratio of positive and negative evaluations holds steady. And fourth, the manner in which variables affect the voting decision might change. For example, some variables (party identification) might decline in importance, while others (constituency attentiveness) might rise.

The preceding pages contain only one piece of evidence for the first possibility: the doubling of positive responses to the contact items in 1978 over those to the "read or heard" item in 1958. As discussed, however, the different question formats, the unexplained doubling for the weak 1978 challengers, and conflicting evidence from other items (name recall, know incumbent) raise doubts about the extent to which real distributional change has occurred.

Similarly, we have found no conclusive evidence that candidates are evaluated any more or less positively today than two decades ago. The evidence is not so much negative as completely ambiguous. Differences in question wording and sequencing, noncomparable filters, and problems with the 1978 challenger sample basically preclude any attempt to compare the relative positivity of candidate images over time.

We have found somewhat more evidence compatible with the third possibility; in certain respects the substance of citizen information and evaluations has changed. Tables 3, 4, 5, and 9 all suggest that varieties of constituent and district attentiveness now loom larger in the memory banks of voters than they did in 1958. Association of House candidates with political parties has correspondingly diminished. Such changes are consistent with theories which posit that today's House incumbents are evaluated according to less partisan and less controversial standards than those of yesterday.

Finally, an analysis of voting behavior in the 1958 and 1978 elections shows considerable continuity, but some change. Party loyalties continue to exert an important effect on the voting as does candidate visibility, variously measured. The decline in the impact of national forces between the two elections is consistent with the argument that modern incumbents have managed to insulate themselves from such forces to a considerable extent. The candidate evaluations that people form mattered a great deal in 1958 and continue to matter a great deal today, though evaluations concerning constituency attentiveness and policy/ideological compatibility appear to matter more than previously. Again, however, one should remember that far more citizens have a party identification and a flicker of recognition of candidate names than have any sense of where the candidates stand on the issues. There is no indication at all that between 1958 and 1978 the United States developed an electorate of Edmund Burkes.

What then do we make of all the preceding? Not so much as I had hoped, I regret to say. This paper is a first step in the attempt to analyze *directly* (rather than by projection of 1978 findings) sources of change in the House elections of the past generation. The topic is an important one, and with further effort and perseverance perhaps others will be more definitive where I have been tentative and exploratory.

CONGRESSMEN AND THEIR DISTRICTS: FREE AGENTS IN FEAR OF THE FUTURE

By Steven V. Roberts
Congressional Correspondent of the
New York Times

In November 1980, fifty-two Republican freshmen were elected to the House of Representatives. Even before they were sworn in, the newcomers were invited to Washington for intensive indoctrination in the fine art of using their new office for maximum political advantage. The agenda included instruction in the bewildering array of tools and techniques now available to lawmakers, from computers and mobile offices to free postage and office supplies, telephone credit cards, television studios, and travel budgets that finance twenty-six trips home every year. One of the most useful perquisites is a newsletter, mailed to the district six times a year. As Rep. Guy Vander Jagt of Michigan, one of the organizers of the seminar, said candidly, "They can be sent to every household, hundreds of thousands of them. Any guy with an ounce of sense makes the newsletter a campaign document."

Those Republican training sessions reflect a basic change in the relationship between many congressmen and their districts. The traditional role of the local political party as "intermediary" or "broker" between legislators and their constituents has virtually disappeared. In most cases today, the members relate directly to institutions and individual voters, through the news media, targeted mail, and personal appearances. Speaker Thomas P. O'Neill, Jr. described the shift this way: "The whole style of politics has changed. We're strong now on dialogue, town meetings, newsletters, giving the public service. You never saw a congressman years ago, but now you see them all the time. It's accessibility . . . . There are no political organizations left anymore, or very few. But these new guys are great salesmen, no question about it."

One result of this changing relationship appears to be an increase in the "awesome power of incumbency," as Representative Vander Jagt put it. In his book, *Congress—Keystone of the Washington Establishment*, Morris P. Fiorina cites the pioneering work of David Mayhew on the "vanishing marginals," and concludes that the percentage of "safe" congressional seats has risen steadily since 1948. Fiorina describes the enormous increase during this period in congressional staffing resources, and the growing allocation of these assets to constituent service. He concludes that these developments have all helped take the guesswork out of congressional elections. "In all likelihood," writes Fiorina, "since the New Deal, the average congressman's desire for reelection has remained constant. What has changed is the set of resources he possesses to invest in his reelection effort. Today's congressmen have more productive political strategies than previously. And these strategies are an unforeseen (at least by us) by-product of the growth of an activist federal government."[1] This "salesmanship" does not always work, of course, and forty-two incumbent lawmakers got knocked off in the last election. One of them, former Rep. John Brademas of Indiana, explained: "The fact is, people were so upset by a combination of inflation, interest rates, and 15 percent unemployment in my district that they weren't focusing on what I'd ever done for the district. Some of the younger voters never even knew what I'd done. It was not a question of forgetting, or being ungrateful, they just never knew."

While the first aim of any lawmaker is to get reelected, the new and more direct relationship between the vote-getter and the vote-giver also carries some distinct benefits for the member's district. As Tip O'Neill mentioned, these new-breed congressmen often function as ombudsmen for troubled constituents whose lives are increasingly affected by the actions of the federal government. James R. Mann, a former representative from South Carolina, points out that even while "less government" and "lower taxes" have become popular political cliches, many voters actually demand more government help for a wider variety of problems. "They sort of treat you like a federal appeals court, when the local government doesn't satisfy them," said Mann, who retired in 1978. "The federal dollar reaches so many areas it's hard to say no. We've seen a steady, increasing involvement of the federal government in everything."

Fiorina argues that congressmen deliberately expand federal involvement as a way of increasing their own value to their constituents, and thus enhancing their reelection chances.[2] But there is no doubt that many voters are also pushing their representatives into this ombudsman or "appeals court" role. As one congressman describes this growing function: "We've become the complaint window in the government department store."

---

1. Morris P. Fiorina, *Congress—Keystone of the Washington Establishment* (New Haven, Ct.: Yale University Press, 1977), p. 36.

2. Ibid., p. 45.

If the new relationship between members and their districts means more accessibility for the public, and more votes for the legislator, another and more disquieting side effect has also developed in recent years. My experience, based on dozens of interviews and visits to congressional districts, indicates that today's congressmen are increasingly vulnerable to the pressures of special interests, advanced direct mail and public relations techniques, and above all, to the vast amounts of money pouring into congressional races from political action committees and other outside sources. The old-style congressman might have been less accessible to the voter who needed a social security check. But he was also less dependent and less fearful of single-issue groups that judged him solely on a few highly selected votes.

When he was retiring before the 1978 election, former Rep. Otis Pike of New York fired this blast at his colleagues: "If there's one thing I fault congressmen on, it's that they're scared to death of the media and their constituents. They want to get reelected so terribly, terribly badly, that they won't say no to anyone." Frank Evans of Colorado, another former lawmaker who withdrew to the sidelines after 1978, described members as "captives" of competing interest groups and added: "You live in a glass house now. You're more visible, more vulnerable, more exposed to criticism than ever."

The elections of 1980 sent a new shudder of concern through many lawmakers, particularly on the Democratic side of the aisle. After he lost his North Carolina seat, Richardson Preyer described the threat this way: "These new public relations techniques, combined with a lot of money, are problems that all office holders must face in the future. Bob Eckhardt [another 1980 loser] says that money in politics is like the pine bark beetle. If the climate is right, and you have enough of them, they'll bring down the tallest tree."

Put another way, the techniques that members can use to reach directly to their districts can be turned against them; the computers that send a newsletter to every house in town can be programmed to send out literature criticizing their votes on abortion or the Panama Canal or anything else. And every round of this battle to touch—and influence—the individual voter costs an accelerating amount of money. A typical comment came from former Rep. Herbert Harris, who lost his seat in northern Virginia last November: "I fear that with the amount of money going into campaigns from special interest groups, an element of representative government is in danger of being lost. It's a very worrisome thing that strikes at the vitals of our system."[3]

This new relationship between congressman and constituent flows from a number of important and overlapping developments. Some changes are clearly symptoms as well as causes, but they are relevant to understanding the thesis of this paper.

Declining Political Parties. Outside Chicago, party organizations have generally ceased to play a major role in selecting and electing congressional candidates. (Even in the Windy City, party wheelhorse Bennett Stewart was unseated by an insurgent, Harold Washington, in the 1980 primary.) The factors are mainly: changing neighborhood patterns, rising educational levels, and above all, the disappearance of patronage.[4] When he was just starting out, Tip O'Neill's political base was strongly rooted in ethnic ties and party loyalties that flourished in his Cambridge neighborhood, and later at Boston College. "I can remember in those days," he once told me, "patronage was the biggest thing in my life, getting people a job." Later I recounted his famous story about the snow buttons this way:

> During the Depression, it seems, various agencies—the Boston Elevated, the Transit Authority, the city of Cambridge—would issue "snow buttons" that entitled the holder to a few days work shoveling snow. Like his father before him, O'Neill cornered the market on buttons, and once the snow started to fall, men would start lining up outside his house at 5 a.m., begging for a chance to shovel snow at $3 a day, $4 if it was a city button. Tip would sit in the kitchen and write down the names as the men trooped through the door; each button meant another link in the chain of loyalty.[5]

They were linked not just to O'Neill, but to the whole party apparatus he represented. When those workers pinned on a snow button, they pinned on a Democratic button as well. Today, the loss of patronage has helped snap the links of party loyalty, and many congressional candidates are "free agents,"[6] as one put it, independent forces with their own personal parties running their own campaigns. Rep. Martin Frost, who represents a

---

3. Quoted in Steven V. Roberts, "Mood of Outgoing Lawmakers Is Sullen," *New York Times*, December 16, 1980. All quotations are from interviews with the author except where otherwise indicated.

4. See extended discussion in Cokie and Steven V. Roberts, "What's Got Into the Voters This Year?", *New York Times Magazine*, June 15, 1980.

5. S. Roberts, "The Politics of Loyalty," *The New Leader*, January 29, 1979.

6. Rep. James Blanchard, quoted in S. Roberts, "Eroding Loyalty Weakens House Leaders," *New York Times*, June 4, 1979

burgeoning district between Dallas and Fort Worth, said, "We had our own precinct captains in every single district, people we recruited ourselves. Basically, we developed our own structure out of necessity."[7]

Of course, patrongage still exists today, but usually in a somewhat different form. Civil service has eliminated many of the jobs the party used to distribute, and tighter bidding rules have made it harder to reward friends with lucrative contracts. Lawyers can still get plum cases from the probate courts, for instance, and municipal insurance deals often get diverted to somebody's nephew, but the mass-scale local patronage that once bound legions of voters to the party has largely eroded.

Accordingly, even veterans who once relied on formal party structures are now forced to adjust. John Brademas, who first ran for Congress from South Bend, Indiana, in 1954, described his 1980 campaign this way: "We had to undertake a lot of activities on our own that were done by the party organization in 1954. We had to implement the business of voter canvasses, telephone banks, and financing the campaign staff to a far greater extent. We financed campaign headquarters in three different counties, and the party shared them. But I paid for them. I had become the de facto party leader."

Expanding Single-Issue Groups and Political Action Committees. Where parties once formulated a series of related policies on a wide range of issues, today's pressure groups have fragmented the entire policy-making process. "With the disappearance of political parties as intermediaries," said Rep. Thomas S. Foley, the new House whip, "you don't have a Republican policy or a Democratic policy. It's the environmental groups or the trade groups who have policies. You have all these separate parties out there now."

The power of these groups has been greatly enhanced by the rise of the political action committees, or PACs, which are now allowed to raise money from corporate employees, for example, or trade association members, and then contribute that money to candidates. John Brademas noted that his $12,000 campaign budget in 1954 had risen to more than $600,000 in 1980, and he blames PACs for the explosion. "The rise of PACs," he said, "which have moved in to fill a vacuum, are a much more important development than people realize."

The Rise Of Television. Television gives "free agent" candidates the mechanism for jumping over the heads of party leaders and organizations,

---

7. Quoted in S. Roberts, "Two Representatives With Style: The Old and the New," *New York Times*, September 1, 1979.

and apppealing directly to voters. As Mayor Jane Byrne of Chicago put it, "The best precinct captain today is the television set. It gets into every home."[8] Not content with what the press picks up on its own, the lawmakers have provided themselves with fully equipped studios on Capitol Hill they can use to beam statements, and whole programs, back home. After the House started televising floor proceedings a few years ago, members had another avenue for reaching out to home viewers and the Senate is likely to start TV this year. While many stations carry only snippets of the floor debate, usually as part of a news broadcast, some cable systems broadcast huge chunks during lax daytime hours. Rep. Tom Tauke told me that two stations in his Iowa district carry House action regularly. Sen. Paul Laxalt of Nevada, one of the shrewder political strategists around, described the growing influence of younger Republican senators this way: "We're a different generation, no doubt about that. We're all here in great part because of the media. We're all comfortable with it, and appreciate its importance."

The Rise of Computers and Direct Mail. This development might be less visible than television, but no less important. In 1980, John B. Anderson constructed a presidential campaign apparatus—and solicited millions of dollars in contributions—mainly through the adroit use of direct mail techniques. In effect, he created a new party that was based on the memory of computers, not precinct captains. Once in office, today's congressmen use computers and direct mail to personalize their relationships with individual voters more precisely than televison ever can. As I once described Rep. Martin Frost's computer operation: "His staff can type in the name of a constituent, for instance, and get an instantaneous readout on every contact with that voter. Another code produces an accounting of all social security cases processed by the office. A third key spews out invitations to a town meeting in a particular part of the district."[9]

New Districts. The balance of political power has shifted from the old cities of the northeast to the surrounding suburbs, as well as to the booming areas of the Sun Belt. The quintessential "free agent" lawmakers often represent these areas of new growth, and the mere fact of mobility has done much to undermine the party structure and foster the notion of every candidate for himself. When people move they leave behind old neighborhoods, old relationships, old institutions—a whole network of ties that

---

8. Quoted in S. Roberts, "Campaign Swings West to Land of Lincoln—and Daley," *New York Times*, March 16, 1980.

9. S. Roberts, "Two Representatives."

shaped their political behavior into a somewhat familiar and predictable pattern. Movement, particularly to a new part of the country, severs those ties, and in an important sense, the "free agent" lawmaker is a direct result of the "free agent" voter.

It is no accident, for instance, that California, the focus of so much internal migration in this century, developed the weakest party structure in the country. Moreover, the growing success of the Republicans in the South can be directly linked to the enormous influx of job-seeking outsiders. After Bill Clements became the first Republican governor of Texas, he attributed his victory to the state's newcomers, who were ready to try on new voting habits along with their new western clothes.

It is not just that people are moving. They are moving to particular areas—the suburbs and the Sun Belt—which lack the traditional structures of the older, urban areas. Tip O'Neill started his career at Barry's Corner in Cambridge, a neighborhood club and social center; as part of that neighborhood, many residents were also part of an ethnic group, a church parish, a political organization, a group of friends and relatives. Martin Frost's district in suburban Texas does not have street corners, let alone political traditions.

The impact of mobility on politics struck me repeatedly during the 1968 campaign. In Philadelphia, for instance, I talked to an Italian grocer who had moved out of the city's old, ethnic South Side to the suburbs on the northern edge of the city. In the old neighborhood, the precinct captain knew his family and made regular house calls; favors given and received over the years had woven an invisible web of loyalty and stability. Now, he did not even know his captain's name. One night in Chicago I talked to an Irish couple who had grown up in Boston as staunch Democrats, but now voted Republican. When did they switch? "Just about the time we moved," the woman remembered. In her tract home in suburban Chicago, no one from the old neighborhood was looking over her shoulder, telling her what to do.

That same evening, I talked to a priest named Pat Brennan who told me that the Roman Catholic church now held "homecoming" masses in these new neighborhoods, appealing to lapsed parishioners who had left their old loyalties behind in the city. I thought at the time that the Democratic party should probably do the same thing; it certainly has the same problem.

New Voters. Many of the voters who help elect the "free agent" congressmen are better educated and more affluent than their parents, and less likely to take political advice from a precinct captain or a parish priest or anybody else. One day in the headquarters of a Chicago precinct organization, a party ward healer named Timothy J. Gibbons explained the development this way:

> The voter has changed. The Democratic party used to be blue collar, but it's getting more sophisticated all the time. We have second and third generation people now and we're running into college graduates. The husband and wife are both working, they read *Time* and *Newsweek*, things like that. And you have TV. Let's face it—today you have to present a good candidate, you can't run the old political hacks. There are four direct phone lines in here. Years ago we had only one, but today, people ask questions. You never heard this years ago. It was heresy.[10]

This new voter, of course, is likely to be a ticket-splitter, the sort of person who seldom looks at party labels and must be reached directly by the candidate. When Rep. Robert W. Edgar first won his seat in suburban Philadelphia in 1974, President Ford carried the district by 35,000 votes; the young Democrat won by more than 50,000 votes. "It was not an attraction to be either Democrat or Republican," remembers Edgar. "People didn't care, and they still don't. They wanted some confidence, almost apart from the issues, that I would be available and accessible, that we'd open government up."[11]

New Problems. In the old days, local party machines took care of local problems—a food basket or a fixed parking ticket, and of course jobs. The history of the political party in this country was written by men like Tip O'Neill, seated in his Cambridge kitchen, recording his daily allocation of snow buttons. Even now, some of that survives in places like Chicago. When Dutch Elm disease ravaged a neighborhood in the southwest corner of the city, ward boss Bill Lapinski went out and bought a machine that uproots tree trunks. It's a small favor, but it keeps people loyal; if the elms of Chicago ever recover, Lapinski could be in trouble.

Today, many of the everyday problems afflicting voters relate to the federal government. At a town meeting I attended in Martin Frost's Texas district, the questions ranged over many topics, from regulation of a local sewage plant by the Environmental Protection Agency, to government research grants and tardy social security checks. Every issue required the intercession of the congressman-ombudsman. No one mentioned snow buttons or Dutch Elm disease the whole evening.

---

10. Quoted in C. Roberts and S. Roberts, "What's Got Into the Voters This Year?"

11. For a discussion of Representative Edgar's career, see S. Roberts, "Representative Edgar: Democrat Trying to Hold His Republican District," *New York Times*, May 15, 1978.

Now that I've described the underlying reasons for this new relationship between congressman and constituent, I'd like to sketch out some of the implications of this new situation. Without making too many value judgments, some of these results would generally be described by political scientists and practicing politicians as positive.

Under the new system, for instance, congressional candidates seldom have to wait their turn, or come up through the party ranks. One can fully apppreciate the value of party organizations, and still recognize that many of them produced real hacks who contributed precious little to the national welfare. To cite one example, many of the Democratic regulars in Philadelphia blindly supported former Rep. Michael Myers last November after he had already been convicted of charges growing out of the Abscam investigations. (He lost to an independent.)

Moreover, the "free agent" newcomers often inject a healthy dose of youth and enthusiasm into the musty halls of Congress. The average age in Congress has been dropping steadily in recent years, and of the fifty-two Republicans elected last fall, seven are under the age of thirty. A good example of a successful insurgent was Andrew Maguire, a former Peace Corpsman and community organizer who "cut in from the side," as he put it, and won the Democratic nomination from a northern New Jersey district in 1974 with no prior campaign experience. "A high risk strategy made sense to me," remembered Maguire, who was a yeasty presence in Congress for six years before losing in the Republican sweep of 1980. "I wanted to do reasonably well in a short period of time."[12]

Moreover, many of these new-style members are "available and accessible" to their constituents, as Representative Edgar put it, listening to their views and helping them with their problems. Morris Fiorina admits to a "cynical" view of all this, and says that congressmen avoid controversial legislative matters—which carry political costs—in order to concentrate on constituent service. "Pork barrelling and casework," he asserts, "are basically pure profit."[13]

But even if these politicians have self-centered motives—and what politicians do not—I think they often provide a real service. For instance, I've taken several trips with Rep. Michael L. Synar through his district in eastern Oklahoma, and he never goes anywhere without being greeted and

---

12. Representative Maguire's career is recounted in S. Roberts, "Second Term Congressman Still Disdains Compromise," *New York Times*, April 17, 1978.

13. Fiorina, *Keystone of the Washington Establishment*, p. 45.

glad-handed, chatted up, and dressed down.[14] One day at a political meeting in Salishaw one of Synar's constituents told me, "The congressman we had before only touched base with a few selected people. Mike has campaigned here, he's our friend." In that district, the federal government has a human face.

Like many younger members, Synar places an enormous emphasis on constituent service, and eight of his fourteen staff members work in Oklahoma, not Washington. Bob Edgar, in a more urban district outside Philadelphia, has made a similar judgment. His aging Republican predecessor had one home office tucked away in an inaccessible government building; Edgar has two district offices, both in highly visible store fronts within walking distance of mass transit terminals. Half of his staff is devoted to casework back home, and as one of them said, "There's no overt connection with politics, but we recognize there is one."

Morris Fiorina documents this trend with statistics comparing 1960 to 1974. In that period, the percentage of congressional staff based in district offices jumped from 14 percent to 34 percent; the number of members with more than one home office surged from 4 percent to 47 percent. Twenty years ago, almost one-third of the members opened their local offices only when they were back home; today that practice has virtually disappeared.[15]

The new breed congressman becomes "accessible and available" in a variety of ways. Several times a year, Synar makes a complete circuit of his sprawling, rural district, one of the largest in the country. But even when he's in Washington, his district staff is in constant motion. After one visit I filed this report on the Synar operation:[16]

> The local coordinator for the Vinita area is Cindy Chestnut, a breezy, fast-talking blonde who calls herself a "barometer" for the congressman. Every week she roams through the towns and villages, stopping at cafes and city halls, taking the pulse and tapping the mood. And every week she gets a new flood of complaints— about social security, veterans benefits, disability payments.

---

14. I wrote a series of six articles about Rep. Mike Synar's education as a freshman in the *New York Times.* They were: "New Congressman Gets a Message: Integrity Is Important," December 12, 1978; "Freshman In House Learns Tough Lesson," January 31, 1979; "House Freshman Builds Support At Home," March 19, 1979; "Freshman Congressman Learns to Settle for Small Triumphs After Enthusiastic Start," May 21, 1979; "Freshman's Progress: Congressman Learns The Power of Interest Groups," Janaury 20, 1980; "An Angry Young Congressman Criticizes Special-Interest Groups," January 11, 1981.

15. Fiorina, *Keystone of the Washington Establishment*, Chapter 7.

16. S. Roberts, "House Freshman Builds Support at Home."

"Money's the name of the game a lot of the time," said Mrs. Chestnut, who is married to Mr. Synar's college roommate. "Federal money reaches almost all of our lives, one way or another."

Like the congressman, she gets frustrated at times. "People want a balanced budget," she said, as a few friends lingered over the luncheon dishes in the Pioneer cafe, "but they don't want you to cut the areas they're interested in."

Joe Hartley, a local lawyer and supporter of Mr. Synar, laughed and added, "When the congressman's in town, everything's a federal problem."

The town meeting, popularized by President Carter, is now a staple for many lawmakers. Rep. Richard Gephardt continues an old campaign tactic, walking door to door through the old Hill section of his St. Louis district and sharing an Italian hero sandwich with the lunchtime crowd that gathers on the steps of the local Catholic church.[17]

In each case, the communication channels work both ways. The lawmaker hears the complaints of his constituents; and the complainers find out that all demands cannot be met, that government must make constant tradeoffs. During our trip to Vinita, Oklahoma, Mike Synar got fed up with city officials who handed him a long shopping list of federal programs. "Don't tell me again you want a balanced budget," Synar said to Bill Castor, the city attorney, "not if you keep asking me for all these things."

As we've noted, the new-style congressman also performs a growing number of specific services for constituents who are frustrated by the normal channels of federal bureaucracy. Some of these services are highly specialized, depending on the district; Bob Edgar's office, for instance, processes many claims for compensation relating to black lung disease, an ailment contracted by coal miners. But many of the problems are universal, growing out of the explosive growth of federal aid—social security, welfare, medicare, veterans' benefits—to poor and needy Americans. "Look at the federal budget," noted a caseworker for Sen. Patrick Leahy of Vermont. "The payments section of Health, Education and Welfare accounts for 40 percent of the budget. All of these people are depending on the federal government and had to have their cases handled."

Ironically, however, aggressive and successful casework often generates even more complaints, and threatens to overload even the most efficient

---

17. See S. Roberts, "An Earful of Grumblings Greets Congress at Break," *New York Times*, August 27, 1979.

office. Dolly McClary, administrative assistant to Martin Frost, confided one day, "Sometimes, I wonder if we've created a monster."[18]

At the same time, the new relationship between lawmaker and citizen carries some significant drawbacks, and one of the main ones was mentioned by Dolly McClary. Good service creates a monster of expectations that cannot be satisfied, a feeling that the federal government—embodied by the congressman—should be able to solve all conceivable problems. "Everybody says they're for a balanced budget," said Rep. Charles W. Stenholm of Texas, "but it's tough to actually make those cuts. Everybody wants to balance the budget on the other guy's program."

Former Rep. Otis Pike says that in 1961, his first year on Capitol Hill, his correspondence with his constituents filled three drawers; in 1978, his last year, the mail filled fourteen drawers. "People expect more and more from government and are willing to do less and less for themselves," said Pike. As an example, he then recalled an incident during a snowstorm in his Long Island district. "Someone called me at home," Pike said, "and complained that the local hardware store was out of shovels. And he wanted to know what Congressman Pike was going to do about it."

Lawmakers often bottle up their resentment against such demanding constituents, but when they leave office, they sometimes let loose. Former Rep. Mendel J. Davis of South Carolina wrote this to a constituent shortly before his retirement: "One of the small but gratifying benefits of leaving Congress is that I no longer have to put up with your unending drivel."[19]

Moreover, being accessible to the voters carries with it a terrible loss of privacy and a punishing schedule that makes anything approaching normal family life impossible. Since the legislator gets paid to take twenty-six trips home every year, he or she is expected to make every Rotary Club lunch and Boy Scout awards dinner; and constituents resent it when their invitations are turned down. "It's very costly to go home for the weekend," explained former Rep. John E. Moss of California. "The government transports me, but not my wife, and her fare isn't even tax deductible." Lloyd Meeds of Washington added: "Every summer you go back to the district to mend fences. You don't go on vacation with your family, like you ought to." Rep. David R. Obey of Wisconsin summed up the problem this way: "The prime condition that affects this place all the time is that members are tired. Life becomes less than human here."

---

18. Quoted in S. Roberts, "Two Representatives."

19. Associated Press, "Congressman Returns Constituent's Barrage," *New York Times,* July 8, 1979.

This constant sense of fatigue is aggravated by the complexity of events and the feeling among many members that they simply cannot keep abreast of all the issues on which their constituents want answers. "Keeping up with what is happening becomes an enormous, steady burden," said Tom Foley, the new Democratic whip. "I'm not whining, that's just the reality of it." Frank Evans of Colorado says that lawmakers feel the strain of ignorance constantly. "You know that people expect you to know a lot about things," the former congressman admitted, "but many times you don't know."

This pressure is compounded further by a pervasive cynicism toward politicians that developed after the Watergate scandal and gained new impetus from Abscam. "Holding office is like a good marriage, there has to be mutual trust on both sides," says John Moss. But many lawmakers feel that trust between the member and the voter has been seriously eroded. "In the post-Watergate era there was a healthy skepticism of politics and politicians," said Lloyd Meeds, "but that's turned now into an unhealthy cynicism. And it's not just me, it's toward all politicians. People shoot you down first and ask questions later, instead of giving you some credence or credibility."

The more direct ties between the people and their representatives have created another monster. The technical advances that allow the member to talk directly to the voters can be turned around, aimed at the member, and used to exert enormous pressure. Television might be the politician's greatest ally, but it can also be a mortal enemy. Herbert Harris says that his opponent last November threw $40,000 into the race in the last week, all for TV time, that the incumbent simply could not match. And when the incumbent is someone like Harris, a free agent with no party base or long-standing political network, he is terribly vulnerable to that sort of blitzkrieg.

Various lobbying groups, particularly on the right, have used TV in an artful way by running paid advertisements on a specific issue—say the Panama Canal treaty. The shows ask viewers to send letters to Washington to pressure the Congress, and money to the organization to pay for the ad. The mail generated by this technique can be enormous.[20]

All politicians use television to broadcast their own messages, through news reports or paid commercials, and so to some extent their complaints have a hollow ring; if you live by the sword of television, you should

---

20. For an example of the use of television advertisements, see S. Roberts, "Panama Treaties at Stake in Bitter Propaganda War," *New York Times*, January 20, 1978.

probably be ready to die by it. But many politicians are increasingly concerned that television seriously distorts the political process and sets up false expectations among the viewers. A typical comment came from Lloyd Meeds: "There is no problem in the world that Starsky and Hutch can't solve in thirty minutes, so people come to believe that all problems can be solved in thirty minutes. People say they want politicians to tell the truth, even when it hurts, but they don't really mean it. If you tell the truth, and it hurts them, they'll vote against you next time."

"It's incredible, the resistance you get in trying to raise any complicated questions," added David Obey. "It's damn near impossible to penetrate the public if you don't take a very black and white, over-simplified approach. And that takes so much out of you emotionally, especially if you're committed."

Similarly, computers and direct mail, which can be used by lawmakers to reach voters, can also be used by special interest groups to reach those same voters and turn them against the congressman. During the past session of Congress, Representative Synar led the fight in favor of toughening fair housing laws, and incurred the wrath of the National Association of Realtors. Even though Synar is a realtor himself and a member of the association, they bombarded his district with literature urging his defeat. "This is an example," said Synar, "of a special-interest group that can get more mail to more people more often than I can as a U.S. congressman, even though I have the frank."

Right-wing groups are not the only ones that play hardball with Congress. Organized labor also has its litmus-test issues, and if you vote against them on, say, raising the minimum wage, they are just as unforgiving as the Moral Majority.

The special interests are not just concerned about elections; they use the same techniques to influence members' votes on legislation. During the fight over a common-site picketing bill, which was ardently sought by organized labor, a group called the National Right to Work Committee targeted key members of Congress and generated a flood of mail opposing the bill. Henry Walther, who heads the committee's direct mail operation, was candid about his purpose. "We want to put the politicians in a position where they have to pay a price, campaign harder to win. They see what can happen to each other if they don't pay attention and they don't want that kind of pain."[21] When the bill reached President Ford's desk, the committee

---

21. Quoted in Ward Sinclair, "Computer Mail Spews a Blizzard of Influence on Congress," *Washington Post*, January 29, 1978.

stirred up an "unbelievable" amount of mail, urging a veto, and when he did reject the bill, the president cited the "vigorous controversy" surrounding it as one of his main reasons.

All politicians know that the "pain" of public pressure comes with the job, but many of them feel that the pain generated by special-interest groups is unfair, because it is based on one issue, and one issue only. But that is what happens when the "broker"—the broad-scale political party with a variety of ideas and issues—dissolves, and the politicians say that in order to meet the computer-based onslaught of special-interest groups, they have to reply in kind, and all over Capitol Hill today, computers are talking to each other.

"This mass mailing is about to wipe us out," said Rep. Roman O. Mazzoli of Kentucky. "It is easy to poke fun at, but I don't know how to respond. They go computer, we go computer. We've reached the point of 1984 already. It is weird, upsidedown, expensive, and almost not productive at all. It is wasteful, debilitating, and time consuming. We go in smaller and smaller concentric circles and one of these days we will eat ourselves."[22]

Special-interest groups have learned another wrinkle that puts additional pressure on the members. Using computerized lists, they can also organize personal visits to the lawmakers by interested constituents. For instance, during the fight over creation of a Department of Education, the National Education Association beseiged the capitol with busloads of teachers, promoting the idea. Other lobbying groups focus on the congressman when he goes back to the district. The forces fighting a hospital cost containment bill, for instance, organized the local citizens who serve on hospital boards across the country, and urged them to lobby against the cost containment bill whenever the local representative showed his face back home.

At election time, these special-interest groups often distribute "report cards" on each member, evaluating him or her in terms of a few, often highly selective votes. The "free agent" congressman is more vulnerable to such attacks because he enjoys virtually no base of party support; the voters judge him as an individual, and those judgments can be deeply influenced by questionable information, pounded home by relentless television and direct mail assaults.

One good example took place in the campaign of 1980. The Republican party and some of its allies made up a report card purporting to evaluate a candidate's support for a stronger defense; all the votes they used for this

---

22. Ibid.

evaluation, however, were budget resolutions, proposed by Republicans, that had no chance of passage. In fact, many of them were deliberately introduced so that Democrats would vote against them—and earn black marks on the report card.

"These public relations techniques have been honed to a fine art," said Richardson Preyer, after his defeat last November. "They take a few votes, and without exactly lying, are able to distort the record."[23]

Television and direct mail campaigns, either on specific issues or reelection campaigns, cost huge sums to stay competitive. And in the absence of party organization—this problem is much worse for the Democrats, because the Republicans can raise a lot of money on the national level—the candidates have to go to the political action committees. By spending so much and raising the ante in the political poker game, the PACs actually make themselves more valuable to the congressmen who need money. Lloyd Meeds retired in 1978 in part because he would have had to raise $250,000 to run again. "There's no way you can raise that without taking it in big chunks," said Meeds. "And when you do that, people are looking for more than just good government. If you take the dough, you're either an ingrate, or obligated to them. And either one is an unsatisfactory position to be in." To Rep. Henry Waxman of California, incurring an obligation is unavoidable. "The special interests pay the cost of the campaign," he pointed out, "and the parties have little impact in that area. The members wind up looking to the special interests for their electoral security."[24]

There is wide agreement on Capitol Hill that the special interests are having a deep, and damaging, effect on the way members vote. Instead of "mutual trust" between the congressman and his district, there is a growing sense of fear, fear that one small slip will incur the opposition of a single-issue group. Mike Synar, an outspoken foe of special-interest influence, said of these groups, "They want me to be overly cautious in everything I do. They want me to fear my constituents. But it's very difficult to get any constituency. You can't legislate out of fear."

Two votes in the lame duck session at the end of 1980 illustrated this spreading fear. On one, senators voted for a bill many felt was unconstitutional, because a negative vote could have been used to label them as favoring school busing for desegregation. As Sen. David Pryor explained, "I just didn't want to have to explain that vote for the next five years." On a juvenile justice bill, an amendment was passed that would require the

23. Quoted in S. Roberts, "Mood of Outgoing Lawmakers is Sullen."

24. Quoted in S. Roberts, "Eroding Loyalty Weakens House Leaders."

placement of juvenile offenders in adult prisons if they violated the terms of their parole. The amendment had been buried in committee, and many members were surprised it passed on the floor. But according to Mike Synar, word went around that the vote would be used by the Christian Voice, a fundamentalist religious organization, in its report card for Congress next year. And many members did not want to risk voting against the organization.

"Members today have a far greater preoccupation with reelection, and that's reflected in their votes," argued John Moss. "There's an increasing reluctance today to cast unpopular votes." John Brademas, the former House whip, sees the same trend. "You don't find some of the members having the convictions and values that run as deep as those in my generation," he said. "It seems the younger members are less willing to bite the bullet and take positions on controversial issues. I'd hate to try to pass the Voting Rights Act today, as we did in 1965. On certain issues you have to vote your conscience, or the national interest, and then go home and justify it and explain it."

This cautiousness within the House is compounded because younger members feel no loyalty to their party, and cannot count on the party for protection or support. As "free agents" they have to fight their own battles, and they are afraid of getting licked. Without loyalty or patronage at his command, how does a leader operate in Congress today? "You have a hunting license to persuade—that's about all you have," said Rep. Jim Wright, the majority leader. "Sometimes you can shame them into doing what's right, but sometimes you can't."[25]

There is a good side and a bad side to almost all of these developments. The energetic newcomer who does not wait his or her turn, and replaces some lifeless old hack, injects a fresh and skeptical view into the mix on Capitol Hill. But in this television age, where political appeal is based on personality rather than party, those insurgents can be turned off by the voters as easily as they were turned on. The result can be a troubling instability, and an appalling lack of institutional memory. One reason President Reagan's budget cuts sliced through Congress so easily was that few members remembered when the programs were enacted; they did not remember, for instance, when hunger really was a serious problem, and they felt no sense of responsibility for the food stamp program that was designed to combat that hunger.

---

25. Ibid.

Speaker O'Neill and other veterans refer caustically to some of these younger lawmakers as "bedwetters". Since they did not have to wait their turn to climb the party ladder, few had legislative experience before arriving in Washington, and thus had seldom been subjected to the kind of white-hot pressure applied by the Reagan administration. As a result, they melted quickly.

What of the future? The most likely result is for a continuation of all the trends I have described—less party loyalty, more independent "free agents," more direct contact between members and voters, more resources devoted to constituent service, more use of direct mail, computers, and television to press home the narrow interest of specialized lobbies, more expensive campaigns, and a growing cautiousness among members who fear these specialized lobbies in an age when the local party "broker" has all but disappeared.

Can anything be done to reverse, or slow down, these less healthy trends? Practically every politician I know would like to see some sort of revival of the political party as a broker, as intermediary, bringing some sense of long-term commitment and stability to the system. The days of the local party boss are probably gone for good, but in recent years the Republicans have started to develop what might be called an "electronic party," a party organized from the top down, not the bottom up; a party linked by computerized mailing lists, not precinct voting lists; a party that advertises itself on national TV, reaching directly into every voter's home; a party that raises money on a national level, and then distributes it to local candidates, instead of the other way around. The Democrats realize they are five to ten years behind the Republicans in creating an "electronic party," but since the last election, many Democrats have realized the need to enter the modern political age and copy some of the Republicans' more successful techniques. Seeing a TV commercial that says "Vote Republican" or "Vote Democratic" is hardly the same as getting a visit from your local precinct captain, but the new-style party might restore come coherence and consistency to a system that now seems almost totally up for grabs.

This has to be backed up with new forms of party activity and service: schools for candidates, media advice, computer time, propaganda packages. As Ann Lewis, the head of the political division of the Democratic National Committee, noted, candidates have to believe they are losing something when they stray from the party, and the party withdraws its help. Now, the cost of being a rebel, particularly within the Democratic party, is almost nil.

Lobbyists and special interests are entitled to free speech like everybody else, but two bills have been proposed that would curb some of their worst excesses. One would require the disclosure of a lobby's membership and sources of funding, so that voters have a chance of knowing who is really behind the blizzard of propaganda they receive.[26] Another would reduce the amount of money a political action committee could give to one candidate, and limit the total PAC contributions one candidate could receive.[27] In the long run, public funding of congressional campaigns—a system that has worked well on the presidential level—is probably the only answer. Otherwise, the members of Congress are likely to grow increasingly fearful of their constituents, and their own shadows.

---

26. For a discussion of lobby disclosure bills, see S. Roberts, "Business is Crying Havoc Over New Lobbying Bill," *New York Times*, May 7, 1978; and S. Roberts, "Lobbyists Join Forces Against Federal Disclosure Law," *New York Times*, March 15, 1979.

27. Public financing of congressional campaigns is discussed in S. Roberts, "House Members Pressing to Curb Special-Interest Gifts," *New York Times*, September 26, 1979.

Response by Hon. Silvio O. Conte
Member, United States House of Representatives

Thank you very much. Let me say at the beginning how pleased I am to participate in this symposium on the United States Congress. As I sat here and I listened, and I kept looking around, it brought back fond memories. Fresh out of the war in the Southwest Pacific, I came here in 1949. In this hall, I sat right over there and took my examination to enter Boston College on a football scholarship. It's the first time I've been back. I don't know whether I was more nervous that day or today. But it's great to hear all these experts. I ran against one in 1958 and beat him, James McGregor Burns. (Laughter)

You know, as I listened to them, I went back to my football days. We had a city rivalry in high school, and everyone predicted that our team was going to lose by three touchdowns on Thanksgiving Day When we got into the fourth quarter in the last two or three minutes, we were behind six to nothing, but it was a moral victory. The quarterback got in a huddle and he looked over to the coach for a signal. The coach was busy and nervous, walking up and down in front of the bench, and he didn't get the signal, so he called one through right tackle and lost a couple of yards. He looked again for another signal, then threw a little shuttle pass. It failed. Then he tried one through the right end, and the man made a touchdown. They kicked the extra point, and we won, seven to six. Everyone was elated. They carried that quarterback around on their shoulders, around the field, and they threw confetti on him—all except the coach. The coach went up to him afterward and said, "You know, John, you're a very lucky boy that we won that ballgame today. You called that play eleven. I told you time and time again in practice it was not a good play; it was a very risky play. Why'd you call it?" The quarterback said, "Well, I was looking for a signal and you didn't give it to me. I got in a huddle and I saw a great big tackle there. He had a six on his jersey, and right next to him was a big guard who had a seven on his jersey. So I called play eleven." The coach said, "Six and seven don't add up to eleven, they add up to thirteen." The quarterback scratched his head, and said, "You know, coach, if I were as smart as you are, we'd never have won that ballgame." (Laughter) I think if I were as smart as these people, I wouldn't be in the Congress today.

I'm particularly pleased to help celebrate the dedication of the Thomas P. O'Neill, Jr., Chair in American Politics. As you all know, Tip's been a very dear friend of mine. We served together in the state legislature in the early 1950s, and we've been long, dear friends in Washington. He and his wife are very dedicated friends of Corinne's and mine, and are our weekly bridge partners. I'm also pleased to share the program with my good friend John Brademas. John and I entered the Congress in 1958 together, became fast friends, and have a great deal of respect for each other. Even though I sit on the other side of the aisle, I feel a terrible void was created in the United States Congress by the loss of John Brademas. He was a tower of strength, a very intelligent congressman, a man of integrity, and a leader. John, we're going to miss you greatly. It also gives me heart to recognize the people of your caliber, position, and talent, who continue to examine and constructively criticize the American political process in the hopes that in some way we will improve it.

I enjoyed immensely the presentation of Professor Fiorina. I've been reading his paper for two days, and it's mind-boggling. And of course it's good to see my friend, Mr. Steve Roberts, who so ably represents the *New York Times* in the Congress. Those gentlemen raise some very interesting and timely questions about many factors that impact on congressmen and their districts today.

Before I react to some of the issues raised in the two papers, I'd like to just take a few moments to talk about how I envision my own role as an elected representative of the First District of Massachusetts. First, let me say that I believe that any legislator worth his salt, or her salt, must approach his or her congressional responsibilities on the premise that public office is really a public trust. This is not simply political rhetoric. It's an important principle that I believe in and that I practice. Regrettably, it's a principle that has been severely tested by the members of Congress. Yet it is also a principle that has weathered the test, will continue, and I support it.

We are here this morning to talk about the relationships that exist between a congressman and his district, as well as the factors that affect those relationships. We must look at the realities and the ideals. In order to do that, from my point of view, we must talk about the public—its needs, its wishes, and the concept of trust that binds a legislator and his constituents together. I do not subscribe to the view that a congressman's role is that of a partisan performing strictly in accordance with the party line. My party feels that way about me. Nor do I completely subscribe to the view that an elected representative is a delegate chosen simply to vote the way the majority of the people in his congressional district want him to vote. I do subscribe, however, to the concept that the most legitimate role for a congressman is that of a trustee—someone who is given power and control over certain resources of this country for the benefit of those who empower him: his constituents.

Today we must be very careful not to fall into the trap of seeking a single, neat definition or description of just how a particular congressman should function. Each congressman represents a very unique district. There are no two districts alike in the Congress. The people's lifestyles vary; their economies vary; their needs vary. Their attitudes toward the federal government vary, and their expectations of their elected representatives seem to change as often as the New England weather. And of course, each congressman has his special style and special interests.

A little of my style, then, is determined by the nature of my district. While there are twelve congression-

al districts in Massachusetts, mine covers more than one-third of the state's land area, and includes eighty-eight towns and cities. It's largely rural, though there are key manufacturing towns like my home town of Pittsfield, and Holyoke. We have industries like the General Electric Company, Sprague Electric, Kollmorgen, and a number of paper-making machinery companies, paper companies, and small tool companies. It also contains a picturesque group of towns and villages endowed with centuries of preserved history, and many small New England farms. In addition, it boasts thirteen outstanding colleges and universities, including the University of Massachusetts, educating tens of thousands of students from across the country. And last but not least, it's a largely Democratic district that has sent a Republican to Congress (had the good sense to do it) for the past twelve consecutive terms—twice with the endorsement of both parties.

Now that kind of diversity means that there are many interests and many issues for me, as a congressman, to master and to attend to. First, I'm a firm believer in providing constituent service. It's important for a congressman to serve his people and to help his people deal with the ever-increasing federal bureaucracy and machinery. Casework is a large part of the service, and it's going on all the time—cases involving medicaid, social security, veterans' affairs, welfare, unemployment compensation, and food stamps lead the lists.

While I believe in this kind of service, I am sometimes concerned about the growing expectation on the part of my people (and the general public) that the federal government should provide the answers for every one of their problems. I'm afraid that, as was said here this morning, we're getting away from people learning to rely upon themselves. As these gentlemen have pointed out, that tendency to always look to Washington contributes to the continued and perhaps ever-growing expansion of the federal government.

I believe in the importance of a congressman being accessible. Accessibility is part of a constituent service. Like the vast majority of my colleagues, I work at being accessible. I make frequent trips back to the district, I hold office hours in towns around the district on a regular basis, and this gives me a direct opportunity to keep in touch with the people, to know how they are reacting to local issues and national events. As Professor Fiorina noted, like many other congressmen I now maintain two district offices to keep in better touch with my district and the people.

Another dimension of the accessibility that I believe in and count on is regular communication with my constituents through the newsletter, radio commentaries, and attendance at public forums. The newsletter, for instance, serves several purposes. It informs my constituents about my activities in Congress. It educates and exposes them to certain issues in government that affect their lives. It serves me by reminding my constituents of the service that I provide to them, and that I continue to seek their support. Now the volume of mail that I receive is astronomical, like all other congressmen. Hundreds and hundreds of letters each day pour into my Washington and district offices. I believe in following up on each of these inquiries as quickly as possible. However, that too demands considerable time and staff support.

As you can anticipate and as these gentlemen suggest, the efforts of a congressman to be accessible and responsive to the constituent creates other problems as well. One that I often attack is properly called "stafflation"—the inflationary increase in congressional staff in recent years. One time I put an amendment on a legislative appropriation bill to create a special workers' compensation insurance so if these staff people trip over each other and get hurt they can be taken care of. The other problem is a form of vulnerability, or in other words, accountability. The more accessible that I am and the more I publicize my views and opinions through newsletters and radio shows, the more I open myself up to attack and criticism by various interest groups. One of the speakers mentioned the debt limit. I voted for the debt limit under Republican and Democratic administrations, and I've been criticized by conservative groups. I voted for foreign aid and led the fight on the floor of the Congress for foreign aid and was highly criticized by my people. But also as a leader—I hope to be perceived as a leader—I've traveled around to different parts of the world and looked at the foreign aid program. I must admit I took biased pictures, but I came back with my films and little projector and spoke to school groups and to church groups, hoping to lead my people on that particular issue.

I'll reserve some of my other observations for later on in the discussion, but before yielding the floor, I'd like to comment quickly on one other theme expressed in the papers today. That is the impression that congressmen spend a considerable amount of their time and energy and incumbent resources focusing on their reelection. That's true. Every representative dedicated to public service

wants to be reelected by the people that he serves. In order to accomplish very much in the Congress, one must achieve some position of responsibility and influence in the committee structure. One must establish true credibility among his colleagues. That takes more than two years. Incumbency benefits not only the incumbent, but also the constituents as well. If it doesn't, you can bet the constituents will demand a change in the next election. Reelection pressures may mean that members feel susceptible to supporting a position that may not always be in direct line with their conscience. When that happens, everybody loses, especially the democratic political process. Fifty-eight percent of the House of Representatives today has eight years of service or less.

Let me just suggest two possible improvements in this regard. One has already been mentioned by Steve Roberts. The first is public financing of congressional campaigns. Public financing has the potential, I believe, to preserve the integrity of congressional elections. The second consideration, which is not discussed too often—and I feel that they should go hand in hand— is a change in the length of the congressional term. It certainly won't happen in my time, but it should be worked on. Two years is just too short in this day and age of television and communication and transportation. Nearly half the term is influenced or shadowed by the incumbent's bid for reelection. Doesn't happen to me, I have twenty-three years in the Congress and eight in the state senate, and I can go my own way, be my independent self, and be the maverick that I am. But a new member going into the House of Representatives, it's impossible today, with all the new things—the polling, the mass mailing, the electronics and all—for him to tend to his work.

I think that's one of the weaknesses of the House of Representatives right now. Everybody wants to be a chief because we've done away with the seniority system. They can dump anybody as a chairman, Democrat or Republican, any time. So we've lost that strength in the Congress, where the ranking member or the chairman of the committee was a strong, powerful individual. He no longer is, because he's afraid that he'll be thrown out by his peers if he doesn't go along with them on the issue that they're interested in. Secondly, these new members coming in are one-issue candidates—whether it's abortion, the Panama Canal, or busing. And they're spending all of their time on TV, and with this other electronic equipment, to get back home to their people to let them know that they're doing everything they can in the Congress on that one particular issue that they got elected on. So I think that a four- or five-year term would be very, very helpful in this regard. Thank you very much.

Response by Hon. John Brademas
Member, United States House of
Representatives, 1958-1980

Mr. Chairman and friends, like my colleagues on the panel, I am enormously flattered to have been invited to join you in this symposium in honor of the remarkable political leader who graduated from this institution, and who has been so significant a figure in the life of our country. Like my colleagues here, Bob Giaimo, Silvio Conte, and Charlie Vanik, I count Speaker O'Neill one of my dearest friends, and I believe history will come to regard him as perhaps the ablest Speaker of this century in the House of Representatives. I can appreciate the pride that all of you here at Boston College must take in him.

I'm also pleased to be here with my colleagues from the House. Bob Giaimo is one of the ablest leaders in the House, and one of the people who got the budget process going. Charlie Vanik is one of the most knowledgeable people on tax law who has ever served in the House. And your own indomitable Sil Conte shows that it is possible to have a civilized Republican in the House of Representatives. (Laughter) So I'm glad to be here with

them, as well as with my old friend, Steve Roberts, of the *New York Times*, and these two distinguished political scientists.

I'd just like to make a few rather random observations about what has been said here today. I'm not going to talk in any systematic manner. I speak from the perspective of someone who has been involved in congressional politics for the last quarter of a century. I first ran for the House in 1954, in a district in northern Indiana, best known perhaps to some of you because it's the location of an establishment called Notre Dame, and I served in the House for twenty-two years. I lost the first two elections, won the third, and, as you know, was defeated last fall. So I have seen in my own political experience some of the changes in the House of Representatives which the earlier speakers have described. I think it might be useful if I follow what Sil Conte said, and just offer the observation that we ought to think for a moment about what it is a representative in Congress is really supposed to be, or to do, or to mean. I always find it useful to reflect on the fact that the proper title of the person who holds that responsibility is United States Representative in Congress from (in my case) the Third District of Indiana. Very often people ask: How do you make up your mind when you decide a tough vote? They mean, of course: Do you vote with your district, or do you vote in the national interest, or do you follow your conscience? I think there is an insufficient awareness that there is a whole series of concerns that go consciously (and probably subconsciously) into the thought processes of a congressman when he or she votes.

Basically a representative has two responsibilities. He has a responsibility to his district; he is a representative of that district. But at the same time, he has a national responsibility, a responsibility to the whole country. And running through a good deal of the changes in the electoral process which previous speakers have described has been, in my opinion, a disconcerting erosion of the capacity of members of Congress to fulfill that responsibility to serve the national interest, to help make policy for a country of 230 million people. Much of what Steve Roberts said I found myself very much at home with. He and I have talked about these matters for some time.

I've seen a sharp increase in the cost of campaigns. My first campaign in 1954 cost about $12,000. This last one cost over $600,000. And I had to have a great deal of attention paid to this matter of fund raising, because of the enormous increase in the cost of campaigning.

I've seen an increase in the role of television. I ran the first campaign for Congress in my district ever run on television . That shows you how relatively young, or how terribly old, I am. The fact is that back in 1954, with three stations and no videotape, I had to run from one station to another to go on live, to make my one-minute or five-minute presentations.

And I've certainly seen a decline in the role of organized political parties. Indiana is a state where patronage was very important at the state level. We're the state that had the famous "two percent club," where if you were on the state payroll, it was expected that you contribute x percent of your salary to the coffers of the state party. And today, to some extent, we still have that kind of an arrangement. Whenever you buy an auto license in Indiana, 50¢ or whatever goes to the county chairman of the party that is in control of the office of secretary of state, or whoever the state legislature decided was going to be in charge of that particular operation. But I've seen in my own political experience the withering away of the local political party. I won't push that too far, because parties still have some consequence. In Indiana, we do have precinct committee men and committee women. But increasingly, in my congressional district, I had to become the de facto party leader. Somebody said, "Brademas, how could you spend over $600,000 in a campaign for the House of Representatives?" Sil might well ask me that question. But in my district, last time, I suppose I had as many as twenty people on the paid campaign staff. I had to put money into voter registration, voter canvassing, paid polling, getting out the vote on election day, using computers for all of that. And a good deal of my expenditures were not directly focused on my own reelection, but rather were investments in what twenty-five years ago the Democratic congressional district party would have handled. But the party does not, for a variety of reasons, have that capability any longer. My defeat last fall will therefore have a marked impact on the future of the Democratic party in my district, because a lot of local Democrats had come to depend on my own capability and that of my supporters to turn out the vote and carry on these party-building functions. In fact,

there is a little subterranean warfare going on right now with respect to who will get his hands on the tapes that have all of the voter data.

I have a district that is different from Sil's, just the other way around really. My district is basically a Republican district, and I was able to represent it for twenty-two years. But one of the problems I had in this last year is, I think, relevant to what Professor Fiorina was talking about, that is, the perception of the candidate by the electorate. I'm not going to try to give you any other than an anecdotal commentary on that phenomenon. But as I looked around at what was going on in my district last year I realized that I was in trouble. Though I'd been the congressman for twenty-two years—and it was hard to go into a community in my district in which you didn't see some physical evidence of my activities in the form of plants, industries, buildings, and all the rest—there were a lot of voters who had no memory of my role in providing these benefits, and indeed *never* knew that I had anything to do with them at all. That is another way of saying that there is a very important electoral problem for an incumbent congressman of some years in educating his constituency about what he's done. It may be that because television has become so important a factor in our lives, and people spend so much time in front of that box, there's not much knowledge about politics, or certainly about substantive issues and substantive achievements.

For example, I put in a good deal of time in helping to write the Education of Handicapped Children Act. That bill touches the lives of any family that has a handicapped child. And you'd be astonished at how many families in our country have handicapped children. But I also have come to the conclusion that a lot of families with handicapped children really didn't know that I had anything to do with the law. One of the members of the faculty here told me about a study done ten to fifteen years ago by Jack Schuster (who used to work for me). Schuster wrote about the extent to which I got support from school teachers in my district because of my hard work on behalf of education. The conclusion of that study was: I got very little. I can only tell you that the world has not changed very much. Think of this, for example. I would have been number two in seniority on the Education and Labor Committee, aside from my role in the House leadership. And I voted constantly with the National Education Association, not so much because the NEA wanted me to, but because my judgment told me to do so, and I

authored a lot of education bills over the years. But the NEA was almost wholly invisible in my campaign for Congress this year. I think they contributed through their PAC about $1,000 to my campaign, and that only after repeated requests. You would have been very hard-pressed to find many active school teachers in my campaign this year. It was very revealing. They just weren't around. So the quid pro quo, if you will, even in respect to a special-interest group that is supposed to be highly sophisticated, is not as evident as you might think.

I was also struck by what Steve Roberts said when he used the phrase "free agent." I think that's a good phrase. I would add another definition, not to replace it but to add another perspective. Members of Congress are in large part, because of these various phenomena we've been discussing, "independent contractors." We're all in business for ourselves, as it were. And having been the whip for a time, I can assure you that the impact of these various developments is felt very powerfully on the floor of the House of Representatives when one goes out to try to persuade people to vote. I'm also struck by the point that was made, I think again by Mr. Roberts, about arousing great expectations on the part of your constituents. One of the problems you have is that if you get pretty good at producing, then people expect you to be able to produce all the time. This problem caused me very great pain last fall, because of the high unemployment in my district. I had come to have a reputation for bringing in projects that meant jobs and business, and indeed Birch Bayh and I were bringing a $140 million gasohol plant to my hometown. But it hadn't got there yet. You couldn't actually see it, it hadn't actually been built yet. But when there's high unemployment—and there was 15 percent unemployment in my district last year, double the national rate—it is enormously difficult to get at people's thought processes.

Another point: I speak here again of my own race for whatever value it may have for political scientists who seek to generalize about these matters. My own district, as I've said, is basically a Republican district. In the twenty-six years I ran for Congress, only *once* was my district carried by the Democratic nominee for president. So presidential years were always uphill for me. But this year, with President Carter being an even weaker Democratic presidential nominee than usual; with inflation being far higher than it's been in a long time; with the hostage crisis intensifying hostility to the Democrats; and then

the Republicans deciding to target my race, putting in far more money than they had ever done before; with an attractive, skilled opposition candidate; then 15 percent unemployment on top of that—it all was too much. Too many negatives came together, and I'm not even talking about the Moral Majority and the National Rifle Association and the others, who I don't really regard as having been decisive. So what happened, I suggest, and especially to Professor Fiorina, is this. In a state like mine there are two levers—there's the Republican lever because they control the state government, and the Democratic lever. In order to split, people have to move back and forth on the two lines. But people were so upset—including blue-collar UAW people, who you would expect to have been strong supporters of mine—about the economic factor, especially high unemployment and high inflation, they just went in and hit that top lever, without thinking. They were *feeling*.

I come back to what Sil Conte said, to which I resonated very strongly, when he remarked upon the peculiar character of his congressional district. The thing that strikes me again and again as I think about the American political system is how enormously complicated it is. When you have a separation of powers constitution, you're already complicating it. When you have weak political parties you are complicating it even more. Then you have these different configurations of forces in each congressional district. Tip O'Neill has one kind of district in Cambridge; Silvio Conte has another kind of district not too far away. But they're different districts, enormously different, in many, many respects. So it ought not to surprise anyone, Professor Fiorina, that it is so difficult to generalize, to get data together that are replicable in one way or another.

Now finally, a word about what we can do about all these matters. Clearly, we've got to recover some role for parties in this country, or the situation that I've been describing, that we've all been describing, is going to get a lot worse. And Mr. Roberts has given us the useful concept of an "electronic party." Politics may also become more ideological in this country—therefore, more issue oriented. A word on public financing. I've been a sponsor of the public financing bill from the start. There's only one reason I was for it—its the only constitutional way (with this Supreme Court) that we can impose a limit on campaign spending. But I'll have to tell you that if we had had a public financing law, I'd have been de-

feated in 1980 even earlier, because I would not have had the opportunity to go out and raise as much money as I did. From the national interest point of view, I'm sympathetic with you. In the short run, I would have been damaged by that. I strongly support the idea of a four-year term. The final thing I would offer as a generalization is this. We have to come back to the question of what it is we expect Congress and congressmen to be. And I have observed increasingly, as others have said here, that Americans have a schizophrenic attitude toward government. On the one hand, they say: "We want government out of our lives and off our backs. And by the way, when are you getting that contract through or that small business loan?" So people have divided desires and that complicates our lives. But I hazard the proposition that if we're going to be able to cope with the problems this country has, a huge country like this with all these crosscurrents of interest, we're going to have to develop ways of making it possible for members of Congress, and in particular of the House of Representatives, to be able to negotiate, to compromise, to accommodate all of these conflicting interests, or the system is going to have a difficult time coping. And I'll go one other step beyond what I've just said, and

I'm reminded of this by Sil Conte's observation on foreign aid. I think that at least some members of Congress have to be able not only to go along, as it were, but to *lead*. That may be the subject for another symposium.

Response by Carole J. Uhlaner,

School of Social Sciences, University of California, Irvine

I will try to be brief, also somewhat more extemporaneous, particularly since, as is usually the case when you're discussing, the papers emphasize points different from those you want to talk about. But bear with me on that. These are two quite different papers, as is obvious. Both are very enjoyable and useful in different ways. Professor Fiorina's paper is enjoyable because of its salutary reminders of the difficulties of data analyses and the limits of them, and his corresponding modesty in discussing the problem. I, on that ground alone, strongly recommend it to all the academics in the group. Mr. Roberts's paper gives us a very enjoyable fleshing out of the congressman's dilemma.

At the same time as the congressman's job has been changing, as Mr. Roberts indicates, political scientists have changed their focus as well. In the old days, the profession looked at roll call votes and thought that what was important about Congress was what happened on Capitol Hill. In more recent years, attention has been turned from Capitol Hill to the district—especially the provision of services and information, and contact of all types. Now these two papers approached the problem of constituent-representative relations in a complementary fashion. Mr. Roberts tells about the attention which congressmen pay to their districts. Professor Fiorina tries to examine, in effect, what attention districts pay to their congressmen. This becomes very circular, because if differences in a congressman's actions do make any difference in constituents' behavior, then we should see differences in the way constituents look at their congressmen, but that might be affecting the way congressmen look at their constituents—anyway, it's two sides of the same puzzle, coming at the same thing.

Mr. Roberts's paper paints a picture of fearful, overworked ombudsmen on Capitol Hill. They fear their dependence on money, especially PAC dollars, which they resent. But at the same time as they complain about PAC money, they try to collect as much of it as they can. And being an overworked ombudsman is a way to establish yourself in your district. But, as Mr. Roberts points out, sometimes this creates a monster. Servicing the demands of a constituency might only lead to further demands on government. So we have two difficult situations here faced by a congressman, both of them in the form of what political scientists call the "prisoner's dilemma." The implication, from what Mr. Roberts has told us, is that all congressmen would be happier if PACs were out of the picture, and if they didn't have to spend lots and lots of money on campaigns. But no single congressman can afford to alienate the groups that provide that kind of money. Even less could any single congressman afford to unilaterally eschew polling, television, direct mail. No one congressman can do this. On the other hand, most of them think that they would be better off if no one did it. So here we have a dilemma. No one can do it alone, they would all like to do it together. The only way you get out of that situation is through an enforceable collective action, like a public financing law. But for that you need strong leadership. A footnote to that—public financing of congressional campaigns may deal with the money problem, but it may accentuate the other problem that Mr. Roberts points out, namely the weakness of the parties.

The ombudsman dilemma creates a similar situation, as Professor Fiorina has pointed out in some of his earlier work. No single district has the incentive to elect a congressman who is not a skilled ombudsman. However, everybody would be better off if the need for ombudsmen, and the amount of bureaucratic red tape, were cut back for everybody at once. Once again, we're in a prisoner's dilemma; without some kind of external sanction, you're caught in a box that you can't really get out of.

One other brief comment on Mr. Roberts's paper. He points out one logical difficulty in dealing with the issue of constituency service and congressmen—namely, if congressmen are really pushing these neutral roles, they should be safer and less fearful. But they're palpably more fearful, even if they may be safer. I suspect that what's going on is that congressmen are being insulated from public opinion as a whole, but are more vulnerable to the special interests. That's just a suspicion. There's a tension there that hasn't quite been resolved.

I think that one of the most exciting parts of Professor Fiorina's paper is the heroic attempt to deal with accountability and data across time, and the data are in fact not very comparable at all. It's a heroic attempt, and I think it's somewhat successful—more than somewhat successful. Professor Fiorina pointed out the two most intriguing results of his research: the changes in the impact of issues on the vote for congressmen, and the changes in the impact of constituency attentiveness on the vote for congressmen. The changes in the impact of issues are particularly nice, because they fit in with what we know has been going on with presidential voting. It's nice to know that, as issues become more important in presidential elections, they also have somewhat greater impact in congressional elections. That makes political scientists feel good, knowing that the world fits together that way. Professor Fiorina clearly finds that constituency attentiveness plays more of a role as well. But I want to point out something that he had to rush over, which is that this constituency attentiveness is not just casework, or the provision of services. In fact, of the people whom he codes as seeing their representative as being attentive to the constituency, by far the larger portion of them, over two-thirds of them, are referring to things like: the congressman listens to the district, the congressman keeps us informed, he stays in touch, he keeps his finger on the pulse. These are not related to providing services. They deal with the more general issue of the presentation of the congressman to the district—the kind of thing that Mr. Roberts talked about.

On Professor Fiorina's basic puzzle—namely that there has been a great increase in staff since 1958, but not that much change in the kinds of things you would think would change, like recognition of incumbents—it could be that part of what's going on is that there hasn't been that much change in service over time. Although there's more staff, maybe not that much more service has been provided to the constituents, and the decline in marginal seats might even have some cause completely independent of the staff and service relationship. In addition, there's always the possibility that 1978 was unusual.

The broader question that all this leads us to is: What are the normative implications, what are the value implications, of what seems to be an apparent increase in the ombudsman role, in constituency service, and in casework? That is to say, what's really going on in the districts anyway? Does all this district attentiveness result in real benefits to people, or is much of it symbolic? And in particular, who are getting the symbolic benefits and who are getting the real ones? Clearly, many of the benefits are symbolic. Richard Fenno's "Congressman E" in *Homestyle* comments that people mainly want a sympathetic ear. They don't necessarily want you to do anything for them, they want you to listen to them. We also know that a lot of the contacts that people referred to are in fact information giving. People are asking for information from congressmen and getting that. We also know that some people get real benefits; they actually get problems ironed out. They get contracts, they get small-level pork-barrel. Who gets which? We know that not all requests could be honored. There are time and staff constraints, like the comments about creating a monster, creating rising expectations. Who are the people whose demands are getting serviced? A great illustration of how service can be symbolic comes from Ireland, where, as I understand from students of Irish politics, backbench members of Parliament spend a lot of their time sitting in the parliamentary library writing letters claiming credit for checks that their constituents would have received anyway, and trying to get their political benefit from this.

So when we focus on constituent relations, we raise in a different context the kind of stratification question that bothers us in other contexts. Who's getting what, and are they getting anything that's real? That requires looking at contacting much more closely than we have. We know that personal contacting of congressmen is not really stratified. There's no real relationship between the usual participation indicators and contacting members of Congress. But we don't know whether or not there's a stratification in terms of the kinds of benefits that people are getting.

The other normative question that we might consider is whether any of this has any impact on that old and now forgotten concern of the discipline, namely what votes are taken in Congress. Is there any kind of relationship between casework and the roll call behavior of congressmen? There might be some kind of circular relationship there, as information is gained, and as pressure is applied, but we don't know. Either casework is irrelevant, though most of the discussion suggests that it's not; or if we believe that the direct relationship between congressmen and constituency is an important development in our political system, we don't know what it means in terms of representation—not representation in terms of reflecting preferences, but representation in terms of access to government goods. If congressmen are important mainly or in large part because of their complaint-window role, we want to know whose complaints get resolved. That has major implications for equality and the other democratic norms of our governmental system.

PART III:
FIRST PLENARY
ADDRESS

What's He Like? What's She Like? What Are They Like?

Richard F. Fenno, Jr.
William J. Kenan Professor of Political Science
University of Rochester

Speaking as someone who studies American politics, I cannot think of a happier occasion than the creation of a powerful incentive for *more* people to study American politics. And that, of course, is exactly what the Thomas P. O'Neill, Jr., Chair in American Politics will be. It is, I think, the special characteristic of the Speakership—and the source of its influence—that its occupant touches more phases of the political process than anyone else in the legislative branch. So, any academic chair named after a Speaker of the House will encourage those associated with it to study the whole of the American political system. At the same time, however, a chair named for the Speaker provides a special invitation to see that larger system through his eyes. We could use the subject of congressional leadership as a window on the wider world of American politics. Or, more narrowly, we might use the perspective of congressional leadership to look at congressional politics. Today, I want to talk about this narrower relationship. And I want to talk as a political scientist to other political scientists. My main point will be simply that if we look at congressional leadership in a particular way, it might make us want to know more about the ordinary member of Congress. And political scientists, I want to suggest, might profitably expend more effort learning about the ordinary members of Congress. A focus on leaders, in short, might end up producing a focus on followers.

Followers and Leaders

This is not a paradox. All of social science tells us that leadership involves a relationship between leader and follower—that one cannot be understood without the other. And all of our studies of congressional leadership point us in the same direction. Studies by Robert Peabody and Nelson Polsby of the way in which House and Senate leaders get elected tell us that the leaders of Congress are chosen by the ordinary members of the Congress, for reasons known only to those members themselves—and with a minimum of outside influence. In most congressional dramas, everybody in the political system can play. But in picking congressional leaders, only the followers can play. To most outsiders, leadership contests are nonevents; inside Congress, they are matters of great intensity—fought "eyeball to eyeball," as one Republican leadership candidate described them in December.

Service and Persuasion

When the ordinary senator and representative chooses among prospective leaders, each member asks this question: "What can he do for me?" or "What will my life be like with him as leader?" The followers think of leadership, therefore, in terms of personal, individual, one-to-one relationships between the leader and each of them. And in so doing, the followers set the basic conditions under which their leaders must function. As one veteran senator put it, "For a leader's job . . . you want a fellow who will treat you fairly. You wonder how a person will conduct himself in the job with particular reference to *you*." And an experienced House member defined leadership the same way. "You only want two things in a leader," he said. "First, someone who will see you and, second, [someone who will] understand your problems." Such is the highly personalized follower's view of congressional leadership.

Not surprisingly, when the leaders talk about their job they stress the same one-to-one relationship with their followers. "There's no mystery about being Senate leader," said Lyndon Johnson. "You've got to be interested in the other fellow's problems." Leaders know that is how they get and keep their jobs. Speaker Carl Albert commented, "The main element in my climb to the leadership is the fact that I've heard more speeches and called more people by their first name. I've always been fascinated by [the members]. . . . There are so many variances and eccentricities." An ordinary member who helped start Albert on his leadership climb—from whip to majority leader to Speaker—agreed. "He's done so many things for so many people, they trust him. . . . They think of him, 'Here's a man I can talk to.' When the members go about picking a leader, they want personal service." A biographer of Sen. Robert Byrd explained his promotion from majority whip to majority leader similarly. "If there was one factor above all others that marked his service as whip, it was that he drove himself from early morning to late evening to meet the personal needs of individual senators."

Congressional leaders move up the leadership ladder from a subordinate position to a higher one—as Byrd did, or as Albert did, or as Robert Michel did. The backlog of personal trust and personal credits they have built up with individual members is taken as a warrant of similar assistance in the future. Speaker O'Neill advanced up the leadership ladder, in this same manner—from whip, to majority leader, to Speaker. He was chosen whip in large part because individual House Democrats felt he would be accessible to them. *Congressional Quarterly* headlined his selection, "New Democratic Whip: Friends In All Factions." When he was later elected majority leader, the man who challenged him and then withdrew said in the caucus, "Tip, I can tell you something that nobody else in this room can. You haven't got an enemy in the place." When he was elected Speaker he told the freshman Democrats, "My policy will be an open door policy. I am easy to talk to." At each rung of the ladder, O'Neill built up enough credits with enough individual members to earn a promotion. And now, at the top of the ladder as Speaker, he continues to devote a great deal of his time to doing what he has always done—helping his followers, one by one.

"When Tip walks onto the floor," says Rep. Joe Moakley, "it's like throwing a piece of sugar at ants. The guys line up to talk to him." And the Speaker says, "I get everybody who has a problem [back home]. It's like a priest hearing confessionals. You can't say no." Speaker O'Neill spends an estimated one in four weekends on the road, visiting in the home districts of from thirty to forty House members each year. What the ordinary members want from their leaders, therefore, is a personal relationship and personal service. And that is what they get. They get it in Washington and they get it back home.

This personal relationship is not, however, a one-way street. While the leaders are doing what their followers most want them to do, they are at the same time learning what they most need to know in order to lead. Sam Rayburn's assistant, D. B. Hardeman, attributed Rayburn's success as Speaker primarily to his "intelligence," because, said Hardeman: "He applied this intelligence to knowing the member and his district, sometimes even better than the member himself." In Lyndon Johnson's words, "A good leader should . . . know the problems of each individual state and the temperament of each individual senator." A good leader, says Robert Byrd, "should understand the problems of individual members within their own respective constituencies. He should know his colleagues, their personalities, their interests." House Majority Leader Jim Wright travelled to the constituencies of eighty-three House Democrats during his first year-and-a-half in office. But he learned about his followers while he served them. "It's fatiguing at times, but richly rewarding," says Wright of his travels. "It helps me in my job, knowing the concerns and aspirations of members. It also helps me to elicit their support for the Democratic program."

Leaders must know their followers as individuals because at some point leadership involves the act of persuasion. Leaders must persuade followers to do something or not to do something—to support or not to support a certain procedure, to vote or not to vote for a certain amendment, or to oppose or not to oppose a certain bill. Persuasion in the Congress is a person-to-person process, done most effectively by someone who knows each individual he is trying to persuade. That is, by a leader who has the kind of knowledge about each follower that Wright and Hardeman and Johnson and Byrd were talking about. The personal, one-to-one relationship which followers expect of their leaders is, then, the same kind of relationship which leaders must seek out if they are to be effective.

So, personal service and personal persuasion are two sides of the same coin for the leader. They require the same concern about individual followers. Either way, from the leader's perspective, the key question about each follower is: "What are his or her problems?" "What does he or she want?" Or to put it most generally, "What's he or she like?" Congressional leaders must answer this question for each senator and representative in order to get their job, in order to keep their job, and in order to do their job. This question—the "What's he like?" or the "What's she like?" question—is, then, a crucial question for congressional leaders. I think it should become more of a political scientist's question, too.

"Mere Anecdotes?"

When I first went to Washington to study Congress in the early 1960s, the people I talked to on Capitol Hill invariably placed great emphasis on this kind of question—on what they called "the human equation" or "the personalities involved." In 1961, John McCormack replied to my questions about assigning members to committees with this typical comment:

> Of course, personality enters in. Like any group of fellas on the corner, you have different personalities. Some members are more popular than others. Some of the members are brilliant but they are lazy. Others are not so brilliant but they develop what they have and they work hard. Some men are eloquent speakers, but they don't have that "it" to make a speech. Others don't speak so

well but they've got the courage to go down and say what they feel. . . . Some members are there for years and years and no one ever knows they are there. But we know they are there, [that] they are doing their job down in committee. . . . We're human beings down here—all different. We take all these things into consideration. You can't help it.

Other Capitol Hill people were more critical. "The trouble with you political scientists," they would say, "is that you don't understand that all these personalities are different." My reaction was to brush aside all such comments—descriptive or critical. I wrote them off as the naturally protective posture of people trying to carve out a part of the process which outsiders, like political scientists, could not hope to penetrate. Even more, I tended to feel that the knowledge they withheld from me was unimportant in the development of theories about congressional behavior. Information about particular individuals, I felt, was grist for the mill of journalists, whose short-run, episodic focus made them more interested in such matters—more interested in "anecdotes" (or as political scientists are wont to say, "mere anecdotes") than in generalizations.

I am no longer convinced of my wisdom in such matters. Why? For one thing, I now believe that my Capitol Hill respondents were telling me something of theoretical importance. They were telling me that the desires and the goals and the abilities of individual members and the relationships of trust, respect, and obligation they establish with one another—leader-to-follower, for example—can be important in legislative politics. It might be difficult (as surely it is) to acquire usable knowledge about individual legislators, but the result might well bring an enhanced understanding of why people do what they do in the legislature. So, the "What's he like, what's she like?" question might be more important than I had thought. And, therefore, answers to that question might lead to generalizations more consequential than I had imagined—generalizations about "What are *they* like?" For that question—*"What are they like?"*—is ultimately the political scientist's question. And I came to believe that our answers to it might be better if we devoted more time looking at individual members.

For another thing, it is a simple fact that some of the most stimulating work on Congress has been produced by journalists—by people who have wrestled quite unabashedly with the "What's he like?" question. And often in anecdotal form. I think of Elizabeth Drew's book on Sen. John Culver, Bernard Asbell's book on Sen. Edmund Muskie, and Jimmy Breslin's book about Speaker O'Neill. Drew described the personal aspects of Culver's effectiveness; Asbell described the priority Muskie placed on achieving his personal credibility among his colleagues; and Breslin described the Speaker's personal approach to consensus building in the House. Political scientists need to know about these things.

Willy-nilly, therefore, we will feed off these studies, just as we have fed off perceptive journalistic studies in the past. Students of Congress should remember that it was a journalist, William White, who set the agenda for twenty-five years of political science scholarship on the Senate with his book, *Citadel*, published in 1956. The echoes of White's ideas on "What are they like?" dominate even the two most recent political science books on the Senate—Ross Baker's *Friend and Foe in the U.S. Senate* , and Michael Foley's *The New Senate*. We should acknowledge our reliance on perceptive journalists. But at the same time we might ask ourselves: Why should we leave the journalists in charge of the "What's he like?" question? And, hence, in charge of the "What are *they* like?" question? Why, indeed, should we leave them in charge of anecdotes? As Raymond Wolfinger has wisely observed, "The plural of anecdote is data." We might have better data if we collected it ourselves.

Of course, political scientists have not totally neglected the "What's he like?" question. Indeed, another reason for entertaining that question lies in the success enjoyed by some political scientists who have done so. For example, David Mayhew's discussion of the advertising, credit-claiming, and position-taking behavior of House members was stimulated by his service in a congressman's office. Morris Fiorina's essay on the importance of constituency service was stimulated by his interviews in two congressional districts. In both cases, the authors began with the "What's he like?" question and moved to "What are they like?" generalizations. They, and others like them, moved the study of Congress forward by making and by pressing such generalizations.

But there is reason to believe that political scientists have just scratched the surface—if only because we have devoted so little time and energy to the "What's he like?" question. Up to now, our major "What are they like?" generalization states that members of the House and Senate want to get reelected. That is, for example, the driving generalization behind the Mayhew and Fiorina studies. For certain, the reelection goal is an important one for our legislators. And no answer to the "What are they like?" question would be complete without the notion that most of them want to keep their jobs. But I doubt that is all there is to it. Members are probably more complicated than that. If Speaker O'Neill knew about each House member only that he or she wanted to get reelected, would the Speaker know enough to keep his job? Or enough to do his job? I doubt it.

Independence

Which leads me to a final reason for looking at individual members. When Speaker O'Neill is asked the "What are they like?" question, he has his own generalization about them. It is that the members are *independent*— significantly more independent than they used to be. "You have such a wave of independence," he says. Or, "They're all independent now." Or, "Years ago, most of them came from their local legislatures. They'd have been seasoned. But now 50 percent of them have never been in public office before. There's a tremendous independence." Or, "They have no sense of party discipline. They run more as individuals." Or, "They're younger. They're better educated. We have more graduates and Rhodes scholars, more doctorates, more master's degrees—people who came into the field of politics as a challenge with the idea that they wanted change—extremely independent." This is the Speaker's constant theme. Robert Byrd echoes the idea for senators. "The emergence of 'the individual' has been a kind of phenomenon," he says.

If legislators are strikingly more independent now—more individualistic—then congressional leaders will have to spend more time than they ever did getting to know the ordinary member—one by one. The individual member cannot so easily be subsumed in a party, or a committee, or a bloc, or a delegation as once was the case. Recent elections, furthermore, have produced increased turnover among the memberships of both chambers. Sixty-one percent of today's House members have served less than seven years. Sixty-two percent of today's senators have served less than seven years. Therefore, as Barbara Sinclair has observed, at the very time it becomes more important for the leaders to know the individual members well, it has become more difficult for the leaders to do so. Thus the "What's he like?" question has become increasingly important *and* increasingly problematic for congressional leaders. So political scientists have yet another reason for spending some time on it.

Knowledge about individual members helps congressional leaders do their job—influencing behavior. More knowledge about individual members might help political scientists do *our* job—analyzing behavior. At present, we are more knowledgeable about legislators in the aggregate than we are about the building blocks that make up these aggregates. Our graduate students are required to learn statistics—the better to manipulate aggregates. But they are not required to talk to politicians—the better to understand aggregates. Would our analyses be improved if more of us actually met our politicians? We can't be sure. Still and all, I should like to tease a few more political scientists into trying.

An Ordinary Member

Let me spend some time with an example. In the 1970s I got to know eighteen members of the House pretty well—by travelling with them in their districts and by talking with them in Washington. Last month, one of those eighteen left Congress. He left of his own volition, at the age of fifty and after only eight years of service. He had no electoral worries. Like most of the 435 members of the House, he remained unknown to the American public outside his district. Nor was he a person of any special influence in the House. He was, in that sense, a perfectly ordinary member of Congress. Because I know him and because he has left public life, I can ask the "What's he like?" question more easily of him than I can of the other members. So I shall. His decision to retire, return home, and resume the private practice of law also gives the question a little extra bite. For his desire to get reelected will not get us very far in answering our question.

His leaving drew one bit of national notice. Otis Pike, a former House colleague and a Democrat, devoted a syndicated column to the retiring member, a Republican. Wrote Pike:

> On the evening of February 6 in the House of Representatives, [he] gave an important speech. It is about war. It should be required reading. [He] is an intellectual, but not an orator. There are better speakers in the House, but none who have more to say. He writes his own speeches and speaks his own mind. It is a superb mind. . . . He is also retiring this year and the Congress and the nation will be the poorer for it. No one in America heard the speech and almost no one outside the Fourth District of Colorado has heard of Jim Johnson.

So, what's he like, Jim Johnson, Republican of Colorado? Like 534 others—complicated. He is a former marine jet pilot who, when asked to speak at a Marine Corps dinner, recited from memory Rudyard Kipling's antiwar poem about "Tommy Atkins." He is a man who, in 1976, could be seen throwing paper napkins at his friends during Colorado State University's raunchy sports banquet and who, in 1980, wanted very much to be the new president of Colorado State University. He is a cofounder of a successful water-toothbrush business, Aquatec, who sits on the Board of Trustees of a Presbyterian seminary. He is a cocktail party charmer who reads each of Shakespeare's histories three or four times a year. He was, according to a man who should know, "the best theologian in the House of Representatives." "Imagine," says House Chaplain James David Ford. "Here I am a Lutheran pastor. I have spent nine years in school studying the Bible. I've travelled all over the world and talked scripture with ministers of all faiths. And I have come here to the House of Representatives to find someone who knows as much about scripture as I do. That's Jim Johnson." And, he adds, "People don't believe it, because he uses such salty language and because he jokes all the time." I have listened to him swap funny stories with people all over Colorado; I have never heard him talk about his religion. As I say, complicated.

"No Big Deal"

Politically speaking, Jim Johnson was nothing if not independent—the very prototype of the House member described by Speaker O'Neill and, thus, very much a congressman of his time. He first ran for Congress in 1966 as a strong opponent of the Vietnam War—in a Colorado district which, said one veteran reporter, "has more lobster pots that it has doves." He lost that year; but he ran again in 1972, as an antiwar candidate, and won. The public mood had changed. But Johnson's persistently dovish views put him permanently at odds with some members of his party in Colorado. Three times the Republican right wing fielded a candidate against him—twice in the primary, once in the general. When he got to Washington in 1973, his first activity was to organize against further American military involvement in Cambodia—a stand that did not endear him to many members of his party in Congress. Johnson had strong convictions on the matter of war and peace. At home and in Washington, his attitude was the same. As he stated it when we first met in 1974: "I don't have any great desire to impose my moral beliefs on other people. But I'm not going to vote with the majority just because they believe something, if I don't believe in it, too. I have no great love for this job. If I lose next time, that's fine. If I win, that's fine too." He had run to make his voice heard on matters of public policy about which he felt strongly and he intended to do just that. "I have spoken up more on the floor and gotten into more debates than almost any other freshman," he said at the end of his first term. "There are issues of life and death importance to the country and I'm not going to sit there and keep still." As I say, independent.

In 1976 he was appointed to the Select Committee on Intelligence to investigate the work of the Central Intelligence Agency. Coming close, as it did, to his strongest policy interests, he regarded that assignment as "the most interesting and important thing I've ever done in my life." Johnson broke with his fellow Republicans on that committee, however, in favoring the publication of the committee's report—a move opposed by the Republican administration. And it was then that *his* leader, John Rhodes, had to cope with the independence of his follower. "Rhodes asked me to back down," he recalls. "I knew I was playing the Democrats' game. But I couldn't change my views. It was the time that my views and Rhodes's views diverged and it was the end of my career within the Republican party." When he made his speech in favor of publishing the report, "I got a standing ovation from the Democratic side. On our side, everybody was silent." When the permanent Committee on Intelligence was set up in 1977, he sought membership on it. But he did not get it.

Jim Johnson was not only independent of party but independent of major interests, as well. Colorado's Fourth District is vast and diverse. It is the district of James Michener's *Centennial*. Covering the top one-third of the state, it is, says Johnson, "four different districts." As he describes them: "The far east is mostly concerned with agriculture; the foothills of the mountains on the east are suburban; the mountain area on the continental divide is mostly tourist, a resort area and small mountain towns which are ranching-oriented; and the far west is agriculture and mineral development." Michener writes that his town, Centennial, stood "at the spot where a man could look eastward and catch the full power of the prairie and westward to see the Rockies. The history of the town would be a record of the way it responded to the impossible task of conciliating the demands of the mountains with the requirements of the prairie." Johnson's home town of Fort Collins stands near that spot and Johnson's job was precisely that of conciliating these diverse interests—sometimes competing with, sometimes oblivious to one another. The nature of these interests put him in the middle of some of the toughest issues of the 1970s—energy, environment, natural resources. When asked by an editor on the front range, "Is it possible for you to represent the western slope and the eastern slope at the same time?" he answered simply, "I don't know. But that's the job I've got." "You do the best you can as a whole," he said later.

> I try not to worry about one group. I try to think of what they want but not their reactions in terms of my career. I'll go home and try to explain it. If you're not fearful about the job, you are more

relaxed in it, more confident. I don't know what it would be like to worry about every vote. Some try to calculate the effect on some group. I don't. It's a wasted mental process. It takes your energy away from the question, "Is this bill reasonable?"

Johnson's reasonability test produced a very checkered, almost inexplicable voting record in Congress. The Colorado Democratic party chairman called him "the greatest enigma in Colorado politics. . . . We don't understand his voting record; the papers don't understand his voting record; the people don't understand his voting record."

When I asked him who his strongest supporters were, he said, "Just personal friends. And the reason is I've never been an ideologue. My voting record is not 100 percent for anything. I think labor has some points. I think the ACA has some points. My ACA rating was 67 percent. The ADA gave me the highest rating of any Republican in the state." His distance from any large interest is reflected by the relatively modest amounts of money he spent on his campaigns: $51,000 to capture the seat in 1972, then $53,000, $65,000 and $92,000 to hold it. In every case, he spent less than his opponent—less than half as much in the year he won the seat and $70,000 less the last time he ran. If there was a group toward which he leaned, it was the farmers. "The farmers are not numerous," he said, "but they are the most important part of the state's economy." For that reason, he went on the Agriculture Committee. But neither the Farm Bureau nor the National Farmer's Union supported him when he won in 1972. As I say, independent.

A distinctive attitude toward the job breaks through in some of these comments. It is that serving in Congress is no big deal. And this attitude underwrites his independence on the job. On the way to a retirement party thrown by his friends in the House, I asked him, "What do you tell your colleagues when they ask about your retirement?" "That I'm tired of it and I want to go home," he said. "Is that taken as a sign of strength or as a sign of weakness?" I asked. "It's not taken any way at all," he said. "It's taken as an event of no great moment." Back home in 1974 when asked by interviewers why people should vote for him, he would reply, "I turn that question back to the voters. If you like my record and accomplishments, vote for me. If you don't, don't." On to the next question. He worked hard to get the job; but he had no sense that, for the benefit of others or of himself, it was important that he keep the job. He appears to have been "hooked" by it only once—after he lost in 1966. "Once you have run for Congress and lost you never get over it," he said. And his wife added, "It was the only thing he had ever failed at in his life." His 1972 success provided the necessary detoxification. And his retirement announcement was characteristically matter-of-fact. "I never intended to make a permanent career in Washington," he wrote, "and it is time to come home to stay." As I say, no big deal.

Citizen-Legislator

We should think of Jim Johnson as a citizen-legislator. He is a man who got agitated about a public problem, went to Washington to see what he could do about it, did what he felt he could do about it, and then returned home to resume his career. From beginning to end, issues of war and peace were the ones that Johnson cared most about. When he decided he could do nothing about these matters, he decided to leave. "The Congress does what the public wants them to do," he said in 1980.

> Right now, the people want a military buildup—the Carter Doctrine, the MX missile. You can feel it coming—rolling, rolling—and there is no way I can make a difference on that issue. It was the war that was the motivating factor for my getting into politics. For a while, we could do something, because the public was opposed to the war. But everything has changed now. There's nothing I can do to advance the things I believe in—the important things.

When President Carter announced his Middle East Doctrine in his State of the Union message, Johnson got up quietly and walked out. But he did not publicize the act. A month later he gave a short speech about it—the one Otis Pike wrote about. "I can make speeches about the important things I believe in and a few people will sit there and listen," he said. "They are polite. But their attitude is, 'There goes Johnson. He's a nut on that subject. We'll let him talk but we won't pay any attention.' Everybody is allowed to be a nut on some subject. But that's all there is to it. You don't get anything accomplished." Persuasion, he says, does not occur on the House floor.

Implicit in his decision to leave Congress rather than to continue such speechmaking is a distaste for publicity seeking and self-advertisement. Whoever heard Jim Johnson's voice in the congressional peacemongering chorus? Otis Pike maybe. A Colorado reporter wrote about his leaving:

> Congress is losing one of its endangered species—a serious legislator who couldn't care less about media coverage. [He] seldom sends out press releases, has only held one press conference in seven years, and doesn't believe in wasting the time of the House with lengthy speeches.

He wanted to accomplish things for his cause, but not through personal publicity. And in that sense, he was not a congressman of his time. He was asked to run for the Senate. He thinks he could have won. Indeed, he has all the qualifications for a Wayne Morse-type role in the Senate. Except the interest. "I don't think I could accomplish any more in the Senate than in the House—not with the public thinking the way it is. Congress just isn't the place for me." The decision to leave Capitol Hill seems final. But, he said later, "If I saw a war starting up some place, I would have no compunction about running again, to make my voice heard." As I say, a citizen-politician.

Johnson's sense of frustration in matters of war and peace was not matched where his committee work—on the Agriculture and Interior Committees—was involved. "I've learned how to work the legislative process and I enjoy it," he said in 1976. He worked well with the Democratic majority, smoothing the way for committee consensus and accumulating a number of concrete accomplishments. For example, "The Democrats let me put my name on the Historic Trails Bill. It's not a great thing. But I'm proud of it." In talking about his decision to leave, he commented in 1980:

> It's not a matter of my being unable to get anything done. It's not sour grapes. I have managed more legislation on the House floor than the whole of my delegation combined. I have my name on more pieces of legislation than any of them. I don't say it isn't worthwhile or that it isn't fun. It is. And I could go on doing that for a long time. But that's not enough.

From his strategic location on two constituency-oriented committees he produced legislative benefits for the Fourth Congressional District—the designation of three wilderness areas, money for local governments from mineral leases, money for water recycling projects, money for the removal of uranium mill tailings. But he hewed to the distinction between the important things and the little things; and he ultimately judged his accomplishments on the important things. It might be correct to say that he had unrealistic expectations in this respect. That may be a problem with citizen-legislators. Still, by all conventional standards, Jim Johnson was an effective member of the minority party in the House.

At home, too, he was an effective politician. He increased his election margin steadily from 51 percent in 1972 to 62 percent in 1978. He assumed the district could be his for a long time. No one disagreed. The district has only had four congressmen since it was created in 1914. Its very diversity makes it both hard to capture and easy to defend. By the time I watched him campaign, in 1974 and 1976, he had developed a relaxed, low-key, comfortable relationship with the bulk of his constituents—as befits a secure defender. "When I first went after the job," he said later, "I went at it like I was killing snakes. Once I got the job, I campaigned the way I liked to." "What I like to do," he said,

> is to get in the car with Mac McGraw [a district representative] and go around to the small towns talking with people like the banker. The banker is central to everything that goes on in town. You can learn more by talking to him for an hour than you can any other way. And there's that sense of community, too, that I feel comfortable with.

The comment reflects a central concern for the *quality* of his constituency relations.

A Sense of Community

Invariably, he did less than his aggressive, more quantitatively oriented campaign staff would program for him. In 1974, he spent an hour talking with a pharmacist in the town of Craig, while a couple of campaign aides sputtered in the cafe next door. Not energetic enough, they said. Too interested in the few on Main Street and not interested enough in the many in front of Safeway, they said. "It doesn't fit my temperament to shake hands without stopping to talk with each person," Johnson commented later. "Then I feel like I can understand them and they understand me. Like that pharmacist in Craig. He disagreed with me on a lot of things and gave me a hard time. But after we talked, he said, 'You've got a tough job. I wouldn't want your job.'" Two years later, we had a replay—with the candidate showing the same disinclination to squeeze every vote out of the situation. On an afternoon when he was scheduled to "hit the bricks" in the business district in Estes Park, he spent the entire time talking to an art gallery proprietor and an artist next door. "He's a lousy campaigner," exclaimed the staffer afterwards. But on the ride home, Johnson again commented on the quality of his constituency relations:

> The attitude I have is that there isn't a grown man or woman alive that isn't worth listening to sometime. People acquire knowledge, skill, and insight in various ways. And there isn't anyone that doesn't have some ideas worth listening to. Some of the Birchers I give short shrift to. But even there I spent two hours talking to five of them over in Ault the other day. And later one of them came back smiling to give me more information. My constituents are tolerant with me because I am tolerant with them. People might not be for me because of some issue, but there isn't any animosity toward me anywhere in this district.

What Johnson valued most about his relationships at home was that "sense of community" about which he spoke—the comfortable feeling that he and his constituents shared enough by way of experience and outlook to talk to one another. "I need that sense of community," he said. But he could not achieve it everywhere. When he left the small towns of the mountains, the western slope, and the eastern prairie, and the small cities of the front range, and went to the mushrooming suburbs nearest Denver, he lost all sense of community. Over on the eastern slope, in Meeker, he had talked in 1974 about the suburban segment of his district.

> I hardly ever campaign there. How can you? It's not a community. The people who work there don't live there. They have no shopping centers where everybody shops. They have no Rotary Clubs or groups like that. It's just a bunch of houses. I went to a picnic there once and they said, "You haven't been here before." "I know it. I know I don't represent the Denver suburbs very well."

Without that sense of community and without community institutions to plug into, he felt lost. When we rode into the Denver suburbs two years later, he exclaimed:

> Now we're coming to the area that gives me the heebie-jeebies. I don't know how to campaign here, so mostly we don't. We come and walk around with our thumb in our ear. . . . The Chamber of Commerce sent out 700 invitations to a meeting and 17 came. We announced that we would be at one of their senior citizen community centers and two people showed up. We went door-to-door and nobody was home—just dogs. There are no community leaders to talk with. We put a district office here, but I don't know that it does any good. . . . They think their representative is Pat Schroeder. It's the most miserable son-of-a-bitchin' place I've ever known.

His inability to identify with the 15 percent of his district only highlights his strong sense of identification with the other 85 percent. His attitude toward most of the district was not fear, but pride. He went out of his way to take me to visit with the grand old man of his district, the man who had defeated him in 1966—Wayne Aspinall. "You get a proprietary interest in your district," he said. "Aspinall had it, too." In 1976, he identified for me the man he hoped would succeed him in Congress, State Senator Hank Brown. Johnson nurtured Brown's candidacy by making him his campaign manager in 1976. Brown was elected to Congress in 1980. As I say, a sense of community.

I have dwelled on this qualitative dimension of Johnson's constituency relations for two reasons. For one thing, it was the quality of this relationship which allowed him to act independently in Washington. He could be a dove in a hawkish district, and he could produce a checkered voting record without worrying about the reaction at home. "There's no reason to fear your constituents," he said in 1976. "There's no reason to look over your shoulder. Cast every vote as you see it and then go home and explain it. People are tolerant. They ask me to explain. They don't say, 'You're a ding-dong.'" I watched him do a lot of explaining at home. His explanations on both sides of the Rockies and in between were devoid of demagoguery. They were as matter-of-fact as he was himself; and they were educative. To complaining cattlemen on the western slope, he said that the dairymen on the eastern slope were worse off. To people in favor of the West Divide Reclamation Project, he said that the people who worried about flooding beautiful country had a point. He told people on the western slope that the Denver Water Board had reasonable people on it; and on the eastern slope he told people it was unfair for them to keep water from the western slope farmers who needed it when Denver had no need for it now. He regularly told one group that another group in the district had a different viewpoint—trying always to engender that essential "tolerance," constituent-to-constituent as well as constituent-to-congressman.

"I think educating your constituency is the most important job we have," he said. On my experience, Johnson did a lot—more than most. In return, he was allowed great freedom of maneuver inside the House. When a newsman asked him to spell out the "guidelines" he used in balancing the wishes of his constituency against his conscience, he could answer this way:

> I don't have a checklist. Are you a flyer? Well, flyers have a checklist they go through. . . . But lawyers don't think in those terms. It's foreign to our experience. I always think people who ask that question don't understand legislation. Legislation is a kind of art. A legislature is a human institution. You have to know what the House is like, what is futile, what is possible. You have to understand when to compromise and on what—or, when not to compromise at all.

The sense of community he established in Colorado undergirded both his legislative freedom and his legislative effectiveness in Washington.

The value Johnson places on that sense of community helps, finally, to explain his decision to retire. For there was a lifestyle element to that decision. "The lifestyle [in Washington] is not compatible with mine," he told a reporter in Colorado in 1976. "I don't like living where I'm not a part of a community, working with the church, the Boy Scouts, the Chamber of Commerce. These bring remuneration to you as an individual. You don't have that in Congress." In 1980 he returned to that theme. "I'll be going back to a rut. But it has a lot of the advantages as well as the disadvantages of a rut. I'll be able to participate in the church, participate in the community. It will be a more wholesome life." Wholesome for him as an individual. For not only did Washington deny him a sense of community; at the same time, it denied him a sense of challenge. Life in Congress did not allow him to engage all his abilities. "I felt I was degenerating," he said of his life on Capitol Hill.

> I was wasting too much time. You don't get out of here till 7:00 and so you go back to your office and drink with your buddies. You drink too much. Traffic is bad, so you wait and you don't get home till 9:00. What kind of family life is that? Most of our time is spent listening to bullshit and jollying. That's fun. But it's not productive work. You aren't using your faculties to the fullest. You degenerate.

"It's a little terrifying," he said, thinking of his return to the law. "You don't have the confidence you did when you first got out of law school. But if you succeed—and I always have—you will have a sense of accomplishing productive work. You will work all day every day and go home at night." When Johnson said about his accomplishments in Congress "it's not enough," he was thinking of personal fulfillment as well as policy achievement. As I said at the outset, complicated.

So what are we to make of this look at one ordinary member of Congress? Not too much. With one case, it is possible to prove everything or nothing. Maybe Jim Johnson is unique. But maybe if we looked at more individual members we would find he is not. We won't know until we try. And I am only suggesting that we try. We might find that he falls into a class or several classes of members about whom we could or should make more general statements—"What are they like?" instead of "What is he like?" At this point we can only guess what these classes of legislators might be. Let me suggest a few.

First, Jim Johnson might belong to a class of members who hold very strong views about certain public policies and whose goals as legislators involve the pursuit of their favored policies. Hence, their behavior as members of Congress can be explained to a large degree by understanding their policy views and the intensity with which they hold those views. At the moment, our political science research seems to be underplaying such people.

Second, granted the independence of present-day legislators, Johnson might belong to a class of members whose independence in Washington is underwritten by the quality of his or her constituency relations at home. If so, we can only understand a member's behavior in Congress by knowing more about the qualitative dimensions of relationships back home. Legislative leaders who travel to the districts of their followers probably know all about these connections. But political scientists might want to collect and codify such matters with our own interests in mind.

Third, Johnson might belong to a class of citizen-legislators, who retain strong ties to their home area and who are either dubious about or opposed to making a career in Congress. If there is such a group of legislators, we might study their effect on the institution. Sen. Henry Bellmon, retiring from the Senate after two terms, suggested in his farewell speech in December that congressional performance would be improved if we had more citizen-legislators and fewer professional legislators. A debate over the limitation on legislative terms seems destined to go on for a while. Political scientists might want to contribute to it by examining the current citizen-legislator class—if such there is. Perhaps they are more independent than others. Perhaps the quality of their constituency relations is different.

Fourth, Johnson may belong to a class of legislators who find the job insufficiently challenging. What they want most is to be pushed to the fullest use of their individual talents and abilities—and they find that they are not. So they lose interest. A newspaperman friend of Johnson's said to me, "I think it's a problem for the country when people of his caliber lose interest. I think that's what happened to Jim. He lost interest." Should we be worried when a Jim Johnson loses interest and goes home? Should we be worried when a legislator loses interest and does *not* go home? Political scientists might want to find out how much legislative behavior is affected by member attitudes toward work and accomplishment, challenge and fulfillment.

Finally, Jim Johnson may belong to a class of legislators who deserve better from the great American public than they get. At a time when Congress is not held in very high esteem and at a time when so much Abscam-fueled street talk concludes that "they are all crooks," an examination of the reality—by classes of legislators—might lead to a different judgment. Perhaps there is a class of members—unknown and unsung, yet complicated, interesting, and able—who are deserving of public confidence. How large a class might that be? Is there anything special about Jim Johnson? Or is he what we have called him, "ordinary," neither more nor less praiseworthy than hundreds of his colleagues? Who knows? There are 535 legislators out there. Political scientists have not spent much time looking at any one of them. Congressional leaders like Tip O'Neill spend a lot of time doing just that. As I say, maybe we should, too.

PART IV:
BUDGET AND FISCAL POLICY

THE CONGRESSIONAL BUDGET PROCESS

Hon. Robert N. Giaimo
Member, United States House of
Representatives, 1958–1980

The budget process has become the Congress's principal instrument for leadership initiatives and democratic decision making on critical economic matters. To students of the political process, this may seem to be an impossible achievement. It immediately prompts the question: How is it possible for such a process to provide a vehicle for strong and aggressive leadership and at the same time be sufficiently open to guarantee widespread participation in the final decisions?

The answer to this question lies in the way the process has developed since the passage of the Congressional Budget Impoundment and Control Act of 1974. In a little more than half a decade, the Congress has come to realize that the only way it can participate effectively in the formulation of national fiscal policy is to have the capacity to view its individual legislative actions within the context of a total fiscal picture. In order for the Congress to develop this capacity, four conditions had to be fulfilled:

1) A clear policy of overall spending and revenue priorities had to be offered.
2) Members had to be informed about and concerned with the policy questions posed in budget resolutions.
3) The majority will had to be expressed in the final decisions.
4) Other relevant decision-making entities within the Congress, especially the spending and revenue-raising committees, had to be bound by the policies and directives contained in budget resolutions.

These conditions could not have been fulfilled without a strong commitment on the part of the leadership, namely the Speaker, the majority leader, and the remainder of the Democratic Steering and Policy Committee to use the budget process to make informed policy choices as to the direction of fiscal policy. And although on the House side, the Republican leadership and members have seldom supported budget resolutions, they have not done so for lack of a commitment to the budget process. Indeed, on all procedural matters they have been virtually unanimous in the support of the process and its continuation. Moreover, these conditions could not have been made without a strong commitment on the part of the entire membership —or at least the overwhelming majority of members—to follow the self-discipline required to translate the policy in budget resolutions into the reality of law.

The Congressional Commitment to the Budget Process

The budget process does not, nor should it ever, depend on the efforts of any individual. In every sense the budget process is and must remain a shared responsibility, a truly collective endeavor. To be effective, the process must have the commitment and support of all members, regardless of how they may view any particular budget resolution.

This is true for some very fundamental reasons. The budget process is the ultimate test of the capacity of Congress to participate fully and meaningfully in the formulation of this nation's fiscal policy. The congressional budget is Congress's principal instrument to exercise control over the direction and impact of that policy. Though its procedures may at times be laborious and lengthy, the budget process is the only way the Congress can take on the Herculean task of establishing national priorities and blending into them the many and diverse interests of this nation. Through the budget process, the Congress can formulate and deliver its message. But with this comes the heavy responsibility of fiscal self-discipline.

Through the many trials which the budget process has faced in the past six years, I have been impressed by the commitment which the majority of members have made to make the process work. The effort referred to as reconciliation is still fresh in my mind. The Ninety-Sixth Congress directed a number of its committees to examine the laws within their jurisdiction and suggest ways in which savings could be achieved. Some felt this could never be accomplished. Yet a majority of members of the House and Senate felt this had to be done in order to break the momentum of federal spending. Reconciliation had its ups and downs as Congress broke new ground, but the result was the Omnibus Reconciliation Act of 1980. This historic bill, which was signed into law on December 5, 1980, will save American taxpayers billions of dollars.

All may not agree on each and every provision of the Reconciliation Act, but who would have thought that eight committees of the House and eight committees of the Senate would, at the direction of their respective bodies, sit down and diligently rewrite basic spending or revenue-raising laws that were within their jurisdiction? To me, it still is almost unbelievable. The passage of the Omnibus Reconciliation Act constitutes a major breakthrough for the budget process, proving that the Congress is capable of decisive and far-reaching action and self-discipline through shared responsibility. That is what the budget process is all about.

The effort to balance the 1981 budget is also a key to how commitment to the budget process has developed. True, both friends and foes labeled the effort as so much election year hoopla, suggesting that the plan proposed in the first budget resolution for fiscal year 1981 was merely designed to camouflage reality. No amount of rhetoric will silence that criticism, but from the perspective of the chairmanship of the House Budget Committee, the effort was a real one, one designed to break the momentum of increasing federal spending year after year.

Unfortunately, the failure to balance the budget blurred the effort, the successful effort, that was made to restrain federal spending. The facts bear this out. For the first time in over a decade, spending in real terms, after accounting for inflation, has actually declined to a negative real growth. Such findings are not surprising if we examine the commitment of the spending committees to stay within the targets set in budget resolutions. It cannot be said too often that the spending committees, and particularly the appropriations committees, have been firm in their commitment to keep spending within overall budgetary limits.

Finally, the budget process has enjoyed widespread commitment, I believe, largely because it has been pragmatic rather than dogmatic—because the participants have relied on reasoned, mature judgments rather than adherence to ideology or one set of economic principles.

Democratic Leadership Commitment to the Budget Process

One cannot discuss the congressional commitment to the budget process without acknowledging the yeoman contributions the Democratic leadership has made to make the budget process work. I think it safe to say that without the strong support of Speaker Thomas P. O'Neill, Jr., Majority Leader Jim Wright, and Chairman Richard Bolling of the Rules Committee and other leaders there would be no budget process with any meaning. Often the Speaker has put himself on the line to ensure the survival of the process because it was the responsible thing to do. Although in the House, debate on the budget has almost always provided the Republicans a forum for achieving new heights of partisanship, the Democratic majority has not shrinked from its responsibility of presenting a budget resolution.

With little or no Republican support for passage of budget resolutions in the House, the burden for carrying the process has been on the Democratic leadership. Some of you may think this an easy task given the large majority the Democrats possessed in the last Congress. Let me just unburden you of that misconception. If you've ever dealt with budgets of any kind, you quickly realize how unpopular it is to say no. No budget ever satisfies everyone. When you consider the size and complexity of the federal budget, the potential for antagonizing members and committees of the Congress and special-interest groups is mindboggling. That budget resolutions have been adopted in spite of these factors is a credit to our Democratic leadership.

In strengthening the budget process the leadership has provided itself with a greater opportunity to influence the direction of public policy. The budget process has become a focal point for the leadership to establish national priorities.

Future of the Budget Process

Without test or trial, the budget process spread to cover almost every facet of legislative activity in both houses of Congress. Does this or that spending bill conform to the budget resolution targets? Does this or that bill break the spending ceiling or violate the revenue floor? Does this bill set an unwarranted budget precedent by creating a new entitlement? These and other pertinent questions were asked every time a bill was considered in committee or on the floor.

These are not fictitious accomplishments. They are factual. Through the budget process, Congress can take pride that it has been able to:

1) Identify our national priorities with greater precision and on a continuing basis.
2) Exercise the difficult choice of determining which goals deserve the highest priority.
3) Determine not only how much it costs to operate the federal government in a given year, but also assess how next year's cost will impact on the cost of government in the second and third and subsequent years.

To me, the real promise of the budget process is even greater than most of us first imagined—that is, it will become an instrument for extending the public's understanding of the decisions that affect them, for allowing more freedom for a creative response to our problems, for providing an opportunity for wider participation in decision making, and for making efficiency and sound management a must for all governmental programs. We should never, never lose sight of the *educational* potential of the budget process. Is that not the promise of representative government?

There is an ominous part of my forecast that I believe I should share with you. If the special interests, particularly those that follow one political persuasion to the exclusion of others, ever gain control over the budget process and make the budget committees a haven for special-interest groups, an enormous evil will be inflicted upon the American people. There are always those special interests willing to conspire to take whatever instruments of power they can to use to their advantage. We must be ready to sound the alarm when such attempts are made. That democracy requires constant vigilance may, to some, be a tired or timeworn cliche; nevertheless it reflects the truth.

Equally dangerous, in my view, is allowing the budget process to become the exclusive domain of "experts" and economic forecasters. I do not question for a moment the need for expertise, for sophisticated analysis, or for the capability to assemble and critically examine complex data. These are musts. But if we permit the experts to call the shots, they will be making our *decisions*. We will assure the destruction of the very foundation of our political system.

On the substantive side, there are two major challenges that will determine the future efficacy of the budget process if the process is to be more than an array of platitudes offered to guide members through the massive details contained in any budget.

First, automatic spending provisions, often referred to as uncontrollables, must be brought under control if there is to be any room to set future spending priorities. Automatic spending now makes up 75 percent of the budget even by the most conservative of estimates. In fiscal year 1981, for example, it will cost over $20 billion to index the social security and federal civilian and military retirement programs. In fiscal year 1982, this cost will skyrocket to almost $30 billion. In fiscal year 1981, we will *automatically* spend over $80 billion on interest on the national debt. Even though the budget process has succeeded in restraining the real growth in federal spending, we may well be past tolerable limits to what one can reasonably expect the federal government to provide. If such control is not forthcoming in the near future, we will surely bankrupt our nation and cause greater inflationary pressure.

And, secondly, nothing is closer to the American people than the government's tax policy. As a matter of sound fiscal policy, a comprehensive review of the tax structure is imperative. Tax burdens fall unfairly on some and not at all on others. Special tax provisions create inequities that are so blatant and obvious that the nation is now confronted with an unhealthy tax attitude. Recently, the Internal Revenue Service estimated that over $90 billion in revenues were lost from *unreported* income. Unless this question is addressed and addressed properly, we will jeopardize the very foundation of our democracy.

In spite of these challenges, I am convinced that the congressional budget process is here to stay. But much work remains to be done. Contrary to what we all heard in the 1980 presidential campaign, federal spending will not be controlled in a year or two simply by cutting waste, fraud, and abuse. Inflation will not be whipped overnight simply by putting government bureaucrats out of business. The solution to these complex problems will require the efforts and will of us all.

CONGRESSIONAL BUDGETS AND FISCAL POLICY

Dennis S. Ippolito
Department of Political Science
Emory University

The 1974 Congressional Budget and Impoundment Control Act was described by its proponents as "one of the most monumental reassertions of congressional prerogatives"[1] and "the most significant reform of the twentieth century."[2] Perhaps its most important and certainly its most challenging provisions related to economic policy leadership. According to Rep. Richard Bolling, one of those who directed the budget reform effort in the House, "the foremost responsibility of Congress must be the determination of macroeconomic budget policy."[3] The main purpose of congressional budgets, he continued, would be to direct fiscal policy through "overall budget aggregates."[4] The procedures and organization put into place by the 1974 budget reform initiative would, it was promised, allow Congress to coordinate its revenue and spending decisions and thereby set coherent—and independent—fiscal policy.

At the time, there was considerable enthusiasm, at least among Democrats, for this generous endorsement of congressional policy-making capabilities. Soon after it was organized, the Senate Budget Committee announced a series of macroeconomic seminars to provide its members with expert opinion on fiscal policy strategies and economic management. House and Senate Democratic leaders eagerly anticipated using their massive post-Watergate majorities to wrest budget and economic policy leadership from the Ford administration. There was even heady talk of a veto-proof Congress that would demonstrate the efficacy of congressional government.

Today, these great expectations have been replaced by confusion and controversy. An independent congressional budgetary process is unable to

---

1. *Congressional Record* 119 (1973): 39344.

2. Ibid., p. 39348.

3. *Congressional Record* 120 (1974): 19673.

4. Ibid.

control spending or deficits. Conventional fiscal policy solutions no longer inspire great confidence. Defenders of the congressional budgetary process have argued rather desperately that it is not a "sham and a fraud and a charade."[5] Representative Bolling now wonders whether annual budgets are suitable instruments for handling economic policy issues and suggests that Congress should somehow formulate long-term economic goals to guide its budget decisions.[6] The second fiscal 1981 congressional budget resolution conceded "the time is right for considering revisions and modifications . . . to improve the congressional budget process."[7]

Some critics contend, however, that the problems Congress faces cannot be resolved by "revisions and modifications." They propose limits on Congress's powers to tax and spend, through either statutory or constitutional formulas that would determine the size of the budget or the balance between spending and revenues. The upcoming debate will no doubt be lively and protracted, and a crucial consideration likely will be the fiscal policy implications of a formula solution. Before Congress embarks on another reform effort, therefore, it might be helpful to examine why its record of fiscal policy management has been so disappointing.

Congress and the Ford Administration

The contrasts between congressional and executive branch fiscal policy choices during the Ford administration emerged fairly quickly and followed predictable lines. Congress supported higher spending levels and larger deficits than President Ford recommended. It also relied more heavily on spending stimulus than tax cut stimulus, again in opposition to Ford proposals. There was, however, a definite congressional sensitivity to the deficit issue, and this led to some initial tentativeness in asserting a distinctive policy approach. Moreover, spending shortfalls in fiscal years 1977 and 1978 resulted in actual deficits that were much closer to the original Ford budgets for those years than to the corresponding congressional budgets. A clear winner in the Ford-Congress fiscal policy disputes was hard to identify, in part because the congressional budget process could not be neatly divided into a macroeconomic stage and an allocative stage, but also because budget totals were affected by economic factors over which neither Congress nor the administration had much control.

---

5. *Congressional Record* 126 (1980): S 14757.

6. *Congressional Quarterly Weekly Report* 37 (1979): 16.

7. H. Con. Res. 448, sec. 6 (1980).

Raising the Deficit

Early in the fall of 1974, the Ford administration singled out inflation as the nation's most serious economic problem and announced that its fiscal 1976 budgetary response would be restraint. If this diagnosis and policy line had been maintained, there might have been sharp and perhaps irreconcilable divisions in Congress over spending control. Divisions did occur, particularly among House Democrats, but they were eased by changing economic priorities and subsequent reversals in budget policy. By November of 1974, unemployment had reached its highest level in fifteen years, and there were fears that it might climb substantially higher during 1975. With a severe recession emerging, there was general agreement that a budget deficit was inevitable, but there was no consensus over its size, the need for accelerated spending on jobs and public works programs, or the appropriate mix between spending and tax stimulus.

When the Senate Budget Committee held hearings on fiscal policy late in 1974, several prominent economists testified that deficits in the $25-35 billion range would be unavoidable during fiscal 1976. This was, as Budget Committee Chairman Edmund Muskie noted, a sharp turnaround from several months previously when the prevailing economic prescription was "large cuts in federal spending and a balanced budget for fiscal 1976. . . ."[8] When President Ford submitted his 1976 budget, he called for modest cuts in spending but also projected a $51.9 billion deficit. Appearing before the Senate Budget Committee, Joseph Pechman of the Brookings Institution criticized the Ford plan as inadequate but congratulated the administration for its "candor and honesty."[9] According to Pechman, this was the first time any administration had given Congress "a set of estimates that are not only consistent, but seem to be a fair appraisal of what the president's program is likely to produce."[10]

Political gamesmanship over the deficit issue, however, quickly put an end to cordiality. In April of 1975, the Office of Management and Budget's revised estimates of the president's budget raised the projected deficit to $60 billion. As Congress prepared to debate its first postreform budget resolution, Ford announced his firm commitment to the $60 billion figure

---

8. U.S., Congress, Senate, Committee on the Budget, *Hearings, The Economy and Fiscal Policy, 1974*, 93rd Cong., 2nd sess., December 11, 12, 17, 18, and 19, 1974, p. 1.

9. U.S., Congress, Senate, Committee on the Budget, *Seminars, Macroeconomic Issues and the Fiscal Year 1976 Budget*, 94th Cong., 1st sess., February 3, 4, and 5, 1975, p. 185.

10. Ibid.

and challenged Congress to match it. Senator Muskie, whose committee was trying to defend a higher deficit figure on the Senate floor, fumed that the president was attempting "to gain some political advantage over the Congress" by publicizing a figure that he and his advisers knew was "not an honest number."[11] The ranking Republican on the Senate Budget Committee, Henry Bellmon, agreed with Muskie that the number was "phony" and sought to persuade his deficit-conscious colleagues that supporting the Budget Committee's higher deficit projection was the only realistic approach.[12] The Budget Committee's report emphasized that Congress was dealing with "a recession deficit, not a spending deficit."[13]

The Senate gave quick approval to the Budget Committee's $365 billion outlay target and $67.2 billion deficit. In the House, the going was much rougher, as Republicans refused to support a comparable deficit and Democratic liberals pressed for more jobs programs and higher spending. For a time it appeared that the House Budget Committee would be unable to report *any* budget resolution to the floor, and it was only after two Republican members decided to "protect the process" that the stalemate was ended. On the House floor, however, the resolution was caught in another conservative-liberal crossfire, and the Democratic leadership intervened to write a majority party budget that finally passed by a four-vote margin. The higher spending and deficit numbers supported by the House were then reduced slightly by the House-Senate conference.

When the second budget resolution for fiscal 1976 was debated later in the year, Congress became a bit bolder, voting to raise outlays almost $8 billion over the first resolution and to increase the deficit to over $74 billion. The Senate Budget Committee judged Congress's "moderately stimulative fiscal policy" course a success.[14] The House Budget Committee agreed the economy was recovering "from the most serious recession of the postwar era."[15] The applause, however, was far from unanimous. Budget committee Republicans, who earlier had argued that fiscal policy was being dic-

---

11. *Congressional Record* 121 (1975): 12656.

12. Ibid., p. 12657.

13. U.S., Congress, Senate, Committee on the Budget, *Report No. 94-77, First Concurrent Resolution on the Budget—Fiscal Year 1976*, 94th Cong., 1st sess., 1975, p. 5.

14. U.S., Congress, Senate, Committee on the Budget, *Report No. 94-453, Second Concurrent Resolution on the Budget—Fiscal Year 1976*, 94th Cong., 1st sess., 1975, pp. 9-13.

15. U.S., Congress, House, Committee on the Budget, *Report No. 94-608, Second Concurrent Resolution on the Budget—Fiscal Year 1976*, 94th Cong., 1st sess., 1975, p. 7.

tated by spending pressures rather than by considered economic judgments, complained that Congress was ignoring its "unprecedented opportunity . . . to take effective steps toward conforming aggregate federal spending and revenues to the requirements of long-term economic stability and growth."[16] A number of Democratic conservatives agreed with this critique, and the conference version of the second budget resolution for 1976 passed the House by only a two-vote margin. Even the Senate Budget Committee finally hedged its claims somewhat, stating that with appropriate estimating adjustments, the congressional budget was "very close to what the president advocated when he 'drew a line' at a $60 billion deficit. . . ."[17]

The accompanying skirmishes on the 1976 budget were inconclusive. None of Ford's spending vetoes, including that of a massive jobs bill, was overridden. Ford's attempts to impose limits on uncontrollable spending programs, however, were rejected. Despite these defeats, the administration claimed that its steady pressure for spending restraint was working and conceded that the "budget process has been beneficial."[18] A spending shortfall that no one anticipated, however, had perhaps the greatest impact, reducing outlays and the deficit by approximately $8 billion below the congressional ceiling.

Deficits and Recovery

Efforts to gain political advantage accelerated during preliminaries for the 1977 budget. In October 1975, Ford proposed a $28 billion tax cut, which he then linked to a $395 billion spending ceiling for fiscal 1977. When Congress simply extended an existing tax cut, Ford vetoed the legislation. A compromise was subsequently worked out in which Ford agreed to a tax cut extension in exchange for a symbolic congressional pledge to consider offsetting spending cuts when the 1977 budget resolution was debated in the spring. Budget committee leaders, however, sharply attacked the administration for trying to circumvent the budget process, which suggested that the spending cut initiative was not totally ineffective.

When the 1977 budget was sent to Congress, encouraging signs of economic recovery loosened the restraints on spending. In its first resolution

---

16. Ibid., p. 82.

17. Senate Budget Committee, *Second Concurrent Resolution—Fiscal Year 1976*, pp. 15-16.

18. *Congressional Quarterly Almanac, 1975* (Washington, D.C.: Congressional Quarterly, Inc., 1976), p. 904.

for fiscal 1977, Congress added almost $20 billion in outlays (as well as over $20 billion in budget authority) and $8 billion in deficit to the Ford budget. The Senate Budget Committee once again claimed that conflicting estimates accounted for most of the difference.[19] Underlying policy disagreements, however, were more substantial. Congress was relying heavily on spending stimulus and counting upon eventual revenue growth to erase the deficit. It was ignoring Ford's proposed cuts in domestic programs, particularly recommendations to restrain certain uncontrollable programs. These differences persisted in the second budget resolution for fiscal 1977. Republican members of the Senate Budget Committee cautioned against an emerging policy of "successive injections of 'fiscal stimulus',"[20] but the lure of election year spending was strong, and Congress passed the first and second 1977 resolutions with relative ease.

Ford's defeat in November eased, at least for a time, the partisan and ideological splits over fiscal policy, but the application of fiscal policy remained frustratingly imprecise. The projected 1977 deficit, which was temporarily increased by almost $20 billion after Jimmy Carter took office, only to be cut back sharply in a "revised third budget resolution," turned out to be well off the mark. Another spending shortfall produced a $45 billion deficit, which was only $2 billion above the original Ford budget. Even the 1978 deficit turned out to be much closer to Ford's projected budget than to those subsequently developed by the Carter administration and Congress.

As shown in table 1, Congress consistently supported higher spending levels and larger deficits than the Ford administration recommended. There was, however, a growing disparity between planned stimulus and actual stimulus. At the same time, these short-term spending patterns were misleading. For fiscal years 1976 to 1978, Congress enacted budget authority that exceeded Ford requests by over $80 billion. Together with the steadily growing portion of the budget labeled "relatively uncontrollable," this indicated that the long-term spending picture would remain highly stimulative.

---

19. U.S., Congress, Senate, Committee on the Budget, *Report No. 94-731, First Concurrent Resolution on the Budget—Fiscal Year 1977*, 94th Cong., 2nd sess., 1976, p. 2.

20. U.S., Congress, Senate, Committee on the Budget, *Report No. 94-1204, Second Concurrent Resolution on the Budget, FY 1977*, 94th Cong., 2nd sess., 1976, p. 54.

Table 1
Fiscal Aggregates, Ford Administration and Congressional Budgets
Fiscal Years 1976-1978 (in billions of dollars)

	President's Jan. Budget	*First Concurrent Budget Resolution*	*Second Concurrent Budget Resolution*	*Actual*
FY 1976:				
Outlays	$349.4	$367.0	$374.9	$366.4
Revenue	297.5	298.2	300.8	300.0
Deficit	–51.9	–68.8	–74.1	–66.4
FY 1977:				
Outlays	394.2	413.3	413.1	402.7
Revenue	351.3	362.5	362.5	357.8
Deficit	–43.0	–50.8	–50.6	–45.0
FY 1978:				
Outlays	440.0	460.95	458.25	450.8
Revenue	393.0	396.3	397.0	402.0
Deficit	–47.0	–64.65	–61.25	–48.8

The New Consensus

Despite the problems encountered during 1975 and 1976, Congress remained confident about its fiscal policy strategy. Indeed, the Carter presidency promised a more cooperative approach to budget policy and a less critical atmosphere in which to apply fiscal stimulus. And, in fact, there was general agreement on fiscal policy throughout the Carter administration. Unfortunately, fiscal policy results were another matter. The inflation rate climbed while the economic recovery slowed, leaving Congress with an exquisitely painful choice of priorities. Spending shortfalls, which some members of Congress had once complained about, soon were replaced by massive and embarrassing overspending. Fiscal policies that Congress and the administration set great store in suddenly appeared economically risky and politically damaging, but spending pressures prevented policy adjustments.

The Stimulus Boost

When the Ninety-Fifth Congress opened in January 1977, there was speculation that the economic recovery might be faltering. Later that month, the Carter administration unveiled a two-year, $31.2 billion stimulus package to spur the recovery. For fiscal 1977, which was already one-third over, Carter proposed an additional $15.5 billion in stimulus, most of it in the form of tax rebates. Congress quickly accommodated this request by passing an unprecedented third budget resolution for fiscal 1977, and at the same time increased Carter's recommendations for spending on jobs and local assistance programs. The third resolution raised the spending ceiling Congress had set several months earlier, lowered the revenue floor, and projected a $70 billion deficit.

This attempt at fine-tuning the economy with what was in effect a quarterly update was defended by House Budget Committee Chairman Robert Giaimo as "a modest, reasonable, balanced approach. . . ."[21] Some members of Congress, however, worried about the long-term consequences of changing "binding" budget resolutions. Rep. Elliott Levitas, a Georgia Democrat, conceded that budget limits should be lifted under "extraordinary and unforeseen circumstances," but questioned whether the available economic evidence required "a wholesale sacking of the budget we pledged to observe."[22] J. J. Pickle, another House Democrat, issued a similar warning about congressional capabilities:

> But I also worry about this Congress and its budget process. If we abdicate now—if we make light of the congressional budget and turn it from a far-sighted economic program into a quarterly economic update—I think we will regret it. We should not jump and jerk with each new wrinkle in the economic indicators. That is what we used to do. Our budget process was conceived. . . to provide for emergencies while fashioning a responsible and responsive economic policy.[23]

These reservations turned out to be prescient, for the Carter administration abandoned its economic diagnosis and withdrew its tax rebate plan soon thereafter. Senator Bellmon complained that Carter's action left "the budget process with egg on its face" and "the Congress with budget targets so loose and inviting that you can see the pressure build hourly to fill the void with cats and dogs on both the spending and revenue side."[24] Amidst embarrassed declarations about the need to preserve congressional inde-

21. *Congressional Record* 123 (1977): 5051.

22. Ibid., p. 5056.

23. Ibid., p. 5052.

24. *Congressional Quarterly Weekly Report* 35 (1977): 776.

pendence, Congress dutifully revised its third budget resolution. By this time, however, another mysterious spending shortfall was emerging. Despite congressional efforts to lower the outlay ceiling accordingly, fiscal 1977 spending turned out to be well below the revised third resolution and the deficit target was missed by almost $8 billion.

The seemingly inherent pitfalls of fiscal policy implementation also affected the 1978 budget. Carter's revisions of the 1978 Ford administration budget included an overall outlay increase of $20 billion and a deficit more than $10 billion higher. Congress proceeded to increase the deficit target by another $7 billion, to just under $65 billion. The second resolution for fiscal 1978 adjusted the deficit and spending figures slightly downward, but the actual deficit for the year was more than $12 billion below the congressional target. Even with a Democrat in the White House, fiscal policy control remained elusive.

The second year of the Carter presidency, however, signaled a growing congressional disquiet with fiscal stimulus. Carter's fiscal 1979 budget promised "a balanced budget in the future if the . . . economy continues its recovery,"[25] but it also recommended a large tax cut and a $60 billion deficit. The budget committees, however, were concerned about the inflationary impact of another large deficit, and there was the additional political problem of defending continued deficits four years into an economic recovery. Budget committee chairmen Muskie and Giaimo met with Carter and reached an agreement to delay the tax cut, thereby reducing its effect on the deficit. The first congressional budget resolution for 1979 actually lowered Carter's overall spending figure by several billion dollars and cut his proposed deficit by a slightly larger amount. Over the next few months, fiscal concerns heightened as California voters approved Proposition 13 and political commentators suddenly discovered a "taxpayers' revolt." Congress finally approved a tax cut, but it was not the type of redistributive tax bill that liberals or Carter had envisioned. A number of policy initiatives, including welfare reform, urban aid, and national health insurance, were abandoned. In the fall, Congress prepared for the midterm election by lowering the deficit to under $40 billion. Most of this reduction was due to revised spending estimates, but there were some important cuts, particularly in jobs programs. The Senate Budget Committee's report on the fall

---

25. *Budget of the United States Government, Fiscal Year 1979*, p.4.

budget resolution highlighted Congress's "Leadership Against Inflation" that was evidenced, it claimed, by this spending restraint.[26]

There was, however, some uncertainty about Congress's actual economic strategy. During 1978, Congress approved the Humphrey-Hawkins Act, which called for reducing the unemployment rate to 4 percent and the inflation rate to 3 percent by 1983. It also passed legislation promising tax and spending reductions for the next several years, and another provision mandating a balanced budget by 1981. At the same time, and perhaps of greater significance, Congress considerably weakened those provisions of the original Humphrey-Hawkins bill that required an "economic objectives" resolution, reported by the Joint Economic Committee, to be adopted prior to the annual budget resolutions.

For the advocates of fiscal restraint, the outcome on the fiscal 1979 budget was somewhat encouraging. Outlays breached the ceiling set in the second fiscal 1979 resolution, forcing Congress to pass a higher "binding" ceiling. With inflation driving up revenues even more sharply, however, the final deficit for fiscal 1979 dropped to $27.7 billion, well below the target Congress had set and more than $30 billion below the original Carter budget.

The Loss of Spending Control

If fortuitous circumstances made the budget process look good in 1978, the events of the next two years shattered most illusions about control of the budget and fiscal policy. The Carter administration opened 1979 by proudly announcing its "lean and austere" fiscal 1980 budget, which met "the president's commitment to hold the deficit to $30 billion or less and to move in the direction of a balanced budget."[27] Congress's first concurrent resolution for fiscal 1980 was seemingly even more impressive, matching the president's spending target and reducing the projected deficit to $23 billion. In the fall, Congress was forced to raise its spending and deficit figures but managed to hold the latter projection to just under $30 billion. In order to do so, however, it had to use economic assumptions and spending estimates that might best be described as optimistic. The optimism was misplaced. Spending estimates continually increased, as did the deficit projection. A third budget resolution for fiscal 1980, which Congress had earlier pledged to avoid, bore little relation to the first. The outlay ceiling was $40 billion

---

26. U.S., Congress, Senate, Committee on the Budget, *Report No. 95-1124, Second Concurrent Resolution on the Budget, FY 1979*, 95th Cong., 2nd sess., 1978, p. 4.

27. *Budget of the United States Government, Fiscal Year 1980*, p. 13.

higher, and the deficit was twice as large. Even this, however, was an underestimate, since the actual deficit for fiscal 1980 finally reached $59 billion.

By the time Congress was forced to revise its "binding" fiscal 1980 resolution, however, congressional Democrats were diverting attention to the "balanced budget" being planned for 1981. The Carter budget for fiscal 1981 was described by the administration as "prudent and responsible."[28] According to the president, it continued "the strategy of restraint [he had] proposed, and the Congress accepted, for the 1980 budget."[29] It also contained, however, a projected deficit of $16 billion. With the inflation rate at the 18 percent mark, House and Senate Democratic leaders quickly convinced Carter of the election year necessity for a balanced budget. The administration dutifully changed its estimates to show a surplus, and the budget committees joined in with balanced budget plans for fiscal 1981.

The first concurrent resolution for fiscal 1981 did contain a modest surplus. Moreover, the budget committees launched a serious effort to tighten spending control by attaching reconciliation instructions to the first resolution. It was soon apparent, however, that even if the reconciliation initiative were a complete success, the 1981 budget would not be even close to balanced. Senator Hollings, who had just succeeded Muskie as Budget Committee chairman, suggested the public might look beyond "a flunking grade on the actual mathematical figure . . . [to] the balanced discipline that's involved."[30] Congress made that hard to do. Action on the second budget resolution was postponed until after the election, thereby preserving the figment of a balanced budget if perhaps risking institutional credibility. (Final consideration of the reconciliation legislation was also left to the lame-duck session.) The second fiscal 1981 resolution increased the spending ceiling by some $20 billion and projected a $27.4 billion deficit. The spending and deficit figures, however, were somewhat shaky. The assumptions on which they were based were questionable. Moreover, there was, as one House member admitted, a "widespread assumption that there will be a third budget resolution giving people another chance to come back and fight another round."[31]

28. *Budget of the United States Government, Fiscal Year 1981*, p. M3.

29. Ibid.

30. *Congressional Quarterly Weekly Report* 38 (1980): 1901.

31. Ibid., p. 3250.

In a situation where budget figures are constantly and dramatically changing, it is difficult to talk about "deliberate" fiscal policy or, indeed, to argue that fiscal policy is much more than a by-product of uncontrolled spending. Yet this is precisely the situation that Congress now faces. During the Carter years, there was an impressive degree of agreement between Congress and the executive branch on fiscal policy (see table 2). The early prescription for strong stimulus gave way to attempted restraint. As it turned out, the spending increases and deficits that emerged with the policy shift can hardly be described as restrained. The virtual indistinguishability of the planned Carter and congressional budgets for fiscal 1980 and 1981—and the extent to which they missed the mark—strongly suggest that spending/deficit problems will not soon disappear despite the recent partisan shifts in Washington.

Table 2
Fiscal Aggregates, Carter Administration and Congressional Budgets
Fiscal Years 1978-1981 (in billions of dollars)

	President's Jan. Budget	First Concurrent Budget Resolution	Actual
FY 1978:			
Outlays	$459.4	$460.95	$450.8
Revenue	401.6	396.3	402.0
Deficit	–57.7	–64.65	–48.8
FY 1979:			
Outlays	500.2	498.8	493.7
Revenue	439.6	447.9	465.9
Deficit	–60.6	–50.9	–27.7
FY 1980:			
Outlays	531.6	532.0	579.0
Revenue	502.5	509.0	520.0
Deficit	–29.0	–23.0	–59.0
FY 1981:			
Outlays	615.8	613.6	(est) 662.7
Revenue	600.0	613.8	(est) 607.5
Deficit	–15.8	+0.2	(est) –55.2

The Fiscal Record

It would be unfair to assign Congress sole responsibility for the budgetary policies of the past several years. Moreover, fiscal policy is not the only determinant of what happens to the nation's economy. At the same time, economic trends cannot be ignored in evaluating Congress's fiscal record and capabilities, especially given the grandiose claims that accompanied passage of the 1974 budget law.

The Policies

First, fiscal policy in the postreform period has been usually, perhaps unprecedentedly, stimulative. The stimulus, moreover, has been primarily on the spending side of the budget. Since fiscal 1976, for example, spending has increased at an average annual rate of over 12 percent. This is well above the rate of increase during earlier periods (see table 3). In addition, revenue growth in the postreform period has averaged more than 13 percent annually, a striking upward movement in what had been a fairly stable trend.

Table 3
Spending and Revenue Trends, Fiscal Years 1951–1980

	Percentage Increase Budget Outlays	*Percentage Increase Revenues*
Fiscal Years:		
1951-1960 (annual average)	8.9%	9.6%
1961-1970 (annual average)	8.0	7.8
1971-1975 (annual average)	10.8	7.9
1976-1980 (postreform annual average)	12.2	13.2

Despite the unusual revenue growth since fiscal 1976, the subsequent deficits have been extraordinarily large. As shown in table 4, the cumulative deficits for the 1950s and 1960s totaled less than $75 billion. The cumulative deficit for the past five years has been just under $250 billion, and the average deficit has been approximately *$50 billion* annually. These figures, moreover, do not include the deficits of so-called off-budget entities, a fiscal subterfuge that was introduced in 1973. If off-budget outlays are taken into account, the average yearly deficit for fiscal years 1976 to 1980 increases to over *$60 billion.*

Table 4
Budget Deficits, Fiscal Years 1951-1980 (in billions of dollars)

Fiscal Years:	Cumulative Deficit*	Average Deficit
1951–1960	$ 14.3	$ 1.4
1961–1970	60.1	6.0
1971–1975	111.1	22.3
1976-1980**	247.0	49.5

*Minus offsetting surpluses.
**Does not include transition quarter spending between fiscal 1976 and fiscal 1977.

The relationship between deficits and outlays has also changed. From 1961 to 1970, for example, deficits represented, on the average, just over 4 percent of total spending. For fiscal years 1971 to 1975, this more than doubled. Since fiscal 1976, annual deficits have represented, on the average, 13.4 percent of outlays (including off-budget entities).

Another factor that must be taken into account in assessing the impact of federal spending is the relationship between spending and gross national product. Both the Ford and Carter administrations advocated reducing federal spending as a percentage of GNP, a policy that would require, of course, keeping spending growth rates below economic growth rates. In his fiscal 1980 budget, for example, Carter stated that this was "equal in importance to a declining deficit" and declared his intention to reduce outlays down to 20.3 percent of GNP by fiscal 1982.[32] Despite the Ford-Carter intentions, and similar advocacy by the Senate Budget Committee, outlays have remained in the 22-23 percent range since 1975. This is, as might be expected, substantially above the level for earlier years.

Economic Indicators

The performance of the economy during the 1970s was disappointing, and there are admittedly numerous factors that must be taken into account in attempting to explain this. When Congress debates fiscal policy, however, it focuses on a few key indicators—economic growth rates, inflation rates, and unemployment rates. Over time, therefore, the movement in these indicators represents a reasonable, if limited, test of how well Congress is achieving its fiscal policy objectives.

32. *Budget of the United States Government, Fiscal Year 1980*, pp. 12-13.

As shown in table 5, the stimulative policies of the past few years appear to have had, at best, mixed success. Economic growth rates, for example, have been roughly comparable to those of the 1950s and 1960s and well above the average real growth for the early 1970s. Unfortunately, the impressive average for the 1976 to 1980 period masks a steady decline from the peak of 5.9 percent in 1976. Recent trends in prices and employment are especially disconcerting. Between 1976 and 1980, the average annual growth in the Consumer Price Index was 8.9 percent, a dramatic change from the 2-3 percent range in which this index moved during the 1950s and 1960s. Moreover, this unusually high rate of inflation has coincided with very high unemployment rates. The 6.8 percent unemployment rate average for the 1976 to 1980 period, in fact, is higher than the rate for any single year between 1950 and 1975, with the solitary exception of 1958 when the rate was also 6.8 percent.

Table 5
Economic Trends, 1951-1980 (calendar years)

Average Annual Rate

	GNP (Real Growth)	Consumer Price Index (Year-to-Year Change)	Unemployment
1951–1960	3.3%	2.1%	4.5%
1961–1970	3.9	2.8	4.7
1971–1975	2.3	6.8	6.1
1976–1980	3.4	8.9	6.8

Sources: Data for 1951-1979 from *Economic Report of the President, 1980* (Washington, D.C.: Government Printing Office, 1980), pp. 205, 237, 263. The 1980 data are based on economic assumptions reported in the second budget resolution for fiscal 1981 (H. Con. Res. 448).

These economic trends have seriously weakened the once widespread consensus on the stimulative potential of fiscal policy. Congress lacks a clearcut strategy for handling growth, inflation, and unemployment problems simultaneously. Indeed, government's ability to "manage" the economy is no longer simply assumed. In the midst of all of this, economic theorists are sending conflicting signals. Demand advocates are split over the stimulative advantages of spending increases versus tax cuts. Supply-side theorists argue the incentive effects of general and targeted tax reductions. There is growing interest in monetary policy solutions. Under these bewildering circumstances, it is not surprising that Congress finds it difficult to fashion a policy response. And even if Congress finally succeeds in doing so, the persistent and massive problem of spending control would seriously threaten that policy's implementation.

Controlling Fiscal Policy

The congressional fiscal policy experiment has not been the institutional boon that many lawmakers once expected. The decision-making process in Congress has probably improved. Members of Congress now routinely consider the economic implications of taxing and spending decisions. Congress must finally set forth its fiscal plan, something it was able to avoid doing prior to the advent of annual budget resolutions.

The problem, of course, is that a better process does not insure better policy, and Congress's record of managing the economy is not very impressive. That the executive branch has not done much better is not an adequate defense. Indeed, it indicates a common shortcoming—an inability to control fiscal policies that result from, rather than harness, spending pressures. It would be unfair to conclude that fiscal policy arguments are simply used to rationalize spending and deficits. The budget committees, for example, have made concerted efforts to reverse spending-generated stimulus. These attempts, however, have been overwhelmed by unanticipated growth in mandatory spending programs, notably indexed entitlements, and by the general reluctance in Congress to restrain these programs. The dramatic disparities between estimated spending and actual spending in fiscal 1980 and 1981, and the resulting reversal in intended fiscal policy, demonstrate conclusively that spending, not fiscal policy, dominates the congressional budget process.

The explosive growth in spending has focused attention on possible changes in the congressional budget process. A number of proposals—such as procedural assists that would give the budget committees more power to enforce spending limits—would leave intact congressional discretion over budget policy. Also on the agenda, however, are more far-reaching measures that would put into effect statutory or constitutional formulas to determine total spending or the balance between spending and revenue.

A relevant consideration in evaluating these various initiatives is their potential impact on fiscal policy options and implementation. Most procedural reforms, for example, would have no particular bearing on the type of fiscal policy Congress adopts, although they might provide a better opportunity to implement policy once it has been decided. The drawback, of course, is that procedural changes are unlikely to solve the kinds of spending problems that have developed recently. So long as those problems persist, fiscal policy will respond to spending pressures.

The formula solutions—balanced budget amendments or GNP-determined limits on spending—would narrow Congress's fiscal policy options. It is important, however, to recognize that each would impose a distinctive limitation. The balanced budget approach prescribes a fiscal policy outcome—no deficits (except, according to most of the current proposals, in cases of national emergency). An expenditure limit would allow deficits but only through tax cut stimulus.

The fiscal policy prescribed by a constitutional requirement to balance the budget raises serious questions, for it would reverse conventional spending patterns. Spending would fall during economic slumps, since revenues would be reduced, and accelerate when economic growth increased revenues. This could be changed by increasing taxes during recessions or cutting them during booms, but such policies would obviously introduce additional complications.

The central assumption of balanced budget proponents is that deficits are the primary cause of our economic and political difficulties. They presumably have in mind that once deficits are precluded, spending will finally be controlled by the political constraints on taxation. Revenue growth during the 1970s, however, suggests that these constraints are not all that formidable. It is possible, after all, to balance the budget at its current share of GNP through either deliberate or inflation-induced tax increases.

More important, the fiscal policy record of recent years strongly suggests that the balanced budget diagnosis is wrong. It is not the desirability of deficits that generates spending, but rather unchecked spending momentum that results in deficits. The core of the fiscal policy problem is spending, not deficits. And it is this problem which is addressed specifically by expenditure limit proposals.

Both statutory and constitutional expenditure formulas would tie spending growth to economic growth by setting a ceiling (for most of the current plans, 20 or 21 percent) on outlays as a proportion of GNP. From a fiscal policy standpoint, this would eliminate spending stimulus as a recession policy. Indeed, just as under a balanced budget requirement, spending growth would decline during slumps and rise during booms. Expenditure limits, however, would not prohibit using compensatory tax adjustments to provide stimulus or restraint. They would also serve to fix the maximum share of resources that could be absorbed by the public sector, further restricting the impact of federal budgets.

The use of compensatory tax policy rather than spending policy may have certain advantages. It would end the confusion between the necessity or desirability of spending programs and the need for economic stimulus. As a political and practical matter, it would be easier for Congress to move tax revenues up or down than to eliminate spending programs once the need for stimulus disappears. With congressional fiscal policy options limited to the tax side of the budget, one of the existing biases for increased spending would be eliminated.

In addition, revenue-based fiscal policy can be implemented quickly, unlike most countercyclical spending programs, thereby reducing fiscal lag. Since revenue estimates tend to be relatively accurate, at least in comparison to spending estimates, fiscal policy implementation is likely to be more precise than in the past. There are objections, of course, that spending stimulus has a greater short-term impact than an equivalent amount of tax stimulus and should therefore be an available option. The supporting evidence, however, is not clearcut, and in any case, the advantages seem marginal at best.

Whether an expenditure limit is desirable or workable on other grounds is another matter, and there is the important choice between a statutory or constitutional route.[33] In terms of fiscal policy considerations, however, expenditure limits should not be summarily dismissed. Under present circumstances, the simple fact is that neither Congress nor the president has firm control of fiscal policy. An expenditure limit would strengthen that control.

The Reagan Plan—A Postscript

The budget cuts sponsored by President Reagan and incorporated into the first fiscal 1982 budget resolution and accompanying reconciliation bill clearly represent a dramatic change in spending policy. The administration's plans for spending reductions in future years are equally substantial.

---

33. For an analysis of the constitutional expenditure limit's political and economic merits, see Aaron Wildavsky, *How to Limit Government Spending* (Berkeley: University of California Press, 1980).

Whether these reductions can be successfully implemented, however, is uncertain. The fiscal 1982 spending estimates, for example, are based upon economic assumptions that are decidedly optimistic. If projected inflation rates, economic growth rates, unemployment levels, or interest rates are inaccurate, fiscal 1982 spending will be higher than initial ceilings indicate, although spending will probably remain well below the Carter administration's January 1981 estimates.

Moreover, the political and economic effects of the fiscal 1982 cuts have not yet been felt. It is entirely possible that once these effects fully materialize, Congress will find it much more difficult to support future reductions of the magnitude the Reagan administration has promised to recommend. Certainly, the budget committees will be hard pressed to match their reconciliation success of this past spring.

The essential point about the fiscal 1982 budget plan, however, is that the congressional budget process did not operate in an independent fashion. The executive branch provided the budgetary program, organized the support for that program, and achieved virtually all that it recommended to Congress. What this suggests is that spending control is possible with appropriate presidential leadership. In the absence of such leadership, Congress lacks the internal cohesion necessary to control politically popular spending programs.

The rationale for a constitutional expenditure limitation is that it insures continued pressure on Congress to keep spending within prescribed limits. Sustained presidential commitment and intervention are much less certain. In the past, unchecked spending momentum has frustrated congressional fiscal policy planning, and the result has been unacceptable spending growth, undesirable economic effects, and congressional vulnerability to presidential attacks. If Congress wishes to chart an independent fiscal policy course in the future, a constitutional spending limit might well provide the necessary institutional protection.

Response by Alice M. Rivlin
Director, Congressional Budget Office

These two presentations, from Chairman Giaimo and Professor Ippolito, reinforce a paradox that I have often thought about as I watched the congressional budget process over the last several years.

On the one hand, the Congress has worked harder on the budget than it ever has before. As has been emphasized at this meeting, the leadership, especially Speaker O'Neill, has twisted arms and gone to great lengths and shown a good deal of courage in keeping the budget process on track and in line. That has involved, as Bob Giaimo knows all too well, endless hours, tight deadlines, difficult decisions, and the need to say no time after time to colleagues and to constituents when it would have been a lot easier to say yes.

On the other hand, despite all this effort, the result has not been to anybody's liking, as Professor Ippolito points out. Despite the Congress's effort, spending and deficits are still too high. There is a sense that somehow the Congress is not doing its job, despite working harder at it. There is enormous frustration within the Congress that the hard work comes to naught, that

the economy and the budget somehow are controlling them. Now why is that, and what's to be done?

To begin with we have to recognize that our current economic problems are just plain hard. It's hard to know what to do. It isn't that there's some simple solution sitting there and the Congress just isn't adopting it. Inflation is an intractable problem that won't yield to quick solutions. The energy crisis is real. Unfortunately, measures taken to relieve one problem often exacerbate another, and then the Congress gets blamed. Not only is it hard to know what to do, but it's very hard to know what will happen if you do something or if you don't.

There is great frustration in the Congress with forecasters, as Bob Giaimo noted, and with good reason. Look only at the history of the fiscal 1981 budget. I can assure Professor Ippolito that people did honestly believe in March and April of 1980 that if they worked very hard at it, given what the economic forecasters then told them, they could balance the budget. And hard at it they did work. The administration and the leadership of Congress met together, going over the budget item by item late into the night to figure a way to pare back spending, to bring the budget into balance on the basis of forecasts that respectable economists were then giving them. The trouble is that the economists were mostly wrong. The economy slipped unexpectedly and rapidly in the second quarter of 1980 into a steep decline—the fastest decline in our economy in any one quarter since World War II. That decline brought with it a lot of changes in the budget that the Congress couldn't control. Unemployment compensation went up and revenues fell off. In the meantime, interest rates were rising so that interest on the public debt went up rapidly, and the Iranian situation was coming to a head. The Defense Department sent ships out to steam around in the Indian Ocean, burning up petroleum at a higher rate and at a higher price than anticipated. As a result of developments over which Congress had no control, the budget got out of balance. Everybody was understandably upset and disappointed that the great effort did not bring about a balanced budget, and frustrated with those who, through erroneous prediction, had said it might.

But such things have to be lived with. In a single year, there's al-ways going to be a lot of uncertainty. The Congress can't change that. What it can do if it wants to, is take steps to change the size and shape of the budget over several years. The big lesson of the budget process so far, I think, has been that there is a lot of momentum in federal spending and that persisting deficits have been largely caused by that momentum in spending. The arithmetic of the budget is simple and dramatic. A quarter of the budget goes for defense. Some of that may be wastefully spent, but there is general agreement that over the next several years we need more defense spending, rather than less, so that is not going to be an area in which we can make cuts. Nine or ten percent of the budget goes for interest on the debt, and there is no easy way in the short run to control that. Nearly half, however, goes for payments to people, mostly to entitlement programs for the aged and the poor—a large part to retirement programs, but also to medicaid and medicare, housing allowances, and other programs that have accumulated over the years. Those are mostly indexed for inflation and they will grow without any action of the Congress over the next several years.

The spending growth in those programs cannot be changed without difficulty. And the budget cannot be brought under control, in the sense of slowing spending growth, without changing those programs. This means that the Congress can't just vote a smaller money total; it has to change the laws that govern who is entitled to benefits and how those benefits are computed. And that's difficult. It means that the Congress is reluctant to change things quickly because people count on having those benefits. They arrange their lives around them, and it's cruel to tell them tomorrow that the benefits aren't going to be there the next day. That's true not only of old people who have arranged their retirement plans around a particular set of benefits. It is also true of students, for example, who have made their plans for an academic career on the assumption that benefits will be available. It means, finally, that those programs cannot be cut without hurting some people directly and making them visibly worse off.

I'm not saying that nothing can be done. As a matter of fact, these programs can probably be cut gradually over the years and fairly substantially. Indeed, some of the student benefits—I hesitate to mention this in a college—are obvious candidates. For example, the social security student benefits were passed many years ago, before a whole set of other student benefits had come into being, and those are perhaps candidates for reexamination. There is a good case at the moment for changing the indexing of social security and other retirement programs, even this year. Real wages have not been rising in the last year and probably will not rise in the next; thus, the incomes of people who are retired are protected to a greater extent than those of wage earners. In short, there is a plausible case for capping such benefits and perhaps for moving in social security and other programs to an indexing system in which you adjust benefits according to a wage index or a price index, whichever is lower. Thus, when real wages are falling, as in a recession, everybody would have to take their cut; retirement benefits would not be protected to a greater extent than the income of wage earners.

Over the last few years, the Congress has practiced budgeting, and now has in place a mechanism for dealing with these kinds of hard choices, if it believes that people want those choices made. I don't think a spending limit or any other artificial device is needed. If the Congress believes that people want it to spend less, Congress will spend less, and the mechanisms for doing that are in place now.

Not that I think the procedures are perfect; I would offer several reforms, many of which are being talked about in Congress at the moment. To begin with, one could make the first budget resolution binding instead of the second, so as to move the enforcement mechanism earlier into the year, and perhaps even dispense with the second resolution. One could, and I think this is particularly important, vote multiyear budget targets, and take them seriously. I think that is one of the lessons of the attempts to deal with the budget for the last several years.

Another lesson is that Congress has too much to do. I'm sure neither Representative Boland nor Bob Giaimo will quarrel with that. It is almost impossible to be a congressman these days—there are too many votes, there are too many issues on which to decide. One way to help reduce that overload within the budget process would be to switch to a two-year budget, to make most budget decisions half as often. I think that might help. Mainly, it would give the spending committees more time to examine the programs. They could do that in the first year of a Congress and then vote a two-year budget as they move on.

But the main point, I think, is that the Congress has over the last several years practiced budgeting, which it never did before, and is now in a position to strengthen its procedures and move ahead to deal with what it perceives as the spending problem.

Response by Hon. Edward P. Boland
Member, United States House of Representatives

Thank you, Professor Ippolito, and Alice Rivlin, and my longtime friend, Bob Giaimo. I was interested at the plenary luncheon to hear Dick Fenno quote Jim Johnson, who said that serving in Congress is not a really big deal. And it really isn't. I've been there, this is my twenty-ninth year starting this year, so it really isn't a big deal. I came to Congress in 1953, with Speaker O'Neill. He and I were members of the state legislature and we parted ways, and I went to an elective office back in western Massachusetts and he stayed in the House of Representatives here and, as you know, became the first Democratic Speaker in the history of the Massachusetts legislature. Then we both arrived in Washington together. They say that institutions are but the lengthened shadows of men. I think this Chair in American Politics will, in some measure and to some degree, lengthen the shadow of this great man in the years to come.

I'm delighted also that those who have structured this symposium have chosen the budget and fiscal policy as one of the subjects to be discussed. Because I know no one who could spend money faster than Tip O'Neill. I always had to keep the bills in the apartment that we shared together, incidentally, for some twenty-four years. I enjoyed listening to Bob Giaimo and Professor Ippolito. I think that Bob Giaimo can brag a bit about the congressional budget process. I think he has a right to brag. He has a right to brag because of the particular staff that has been structured since the passage of the Budget and Impoundment Control Act in 1974. And particularly the staff leadership that has been given to that process by Alice Rivlin. No one in Washington knows more about the budget process than Alice Rivlin. She's been in the middle of all of it. Without the kind of advice and counsel she has given to the Congressional Budget Office, it might very well be that the budget process would be a lot of rhetoric and perhaps not as effective as some of us in Congress believe it to be. So the process really is not irrelevant. I shudder to think what kind of shape we'd be in without it.

The Appropriations Committee came into being 116 years ago, back in 1865. Up to that time, the tax-writing committee of the Congress was also the spending committee—the Committee on Ways and Means. But that was split in that year, and the Appropriations Committee was created. And ever since that time, it's had its ups and downs. Since 1920, the committee has exercised, I think, a degree of responsibility in spending that has showered some praise upon the Congress. I might agree with Professor Ippolito when he talks about the fact that we have lost control over fiscal policy. That could be so. Perhaps we've lost control of it because spending is out of control. I would be the first to agree with Bob Giaimo that the budget is fundamentally out of control. It's largely out of control because entitlements and indexing and mandatory programs and previous spending commitments have contributed to the inability to control it. That's the fault of the House itself. That's the fault of Congress. So I guess we can afford to brag about the reconciliation process. Last year was the first time it was used. It's part of the Budget and Impoundment Control Act of 1974, and it was exercised in the lame-duck session of the last Congress. I think something was accomplished by it. If I recall correctly, it was a reduction of $8 billion. Congress said to eight committees in the House and Senate:

"Go back and look at your authorizations again and come back with a reconciliation bill that gives us this reduction or we're going to face a greater problem in the area of deficits."

But let's not get too carried away by it. It was the first time we've tried it and it's been successful. I think that the House and the Senate deserve credit for it, although it kind of reminds me of the fellow who brags about the fact that over the years he's lost 700 pounds dieting. But the problem is that he is now 50 pounds heavier than when he began his first diet. I don't want to bore you with a lot of statistics, but let me give you a couple of points. You've heard that roughly 77 percent of the federal budget is uncontrollable. I think Dennis Ippolito would probably agree with that figure; it's the figure that's pointed to by the experts on the budget and by those of us who have something to do with the budget, and also by the House Budget Committee. But maybe more critical is the fact that 58 percent of the budget has built-in indexing. So that means, to offset inflation, provisions are made for an equal amount to be added to the various programs, which of course just tends to double the rate of increase. I think it can be said that indexing is about as helpful as using gasoline to put out a fire. Indexing is at the very heart of the budget control problem, and it will probably be the toughest nut to crack.

I think most of us can agree on the problem. What about the solution? Here I am afraid that we have to borrow a line from our comic-strip friend, Pogo: "We've met the enemy and he is us." The Congress as an institution and members as individuals still haven't summoned the will to say no, and nobody on this panel would disagree with that. Dick Bolling, who was one of the key framers of the 1974 Budget Act, hit it right on the mark. He said that the problem isn't with the process; that will work if the will is there to make it work. I could put it another way. The problem isn't that the Congress can't control the budget. The real problem is that we can't control the special interests, and until we can solve that problem, we will continue to have a hemorrhaging budget.

Let me turn now to some of the issues concerning the budget process that involve the Appropriations Committee, and some of my thoughts on what we may want to do to help that process become more effective. Let me begin by saying a word about the Appropriations Committee in relationship to the Budget Committee. When the 1974 act was adopted, many critics

felt that the Budget and Appropriations Committees would be at each other's throat within a few weeks. Well, that hasn't happened. In fact, I believe that the members of the Appropriations Committee have leaned over backwards to help the process work. The fact is, the two committees are and should be natural allies. Of course, that doesn't mean that everything is okay, because it isn't. Let's look at what's involved from the perspective of the Appropriations Committee. Probably the most severe problem that has emerged before the Appropriations Committee in the new budget process is one of timing. For a variety of reasons that even the Budget Committee cannot control, that committee has been unsuccessful in meeting the schedules envisioned in the Budget Act. I believe that an important cause of this is that budget resolutions have become entangled by the consideration of individual budget line items.

Another drag in the budget process is the move toward more and more annual authorizations. We now have something like 100 authorization bills introduced each year. This has virtually strangled the congressional legislative machinery. The system just cannot digest the increased legislative volume represented by the proliferation of annual authorizations, and the victim is the congressional budget process, because there is no time to get everything done. If the budget process is going to work, solving the timing problem is absolutely essential.

What about entitlements? That has been mentioned here. One of the most important objectives of the Congressional Budget Act was to eliminate the fragmentation of the congressional budget decision-making process. It got rid of the so-called backdoor spending devices—contract authority, borrowing authority, etc. While these changes have been helpful, the fact remains that the programs not subject to annual review in the regular authorization and appropriations process tend to remain virtually uncontrollable and continue to grow at a much faster rate than those programs which Congress controls in the appropriations process. As I said earlier, about 58 percent of those programs are adjusted automatically alone—think of it—by price indexes. These include food stamps, school lunch, veterans' survivors' pensions, civil service retirement, railroad retirement, social security, supplemental security income, black lung benefits, Older Americans Act programs, and child nutrition. Now many of these programs are worthwhile. We'd all like

to have them. But I think in order to have an effective budget process and control spending, you have to have priorities. We've got to weed out those programs that are less justifiable.

Let me just give one example. It's a small one, but it's an important one. For as many years as I can remember, the president has proposed to the Congress the elimination of flight and correspondence training from the GI bill. Flight training, for example, was instituted after World War II as a legitimate use of veterans' GI bill benefits. Today we have roughly 2,000 commercial airline projects. The training of new pilots from the GI bill has got to be a lower priority. Last year, in the fiscal year 1981 Housing and Urban Development and Independent Agencies appropriations bill, we tried to eliminate flight and correspondence training through a limitation. We weren't able to eliminate it; the Senate Veterans' Affairs Committee wanted the program to continue. We did, however, reduce the federal contribution from 90 to 60 percent. The point of the story is that these are the kinds of entitlement programs that need to be looked at, and that has got to be done on an annual basis.

Let me conclude with some ideas on solving some of these problems I have just outlined. To begin with, I would strongly recommend (and I think Bob Giaimo and Alice Rivlin will support this) that we have only one budget resolution before the fiscal year begins. This would help the timing problem. It would make the first resolution binding and tie the reconciliation procedure to that resolution. The fact is that the second budget resolution has become more or less superfluous in that it simply rubberstamps that which has already been approved in many of the appropriation bills.

Next, I would structure the process in a way to cut down on the number of line items in the budget resolutions through some mechanism that permits members to vote on the comparative size of the various budget functions. In other words, the resolution would be centered on a debate as to whether or not the income security function of the budget should capture 50 percent of the total, or 49 percent,

as opposed to the defense function taking 20 percent, or 25 percent. If that approach is adopted, then we could focus the debate on the macroeconomic objectives of the federal budget, without time-consuming discussion on the mechanisms of federal programs.

Next perhaps we should consider going back and taking another look at the possibility of one general appropriation bill in each year. We did this in only one year—1950. It didn't work then, largely because many of the subcommittee chairmen of the Appropriations Committee didn't like it. But I think it has some real positive benefits that we should examine. To begin with, it would give the members an opportunity to look at the entire budget and weigh adding money for x and taking it away from y. It would involve the actual dollars that a program or an agency receives. Thank you very much.

PART V:
REFORMING
CONGRESSIONAL
PROCEDURES

ASSESSING CONGRESSIONAL CHANGE, OR WHAT HATH REFORM WROUGHT (OR WREAKED)?

Leroy N. Rieselbach
Department of Political Science
Indiana University

Barely a decade ago, as Congress entered the 1970s, the scholarly consensus described the national legislature as stable or "institutionalized." Its internal structure, though complex, was relatively fixed, with virtually autonomous committees assuming the central position; its customary modes of conducting business, in keeping with widely shared norms— e.g., specialization and reciprocity —were broadly accepted. Its members were "careerists," eager and able to sustain their incumbency and more than willing to allocate authority using automatic criteria (e.g., seniority). In short, while certainly not static in any sense, the Congress was at least predictable.[1]

Ten years later, as the 1980s unfold, Congress seems singularly unpredictable. Indeed, as is so often the case with academic consensus, the seeds of change had been sown by the time the original generalizations appeared in print. In the congressional case, the Vietnam War, clearly revealing legislative impotence vis-a-vis the executive, planted the seed for reform firmly in some legislators' minds. The liberal Democratic Study Group (DSG) nurtured the idea, which first bore fruit when the Congress enacted the Legislative Reorganization Act of 1970. Watergate, and policy problems that appeared intractable, like energy, extended the growing season, and reformers harvested a bumper crop of changes during the ensuing years. But they did not inevitably reap what they had intended to sow (in fact,

---

I am grateful for Lawrence C. Dodd's insightful commentary on the first draft of this paper.

1. N. W. Polsby, "The Institutionalization of the House of Representatives," *American Political Science Review* 62 (1968): 144-168; D. R. Matthews, *U. S. Senators and Their World* (Chapel Hill, N.C.: University of North Carolina Press, 1960), ch. 5; C. S. Bullock III, "House Careerists: Changing Patterns of Longevity and Attrition," *American Political Science Review* 66 (1972): 1295-1300; D. R. Mayhew, *Congress: The Electoral Connection* (New Haven, Ct.: Yale University Press, 1974).

they did not always seem to be certain about what they had set out). There were weeds, of one sort or another, in each year's crop. This essay seeks to describe and assess—at some peril, and perhaps prematurely—the impact of change on the contemporary Congress.

Change and Reform in the Seventies

To chart the course and consequences of congressional change, even its procedural forms, is no easy task. For one thing, *reform*—defined as *intentional* efforts to reshape institutional structures and processes—is only one, and perhaps not even the most important, facet of change—seen, more broadly, as any shift, intentional or inadvertent, in fundamental organizational patterns. The latter may reflect extralegislative forces such as major events, including the emergence of new policy issues, and election results, which may bring newcomers with different backgrounds, experiences, and perspectives to the legislature.[2] Thus, external events and personnel turnover, neither planned nor predictable, may contribute as much or more to legislative change as any self-conscious reconstruction of rules and procedures.

Second, because the members of Congress are the chief agents of reform—unless and until they choose to act, there will be no reform[3] —it is not surprising to find that they reform their institution in the same fashion that they make other decisions. That is, the lawmakers treat reform, like other, more "substantive" issues, in incremental style. They are seldom, if ever, moved by broad visions of what the ideal Congress might be; rather they respond in the short run, to circumstances of the moment. Reforms tend to be political, pragmatic, and more-or-less spontaneous reactions to seemingly irresistable forces; they have been piecemeal, not wholesale; individually modest, not radical; ad hoc, not the products of comprehensive planning.[4]

In addition, the reformers' motives are both mixed and not necessarily

2. D. W. Rohde and K. A. Shepsle, "Thinking About Legislative Reform," in *Legislative Reform: The Policy Impact*, ed. L. N. Rieselbach (Lexington, Mass.: Lexington Books, 1978), pp. 9-21.

3. C. O. Jones, "Will Reform Change Congress?", in *Congress Reconsidered*, ed. L. C. Dodd and B. I. Oppenheimer (New York: Praeger, 1977), pp. 247-260.

4. For a fuller discussion of the matters raised in this and the preceding paragraph, see L. N. Rieselbach, "Legislative Change, Reform, and Public Policy," in *Encyclopedia of Policy Sciences*, ed. S. Nagel (New York: Marcel Dekker, forthcoming).

"pure," making it difficult to determine precisely the purposes of the changes they propose. Some ostensible goals are far easier to defend than others; the rationale for institutional engineering may belie its true intent. For example, who can protest the desire of Congress to regain public prestige, lost during the late 1960s?[5] Similarly, it is hardly controversial to seek to make the legislature more effective or more efficient in producing public policy. It is, however, somewhat riskier to propose reforms that increase legislative influence relative to the executive. There are those who prefer presidential to congressional power. Likewise, to suggest reforms to bring about desired policy results, or to reverse unfavorable outcomes, is likely to elicit opposition from those satisfied with the legislature's current output (or lack thereof). Finally, there are personal considerations—the desire to improve one's electoral or legislative power situation—that may underlie reform sentiments but which are seldom openly advertised.

Overall, then, it is hard to know with certainty what reformers sought to accomplish. The reforms they did adopt, implemented incrementally and sequentially over a half decade, were compromises, not always consistent with one another. Their efforts, moreover, are hard to distinguish from the consequences of other, unplanned changes that occurred over the same period. These arguments make treacherous any effort to specify precisely what the reforms of the 1970s actually produced. Nonetheless, this disclaimer notwithstanding (valor being the lesser part of discretion), it is possible to identify four separate sets of reforms, each focusing on a different aspect of legislative performance, and each contributing to the current state of congressional performance.[6]

5. G. R. Parker, "Some Themes in Congressional Unpopularity," *American Journal of Political Science* 21 (1977): 93-109.

6. A number of useful sources describe the developments of the 1970s, discussed in this section. See especially: L. C. Dodd and B. I. Oppenheimer, "The House in Transition," in Dodd and Oppenheimer, *Congress Reconsidered*; N. J. Ornstein, ed., *Changing Congress: The Committee System*, Annals of the American Academy of Political and Social Science 411 (1974): 1-176; N. J. Ornstein, ed., *Congress in Change: Evolution and Reform* (New York: Praeger, 1975); N.J. Ornstein and D. W. Rohde, "Political Parties and Congressional Reform," in *Parties and Elections in an Anti-Party Age*, ed. J. Fishel (Bloomington, Ind.: Indiana University Press, 1978), pp. 230-294; S. C. Patterson, "The Semi-Sovereign Congress," in *The New American Political System*, ed. A. King (Washington, D.C.: The American Enterprise Institute, 1978), pp. 125-177; L. N. Rieselbach, *Congressional Reform in the Seventies* (Morristown, N.J.: General Learning Press, 1977); S. Welch and J. G. Peters, eds., *Legislative Reform and Public Policy* (New York: Praeger, 1977).

"Sunshine" Reforms: Increasing Congressional Accountability

One set of reforms sought to counter an increasingly hostile public opinion. Not only policy failure but also a series of scandals (from Adam Powell to Abscam, featuring nontyping typists and aquatic exhibitionism in the Tidal Basin, along with ordinary, old-fashioned corruption) and apparent conflicts of interest combined to reduce the prestige of Congress. Paradoxically, while constituents retained considerable confidence in their own individual representatives, they concluded that Congress collectively was performing poorly.[7] To remedy this situation and restore popular approbation, Congress adopted a series of reforms designed, in large part, to expose its operations to public scrutiny. To the extent that citizens could discover what their representatives were doing, and satisfy themselves that these activities were ethically beyond suspicion, they would be able to hold Congress accountable and accept the legislature as legitimate and untainted.

First, members of Congress concluded that they should conduct the public's business in public.[8] The Legislative Reorganization Act of 1970 decreed that legislators vote publicly in committee and on the floor. Committee roll calls are recorded and made available; new requirements for recording teller votes reduce the likelihood that lawmakers can avoid going "on the record," individually, during debate and preliminary floor consideration of legislation.[9] The committee process was opened up as well. All sessions, including markups and conference committee meetings, are to be public, unless a majority votes, in public, to close them. While executive sessions on secret or controversial matters remain possible, the burden of proof now rests with those who would exclude outside observers.

Second, both the House and Senate adopted codes of ethics, including financial disclosure provisions, designed to deter or expose conflicts of interest. Members are required to report gifts they (and their employees)

---

7. R. F. Fenno, Jr., "If, as Ralph Nader Says, Congress is 'The Broken Branch,' How Come We Love Our Congressmen So Much?", in Ornstein, *Congress in Change*, pp. 277-287; G. R. Parker and R. H. Davidson, "Why Do Americans Love Their Congressmen So Much More Than Their Congress?", *Legislative Studies Quarterly* 4 (1979): 53-61; T. E. Cook, "Legislature vs. Legislator: A Note on the Paradox of Congressional Support," *Legislative Studies Quarterly* 4 (1979): 43-52.

8. C. S. Bullock III, "Congress in the Sunshine," in Rieselbach, *Legislative Reform*, pp. 209-221.

9. N. J. Ornstein and D. W. Rohde, "The Strategy of Reform: Recorded Teller Voting in the House of Representatives" (Paper presented to the annual meeting of the Midwest Political Science Association, 1974).

receive, to reveal their holdings in property and/or securities, and to acknowledge their debts. Moreover, members are limited (to a sum not more than 15 percent of their salaries) in the outside income they can earn while serving in Congress. Such disclosures should enable concerned citizens, or enterprising journalists, to discover to whom, if anyone, members are financially beholden, and to assess the extent, if any, to which members' personal interests impinge on matters about which they must vote or otherwise act.

Third, the Federal Election Campaign Act of 1971, as amended in 1974, 1976, and 1979, and as interpreted by the Supreme Court in *Buckley* v. *Valeo* (1976), established a congressional election system that limits contributors' donations but not candidates' expenditures (and the latter can give whatever of their own funds they want to their own campaigns). Political action committees (PACs) have superceded individual contributors as the main source of congressional campaign funding; they can give $5,000 to any nominee while individual donors are limited to $1,000.[10] Disclosure is central to the new election system. Candidates must report in detail the sources of their funds and the uses to which they put their money.

On their face, these "sunshine" reforms—open procedures in Congress, ethics codes, and campaign regulation—seem suited to achieve their avowed purpose. They should make it possible, though not always easy, for the public to assess the extent to which members of Congress act on the basis of self-serving rather than public-regarding considerations. Yet other motives may have lurked beneath this rationale. Though little noted, there were clear implications for the political parties implicit in mandating that Congress perform in public; the more visible any action, the less the ability of the party leaders to influence it.[11] Likewise, financial disclosure may have indirect effects on the substance of policy. It may be more difficult for members, forced to acknowledge the sources of their funds and obligations, to support the programs of those to whom they are indebted. Similarly, controls on campaign funding have an obvious impact on election results; given the well-documented advantage of incumbents (at least in the House), limits on challengers' ability to fill their campaign coffers work to

---

10. See H. E. Alexander, *Financing Politics: Money, Elections and Political Reform*, 2nd ed. (Washington, D.C.: Congressional Quarterly Press, 1980); and G.C. Jacobson, *Money in Congressional Elections* (New Haven, Ct.: Yale University Press, 1980).

11. L. A. Froman and R. B. Ripley, "Conditions for Party Leadership: The Case of the House Democrats," *American Political Science Review* 59 (1965): 52-63.

buttress the electoral position of sitting members.[12] In sum, even so praise-worthy a set of reforms as increasing congressional visibility, and thus accountability, may conceal "baser" intentions.

Reforms for Institutional Power: Challenging the Executive

A second set of reforms was aimed directly at the executive branch, seeking to reassert atrophied legislative powers. Presidential assertiveness and congressional acquiescence combined, in the critics' view, to create an imbalance between the two branches. The "imperial presidency," symbolized by Vietnam and Watergate, suggested that the legislature had lost, or ceded, many of its traditional powers: to declare war, to control the federal purse strings, and to oversee the bureaucracy. Reform would allow and stimulate Congress to reclaim its rightful role in the policy process, imposing its preferences on the presidency when it seemed sensible to do so.

Congress, acting on this assumption, took a number of steps to buttress its own position relative to the executive. It moved against the president's military position in 1973; it enacted, over Richard Nixon's veto, the War Powers Resolution to circumscribe the commander-in-chief's authority to commit military forces to combat.[13] The legislation empowered Congress to compel the executive to withdraw any troops sent into the field within sixty days (or ninety days in special circumstances).[14] In theory at least, the president should cultivate congressional approval before sending troops

---

12. G. C. Jacobson, "Practical Consequences of Campaign Finance Reform: An Incumbent Protection Act?", *Public Policy* 21 (1976): 1-32. The political alignments on issues of extending campaign finance reform—to reduce PAC contribution levels or to expand the system of public financing to congressional elections—nicely illustrate the problem of incompatible intentions. Republicans, the legislative minority throughout this period, vigorously opposed many features of the scheme enacted as well as proposals to enlarge it. They feared that the restrictions on fund raising would entrench the majority Democrats permanently. The Republican position, now that the party has won the Senate and aspires to take the House in the near future, bears watching. On the one hand, as incumbents, limits on funding should benefit them; on the other, as the "in party" *and* the ideological favorite of the burgeoning number of corporate PACs, they stand to gain a decisive advantage in contributions under the present arrangements. In either case, the usual justification in terms of visibility and accountability may have little to do with the ultimate choice.

13. There are those, it should be noted, who argue that by giving the executive virtual carte blanche for the sixty-day period, Congress actually enlarged presidential power.

14. T. Franck and R. Weisband, *Foreign Policy by Congress* (New York: Oxford University Press, 1979); P. Holt, *The War Powers Resolution* (Washington, D.C.: The American Enterprise Institute, 1978).

into battle; without consultation, there is real risk of legislative reversal of the chief executive.[15]

The Budget and Impoundment Control Act of 1974 constitutes a second congressional effort to enhance the legislature's authority. Acknowledging past failure to exercise effective control over federal expenditures, the law created new budget committees in each chamber; provided them with a powerful analytic agency, the Congressional Budget Office (CBO), capable of competing with the Office of Management and Budget; and charged them with imposing fiscal discipline on an archaic budgetary process.[16] The product of the new scheme is, potentially, a coherent, unified budget that compares revenue and expenditure totals, thus presenting a clear picture of the deficit (or surplus), and that does so on a fixed timetable. The act sought to enable Congress to centralize and coordinate its consideration of the budget and, in consequence, to compete on even terms with the executive for fiscal supremacy. Tacked on to the bill, as Title X, were major restrictions on the president's power to impound funds Congress has duly authorized and appropriated.[17] Enacted specifically in response to Richard Nixon's aggressive use of impoundment for policy rather than routine administrative purposes, these new provisions made it considerably more difficult for the president to regulate the flow of federal funds.[18]

In addition, to remedy disadvantages in information and analytic capacity, to generate independent expertise to countervail that readily available to the executive, Congress moved to enlarge its data resources. It established two new agencies—the Congressional Budget Office, as a part of the new budget process, and the Office of Technology Assessment (OTA)—to

---

15. Interestingly, Congress was apparently worried about its collective capacity to oppose the president; it framed the statute so that legislative *inaction* triggers the troop withdrawal. That is, while the chief executive can introduce troops into hostilities on his own initiative, he is obligated to withdraw them unless Congress acts positively—declares war or enacts some legislative authorization of the conflict—to approve the commitment.

16. J. Havemann, *Congress and the Budget* (Bloomington, Ind.: Indiana University Press, 1978).

17. L. C. Dodd and R. L. Schott, *Congress and the Administrative State* (New York: Wiley, 1979); L. Fisher, *Presidential Spending Power* (Princeton, N.J.: Princeton University Press, 1975).

18. Here, too, the law was written to permit Congress to have its way with a minimum of effort. To rescind—that is, cancel—appropriations, the president must secure an approving resolution from both houses; inaction by either house obligates the chief executive to spend the money. To defer—that is, delay—expenditures is less difficult; a presidential request to defer is approved automatically unless either house votes a resolution of disapproval.

advise on the potential impact of various scientific programs; and it strengthened two old ones—the Congressional Research Service (CRS) (formerly Legislative Reference Service) of the Library of Congress, and the General Accounting Office (GAO). It also greatly enlarged members' personal and committee staffs, making available many more experts.[19] The legislature has also sought to harness computers to its information needs.[20] In these ways, Congress can claim to have positioned itself to compete more effectively with the executive; it need no longer defer so readily to an administration presumed to possess superior information.

Finally, Congress began to assert, more forcefully than in the previous decades, already established powers. The Legislative Reorganization Act of 1946 formalized the legislature's obligation to exert "continuous watchfulness" over the agencies and bureaus of the executive departments.[21] Greater information resources and an enlarged number of vantage points, particularly in more independent subcommittees, stimulated increased congressional surveillance of the administration.[22] Even the seemingly sacrosanct Central Intelligence Agency came in for substantial scrutiny. Watergate revelations triggered major investigations of the CIA, which led directly to House and Senate creation of intelligence committees, charged to oversee the intelligence community. In addition, a 1974 amendment to the foreign aid bill (the Hughes-Ryan amendment) required the CIA to report "covert operations" that it conducted, or had carried out on its behalf, to "the appropriate committees of the Congress," four in each chamber. More specifically, Congress came increasingly to employ the legislative veto during the 1970s. Found in a variety of forms,[23] the veto

---

19. J. W. Fox and S. W. Hammond, *Congressional Staffs: The Invisible Force in American Lawmaking* (New York: Free Press, 1977); M. J. Malbin, *Unelected Representatives: Congressional Staff and the Future of Representative Government* (New York: Basic Books, 1980).

20. S. E. Frantzich, "Computerized Information Technology in the U. S. House of Representatives," *Legislative Studies Quarterly* 4 (1979): 255-280.

21. M. S. Ogul, *Congress Oversees the Bureaucracy: Studies in Legislative Supervision* (Pittsburgh, Pa.: University of Pittsburgh Press, 1976).

22. J. D. Aberbach, "Changes in Congressional Oversight," *American Behavioral Scientist* 22 (1979): 493-515; Dodd and Schott, *Congress and the Administrative State*, ch. 6.

23. Both chambers, either house, or even a single committee—through requirements that an agency "come into agreement" with it before acting—can exercise the veto, usually by enacting resolutions of disapproval (although the statute many permit inaction to indicate disapproval) within a specified (usually between thirty and ninety days) period. The one-house veto, providing for either House or Senate to block executive action, remains con-

reserves to Congress, or some part of it, the opportunity to block or delay executive actions—reorganizations, arms sales, agency regulations—within a specified time period. Fundamentally, the veto permits the legislature to prevent executives from acting, though they are authorized by law to do so, when some significant number of lawmakers disagrees with the proposed administrative conduct. Both the War Powers Resolution and the impoundment title of the Budget Act contain congressional veto provisions, as do more than 150 other statutes, many enacted since 1975.[24]

Here, too, a convenient justification for congressional challenge to the executive seemingly provides the basis for reform. To redress the imbalance in institutional power between the two elected branches requires reassertion of legislative authority over military, budget, and administrative matters. But here, too, other purposes may well have supplemented the avowed justification. Ideological intentions figured prominently in both the war powers and budget bills. Those, mainly liberals, who opposed involvement in Southeast Asia led the fight to curb the commander-in-chief. Liberals and conservatives, for quite different reasons, joined forces to support budgetary reform. The former expected the new process to provide more funds for social programs and less for defense; the latter hoped for the reverse and, in addition, were eager to see the budget committees control spending—particularly of the "backdoor" variety—and balance the budget.

The Budget Act also involves considerations of policy effectiveness and personal power. To the extent that the new budget committees can seize control of the budget process, they may be able to centralize congressional operations; their proposals, in effect, would be the legislature's financial decisions. Such circumstances would certainly expedite budgeting, but would exact a major price from the traditionally powerful revenue and

---

troversial; all recent presidents have resisted it, as an unconstitutional derogation of the separation of powers principle, but the courts steadfastly refused to resolve the issue. In December 1980, however, a federal appeals court ruled that a one-house veto provision that permits either chamber to reverse orders of the Immigration and Naturalization Service violates the separation of powers principle. If the Supreme Court sustains the decision, the executive's position relative to Congress would be greatly strengthened.

24. J. R. Bolton, *The Legislative Veto: Unseparating the Powers* (Washington, D.C.: The American Enterprise Institute, 1977); R. S. Gilmour, "The New Congressional Oversight and Administrative Leadership" (Paper presented to the Everett McKinley Dirksen Congressional Leadership Research Center—Sam Rayburn Library Conference, Understanding Congressional Leadership: The State of the Art, 1980); W. P. Schaefer and J. A. Thurber, "The Causes, Characteristics, and Political Consequences of the Legislative Veto" (Paper presented to the annual meeting of the Southern Political Science Association, 1980).

appropriations panels. Members of the latter, quite obviously, have a stake in resisting the budget committees, and much of the early experience under the 1974 act has reflected maneuvering among the old and the new committees.[25] Use of the legislative veto involves similar possibilities. If granted to full chambers, the veto may help Congress centralize control over a sprawling bureaucracy; if committees or subcommittees—in reality, perhaps, their chairpersons—exercise the veto, the device will enhance the authority of congressional participants in those now widely noted and ubiquitous "cozy triangles" or policy subgovernments.[26] Schaefer and Thurber argue that the veto is more likely to facilitate member reelection goals and personal power, among other things, than to promote coordinated congressional control of administration.[27] Again, a relatively acceptable motive—to redress legislative grievances against a too-powerful presidency—may conceal almost as much as it reveals about the intent of congressional reformers.

Reforms for Internal Efficiency: Centralizing Congress

A third cluster of reforms was a response to a perceived inefficiency in congressional performance. A decentralized decision-making structure impeded coherent policy formulation, and the reformers professed a desire to make it easier for Congress to act. These reforms sought to strengthen the party leader and to reduce the possibilities for minority obstructionism. Most of the action was in the House, where a few steps were taken to

25. L. T. LeLoup, "Budgeting in the U. S. Senate: Old Ways of Doing New Things" (Paper presented to the annual meeting of the Midwest Political Science Association, 1979); idem, "Process Versus Policy: The U. S. House Budget Committee," *Legislative Studies Quarterly* 4 (1979): 227-254. Indeed, the House sought to protect its major financial committees. Appropriations and Ways and Means members were to sit on the Budget Committee, and service on the latter was limited to two (later increased to three) terms. The House Budget Committee, under these constraints, would be less likely to emerge as a challenger to the customary wielders of budgetary influence.

26. R. B. Ripley and G. A. Frankin, *Congress, the Bureaucracy, and Public Policy*, rev. ed. (Homewood, Ill.: The Dorsey Press, 1980); R. H. Davidson, "Breaking Up Those 'Cozy Triangles': An Impossible Dream?", in *Legislative Reform and Public Policy*, ed. S. Welch and J. Peters (New York: Praeger, 1977), pp. 30-53.

27. Schaefer and Thurber, "Legislative Veto"; see also M. P. Fiorina, *Congress—Keystone of the Washington Establishment* (New Haven, Ct.: Yale University Press, 1977); and idem, "Control of the Bureaucracy: A Mismatch of Incentives and Capabilities," in *The Presidency and the Congress: A Shifting Balance of Power?*, ed. W. S. Livingston, L. C. Dodd, and R. L. Schott (Austin, Tex.: Lyndon B. Johnson Library, 1979), pp. 124-142.

enlarge the capacity of the majority Democrats to impose some partisan discipline.

Specifically, the party—the caucus and its leader, the Speaker —was granted additional authority while the committees, the chief roadblocks to legislative responsibility, were in some ways brought to heel. Party power was enlarged on several fronts. The caucus won the right to determine who would chair the committees, breaching the seniority rule; in 1975, it actually ousted three elderly southern oligarchs from their posts.[28] Appropriations subcommittee chairs were also subject to caucus scrutiny. In addition, the Democrats created a Steering and Policy Committee that, eventually, came to make committee assignments as well as to advise on party policy positions. Finally, the caucus assumed the power to instruct the Rules Committee, to prevent favored programs from expiring in that sometimes defiant committee.

The Speaker's new authority included personal power to appoint Rules Committee members, to yoke that panel firmly to the leadership. He was also given a major voice in the new Steering and Policy Committee. Half its members were his appointees and, presumably, loyal supporters. In addition, the Speaker was granted new ability to regulate the flow of legislation to and from committee consideration, and to create ad hoc committees to facilitate coherent treatment of complex policy issues. Finally, the leadership began to supplement existing techniques of vote gathering with the use of informal task forces as a means to increase party cohesion. On the Senate side, a modest committee reform, which a Temporary Select (Stevenson) Committee to Study the Senate Committee System proposed, and the chamber accepted in 1977, gave the leadership some new controls over bill referrals and scheduling.[29]

A few other reforms with implications for efficiency were adopted in the

---

28. B. Hinckley, "Seniority, 1975: Old Theories Confront New Facts," *British Journal of Political Science* 6 (1976): 383-399.

29. B. I. Oppenheimer, "The Changing Relationship Between House Leadership and the Committee on Rules" (Paper presented to the Everett McKinley Dirksen Congressional Leadership Research Center—Sam Rayburn Library Conference, Understanding Congressional Leadership: The State of the Art, 1980). At the start of the Ninety-Seventh Congress, Speaker O'Neill enlarged the Steering and Policy Committee from twenty-four to thirty. The top five party leaders, thirteen Speaker's appointees, and twelve members whom the caucus elects from geographical regions constitute the committee (*National Journal* 12 : 2137). Needless to say the Speaker's influence would be felt on the panel. See also D. Vogler, "The Rise of Ad Hoc Committees in the House of Representatives: An Application of New Research Perspectives" (Paper presented to the annual meeting of the American Political

1970s. As noted, the new budget process contains considerable potential for centralization. A series of rules changes, largely directed to eliminate dilatory tactics, was designed to curtail the minority's ability to subvert the majority. The most significant of these, of course, is the weakening of the Senate filibuster. The number of votes needed to end debate was reduced from two-thirds of those present and voting (a maximum of sixty-seven; sixty-four or sixty-five under ordinary circumstances) to a constitutional three-fifths majority (sixty votes). The possibilities for a postcloture "filibuster by amendment" were largely eliminated by a 1979 change that mandated that the vote on final passage must come within 100 hours after cloture is invoked.[30]

Finally, both chambers sought to realign and rationalize their committee jurisdictions. In the House, the defenders of the status quo managed to remove all but the most routine features of the Select (Bolling) Committee on Committees' 1974 reform proposals, substituting a much milder set of changes that the caucus's (Hansen) Committee on Organization, Study, and Review suggested. The resulting reform was more cosmetic than anything else with respect to committee jurisdictions. In the Senate, the reformers fared better; they won approval of modest but meaningful committee changes. The number of committees declined from 31 in the Ninety-Fourth Congress to 24 in the Ninety-Fifth. Subcommittees declined from 174 to 117. In consequence senators had an average of eleven full and subcommittee assignments in the latter Congress, down from eighteen in the former. More importantly, jurisdictions were rationalized somewhat, though considerably less than the Stevenson Committee initially proposed.[31]

Like popular approval and reviving the separation of powers, efficiency (or effectiveness or responsibility) provided a convenient and acceptable

---

Science Association, 1978); L. C. Dodd and T. Sullivan, "Partisan Vote Gathering in the U. S. House of Representatives: Concepts, Measures, Models, and Propositions" (Paper presented to the Everett McKinley Dirksen Congressional Leadership Research Center—Sam Rayburn Library Conference, Understanding Congressional Leadership: The State of the Art, 1980); B. Sinclair, "The Speaker's Task Force as a Leadership Strategy for Coping with the Post-Reform House" (Paper presented to the annual meeting of the American Political Science Association, 1980); J. H. Parris, "The Senate Reorganizes its Committees," *Political Science Quarterly* 94 (1979): 319-337.

30. See *Congressional Quarterly Weekly Report* 33 (1975): 2721-2722; and 37 (1979): 319-320.

31. R. H. Davidson and W. J. Oleszek, *Congress Against Itself* (Bloomington, Ind.: Indiana University Press, 1977).

justification for reform. As with these other structural alterations, strengthening the parties and the Speaker of the House, undercutting minority power, and reorganizing committee jurisdictions had implications beyond efficiency. Centralization in general should increase the influence of Congress against the executive; a strong legislature is better situated to impose its preferences on the administration. A disciplined legislature, enacting programs, should also look good to the citizens, leading to a rise in its popular standing. More significantly, of course, policy and personal goals may also be achieved. Those in command of an efficient policy process—the party leaders—will have a loud voice in the programs such a process produces as well as considerable personal power to promote their own purposes. Jurisdictional realignments, especially in the Senate, did move programs from one committee to another. That so many more moves were rejected, however, makes clear that whatever the intrinsic attractiveness of arguments about effectiveness, it will readily yield in the face of practical pressures relating to influence and ideology.[32]

Reforms for Internal Influence: Democratizing Congress

Last, but by no means least, dissatisfied lawmakers were unwilling to forego the opportunity to improve their own positions in Congress. Many members, especially the liberal and junior legislators, chafed under the restrictions on their participation and policy influence that the old, committee-dominated regime imposed. The committee chair, often in collaboration with the ranking minority member, dominated the panel. Strengthening the parties through centralization was one way to circumvent recalcitrant committee leaders, but the reformers were not content to rely exclusively on such steps. They quickly seized on the reform mood to impose reforms that enhanced their own individual circumstances. In so doing, they adopted decentralizing changes that frequently ran counter to other changes, especially because much influence that previously rested with committee chairpersons now devolved to autonomous subcommittees.

Substantial pieces of committee power were reallocated to the rank-and-file. Such shifts were particularly pronounced in the more hierarchical House, where first of all members were limited to one subcommittee chair

---

32. Committees with strong subsystem allies—external clienteles and sympathetic bureaucrats—like Veterans' Affairs were successful in fending off proposed changes that would have cost them their influence if not their very existence (see ibid.; and Parris, "The Senate Reorganizes its Committees").

each. In addition, no individual could select a second subcommittee assignment until each full committee member had secured one subcommittee position. Equivalent changes in the Senate —limiting chairmanships and allocating subcommittee assignments more equitably—effectively guaranteed that in each chamber members could gain a "piece of the action," in a subcommittee, earlier in their careers.

The House went further. The Democratic Caucus, in 1973, adopted the "subcommittee bill of rights" to protect the independence of sub-committees.[33] The bill of rights required that subcommittees have fixed jurisdictions and that legislation on these subjects be referred automatically to them. It permitted subcommittees to meet at the pleasure of their members, to write their own rules, and to control their own budgets and staffs. Moreover, two years later, the caucus mandated that all committees with more than twenty members create a minimum of four subcommittees. The upshot of these changes has been to establish an "institutionalized" sub-committee system, with active, permanent, and independent panels.[34] Subcommittee members are strategically located to exert considerable influence over matters in their jurisdiction (though such areas may be quite narrow). Resources were also distributed more evenly in the Senate; for instance, in 1975, S. Res. 60 gave each senator a staff assistant for each committee on which he or she served, to aid with committee work.[35]

In sum, these changes have made the House more like the Senate.[36] Both chambers are decentralized. Committee chairpersons must, under threat of ouster, share their authority with full committee majorities and subcommittee leaders. In general, more people, operating from more secure power bases, now have the potential to shape legislative activity. This influence is entrenched in autonomous subcommittees. These reforms do democratize Congress, but they also serve other purposes as well. For the individual member, ensconced in a subcommittee seat that carries with it staff and

---

33. D. W. Rohde, "Committee Reform in the House of Representatives and Subcommittee Bill of Rights," *Annals* 411 (1974): 39-47; N. J. Ornstein, "Causes and Consequences of Congressional Change: Subcommittee Reforms in the House of Representatives, 1970-1973," in Ornstein, *Evolution and Reform*, pp. 88-114; and the sources cited in note 6.

34. S. H. Haeberle, "The Institutionalization of the Subcommittee in the U. S. House of Representatives," *Journal of Politics* 40 (1978): 1054-1065.

35. S. W. Hammond, "Congressional Change and Reform: Staffing the Congress," in Rieselbach, *Legislative Reform*, pp. 181-193.

36. R. B. Ripley, *Power in the Senate* (New York: St. Martin's, 1969).

other resources, policy influence is a real possibility. So, too, is participation in cozy triangles; since the subcommittee has jurisdiction, its members can contribute to the policy that the subsystem manages. And of course policy influence is readily convertible, through advertising and credit claiming, into reelection currency.[37] Democratization, in short, is readily defensible (who can quarrel with the values of equality and participation), but it also entails other, more mundane and personal political considerations.

Other Congressional Change: New Members and New Issues

Whatever the difficulties—and there are many—in disentangling real motives from rationalization for these four sets of congressional reforms, the problem is further compounded because reform, as a conscious effort, is deeply enmeshed in, and influenced by, broader currents of change. Not only must analysts seek to assess the effect of a multitude of reforms, adopted over a period of time, for a variety of reasons; they must also try to separate the impact of reforms, whatever intentions underlie them, from other, unplanned and unpredictable forces. Two such forces—member turnover and agenda change—seem particularly important for understanding recent congressional change.

In the 1960s, when Polsby wrote, congressional membership was indeed stable. Turnover was low. In the Ninety-First House, elected in 1968, there were thirty-six freshmen (twenty-three members of the Ninetieth retired; thirteen lost their reelection bids); 8 percent, that is, were serving their first term while 18 percent were in their tenth term or beyond. A decade later, in the Ninety-Sixth House, there were seventy-seven freshmen (18 percent) replacing forty-nine retirees and twenty-four election losers, and members with ten or more terms of service constituted 13 percent of the House. In the Senate, the story is the same. Turnover increased dramatically. In the Ninety-First Senate, there were fourteen freshmen (replacing six retirees and eight losers); in the Ninety-Sixth, there were twenty (succeeding ten retirees and ten election victims). From an alternative vantage point, 31 percent of the Ninety-First Senate had less than a full term of service, while ten years later the figure was 48 percent.[38] There was, in short, an infusion of much "new blood" in Congress during the 1970s.

---

37. Mayhew, *The Electoral Connection*; see also Fiorina, *Keystone of the Washington Establishment*.

38. J. F. Bibby, T. E. Mann, and N. J. Ornstein, *Vital Statistics on Congress, 1980* (Washington, D.C.: The American Enterprise Institute, 1980), tables 1-7, 1-8, 3-6, and 3-7. Any two

New members created new conditions, propitious for reform, in Congress. Many of the newcomers were young, and relatively liberal— persons who, in consequence of the Vietnam and Watergate traumas, were loath to accept the legislature as it was. Indeed, many of them had campaigned against Congress and felt obliged to carry out their reform suggestions. They were reluctant to adhere to the norms that characterized Congress, declining in particular to serve an apprenticeship or to defer mindlessly to presumed committee expertise.[39] These newcomers, numerous and independent-minded, were the catalysts for reform; they both created and channelled the reform movement, and without their presence in Washington, the history of the decade would most certainly have been different.

The period also saw the emergence of a host of new issues, or old issues in new guises. Old rules of thumb, "standing decisions," were of little or no help on these questions. Watergate, in its myriad manifestations, was unprecedented; Vietnam aroused passions unlike those known previously. The Arab oil embargo unleashed an unanticipated and unmanageable (in the short run at least) "energy crisis." "Stagflation," an undiagnosed economic malady, left the nation pained with simultaneous inflation and high

---

Congresses are, of course, not perfectly typical. Here, however, the evidence of high turnover is clear. In the House, for instance, the percentage of representatives with three or fewer terms of service (the relatively junior) was 37 in the Ninety-First Congress; 34 in the Ninety-Second; and 37 in the Ninety-Third; for the three subsequent Congresses, the figures were 44, 49 and 50. It is worth noting that the basis for this high turnover in the two chambers differs markedly, especially since 1976. Before that year, incumbents had good prospects for reelection; from 1966 to 1974, for example, never less than 88 percent of House incumbents or 71 percent of sitting senators who sought another term were successful (the mean success rates for these five elections were 92 percent in the House and 79 percent for the Senate). Since then, however, the situation has changed: House incumbents continue to succeed in retaining their seats; over 90 percent of those running won (even in the face of the Reagan 1980 landslide, 90.3 percent of House incumbents held their positions). In the Senate, in sharp contrast, the incumbent advantage declined drastically. The 1976, 1978, and 1980 elections saw the incumbent success rate fall to 64, 60, and 55.2 percent, respectively. Thus, House turnover reflects voluntary departures from Congress, while Senate membership change reflects the voter's preferences more directly. In any event, turnover has increased substantially.

39. Compare H. B. Asher, "The Learning of Legislative Norms," *American Political Science Review* 67 (1973): 499-513; D. W. Rohde, N. J. Ornstein, and R. L. Peabody, "Political Change and Legislative Norms in the United States Senate" (Paper presented to the annual meeting of the American Political Science Association, 1974); J. Fishel and B. A. Loomis, "Old Norms and New Members in the New Congress: Change and Continuity, 1965-1976" (unpublished manuscript, n.d.); with Matthews, *U. S. Senators and Their World*, and R. F. Fenno, Jr., "The Internal Distribution of Influence: The House," in *The Congress and America's Future*, ed. D.B. Truman, 2nd ed. (Englewood Cliffs, N.J.: Prentice-Hall, 1973), pp. 63-90.

unemployment. And emotional matters, like busing and abortion, engaged new "single-issue" pressure groups and subjected members of Congress to new forms of external influence. This altered agenda created new conditions for Congress. The need to deal with (or to duck) these matters colored the climate in which the legislature acted, including the sorts of reforms various members envisioned.

Summary

It is indisputable that considerable congressional change occurred during the 1970s; procedural reform was prominent, but not exclusive, among these changes. Acting in its usual fashion—that is, sequentially and incrementally, without much overall coordination— Congress enacted four distinct sets of reforms: to regain public approval, to restore its competitive position against the executive, to render its internal operations more efficient, and to reallocate internal influence. Each set seems to have served purposes other than these commonly cited justifications; members pursued these reforms for mixed motives. Finally, these consciously adopted reforms were passed in the context of, and shaped by, a broader set of unplanned changes, reflecting both substantial membership turnover and an agenda filled with new and challenging issues. The precise impact of reform, as distinct from all forms of change, is extraordinarily difficult to specify precisely.

Change, Reform, and Congressional Performance

It is nevertheless possible—though hazardous, given the recency of the developments—to use some admittedly incomplete and impressionistic evidence to outline and evaluate what reform has accomplished. The obvious generalization is the easy one—the results of reform have been many and varied. Reformers' intentions have sometimes been realized, and sometimes not; in other instances, their efforts seem to have produced quite unintended, and often undesirable, consequences. Moreover, this seems to be the case within each of the four categories of reform outlined previously.

A More Accountable Congress?

In a simple sense, requiring Congress to act in the sunshine has achieved its purpose. It appears that the public has substantially increased opportunities to inform itself about congressional deliberations and commitments. Each type of reform has done a good deal to open up legislators' activities and accounts to citizens and the media. The vast majority of congressional proceedings—from subcommittee to conference committee—are now public sessions; more than 90 percent of committee meetings are open. Members duly file, and the media publicize, their financial disclosure data. Similarly, the Federal Election Commission collects and disseminates candidates' campaign finance information. Yet these reforms have produced unforeseen side effects that appear to alter congressional performance.

Visible legislative operations, for example, have had repercussions that some observers find disturbing. For one thing, there is little if any persuasive evidence that citizens, in fact, do pay greater attention to Congress. For another, with committee proceedings and voting now matters of public record, lawmakers can no longer hide behind closed doors and unrecorded votes; they must act in the open. With constituents and campaign contributors watching, they must take care to protect their electoral flanks. As single-issue groups and PACs become more numerous and more forceful, sitting legislators may be less willing to risk offending any potentially decisive electoral force. Prudence dictates caution, and lawmakers may feel obliged to resist party or presidential calls for support. Where previously members could help out undetected, in the quiet of the committee room or on a standing or teller vote on the floor, at present there are dangers in doing so.[40] The observer, more likely a group than a citizen, has greater influence in the more public setting of contemporary congressional politics. Members may be loath to act at all, preferring to entrench themselves electorally by being ombudsmen, by claiming credit for serving the district, or by limiting their policy making to "position taking," choosing sides on substantive questions only when it is safe to do so or obfuscating their stands to minimize the risk of being caught on the wrong side of a policy issue that turns out to be controversial.[41]

Neither has financial disclosure, which House and Senate ethics codes mandated, had much visible effect. There is scant evidence that members

---

40. Froman and Ripley, "Conditions for Party Leadership".

41. Fiorina, *Keystone of the Washington Establishment*; Mayhew, *The Electoral Connection*. The party leaders recognize this caution clearly. As House Speaker O'Neill has noted, "Members are more home-oriented. They no longer have to follow the national philosophy of the party. They can get reelected on their newsletter, or on how they serve their constituents" (I.B. Arieff, "House, Senate Chiefs Attempt to Lead a Changed Congress," *Congressional Quarterly Weekly Report* 38 [1980]: 2695-2700).

are forced to think twice before they act in ways that might leave them vulnerable to charges of conflict of interest. There has been no diminution in the frequency of ethical problems representatives and senators have encountered since the codes were adopted. In the recent period, the House has censured Charles Diggs and Charles Wilson for their financial dealings, and expelled Michael Myers, snared in the Abscam net; the Senate "denounced" Herman Talmadge. Others involved in Abscam have chosen to resign, presumably to avoid expulsion. But if there has been no reduction in malfeasance in the immediate postreform period, the future may be more promising. In 1980, the voters delivered a resounding verdict (matched only by those in the courts), retiring from office all save one of those accused. Still, these are dramatic cases—featuring videotapes of money changing hands and allegations of coat pockets stuffed with cash —and the effect of disclosure statutes on more mundane conflicts of interest (e.g., self-serving, but legal behavior) remains problematic.

Finally, campaign finance reform has led to paradoxical results. On the one hand, the new election system—with limits on contributions, but none on expenditures, and with full disclosure provisions—has seemingly helped to entrench incumbents, especially in the House. With presidential campaigns now federally funded in full, private groups, particularly the newly legitimized PACs, have channeled their resources into congressional contests. Federal Election Commission and Common Cause studies suggest that these donors have preferred the safe course of contributing to incumbents, who hold potentially powerful positions in Congress, to the riskier strategy of funding challengers, who might someday hold prominent posts.[42] Incumbents start with sizable advantages, inherent in the perquisites of office, and unless their opponents can raise and spend significant sums—probably more than $200,000—their prospects range from dismal to nil.[43] Jacobson concludes that "any measure that limits the

---

42. Jacobson, *Money in Congressional Elections*; Alexander, *Financing Politics*. This concentration of contributions to sitting members many alter in the 1980s. The rise of ideological groups, such as the National Conservative Political Action Committee (NCPAC) and the evangelical Christian movement's Moral Majority (see the four-part series, *New York Times*, August 17-20, 1980), that support challengers, or at least oppose incumbents, became visible in 1980. Preliminary figures for that year indicate that PACs have begun to give greater support to "out party" candidates; while incumbents still received greater contributions, their advantage was sharply reduced (see *National Journal* 12 [1980]: 1851).

43. Mayhew, *The Electoral Connection*; Fiorina, *Keystone of the Washington Establishment*; Jacobsen, *Money in Congressional Elections*.

money available to candidates benefits incumbents."[44] Certainly, contribution controls appear to have hindered hard-pressed House challengers. Senate contests, by contrast, tend to be more competitive. Challengers are more visible and attractive, better able to solicit the funds they need, and in consequence more likely to unseat the incumbent.[45]

On the other hand, public scrutiny—the combination of campaign finance and personal disclosure requirements—has made life more difficult for members of Congress and record numbers have chosen to retire rather than risk the relentless exposure of their daily routines, and those of their families, to popular examination. Moreover, many of those leaving are relatively young—in their fifties —and have substantial seniority, already holding positions of some prominence and power in Congress. The rise of aggressive investigative reporting in the wake of Watergate no doubt accounts, in part at least, for the increase in attention to the personal lives of legislators; events formerly left unreported—alcoholism, family problems, financial dealings, even brushes with the law—are now fair game for the media. In any case, many lawmakers have found the rewards of legislative service lacking and have chosen to pursue their careers elsewhere.[46] In the four elections from 1966 through 1972, House retirements averaged 18.5, while a mean of 4.75 senators declined to seek reelection; for the subsequent four elections, 1974 to 1980, the figures were 43.3 and 7.5.

In sum, while congressional activity is certainly more accessible to citizens, the fragmentary evidence accumulated in the short time the sunshine reforms have been in effect suggests that the public is not really more aware of, or more sympathetic to, Congress or its members, their activities, or their performance. Citizens seem no better able to *recall* the incumbent's name, though more can *recognize* it when it is presented to them; there has been no visible increase in issue-based voting in congressional elections.[47] Incumbency and partisanship more than policy positions shape voter con-

---

44. Jacobson, *Money in Congressional Elections*, p. 194.

45. B. Hinckley, "House Reelections and Senate Defeats: The Role of the Challenger" (Paper presented to the annual meeting of the American Political Science Association, 1979).

46. For example, Rep. John J. Cavanaugh, thirty-five years old, well regarded in his district and in the House, retired in 1980 after two terms, in part because "the continuous campaigning is debilitating and the campaign financing is corrupting" (B. Gamarekian, "A Congressman Who's Going Home Again," *New York Times*, August 31, 1980, p. 20). See also Rep. Otis Pike's "retirement speech" (*Congressional Quarterly Weekly Report* 36 [1978]: 528-529).

47. J. A. Ferejohn, "On the Decline of Competition in Congressional Elections," *American Political Science Review* 71 (1977): 166-176; T. E. Mann, *Unsafe at Any Margin: Interpreting*

sideration of Congress and congressional candidates. The *potential* for citizen-enforced accountability is real, but unrealized. In fact, visibility may contribute to legislative inertia. Rather than acting publicly lawmakers may find it safer not to act at all.

An Institutionally More Powerful Congress?

Nowhere is the difficulty in disentangling the effects of reform from those of more general change more obvious than in the effort to evaluate the impact of the congressional challenge to the executive branch. The War Powers Resolution and the Budget Act were passed during a period of popular discontent, rapid turnover in Congress, and a scandal-ridden and politically vulnerable presidency. Moreover, there has been (fortunately) no clear test of the War Powers Resolution and the new budget process has not yet fallen into a clearly established pattern.

Nevertheless, the available evidence suggests that Congress has not yet used its newly claimed authority to impose its will on the executive, especially in the military realm. On five occasions, the president has felt obliged to report to Congress in compliance with the War Powers Resolution. Only two were controversial: Ford's recapture of the ship *Mayaguez*, seized by Cambodia, and Carter's abortive effort to rescue the American hostages in Iran. Each episode lasted only a few hours; neither really offered Congress a chance to act in any meaningful fashion. Each president complied with the letter, if not the spirit, of the statute; and in Carter's case, legislative acquiescence with minimal protest is not a promising precedent, given the long planning period during which the administration could easily have consulted with appropriate members of Congress.

In reality Congress has the opportunity to participate in military policy making only when troops remain in the field for substantial periods. In these circumstances, Congress can act decisively, ordering the troops home if it wishes, or by default, doing nothing and thus requiring the president to cease military operations. The issue, of course, is whether the legislature will act, imposing its preferences on the commander-in-chief, who will most certainly invoke the "national interest," the nation's prestige and

---

Congressional Elections (Washington, D.C.: American Enterprise Institute, 1978); K. L. Tedin and R. W. Murray, "Public Awareness of Congressional Representatives: Recall versus Recognition," *American Politics Quarterly* 7 (1979): 509-517; T. E. Mann and R. E. Wolfinger, "Candidates and Parties in Congressional Elections," *American Political Science Review* 74 (1980): 617-632.

honor, and the gravity of the situation. There is no cause to believe with certainty that members of Congress would, in such circumstances, be prepared to run the risk or assume the responsibility for overruling the chief executive.

More speculatively, the War Powers Resolution may be significant less after the fact of military involvement than as a prior deterrent to precipitous, or dubious armed intervention. Presidents can never be entirely certain that Congress will approve their actions, and they may calculate carefully about congressional response before commiting troops. For example, there was widespread speculation that the Ford administration was considering direct intervention, in 1974, in the civil war in Angola. The foreign policy committees of Congress, especially the Senate Foreign Relations Committee, became increasingly concerned, given the perceived lessons of our Indochina involvement, that American commitment of money and military supplies might escalate into military support of our favored faction. Such forthright expression of concern may well have contributed to executive caution. No use of American troops was ever officially proposed.[48] Whether such actions truly constrain the president is difficult to determine; if they do, whether this is desirable depends on the observer's view of the president and/or the policy that military intervention would seek to pursue.

More generally, Congress's success in imposing its military and foreign policy judgments on the executive is uneven. On the one hand, Congress has flexed its institutional muscle frequently. The Senate refused to ratify SALT II; the legislature has repeatedly blocked or delayed (using the legislative veto) arms sales, the export of nuclear materials, and numerous treaties with neighboring nations (e.g., maritime treaties with Mexico and Canada failed in 1980). Franck and Weisband see in these actions a beneficial and enduring reassertion of congressional foreign policy powers.[49]

On the other hand, some signs point to a revival of legislative deference to the executive. Heightened conflict with the Soviet Union has undercut

---

48. Just to be certain, Congress added an amendment, by overwhelming margins in each chamber, to the Defense Department appropriations bill forbidding the expenditure of any funds for "any activities involving Angola directly or indirectly." Since CIA funds were hidden in the DOD appropriation, this action removed the legal basis for either overt or covert intervention in Angola.

49. Franck and Wiesband, *Foreign Policy by Congress*; see also C. V. Crabb, Jr., and P. M. Holt, *Invitation to Struggle: Congress, the President, and Foreign Policy* (Washington, D. C.: Congressional Quarterly Press, 1980).

liberal attacks on the defense budget; military spending seems certain to rise precipitously, and lawmakers may well give greater credence to the views of the professional military. For instance, Congress backed away from a comprehensive charter to regulate CIA intelligence activities, and while it did assert its right to prior notice of covert operations overseas, it also softened the Hughes-Ryan amendment, reducing from eight to two (the intelligence committees) the number of committees that the president must inform about CIA covert activities. Similarly, the fiscal 1981 foreign aid authorization bill relaxed a number of constraints on presidential discretion, enacted in response to the Indochina conflict, to employ aid funds flexibly. Furthermore, domestic problems with obvious electoral implications—the economy, or another energy "crisis"—may lead members to redirect their attention to the home front, leaving international matters to the executive.

In sum, while presidents can no longer count on customary congressional acquiescence to their foreign policy initiatives, the legislature's assertiveness may reflect less structural reform than more basic, evolutionary change—more members more willing, under the stimulus of political circumstances, to use basic legislative prerogatives to challenge the administration. Should membership and situations alter, the old pattern of congressional subordination might readily recur. Members' policy preferences and political purposes, more than institutional reassertion against the executive, may well be the decisive determinants of congressional performance.

Assessment of the new budget process yields a similar picture, complicated because the reforms have led to somewhat different results in the House and Senate. On the whole, Congress has observed the form of the new scheme. It has for the most part formulated a coherent budget, specifying revenues, outlays, and the size of the deficit. But it has done so with some departures from the prescribed timetable. Moreover, the Congressional Budget Office, "now considered the best source of budget numbers in Washington,"[50] provides the lawmakers with invaluable data with which to formulate independent budget proposals.[51] At a minimum, the Congress now looks at the federal budget from a far broader perspective than it did previously.

---

50. A. Wildavsky, *The Politics of the Budgetary Process*, 3rd ed. (Boston: Little Brown, 1979), p. 246.

51. J. A. Thurber, "New Powers of the Purse: An Assessment of Congressional Budget Reform," in Rieselbach, *Legislative Reform*, pp. 159-172.

The Senate seems particularly well positioned to make the process work. Its Budget Committee, a permanent panel, prospered under bipartisan leadership from Sens. Edmund Muskie, the chair, and Henry Bellmon, the ranking minority member. The committee has been cautious, careful to conform to the chamber's norms, to accomodate Senate power centers, and to avoid posing direct challenges to the existing committees. The full chamber, in consequence, seems satisfied with the operation of the new process.[52] Whether satisfaction will survive in the Ninety-Seventh Congress, with Republican control placing Pete Domenici in the chair and Ernest Hollings in the ranking minority member's seat, is another matter. The situation in the House is quite different. Motives beyond a more rational budget process seem to have induced the lower chamber to seek to limit the potential of its budget committee. That panel, with its restrictions on members' continuous service and required representation of other revenue-related committees and the party leadership within its ranks, has become a partisan and ideological battleground. Because it does not offer long-term possibilities for internal influence, committee assignments have tended to go to liberal Democrats and conservative Republicans who, in pursuing their policy predilections, have left the panel polarized and volatile.[53] Partisanship has, in fact, threatened the process in the House, which has been hard pressed to comply with the act, often passing the budget resolutions late and by slender margins.

In the final analysis, of course, the question is whether the revised procedures influence budgetary decisions, and here the evidence is neither clear nor consistent. Some observers suggest congressional budgets for fiscal years 1976 and 1977 differed "significantly" from President Ford's proposals, but to what extent the variance reflects natural enmity between branches controlled by opposing political parties rather than the budget

---

52. LeLoup, "Budgeting in the U. S. Senate." This is not to suggest that there was no conflict between the Budget Committee and other committees (see, for example, L. Fisher, "Congressional Budget Reform: Committee Conflicts" [Paper presented to the annual meeting of the Midwest Political Science Association, 1975]; C. Rudder, "The Impact of the Budget and Impoundment Control Act of 1974 on the Revenue Committees of the U. S. Congress" [Paper presented to the annual meeting of the American Political Science Association, 1977]; and Havemann, *Congress and the Budget*). It is to suggest rather that the Senate panel sought accomodation rather than confrontation during the early phases of the new process. See also Wildavsky, *The Politics of the Budgetary Process*; and Thurber, "New Powers of the Purse".

53. LeLoup, "Process versus Policy"; Fisher, "Congressional Budget Reform."

process itself remains difficult to determine.[54] In contrast, other analysts, looking at later years, find congressional impact moderate to low during the Carter administration. Huddleston claims that the act has produced "no major shifts in spending priorities."[55] Since it is impossible to divine "what might have been" without the reforms, the most reasonable conclusion seems to be that the new procedures have put the Congress in a better position to assert and sustain its positions if, and when, it chooses to do so.

More important, perhaps, the ability of the budget committees to impose their preferences on the standing committees, and thus to centralize the budget process, may be increasing. In attempting, admittedly for election year political purposes, to balance the fiscal 1981 budget, the committee used a "reconciliation" procedure, never previously invoked, to force eight substantive committees in each house to reduce expenditures. When the House Education and Labor Committee balked, the Senate budget panel successfully urged the upper chamber to reject a conference report on higher education legislation, forcing the House to make the cut.[56] Congress, after considerable acrimony and the largest conference in history (with more than 100 participants), cleared a reconciliation bill that saved some $8 billion—although less than the first budget resolution had sought and insufficient to achieve a balanced budget.[57] Should such precedent become firmly established, budget committee superiority to the authorizing bodies might enable the former to dominate the budget decisions both within Congress and against the executive.[58]

With respect to impoundment, the Budget Act has had a clear and

---

54. J. P. Pfiffner, "Executive Control and the Congressional Budget" (Paper presented to the annual meeting of the Midwest Political Science Association, 1977); Thurber, "New Powers of the Purse"; A. Schick, "Whose Budget? It All Depends on Whether the President or Congress is Doing the Counting," in Livingston, Dodd, and Schott, *The Presidency and the Congress*, pp. 96-123.

55. Wildavsky, *The Politics of the Budgetary Process*, pp. 254-262; LeLoup, "Budgeting in the U. S. Senate," and idem, "Process versus Policy"; M. W. Huddleston, "Training Lobsters to Fly: Assessing the Impact of the 1974 Congressional Budget Reform" (Paper presented to the annual meeting of the Midwest Political Science Association, 1979).

56. *Congressional Quarterly Weekly Report* 38 (1980): 2758.

57. Ibid., pp. 3487-3488.

58. The future of reconciliation remains cloudy. Policy and reelection goals led members to use the reconciliation bill to enact substantive provisions (e.g., authorization of child nutrition programs) as well as the required revenue matters. Numerous lawmakers argued that this undercut the purposes of the reconciliation process and suggested the procedure itself needs reform.

pronounced effect. The president is now considerably less able to regulate the flow of federal funds. Impoundment for policy purposes, as Richard Nixon practiced it, is now virtually impossible without legislative acquiescence, and the burden has been transferred to the executive to win that approval.[59] When Congress appropriates, it is far more probable that the funds will be spent. Yet the anti-impoundment provisions have had unintended consequences as well. Traditionally, impoundment was a useful and noncontroversial device that promoted efficient administration. Now all matters, even the most routine deferrals, must be reported to Congress; members have complained that many hours are wasted on relatively trivial items, a concern that bureaucrats share.[60] More seriously, the law appears to give the president an opportunity to delay expenditures, temporarily at least, for policy purposes, authority never previously acknowledged. That is, the chief executive can propose rescissions that effectively withhold funds for the forty-five days until congressional inaction compels their release.[61] Overall, the Budget Act improves the legislature's chances to impose its priorities, if it is determined to do so. Whether it is, and what such decisiveness will accomplish over the long haul, of course, remain unclear.

Similar uncertainties appear about the results of the "information revolution." From one perspective, it is incontrovertible that members of Congress have substantially greater quantities of data than ever before. Enlarged staff resources, new agencies (Congressional Budget Office and Office of Technology Assessment), more effective old support facilities (General Accounting Office and Congressional Research Service), and increasing computer technology combine to expand enormously the congressional capacity to engage in serious analysis, which can sustain legislative alternatives to executive initiatives. These developments, however, are not necessarily an unmixed blessing.

For one thing, members of Congress may not have adequate incentive to seize these new opportunities. Fundamentally, in some, perhaps most, circumstances, senators and representatives are politicians rather than objective analysts. They may well be searching less for optimal policies than

59. W. G. Munselle, "Presidential Impoundment and Congressional Reform," in Rieselbach, *Legislative Reform*, pp. 173-181.

60. Pfiffner, "Executive Control and the Congressional Budget"; Wildavsky, *The Politics of the Budgetary Process*, p. 240.

61. Schick, "Whose Budget?", pp. 112-113.

for programs that will serve their political purposes. They want ideas that will satisfy their constituents—voters and supporting interest groups. They need solutions that will survive the bargaining and compromising of a decentralized legislature. Policy analysts who do not recognize the political needs of their principals will find their advice ignored. Where politics and analysis merge, the latter may be of considerable use to legislators; where they diverge, analysis is likely to receive low priority.[62]

Moreover, information that these reforms make available may actually distract lawmakers from programmatic activities. Too much data, "information overload," may overwhelm members. They may not know how to cope with what is available to them and they may be increasingly inclined to look to staff for substantive guidance.[63] Conversely, staff personnel who are prepared to be "entrepreneurs" rather than impartial "professionals" may come to play powerful roles.[64] Dependence on the experts may undercut the members' ability to exercise genuinely independent judgments. Finally, there is an information management problem; members may spend more time and energy administering large staffs than they do using the data that their information resources supply. While some offices now employ professional managers,[65] the risk remains that organizational confusion and chaos will intrude on legislators' ability to engage the substance of policy questions.

Finally, it is not certain that for all the increased attention Congress has paid to gaining control of a "runaway" bureaucracy, much has been accomplished. There has been more oversight activity—more hearings, more reports required, more legislative-bureaucratic contacts—but not necessarily more influence exerted, at least not coordinated management of the executive agencies.[66] This situation probably serves the purposes of most members of Congress; they prefer their personal power—for policy or reelection reasons—over some small segment of the bureaucracy to broader

---

62. On these matters, see C. O. Jones, "Why Congress Can't Do Policy Analysis (or words to that effect)," *Policy Analysis* 2 (1976): 251-264; A. Schick, "The Supply and Demand for Analysis on Capitol Hill," *Policy Analysis* 2 (1976): 215-234.

63. Malbin, *Unelected Representatives.*

64. D. E. Price, "Professionals and 'Entrepreneurs': Staff Orientations and Policy Making on Three Senate Committees," *Journal of Politics* 33 (1971): 316-336.

65. Hammond, "Congressional Change and Reform."

66. Dodd and Schott, *Congress and the Administrative State,* chs. 5-6.

forms of institutional control.[67] It is not that the legislature lacks the capacity to exercise significant oversight; rather members lack the incentives to conduct that oversight in ways that impair the cozy subsystem relationships that permit them to realize goals other than challenging the executive branch.[68]

Similar considerations undercut forceful use of the congressional veto. Congress increasingly reserves for itself the right to block bureaucratic actions, but it has actually vetoed few executive proposals. Its ability to do so, of course, may induce administrative caution, but particularly in domestic affairs there have been relatively few direct confrontations. Congress did veto four Education Department regulations and made its position stick, but on balance members seem content to protect or enhance their individual contacts with agencies of particular concern rather than engage in severe interbranch conflicts.[69] Again, motives beyond the original justification color the use of the veto.

In sum, Congress in the 1980s is better equipped institutionally to challenge presidential leadership. The reforms it has adopted—the War Powers Resolution, the Budget Act, strengthened analytic capacity—have placed the national legislature in a strong position to define and fight for its own priorities. But capability and its use are not necessarily synonymous. Whether Congress will, in fact, challenge the executive depends equally on less tangible factors—members' willingness to mount the attack, and events encouraging them to take up arms. This suggests, of course, that Congress can, but only sometimes will, marshal its available institutional might to do battle with the administration.

A More Effective (Centralized) Congress?

Congressional reformers sought not only to rearm the legislature against the executive, but also to reallocate authority internally. The standing committees, and their allegedly autocratic chairpersons, were the chief

---

67. Where some form of institutional control does seem warranted, Congress has increasingly used "riders" on authorization or appropriations bills to prohibit spending for particular purposes (e.g., to bar the Justice Department from committing money to institute any legal proceeding to require busing for desegregation) instead of the legislative veto.

68. Dodd and Schott, *Congress and the Administrative State*; Fiorina, "Control of the Bureaucracy."

69. R. E. Cohen, "Congress Steps Up Use of the Legislative Veto," *National Journal* 12 (1980): 1473-1477.

targets of reform. One thrust of the attack on the committee oligarchs—probably the least important—was to strengthen the political parties. More coheisve, centralized parties would be better able to move a program through Congress efficiently and effectively, to overcome the opportunities for delay and defeat built into a fragmented, pluralistic institution. In reality, the legislators were unwilling to surrender more than a modicum of their individual freedoms to the party leaders, and the movement toward centralization has proved halting at best. The parties, on balance, remain weak.

There have been some specific successes, however. Using its newly won right to approve committee chairpersons, the House Democratic Caucus did remove from their posts three elderly and supposedly arbitrary committee chairmen—W.R. Poage of Agriculture, Edward Hebert of Armed Services, and Wright Patman of Banking and Currency—but little or no change in committee factional alignments, leadership patterns, or policy outcomes seems to have followed. Most committees, even with new leaders, seem to have acted in the customary fashion.[70] About all that can be said is that committee chairs are now on notice that they have no guarantee of retaining their positions, a fact that may shape the ways they use the powers available to them. The same is true at the subcommittee level; in 1979, there were three violations of the seniority principle in choosing chairs for the roughly 140 House subcommittees.

The caucus also won one significant policy victory. In 1975, it voted to instruct the Rules Committee to permit an amendment repealing the oil depletion allowance, previously defeated in the Ways and Means Committee, to be offered on the floor—where it passed and eventually became law. But in general, the caucus has been unwilling or unable to impose discipline on its majority, leaving individualism to flourish.

The Speaker, too, has made successful but infrequent use of his new powers. While the Rules Committee, whose majority membership the Speaker controls, most often supports the party leadership, even it balks from time to time.[71] For example, in 1980 the panel refused to comply with

---

70. J. K. Unekis and L. N. Rieselbach, "The Structure of Congressional Committee Decision Making" (Paper presented to the Everett McKinley Dirksen Congressional Leadership Research Center—Sam Rayburn Library Conference, Understanding Congressional Leadership: The State of the Art, 1980); J. Berg, "The Effects of Seniority Reform on Three House Committees," in Rieselbach, *Legislative Reform*, pp. 49-59.

71. S. Bach, "The Structure of Choice in the House of Representatives: Recent Use of Special Rules" (Paper presented to the annual meeting of the American Political Science Association, 1980); Oppenheimer, "House Leadership and the Committee on Rules."

Speaker O'Neill's request for restrictions on amendments to the fiscal 1981 budget reconciliation bill. Similarly, the Speaker used his power to establish ad hoc committees to promote passage of an Outer Continental Shelf Act (in 1975 and 1976) and President Carter's energy package (in 1977) when committee conflict threatened to make concerted and comprehensive action impossible.[72] More commonly, such intrusion into standing committee jurisdictions and authority has seemed too risky, too unlikely to overcome the divisive and divergent preferences of numerous individual members.

The Speaker's enlarged bill referral powers may even have had counterproductive consequences. While he can (and did—4,148 times in the Ninety-Fifth Congress) refer bills to several committees and impose time limits on their consideration of the bills, multiple referrals greatly exacerbated the problem of coordinating congressional activity.[73] Uslaner reports that multi-referred legislation lingered substantially longer in committee and was significantly more likely to be amended and less likely to pass if it did reach the floor.[74] Far from providing centralization, the Speaker's referral authority encouraged House committees to assert their authority; indeed Oppenheimer argues that pressing jurisdictional claims provided full committee chairpersons with an opportunity to compensate for their otherwise declining influence.[75] In any case, House leaders' new powers appear inadequate to overcome the decentralizing forces that the reform movement also unleashed. And in the already individualistic Senate, Peabody finds an equivalent decline in the leaders' ability to manage the chamber.[76]

Finally, procedural reforms have produced only minimal effects; and entangled in broader changes, some of these have been unanticipated. Dilatory tactics are more difficult to use, and legislation is somewhat less likely to get enmeshed in parliamentary thickets in the House. In the

---

72. E. M. Uslaner, "The Congressional War on Energy: The Moral Equivalent of Leadership?" (Paper presented to the Everett McKinley Dirksen Congressional Leadership Research Center—Sam Rayburn Library Conference, Understanding Congressional Leadership: The State of the Art, 1980); B. I. Oppenheimer, "Policy Effects of the U. S. House Reform: Decentralization and the Capacity to Resolve Energy Issues," *Legislative Studies Quarterly* 5 (1980): 5-30.

73. Uslaner, "The Congressional War on Energy," p. 12.

74. Ibid., p. 13.

75. Oppenheimer, "U. S. House Reform."

76. R. L. Peabody, "Senate Party Leadership: From the 1950s to the 1980s" (Paper presented to the Everett McKinley Dirksen Congressional Leadership Research Center—Sam Rayburn Library Conference, Understanding Congressional Leadership: The State of the Art, 1980).

Senate, however, the new cloture procedures have not facilitated more rapid processing of bills. This is not because cloture has not been invoked; it has been used more successfully in recent years.[77] Rather, the norms governing the conduct of filibusters have changed markedly. Historically, unlimited debate was reserved for major matters—those about which an intense minority felt passionately.[78] At present, by contrast, any topic seems fair game for extended debate, led by a handful of senators or on occasion a single member. Norm changes condoning seemingly frivolous filibusters have undercut the intended effect of rules reforms. It may be that in the 1980s, now that the Senate has curbed the postcloture filibuster, the reform will produce its intended effect. In the 1970s, however, despite the revisions of Rule 22, the filibuster—conducted or merely threatened—shaped Senate floor action.

On balance, while the reforms for efficiency provided party leaders with some new authority, the net impact of these powers has been marginal at best. In fact no serious effort to create strong, much less responsible, parties was undertaken because other goals— individual influence, for ideological or electoral purposes, in particular—seem to have weighed more heavily with the members. Party leadership is left with a few carrots and an occasionally available small stick to bargain and cajole support from their rank-and-file, from whom they have little tangible power to compel allegiance. Legislative efficiency, however desirable and defensible in the abstract, fades in the face of other, more immediate incentives.

A More Democratized (Decentralized) Congress?

Basic to the leadership's inability to centralize operations is the devolution of much of the authority formerly lodged in full committees to subcommittees. Reformers did reassign some powers upward to the party leadership, but they took advantage of full committee vulnerability to reallocate even more influence downward to themselves. The limits on subcommittee chairmanships and the subcommittee bill of rights, in particular, were

77. See *Congressional Quarterly Almanacs* for 1977 (p. 813) and 1979 (p. 13); *Congressional Quarterly Weekly Report* 38 (1980): 1618, 2252, 2247, and 2453; and P. D. Renfrow, "The Senate Filibuster System, 1917-1979: Changes and Consequences" (Paper presented to the annual meeting of the Southern Political Science Association, 1980).

78. R.E. Wolfinger, "Filibusters: Majority Rule, Presidential Leadership, and Senate Norms," in *Congressional Behavior*, ed. N.W. Polsby (New York: Random House, 1971), pp. 111-127.

designed to open up new avenues of participation and influence. Viewed narrowly, these reforms accomplished their purposes, but from a broader perspective their proponents may have won the battle but lost the war.

At the most fundamental level, the subcommittee reforms did enable more (and junior) members to accede to positions of potential power. Limiting individuals to a single subcommittee chair opened up at least sixteen leadership positions to those previously denied such posts.[79] Moreover, the number of subcommittees grew in the House— from 116 in the Ninety-Second Congress to 134 in the Ninety-Sixth— providing additional positions for still more majority members.[80] Finally, the new subcommittee chairpersons are more liberal, more typical Democrats, making the House leadership more representative of the party.[81] Yet there are limits to the impact of reform here: Stanga and Farnsworth suggest that, though wounded, seniority survives, and much of the reform-induced change is concentrated in a few committees.[82] That is, exclusive House committees remain the province of senior members, and on other panels there has been only modest reduction in the seniority of subcommittee chairpersons. Within these limits, however, it seems safe to say that more members have some subcommittee seat from which to seek influence than was the case in the prereform period.

More importantly, perhaps, most subcommittees are independent. Subcommittees are often active; they are frequently expert (with their own staffs); and they are protected from outside interference by guarantees of jurisdiction, control over their own rules, and adequate budgets. Indeed, Deering and Smith find that party leaders do not often seek to impose discipline on the subcommittees; they most regularly confer with subcommittee chairs on procedural matters, like scheduling, and only rarely lobby the subcommittees with respect to the content of policy.[83] In fact, the most

79. Ornstein, "Subcommittee Reforms in the House of Representatives"; J. E. Stanga and D. N. Farnsworth, "Seniority and Democratic Reforms in the House of Representatives: Committees and Subcommittees," in Rieselbach, *Legislative Reform*, pp. 35-47.

80. C. J. Deering and S. S. Smith, "Majority Party Leadership and the Effects of Decentralization" (Paper presented to the Everett McKinley Dirksen Congressional Leadership Research Center—Sam Rayburn Library Conference, Understanding Congressional Leadership: The State of the Art, 1980).

81. Ibid.

82. Stanga and Farnsworth, "Seniority and Democratic Reforms."

83. Deering and Smith, "Majority Party Leadership."

common communications between party and subcommittee leaders find the latter placing demands on the former. Such policy-related contact as the party leaders choose to initiate is limited to issues of major significance and often takes place after the subcommittee has completed action. In general, the leadership "neither desires to influence nor is capable of influencing the specific legislative outcomes of the vast majority of subcommittee deliberations...."[84]

Such subcommittee autonomy—though the evidence remains sketchy —suggests that structural change has produced more fragmentation than centralization. Party leaders simply cannot impose their preferences on independent subcommittees. In consequence, there are at present more individuals and power centers to deal with in coordinating congressional policy-making activities. Concomitantly, the legislature's ability to act at all, much less decisively, may have declined as a result of reform. A decentralized institution further fragmented, for whatever motives, may find it nearly impossible to integrate small increments of power sufficiently to produce decisive action.

Moreover, reform does not have consistent effects throughout the legislative institution. Because explicit structural shifts coexist with a variety of other changes, all of which impinge differently on the various elements of legislative organization, it is hardly surprising to discover that reform and change combine in numerous ways within different units of Congress. Fenno has made clear that congressional committees vary along a number of dimensions—the members' personal goals, the environmental context within which the committee works, a panel's "strategic premises" (decision rules or norms), and its decision-making processes (specialization, partisanship, participation)--that together shape the decisions they make.[85] In short, committees differ, and change—events that alter environmental forces, the rise and fall of leaders, membership turnover, and the like—has a different impact on them.

For instance, Ornstein and Rohde find that the reforms of the 1970s combine with membership turnover in distinctive ways. The House Agriculture Committee "implemented the full array of subcommittee-strengthening reforms," experienced major personnel change, and got a new chairperson, in the process becoming ideologically more moderate and

84. Ibid., p. 36.

85. R. F. Fenno, Jr., *Congressmen in Committees* (Boston: Little Brown, 1973).

regionally balanced. Yet despite these major alterations, because the new members' goals varied little from the motivations of the members they replaced, "little overt change in behavior or policy outputs occurred...."[86] They also find that reforms have increased the autonomy of most, and the activity of many, subcommittees on the House Commerce and Government Operations Committees without significantly altering policy-making behavior. Indeed, on the former, the shifts have, if anything, inhibited policy activities.[87] On the House Foreign Affairs Committee, new members and new rules put liberal members into prominent positions in subcommittee, and pressured the committee chair into joining the more active panel members in placing more restrictions on presidential foreign policy leadership.[88] In short, change and reform in varying forms and combinations produced behavioral shifts in some committees and none in others.[89] The House Ways and Means Committee offers a clear instance of the unintended and negative consequences of reform. Long a target of liberal hostility during Wilbur Mills's lengthy and successful tenure as chairman, the committee suffered the wrath of the reformers when circumstances were conducive—when Mills's personal problems left him and his panel vulnerable. Mills was, in effect, forced from the chair and Ways and Means was stripped of its committee assignment powers, required to create subcommittees, enlarged from twenty-five to thirty-seven members, and deprived of some procedural protection (the "closed rule") for the legislation it reported. The upshot was that the new Ways and Means chair, Al Ullman, failed to sustain the bipartisan consensus that had characterized the committee.[90] The panel began to divide along party lines,[91] and it suffered a

86. N. J. Ornstein and D. W. Rohde, "Shifting Forces, Changing Rules, and Political Outcomes: The Impact of Congressional Change on Four House Committees," in *New Perspectives on the House of Representatives*, eds. R.L. Peabody and N.W. Polsby, 3rd ed. (Chicago: Rand McNally, 1977), pp. 186-269, esp. pp. 227-229.

87. Ibid., pp. 237-252.

88. Ibid., pp. 252-261. See also F. M. Kaiser, "Congressional Change and Foreign Policy: The House Committee on International Relations," in Rieselbach, *Legislative Reform*, pp. 61-71.

89. See also Berg, "The Effects of Seniority Reform," and C. J. Deering, "Adaptation and Consolidation in Congress's Foreign Policy Committees: Evolution in the Seventies" (Paper presented to the annual meeting of the Midwest Political Science Association, 1980).

90. Fenno, *Congressmen in Committees*; Unekis and Rieselbach, "Congressional Committee Decision Making."

91. G. R. Parker and S. L. Parker, "Factions in Committees: The U. S. House of Representatives," *American Political Science Review* 73 (1979): 85-102; Unekis and Rieselbach, "Congressional Committee Decision Making."

series of humiliating defeats on the floor.[92] Rudder concludes that the ability of the Ways and Means Committee to carry its proposals on the floor has been seriously impaired.[93]

Planned reform and other elements of change mix in distinctive fashions to influence performance at the subcommittee level as well. Price, examining the variety of changes that affected the House Commerce Committee, attributes the shift in behavior of that body's Subcommittee on Oversight and Investigations to the accession of John Moss to the subcommittee chair. Though replacing the sitting chairperson was one part of a thoroughgoing reform—the parent Commerce Committee rewrote its rules and reallocated its resources to accomodate its subcommittees—Price concludes that Moss was responsible for significant change. His "goals and methods as a leader-...made for alterations in the subcommittee's product and performance."[94] Malbin reaches a similar conclusion. Subcommittee activity reflected Moss's legislative interests; reform per se was less critical.[95] Again, the moral seems clear. Reform and more general change combine distinctively to influence subcommittees and full committees differently.

On balance, insofar as fragmentary evidence permits generalization, the reformers' desire to spread influence more widely within Congress, especially in the House, has been realized—but at a price. More members can and do participate more fully in congressional affairs; more hold institutional positions that sustain that participation. Committees and subcommittees are distinctive units in an increasingly decentralized structure. By multiplying the number of power centers, reform and change have jointly increased the need for elaborate bargaining and compromise to reach agreement, and have made that agreement more difficult to attain.

Summary

It is scarcely surprising to discover that reform, adopted piecemeal over

---

92. C. E. Rudder, "Committee Reform and the Revenue Process," in Dodd and Oppenheimer, *Congress Reconsidered*, pp. 117-139; C. E. Rudder, "The Policy Impact of Reform of the Committee on Ways and Means," in Rieselbach, *Legislative Reform*, pp. 73-89; Oppenheimer, "U. S. House Reform."

93. Rudder, "Reform of the Committee on Ways and Means."

94. D. E. Price, "The Impact of Reform: The House Subcommittee on Oversight and Investigations," in Rieselbach, *Legislative Reform*, pp. 113-157, esp. p. 154.

95. M. J. Malbin, "The Bolling Committee Revisited: Energy Oversight on an Investigative Subcommittee" (Paper presented to the annual meeting of the American Political Science Association, 1978).

an extended period and imbedded in a series of broader and more basic changes, has produced widely varied and often unanticipated consequences. In many instances, these consequences are at cross-purposes, and in toto may have contributed to the destabilizing, or "deinstitutionalization," of Congress.[96] The legislature is certainly more accessible to the public, but that very visibility has exposed members more frequently to external influences, and lessened an already limited basis for party leadership. The legislature is surely better able to challenge the chief executive, but other incentives and the lack of supportive external forces often seem to deter it from doing so. Congress did grudgingly grant its leaders additional authority that potentially might increase centralization and thus efficiency, but these powers have proved weak, perhaps because the membership really preferred decentralization. This they have attained—Congress is surely more democratized than it was in the 1950s and 1960s—but at some significant cost in their ability to mobilize and integrate their resources in the service of institutional power and programs. In short, reform undertaken for mixed motives has produced mixed results.

Conclusion: The Results of Reform

This review of developments and consequences of a striking period of reform makes clear, at the very least, that conscious effort to redesign Congress is part of, and quite similar to, the general pattern of American politics. Both as a substantive issue and as a means to an end—an altered and presumably improved Congress—reform is best understood as an integral element of an ongoing political system, characterized as much by unplanned change, or evolution, as by any revolutionary recasting of legislative institutions. This central fact goes far to explain both the nature of the reforms adopted and the consequences of those reforms for policy formation, enactment, and implementation.

As a subject of the legislative process, reform looks very much like most other policy domains. Legislators are the prime movers for reform, and they tend to treat it as they treat other matters. While they like to cloak reform in respectable garb—public approval, balance of institutional powers, efficiency, and democracy—they are not unaware of its power, policy,

---

96. T. E. Cavanagh, "The Deinstitutionalization of the House" (Paper presented to the Everett McKinley Dirksen Congressional Leadership Research Center—Sam Rayburn Library Conference, Understanding Congressional Leadership: The State of the Art, 1980).

or reelection implications. Reform has reflected all these needs, and in sum, it has been both "idealistic" and simultaneously "political."

The fate of the reform impetus, when the conditions that precipitated it faded in intensity and receded into history, makes clear the incremental nature and ephemeral quality of reformism. After 1977, members seemed to feel that enough had been done. To be sure, some conditions demanded response. The loophole in the Senate filibuster rule was quickly closed. When ethical failings surfaced, the members moved rapidly to censure, denounce, or expel their wayward colleagues. But on the whole the reform spirit flagged. A series of proposals—from the House (Obey) Commission on Administrative Review (1977) and the (Patterson) Select Committee on Committees (1979-80)—designed to clarify the confusing committee jurisdictions, to create an Energy Committee, and in general to make the House more efficient, were brushed aside after perfunctory consideration. Similar but even more modest moves in the Senate met the same fate. In the absence of numerous facilitating conditions—supportive members, the press of public opinion, the stimulus of national and international events—reform is likely to founder. Such conditions were present between 1970 and 1977, but faded rapidly thereafter; the tide of congressional reform ebbed with them.

Given that reform programs resemble other policy areas in terms of their incremental content and mode of adoption, it is not surprising that their impact has been uncertain and unpredictable. The numerous reforms adopted in Congress have often been incompatible. Reformers have won some victories and suffered some reverses, often discovering that their alterations have led to quite unexpected and frequently undesirable results. Indeed, such is the case with each set of reforms Congress enacted.

On balance, Congress has become more decentralized, more responsive to a multitude of forces inside and outside its halls, and as a result more hard-pressed to formulate and enact coherent, responsible public policies. Structural change has enlarged the number of power centers (in particular the subcommittees) involved in making policy, and party power cannot mobilize them in support of programs that either challenge or sustain the president. "Sunshine" changes have left members visible and exposed to attentive publics, most often organized interests. More independent members, faced with more difficult policy choices (the "politics of scarcity" requires allocation of sacrifice rather than dispensation of largesse) on issues that evoke great emotion (abortion and energy, for example) find it politically expedient to avoid risky actions. To do so, of course, is to duck controversy: to defer to others, to delay, or to obfuscate. In consequence, Congress enters the 1980s seemingly less willing or able to frame and fight for its preferences. Paradoxically, greater individual influence adds up to reduced institutional authority.

What does the future hold? Since reform in the last analysis accomplishes what the members make of it, much will depend on the determination of the lawmakers themselves. The ways in which they choose to use the resources available to them will largely establish not only what Congress does in the years ahead but also the legislature's place in the political order. In a series of insightful but pessimistic essays, Dodd argued that reform and change have combined to wreak havoc with Congress.[97] Without fundamental constitutional change, he suggests, the legislature's "serious incapacity to act may lead to a widespread questioning of its legitimate role in national governance."[98]

Others may hope for better things. Change and reform, from this perspective, may merge to create a Congress both eager and able to use its altered structures to play a creative role in American politics. More dedicated and intelligent members should have the courage and the capacity to act in the national interest, to seize control of economic or military policy when they sense it necessary, and to play a generally constructive part in federal policy making. Congress, then, may be expected to rise to the challenge when its members' incentives and motivations move them to capitalize on the authority constitutionally and politically available to them.

Reality, in all likelihood, lies between these extremes. Incremental, pluralistic politics will probably survive, and Congress will no doubt continue to operate within this framework. Acting to attain numerous and contradictory goals, members espousing various viewpoints will dodge some issues and confront others, as changing political circumstances and personal situations dictate. Compromise and coalition building will continue to be the congressional modus operandi. Whether this is sufficient to meet the nation's needs requires a clearer crystal ball than is currently available. In

---

97. L. C. Dodd, "Congress and the Quest for Power," in Dodd and Oppenheimer, *Congress Reconsidered*, pp. 269-307; idem, "Congress, the Presidency and the Cycles of Power," in *The Post-Imperial Presidency*, ed. V. Davis (New Brunswick, N. J.: Transaction Books, 1980), pp. 71-99; and idem, "Congress, the Constitution, and the Crisis of Legitimation," in Dodd and Oppenheimer, *Congress Reconsidered*, 2nd ed. (Washington, D. C.: Congressional Quarterly Press, 1981), pp. 390-420.

98. Dodd, "Congress and the Crisis of Legitimation," p. 415.

any case, one conclusion seems certain. The old order is gone. Change and reform have wrought basic shifts in Congress; the stable, institutionalized legislature of the 1960s, which Polsby described so well, has vanished. The reformed Congress of the 1980s is clearly different, but it is not necessarily better.

Epilogue: Change, Reform, and the Reagan Regime

At first blush, it may appear that congressional performance in the first six months of the Reagan administration undercuts the analysis of the previous paragraphs. After all, despite the many changes and reforms of the 1970s, Congress deferentially and efficiently enacted the new president's budget and tax programs. In reality, the events of 1981 underscore and dramatize the central strand of this assessment of legislative change. Congress remains a powerful institution that can, and will, do what its members want to do. When a majority forms, whatever the intentions of the individuals who comprise it, that majority can have its way. It is obvious that a determined majority was eager to implement the Reagan economic vision in the first days of the Ninety-Seventh Congress.

It would be premature, however, to conclude that congressional change has led nowhere, that the old, prereform mode of conducting business has returned to Capitol Hill. In fact, an extraordinary concatenation of circumstances facilitated passage of the Republican economic package. The 1980 election was central. If Ronald Reagan's landslide victory conferred any mandate at all, it was surely that new economic policies were worth trying in order to remedy the most conspicuous failures of the Carter administration. The voters enlarged the Republican congressional ranks, giving the party a clear majority in the Senate and a near one in the House. In addition, the revived GOP lawmakers were eager to reverse past programs, to solidify their party's status in the nation, and in consequence to support their president. The election results, combined with the usual honeymoon period of a new administration, put Reagan in a solid position to press his programs vigorously.

This he did, with exceptional political skill. In placing high, almost exclusive, priority on economic matters, the administration chose the policy area most likely to maximize its support. In devising an innovative use of the 1974 Budget Act's reconciliation procedure, which the framers of the statute seemingly had not foreseen, the administration structured the issues in a singularly advantageous fashion. In capitalizing on the Republican readiness to back him, Reagan exploited his personal abilities as a "communicator," both in personal contacts with lawmakers and in use of the media, particularly television, to energize citizen sentiment. Finally, in winning the necessary votes to build a majority in the House, the president proved himself adept at good, old-fashioned horse trading. Budget concessions to sugar and peanut growers and tax breaks for oil, banking, and trucking interests produced Democratic defections sufficient to create a successful coalition.

Reagan's was indeed a virtuoso performance, but the conditions that made it possible are unlikely to recur, at least in such pure form. When social, environmental and international issues—which split each party, arouse strong ideological emotions, and/or engage interregional conflicts—work their way to the top of the political agenda, as they inevitably will, the "real" Congress may become visible. On these matters—which divide the public and the politicians in a way that economic matters do not (who in principle favors big deficits and high taxes?) and which cannot be conveniently packaged for prompt and efficient legislative consideration—committee rivalries, reelection concerns, and policy individualism are likely to surface. The genuine effects of change and reform may well appear, as predicted, in these more ordinary contexts. Indeed, the extent to which the economic legislation bears Congress's distinctive stamp is often overlooked; virtually no aspect of the budget or tax bills is exactly as the president originally proposed.[99]

In short, it is too soon to discount the impact of recent reform and change in Congress. The legislature remains fundamentally a representative institution, attuned to citizen preferences.[100] Where there is consensus in the country, Congress will reflect it; no institutional structures or processes can keep it from acting decisively when a majority of members, for whatever motives, want to do so. Where agreement is lacking, as it continues to be on most matters, conventional congressional politics is likely to emerge. On such divisive issues, the changes—evolutionary or reform-induced—described above, particularly increased decentralization and greater member independence, may make congressional action more difficult. Thus, de-

---

99. See "Reconciliation Roundup," *Congressional Quarterly Weekly Report* 39 (1981): 1463-1516.

100. R. F. Fenno, Jr., "Strengthening a Congressional Strength," in Dodd and Oppenheimer, *Congress Reconsidered*, pp. 261-268; B. Hinckley, *Stability and Change in Congress*, 2nd ed. (New York: Harper & Row, 1978).

spite the Reagan regime's dramatic early triumphs, the odds continue to favor instability and uncertainty in Congress's behavior; if such is the case, reform and change will have contributed significantly to the shape of legislative politics.

A VIEW FROM THE TRENCH: REFORMING CONGRESSIONAL PROCEDURES

Thomas R. Wolanin
Staff Director (1977-1981)
Subcommittee on Postsecondary Education
United States House of Representatives

The purpose of this essay is to present a view from inside the Congress on the past course of congressional reform, its impact, and the needs for reform in the future. To begin, let me make clear my perspective. The focus will be on the House of Representatives because I know more about it, and more importantly, because the House, for the past twenty years, has been the most reformed and the most in need of reform. In addition, the size of the House increases the importance of rules and procedures rather than informal norms in determining its performance as a legislative body.

My particular trench is one of the 157 subcommittees of the House. Subcommittees are perhaps the most important institutions within Congress in initiating and shaping legislation. They have therefore been justly characterized as the "miniature legislatures of Congress."[1] While the vantage point of the subcommittee is well suited to viewing the legislative process, it also produces a different slant than a full committee, personal staff, or leadership staff position would.

The subcommittee on which I served as staff director from 1977 to 1981, the Subcommittee on Postsecondary Education of the House Education and Labor Committee, is in some respects a typical subcommittee. It is, like most subcommittees, a legislative subcommittee of an authorizing committee. Its jurisdiction and workload—the Higher Education Act, the National Foundation for the Arts and Humanities Act, the Library Services and Construction Act, the Arts and Artifacts Indemnity Act, the Museum Services Act, and some related measures—is neither excessively broad nor narrow by House standards. Issues before the subcommittee, such as student aid policies to achieve equal educational opportunity, federal initiatives to accommodate nontraditional students in postsecondary education, and the appropriate federal role in supporting the arts and humanities, are

---

1. George Goodwin, Jr., *The Little Legislatures: Committees of Congress* (Amherst, Mass.: University of Massachusetts Press, 1970), p. 45.

also about middling in terms of their visibility and level of controversy: neither invisible nor in the daily headlines.

In some other ways the subcommittee is atypical. In recent years it has been very successful. Three major pieces of legislation—the Middle Income Student Assistance Act, the Education Amendments of 1980, and the Arts and Humanities Act of 1980—were initiated by the subcommittee, and enacted without substantial change in the past three years. In the Ninety-Sixth Congress, the subcommittee achieved its entire legislative agenda. In addition, the subcommittee operates in the context of a full committee, the Education and Labor Committee, which was more thoroughly reformed earlier than any other committee in the House. Thus, my experience and the experience of the subcommittee has not been one of frustration in recent years, and this probably produces less enthusiasm for reform than might be the case with less achievement and more frustration.

My perspective is also specialized in that I work for the majority (i.e., Democratic) side of the subcommittee and the subcommittee deals exclusively with issues of domestic rather than foreign policy. In that the majority *is* the majority, and most issues before the Congress are domestic rather than foreign, the perspective is again more typical than not, although hardly universal.

The common sense of the term "reform" is to improve or to remove faults and abuses. Reform is change toward a better or more desirable state. It therefore seems apparent that judgments cannot be made about the success of past reforms or the need for future reforms without specifying the goal. The goal, in this case, is the answer to the question "What kind of House of Representatives do we want?" in terms of its processes and procedures as opposed to the public policies it produces.

The body of this essay is organized with this question as a starting point. It proceeds then to an enumeration of the reforms enacted since 1946, the impact of the reform thus far achieved, and the need for additional reforms.

What Kind of House of Representatives Do We Want?

The processes and procedures of the House of Representatives should have the following six characteristics:

1) *The processes and procedures of the House should be democratic.* Decisions should be made by majority rule. Implicit in this principle is that each member should have equal weight in each decision or at least equal weight in selecting those who have more than equal weight. Decisions are, there-

fore, based on the consent of the members, and this consent is expressed through processes and procedures that provide an adequate opportunity for each member to participate in the decisions.

2) *The processes and procedures of the House should protect minority rights.* While the majority should rule, the minority, either as a party or as a faction with respect to a particular issue, should have an opportunity to be heard. Majorities should not be able to easily or lightly run over minorities, especially intense minorities. In short, the processes and procedures should be fair.

3) *The processes and procedures of the House should enable the House to effectively carry out its constitutional responsibilities.* The House should work as a legislative body. The timing of decisions should reflect the urgency of the issue. The attention and resources devoted to the consideration of an issue should reflect its importance as a matter of public policy. In other words, the House's deliberations should reflect the priority of public policy issues, and they should be timely.

4) *The processes and procedures of the House should permit and facilitate members being held accountable for their actions by their constituents.* It is central to a democracy based on representation that those being represented have the opportunity to know what their representatives are doing in their official capacity.

5) *The processes and procedures of the House should facilitate informed decision making.* The House should be a deliberative body. Decisions made by the House should conform to the public's expectations of a process that makes legitimate decisions. Such a legitimate decision-making process includes two basic elements. First, decisions should be made with access to the best available information and analysis. Second, decisions should be made with an opportunity for the views of all of those interested to be heard.[2]

6) *The processes and procedures of the House should facilitate unbiased decisions.* Each member should be equally beholden to each of his or her constituents or able to exercise unbiased judgment on their behalf. This implies that a member's constituents should each have an equal role in congressional elections and that special-interest groups should not wield disproportion-

---

2. For a further discussion of public expectations of a legitimate decision-making process, see Thomas R. Wolanin, *Presidential Advisory Commissions: Truman to Nixon* (Madison, Wisc.: University of Wisconsin Press, 1975), pp. 37-40.

ate influence in elections or the legislative process. It further implies that members should not be subject to corrupt influences or be so preoccupied with interests outside of their official responsibilities that they cannot exercise unbiased judgment. Finally, it means that incumbents should not have unfair advantages over challengers.

It is obvious that these six characteristics are to some extent in conflict with each other. Maximizing some of these goals would diminish others. The tension between majority rule and the protection of minority rights is a classic dilemma of democratic theory. Furthermore, it has frequently been argued by some opponents of reform that measures to insure majority rule, minority rights, and accountability excessively diminish the capacity of the House as an institution to carry out its legislative tasks. For example, it is argued that open hearings, markups, and conferences impede the candid negotiations that are required to achieve consensus and action. Thus, the ideal reformed House of Representatives would have a balance of these six characteristics rather than a maximization of each.

How Has the House Been Reformed?

This survey of reforms spans those enacted since the Legislative Reorganization Act of 1946 (the La Follette-Monetary Act) which was the first attempt at comprehensive reform of the modern Congress.[3] In fact, the most significant reforms have been achieved in the past twenty years, and if the fight to expand the Rules Committee is excluded, it is the past decade that has witnessed the fruition of reform efforts.

The enumeration of reforms is grouped in terms of the six characteristics of a reformed House and subsets of them. The intention is to show change toward achieving the six goals. Clearly, the placement of a particular change is arguable in some cases, and a few changes have been placed under more than one goal. The primary emphasis is on changes in the rules of the House of Representatives and the rules of the Democratic Caucus. The lack of attention to changes in the rules of the Republican Conference only reflects the fact that the Democrats have controlled the House in every Congress since 1946 except two. It should be noted, however, that changes in the rules of the Republican Conference generally parallel those adopted

---

3. For a brief survey of reform efforts prior to 1946, see *Congress and the Nation* (Washington, D.C.: Congressional Quarterly Service, 1965), 1: 1410-1418. For a more detailed examination of change and reform of the House of Representatives prior to 1946, see George B. Galloway, *History of the House of Representatives* (New York: Thomas Y. Crowell Co., 1962).

by the Democratic Caucus. Indeed, the Republicans enacted some of the reforms earlier than the Democrats.[4]

Democratization

Democratizing the choice of committee chairman

- 1969 - Democratic Caucus approval of lists of committee chairmen and members.

- 1971 - Democratic Committee on Committees need not follow seniority in recommending committee chairmen.

- 1971 - Separate vote on committee chairmen by the Democratic Caucus could be demanded by ten members.

- 1973 - Automatic separate vote on each nominee for committee chairman in the Democratic Caucus and secret ballot on demand of one-fifth of those present.

- 1975 - Nominations permitted for committee chairman from the floor of the Democratic Caucus as well as from the Committee on Committees if the latter's first nominee is defeated.

- 1975 - Appropriations subcommittee chairmen selected in same manner as full committee chairman by the Democratic Caucus.

Limiting the power of committee chairmen

- 1946 - Committees required to fix regular meeting dates and keep records of their actions.

- 1966 - Education and Labor Committee revolt against Chairman Adam Clayton Powell, Jr.

- 1970 - With the authorization of a committee majority, a committee member can move the consideration of a bill reported from the committee if the chairman fails to do so within seven days after a rule is granted.

- 1971 - Democratic subcommittee chairmen guaranteed at least one staff person for each subcommittee.

---

4. The compilation of reforms was gleaned from *Congress and the Nation*, volumes 1, 2, 3, and 4 (Washington, D.C.: Congressional Quarterly Service, 1965, 1969, 1973, and 1977); *Congressional Quarterly Almanac*, volumes 33, 34, and 35 (Washington, D.C.: Congressional Quarterly Service, 1978, 1979, and 1980); and Democratic Study Group, *Special Report: Reform in the House of Representatives*, No. 96-41, December 1, 1980.

- 1973 - Democratic caucus created on each committee with the authority to select subcommittee chairmen, establish party ratios, and establish sub-committee budgets.

- 1973 - Subcommittee bill of rights of the Democratic Caucus requiring that all legislation referred to a full committee be referred to an appropriate subcommittee within two weeks, guaranteeing an adequate budget for each subcommittee, and authorizing subcommittees to meet, hold hearings, and report to the committee on all matters referred to it.

- 1973 - Bidding process for selection of subcommittee chairmen and ratification by the committee Democratic caucus.

- 1973, 1975 - Bidding process based on seniority for establishing sub-committee membership.

- 1974 - Democratic Caucus requires each committee (except Rules and Budget) to establish at least four subcommittees.

- 1976 - Democratic caucus of each committee determines number and jurisdiction of subcommittees.

- 1977 - Votes for subcommittee chairmen in committees by secret ballot.

Limiting the ability of the Rules Committee to obstruct legislation

- 1961 - Expansion of the Rules Committee from twelve to fifteen members.

- 1965-1967 - "Twenty-one day rule" permitting the Speaker, with the approval of a majority of the House, to bring a measure before the House if the Rules Committee has failed to act on it in twenty-one days. (A weaker version was in effect 1949-51.)

- 1965 - Permit Speaker with the approval of majority to send legislation to conference. Previously unanimous consent or a rule from the Rules Committee was required.

- 1975 - Democratic Speaker given power to nominate chairman and Democratic members of the Rules Committee.

Dispersing the positions of power among more members

- 1971 - Democratic member may not chair more than one legislative subcommittee.

- 1971 - No Democratic member may serve on more than two legislative committees.

- 1973 - Committees designated as exclusive, major, or nonmajor. Democratic member may be a member of one exclusive committee, one major and one nonmajor committee, or two nonmajor committees.

- 1973 - Each Democratic member guaranteed an assignment to an exclusive or major committee.

- 1975 - Chairmen of exclusive or major committees may not chair any other committee or serve on any other exclusive, major, or nonmajor committee.

- 1977 - Democratic members may not chair more than one legislative or nonlegislative subcommittee.

- 1978 - Democratic full committee chairmen may not chair a subcommittee on a committee other than the one they chair.

- 1979 - Democratic members may not serve on more than five subcommittees of standing committees.

- 1979 - Democratic members may protect their membership on only one subcommittee that they served on in the previous Congress.

- 1979 - Democratic chairmen of standing committees may not chair any other committee (with limited exceptions).

General democratization

- 1969 - Democratic Caucus required to meet monthly.

- 1969 - Items can be placed on the agenda of the Democratic Caucus by individual members, not only by the leadership.

- 1970 - Proxy voting limited to the specific matter before a committee.

- 1971 - Fifty percent of a state delegation can nominate a member for a committee assignment as an alternative to nomination by the Committee on Committees.

- 1977 - Election of the chairman of the Democratic Congressional Campaign Committee by the Democratic Caucus rather than by the committee.

- 1977 - Members permitted to have one staff member on the House floor when the member has an amendment under consideration.

- 1977 - Speaker required to name conferees from among members primarily responsible for the legislation and, to the fullest extent feasible, include principal proponents of major provisions of the bill passed by the House.

- 1978 - Members may not be excluded from any committee or subcommittee hearing (except Ethics) even if the hearing is closed.

Minority Rights

- 1970 - Guarantee of at least ten minutes of debate on amendments printed in the *Congressional Record* at least one day prior to debate on a measure.

- 1970 - Guarantee of at least three days to file minority views to committee reports.

- 1970 - Minority permitted to call witnesses during at least one day of hearings on a measure.

- 1970 - Debate time on conference reports required to be evenly divided between the majority and the minority.

- 1975 - Minority party guaranteed at least one-third of committee staffs.

An Effective Process

Strengthening the Democratic Caucus as an agenda-setting institution

- 1969 - Democratic Caucus required to meet monthly.

- 1969 - Items can be placed on the agenda of the caucus by individual members as well as by the leadership.

- 1969, 1972, 1973, 1975, 1979 - Resolutions urging or instructing committees to bring matters before the House and endorsing legislative policies on issues such as welfare, American military involvement in Indochina, the oil depletion allowance, and public financing of congressional elections.

Strengthening the leadership

- 1973 - Democratic Steering and Policy Committee created consisting of the Speaker, majority leader, caucus chairman, twelve members elected from regions, and eight members appointed by the Speaker. The committee makes recommendations on legislative priorities and party policy.

▪ 1973 - Speaker, majority leader, and caucus chairman added to the membership of the Democratic Committee on Committees (formerly exclusively the Democratic members of the Ways and Means Committee).

▪ 1974 - Speaker authorized to refer bills to more than one committee for joint or sequential consideration.

▪ 1975 - Speaker given power to nominate chairman and Democratic members of the Rules Committee.

▪ 1977 - Speaker authorized to set time limits for joint or sequential consideration of legislation by committees.

Expediting the business of the House and limiting dilatory tactics

▪ 1970 - Committees permitted to sit without special leave while the House is in session, except during the consideration of amendments in the Committee of the Whole.

▪ 1970 - Quorum calls can be suspended after a quorum is obtained.

▪ 1970 - Reading of the *Journal* can be dispensed with unless ordered by the Speaker or a majority of the House.

▪ 1970 - Electronic voting on quorum calls and roll call votes authorized.

▪ 1977 - Cluster recorded votes on rules permitted.

▪ 1977 - Committees permitted to meet during debate on amendments in the Committee of the Whole except on the objection of ten members (rather than only one).

▪ 1977 - Quorum calls in the Committee of the Whole limited.

▪ 1979 - Deferral and clustering of recorded votes on passage of bills and conference reports permitted.

▪ 1979 - Rules changes to expedite the business of the House, e.g., providing for only one vote to establish a quorum at the beginning of a legislative day, and permitting a short period of five minutes on some recorded votes.

▪ 1979 - Number of members required to request a recorded vote in the Committee of the Whole increased from twenty to twenty-five.

Rationalization of committee structure

- 1946 - Legislative Reorganization Act reduces the number of House committees from forty-eight to nineteen and realigns their jurisdictions.

- 1974 - Significant realignment of House committee jurisdictions.

General effectiveness

- 1946 - Congressional consideration of private bills for pensions, tort claims, and correction of military records eliminated.

- 1971, 1973, 1975 - Democratic Caucus action with respect to committee ratios to insure representation of Democrats in proportion to their numbers in the House and to insure working committee majorities.

- 1974 - Budget and Impoundment Control Act creates a mechanism for congressional decisions on macro-budget priorities—including spending, revenues and deficits, establishment of a timetable for the consideration of authorizations, appropriations, and new entitlement authorities—synchronized to their relevance to macro-budget decisions.

- 1974 - Early organization of the Congress in December and January following elections.

- 1978 - Unlimited number of cosponsors on legislation permitted.

Accountability

- 1970 - Votes on amendments in the Committee of the Whole would be recorded.

- 1970 - Radio and television coverage of House committee hearings permitted.

- 1970 - Roll call votes in committees must be made available to the public.

- 1973 - Required a separate roll call vote to close a committee meeting or hearing.

- 1975 - Required a separate vote each day a committee hearing or meeting is closed.

- 1975 - Conference meeting could only be closed by a majority vote of the House or Senate conferees.

- 1977 - Conference meetings could only be closed by a roll call vote of the full House.

- 1978 - Television coverage of the floor of the House.

Informed Decision Making

- 1946 - Witnesses required to submit written testimony in advance of hearings insofar as possible.

- 1946 - Increased committee staffing; expanded frequently and substantially since 1946.

- 1946 - Legislative Reference Service established in the Library of Congress (now the Congressional Research Service).

- 1946 - Committees directed to exercise "continuous watchfulness" (oversight) of execution of the laws by the executive branch.

- 1970 - Conference reports must be available and printed in the *Congressional Record* three days prior to floor consideration.

- 1970 - Five copies of amendments offered in the Committee of the Whole must be made available to the committee managers.

- 1971 - Printed copies of committee reports must be available three days prior to House consideration of a measure.

- 1974 - Congressional Budget Office created.

Unbiased Decisions

- 1958 - Code of ethics for federal officials (without legal force).

- 1966 - Creation of Select Committee on Standards and Conduct.

- 1967 - Standing Committee on Standards of Official Conduct created to develop a code of ethics.

- 1968 - Code of Official Conduct adopted including limited financial disclosure.

- 1977 - Use of franked mail limited with respect to postal patron and mass mailings.

- 1978 - Adoption of stricter code of ethics including financial disclosure, prohibition of unofficial office accounts, and limitation on outside earned income.

- 1980 - Any subcommittee or committee chairman who is indicted, convicted, or censured must immediately cease to exercise the powers of chairman either temporarily (in the case of those indicted) or permanently (in the case of those convicted or censured).

The Impact of Reform

The House of Representatives is very different from what it was twenty or even ten years ago. A member who returned after an imaginary twenty-year Rip Van Winkle slumber would be bewildered and disoriented by TV cameras, electronic voting, clustered votes, committee chairmen who speak politely to freshmen, three-term members chairing subcommittees, recorded teller votes, a budget process, financial disclosure, a Rules Committee that operates in cooperation with the leadership, and open conferences.

In particular, the most frequent criticism of the House before 1970 was the concentration of arbitrary power in committee chairmen who were chosen by the seniority system and beyond democratic control.[5] While seniority is still the general rule in the selection of committee and subcommittee chairmen, these chairmen hold power at the pleasure of their fellow Democrats. The rejection by the Democratic Caucus in 1975 of three members, entitled by seniority to chair committees, gave dramatic and enduring substance to this change. The power of chairmen to control their committees regardless of the wishes of the committee members or the House as a whole has been drastically curbed. Power is now widely dispersed among the members both through the availability of choice committee assignments and subcommittee chairmanships to junior members, and through the participation of members in the caucuses of the committees and the House.

Gains have been made in insuring the protection of minority rights. However, this has not been widely perceived as a major problem of House

---

5. See, for example, Richard Bolling, *House Out of Order* (New York: E.P. Dutton and Co., 1966), pp. 38-41 and 221-234; and John V. Lindsay, "The Seniority System," in *We Propose: A Modern Congress*, ed. Mary McInnis (New York: McGraw-Hill Book Co., 1966).

procedures. In fact, the complexity of the legislative process, and the opportunities its procedures provide for delay and obstruction by intense minorities, most notably the Senate filibuster, has more frequently been decried.

The Democratic Caucus has evolved into an institution with agenda-setting potential. The Democratic Steering and Policy Committee "shall serve as the Committee on Committees and shall make recommendations regarding party policy, legislative priorities, scheduling of matters for House or caucus action, and other matters as appropriate to further Democratic programs and policies."[6] This body, which is balanced with the leadership and appointees of the Speaker and members elected regionally, can be both a legitimate and effective mechanism for coordinating and leading the House. Its power as the Committee on Committees provides it with an important base of real institutional power.

The new budget process sets an orderly agenda for the consideration of authorizations, appropriations, and new entitlements. It also provides the Congress with an opportunity to set program priorities based on the consideration of macroeconomic variables—unemployment, inflation, energy prices, federal deficits, federal borrowing, etc.

The business of the House is transacted more expeditiously without compromising either minority rights or the deliberateness of the process. Electronic roll call votes and cluster voting are among the most obvious timesavers.

The ability of the general public (and their ardent surrogates, the press) and of a member's constituents and opponents to know what a member is doing with respect to significant public policy issues is greatly enhanced. Recorded votes on amendments in the Committee of the Whole; open hearings, markups, and conferences; and reports on votes in committee make the House more accountable. Public disclosure of outside interests and income has the same effect. The televised proceedings of the House have, I am told, come to rival the soap operas on a few cable television networks. (I might note, parenthetically, that my perception is that while televising the proceedings of the House provides some good film clips for the nightly network news, its primary effect is to promote more informed decisions on the floor. Members can work in their offices with one eye and ear on the television. When they dash to the floor in response to the bells for a vote, they probably have a much better idea of the tenor and substance of

---

6. *Preamble and Rules Adopted by the Democratic Caucus*, p. 5.

the debate on an issue than before televised proceedings. On unfamiliar issues, there is probably less reliance on a quick word from a colleague or a glance up at the names and lights to see how the state delegation is voting.)

Congressional decision making is also more generally informed. Guaranteeing the availability of committee and conference reports prior to floor action is highly desirable. However, the most significant changes are the availability of timely and viable information from the Congressional Budget Office and the development of legislative computer and information technology. Equally important is the expansion of committee and personal staffs to analyze and organize the mass of information that bears on any issue. House committees had about 150 staff employees in 1946, 900 in 1973, and 2,000 in 1979.[7]

Creating an unbiased process in the House of Representatives in some respects takes us far afield from the topic of congressional procedures. Such a process would be based on the participation of voters able to fully exercise their voting rights in districts that are fairly apportioned by numbers and are not gerrymandered. It would also require a system of campaign financing that did not permit narrow interests to exercise undue influence. Incumbents should not have unfair advantages over challengers. It is my sense that the resources at the command of individual members—staff, district offices, travel to the district, office allowances, etc.—have generally kept pace with the demands and expectations of constituents for services, information, and personal contact. Sufficient resources are available to get the job done without excessive opulence or payroll padding—although I do sometimes wonder whether the House needs quite as many doorkeepers and garage attendants, but maybe that is because I am on a committee staff. It is, of course, very difficult to draw the line between resources to serve the public adequately and resources that only help insure reelection. Reforms in the use of the frank have certainly restrained the unfair use of mass mailings as an incumbent advantage.

The adoption of a code of ethics, the creation of a committee to enforce it, and above all, public disclosure of outside interests and income has served to improve ethical standards in the House. Changes in the composition of the House—younger, better educated, more issue-oriented and less party-connected members—while certainly not unmixed blessings, have also had positive effects in the same direction.

---

7. "Congressional Staff Cuts," *Congressional Record*, January 6, 1981, p. H 49.

The Unfinished Reform Agenda

Democratization

The seniority system insures continuity of control of committees and subcommittees by experienced members. It also mutes the competition and conflict based on personal ambition that would otherwise dominate the choice of members to occupy institutional positions of power. Thus, the seniority system promotes institutional effectiveness. The reforms of the past decade have tempered this system with democratic control at both the caucus and the committee level. Additional proposed changes in the seniority system are of two kinds: first, to promote or require competition for the chairmanship (e.g., an automatic contest among the three most senior members of a committee); or second, to limit the tenure of chairmen (e.g., an age limit, a limit on years of service as chairman, or mandatory rotation of the chairmanship among the three most senior members). In my view, an appropriate (if not perfect) balance has been struck between democratic control and institutional effectiveness with respect to the seniority system. Mandatory contests for chairmanships would introduce unnecessary conflict into a body the fundamental task of which is to build a consensus on a very wide range of complex and divisive issues. Mandatory limits on the tenure of chairmen is both fundamentally antidemocratic (potentially denying the caucus the member preferred by the majority) as well as a mindless disregard for past legislative performance. Chairmen who are ineffective, outside the party consensus, or too old to carry on can be and have been successfully challenged and replaced.

Other suggested changes alleged to enhance democratic control such as election of the majority whip or a prohibition on proxy voting fall, in my mind, into the class of debatable propositions rather than crying needs.

Minority Rights

There are not apparent to me either any strong needs or front-burner proposals in this area. (Republicans dissatisfied with the committee ratios might disagree.)

An Effective Process

Curbing the power of committee chairmen, recording teller votes, guaranteeing the rights of subcommittees, and widely dispersing institutional positions of power and authority among the members has produced an entrepreneurial House of Representatives. The successes of the Subcommittee on Postsecondary Education were produced in large part by consensus building within the subcommittee and its parent full committee and negotiations with the Budget Committee. The timing of full committee, Rules Committee, and floor consideration were either automatic (being done in the order of our request, like service in a busy bakery), or the result of the entrepreneurial ability of the subcommittee chairman to navigate the process and successfully assert the priority of our legislation. Decisions to speed up or slow down were made entirely by the subcommittee on the basis of *its* calculations on how to enhance the prospects of *its* agenda. The only real constraint on timing was the fixed deadlines of the budget process. Timing of legislative action was not significantly influenced in most cases by a broad agenda of legislative priorities or a strategic relationship of various legislative measures. The content of the subcommittee's legislation was also left almost entirely to its own ability to resolve the conflicts in its political environment.

This situation was both happy and perfectly appropriate in the case of legislation emanating from the Subcommittee on Postsecondary Education. It is also true that legislation dealing with more highly charged and visible issues (e.g., energy and taxes) is more subject to having its content and timing influenced by broad priority setting. However, the experience of the Subcommittee on Postsecondary Education seems more common than not and also seems to illustrate a serious general problem of the House—the attention and resources of the House are not sufficiently allocated to issues in proportion to their urgency and importance. It seems to me that the House would benefit from a managed marketplace, rather than Adam Smith's unseen hand, or to borrow some terms from Lenin, a larger measure of "democratic centralism" should replace "spontaneity" and "adventurism." The institutional mechanisms for the leadership to set priorities, control timing, and allocate resources exist—the Rules Committee, the Democratic Steering and Policy Committee, and the caucus. It could be argued that the problem is a lack of leadership skill in using these mechanisms. It might be observed also that the preponderance of junior members in the House who won their seats mainly by their wit, skill, and entrepreneurial ability produces a distinct lack of *followership*. It could also be noted that for the last four years President Carter failed to set a national agenda and to communicate that agenda to the Congress. However, in my view, the basic problem is the absence of a national consensus on what our policies should be. The Congress has been receiving conflicting signals:

reduce inflation and unemployment, balance the budget and cut taxes, but do not cut my programs; make the tax system fairer, but do not plug my loophole; increase personal security and fight crime, but do not enact gun control; strengthen national defense but no draft; solve the energy crisis but put nuclear power on hold; increase competition but protect *me*; increase productivity but give me more days off; get government off my back, unless I live near Love Canal, Mt. St. Helens, or Three Mile Island, or unless I drive a Pinto, am afflicted by the effects of a drug or unhealthy working conditions, or was fleeced in a shady business deal—in which case government has been derelict for not safeguarding and assisting me enough.

In sum, the basic shortcoming of the House as an effective legislative body is not amenable to solution by either tinkering with or transforming the rules and procedures. How to create a national consensus is a question for which I have no simple answer and which is also far beyond the scope of this essay.

Everyone is familiar with the pinball existence of members of Congress, bouncing between several subcommittees, at least two committees, conferences, office work, constituent visits and the floor schedule. For example, "in 1977-78, there were 7,000 committee and subcommittee meetings, 5,000 of which presented scheduling conflicts for the members."[8] Improvements in the allocation of the committee workload and coordination of the committee and floor schedules would clearly improve the effectiveness of the House as well as the ability of members to make informed decisions. There are no simple remedies but this is clearly an area where reform efforts should concentrate.

There are incessant calls to improve the effectiveness of the House by reallocating jurisdictions among the standing committees to make them better conform to the nature of public policy issues (e.g., an Energy Committee and consolidation of transportation, health, and environmental jurisdictions) or to more equitably distribute the legislative workload. The issues of public policy can obviously be sliced in many different ways and there is no "correct" or final resolution. This area requires continuing attention.

With respect to the allocation of the legislative workload, the most glaring problem is the overload of the Ways and Means Committee. It is centrally involved in health, welfare, income security, energy, compensating and combatting unemployment, foreign trade, all issues using tax incentives or

---

8. Bill Frenzel, "House Reforms and Why They Haven't Worked," *Commonsense* 3 (1980): 32.

the support of designated taxes, in addition to revenue raising and macroeconomic policy. The power of the committee has been curbed specifically through restrictions on the use of the closed rule (1973), and by the transfer of the Committee on Committees' functions to the Democratic Steering and Policy Committee (1975), as well as by the other reforms that increased democratic control of all committees. The expansion of the Ways and Means Committee in 1975 modified its balance of power to more closely reflect the balance in the full House. The 1974 rule change requiring each committee to establish at least four subcommittees forced the Ways and Means Committee to allocate its responsibilities among subcommittees. The fall from power of the committee's long-time chairman, Wilbur Mills, as well as the development of the budget process, have also diminished its influence. The committee nevertheless remains overloaded with critical issues and is a bottleneck preventing the timely consideration of some important questions.

Accountability

The most frequently heard suggestion in this area is to make the *Congressional Record* more accurately reflect what was actually said during the floor debate, as opposed to the current lenient interpretation of "revise and extend". The practice of "bulleting" statements no part of which was said is one recent change in this direction. The practice of periodically interspersing the *Record* with the time of day provides the careful reader with a clue that there is more printed than could possibly have been said. Permitting only grammatical revisions of what was actually said, and distinguishing by typeface or "bulleting" the verbatim proceedings from other insertions, would somewhat improve the public's ability to know and judge what transpired on the floor. However, if the courts, the executive branch, and the public distinguished, in weighing congressional "intent," between what was actually said and other material, there might be a greater tendency to drone all the way through long explanatory statements. This would not be the most productive use of the House's time in most instances. Enhancing accountability by refining public disclosure of outside income and interests and campaign contributions, as well as requiring that subcommittee and committee votes be published in the committee reports, are also worth serious consideration.

Informed Decision Making

Improving the scheduling practices of the House and more effectively devoting the time and resources of the House to issues in terms of their priority would very significantly improve the ability of members to make informed decisions. Both the Congressional Research Service and the Committee on House Administration provide technical assistance and in-service training for congressional staffs to upgrade their ability to manage the deluge of fact and opinion that flows over them, and to manage their offices and their legislative responsibilities. It strikes me, however, that congressional staff need to have more training to deal with the complicated procedures of the House, particularly compliance with fiscal and financial reporting requirements, and with the information technology and data processing capability that is available. I am, on the other hand, very skeptical of proposals to introduce an analogue to the civil service, including prohibition of employment discrimination, into congressional staffing. Since staff members act in many cases as surrogates for their employers, doing what they would do could they defy the laws of physics, the staff must be directly accountable and responsive to the members.

Unbiased Decisions

The ethics of members of Congress could certainly be improved, but whose could not? It is not my experience or impression that betrayal of the public trust is widespread by members of Congress. In fact, my experience has provided very few illustrations of even slight deviations from scrupulous integrity. I might note in passing that I view Abscam as an example of criminal behavior by the FBI rather than by members of Congress. The Committee on Standards of Official Conduct could perhaps be strengthened as a monitor and enforcer of ethical behavior. However, the fundamental problem is the inherent difficulty in having vigorous self-policing among a group of peers and colleagues. This difficulty is evident not only in Congress but also among doctors, faculty members, students, policemen, lawyers, and the military, to name only a few. The usual solution, external review, would risk breaching a fundamental principle of American constitutional government, the separation of powers, as well as infringing on the constitutional right of each House to "punish its members for disorderly behavior."[9] Aggressive disciplining of members, including expulsion, also

---

9. U.S., Constitution, Article I, Section 5.

seems to diminish the sovereign right of the people to be represented by members of their own choosing according to *their* standards. I place my primary reliance for ensuring congressional behavior that is faithful to the public's trust in effective public disclosure of outside income and interests, staffing practices, and campaign finances, the vigilance of the press, and the public and the ballot box.

In summary, my view is that future reform of the House is a matter of trench warfare and incremental advances over difficult terrain, rather than sweeping Napoleonic campaigns across the political landscape. But this might be the natural result of viewing events from the trench itself, rather than from a command post on the top of the mountain.

Response by Kenneth W. Hunter
Senior Associate Director
Program Analysis Division
United States General Accounting Office

Both papers do an excellent job of documenting and describing what has been a decade plus of extremely active change. I would make one observation about the hows and whys of reforming that I don't think was made explicit in either paper. My belief is that we are in the *middle* of an era of reform, which is what complicated these gentlemen's task, and made it almost impossible for them to really assess and project very well from their research. My own feeling is that it takes about twenty to twenty-five years to accomplish a group of reforms— starting from an event, at which it was generally recognized that significant change was needed, to the point at which the new procedures are accepted by the leaders and members as the normal operations. That's obviously a long enough time period for there to be a generation change also. If I am right and if the event or events that started this particular era occurred in the late 1960s and early 1970s, then this group of reforms will not be completed until sometime around 1990. Therefore one of the interesting

questions is what the results of these reforms will be in terms of the type of Congress and its capabilities in 1990. Will it be a Congress that can deal with the issues of the 1960s? The 1970s? The 1980s? Or the 1990s and beyond? Some evidence that this reform era is not complete can be derived by looking at the number of bills and other actions that are being considered for further reform. Many of them are simply adjustments to the basic reforms which I think these papers categorize extremely well. People are not happy with the interim results.

Let me at this point inject another perspective that deals more with the policy environment in which the remaining steps in this group of reforms will be carried out. There is pressure for less government; there are other pressures for more government, and there are some pressures for smarter government. If we categorize the current crop of refinements to the procedures, those that are pushing or based upon the less-government argument include the constitutional or other procedural requirements for a balanced budget, the proposals for sunset legislation, or automatic termination, and the legislative veto.

There are another group of practices which do not get labeled reforms but which are in the direction of more government. These are illustrated by the extent to which programs and spending and other activities have been created outside of the regular discipline of the process. And we refer to these in the case of programs for assistance to business-type activities, which in my judgment also have the same characteristics of an entitlement, and those are credit programs, loan guarantees, and tax preferences. These don't count in regular outlay numbers, so they get less visibility, but are in fact demands for more government assistance. And of course there are demands for protection through regulations. In all of these cases, the pressure is high for more government involvement.

There are also a group of refinements which fit better into the categories which these papers deal with: the thrust toward a smarter government. One of them that is a refinement of the budget process is to shift to a longer period for authorizations and appropriations—say, a two-year budget, or greater use of two-year authorizations and appropriations, so that Congress would have to deal with fewer

things each year. Similarly, another one that falls into that category is to eliminate the deferral process under the Budget Act. Third would be to include credit and tax programs in the budget process more fully. All of those are refinements of the budget process. The fourth in the oversight category is the type of refinement that the oversight reform or sunset review bill would institute, which is based primarily on the agenda-setting activities. The fifth is regulatory analysis, and I make quite a distinction between analyzing what the potential impact of regulation would be before decisions are made, and the legislative veto after the fact—that's a little late. It's also very difficult. Now the sixth area is the information overload issue.

Each one of these reforms has been laid on top of the existing process and nothing has been eliminated. That's even complicated further by the reporting requirements which have become boilerplate, so Congress is getting inundated with paper and we need to do a housekeeping job on some legislation to get rid of a large number of reports that are not going to be relevant to the 1980s and 1990s.

The seventh is not a reform of the Congress but an attitude, a belief that there is a fixed amount of power, and if Congress gets some, then somebody else is losing it. We might reject that and say that, to the extent that all of the institutions are strengthened, then each will be able to take on and carry out their own functions more effectively and thereby strengthen the others also, which is a different concept. And with that I would like to quit.

Response by David W. Brady
Department of Political Science, Rice University

When I was first called to participate in this panel, I was worried
about two things. One was that it
would actually be about congressional procedures, which is somewhat dull. And second that I would
be the token southerner, and that
turns out to be true. Now the comment about procedure, I think, is
relevant, because hardly anyone
would really come to listen to a talk
about congressional procedures
unless we thought they were related to something more important—like how congressional procedures affect public policy, pres-
idential-congressional relations,
the ability of Congress to aid in conflict management, systems change,
and so on. Fortunately, these papers dealt with exactly that.

I think what is most interesting
about the papers is the assumptions
each makes regarding procedures
and their effects. Thus I begin my
response by defining procedures,
and then turn to constraints upon
those procedures, and finally deal
with the question of what Congress
has done and what difference it
makes.

For simplicity's sake I divide procedures into two sorts: one, horizontal organizational procedures,
by which I mean simply how legislation passes from the Speaker to
committee and from committee to
subcommittee and so on; and
second, vertical procedures, the
organizational capacity of the Congress to integrate and process information. Another way to put that
is the extent to which procedures
centralize power in the leadership.
Questions of integration and procedure lead, as both papers indicate,
in various ways: to questions about
the relationship between parties
and committees, or the relationship
between the Speaker, as the leader
of the party system, to the committees. The important question about
congressional reform is to what extent reform improves either congressional integrative capacity and/
or its division of labor. My comments on these papers must be
viewed in light of the above. '

While both these papers are concerned with the reforms of the
1970s, reform in Congress does not
take place in a historical vacuum.
The same reforms, and the same
questions, have come up at various
times. And once again, when reforms are discussed, there's a

general feeling among lots of people—both among representatives and senators themselves, and among constituents and observers—that Congress is in trouble. I think that these papers make the assumption that Congress is in some trouble, and that the reforms of the 1970s try to address the perceived difficulties. Then the authors attempt to ascertain what has been achieved.

Before you can really decide what effect these reforms have had on Congress, I think you have to talk about this: What are the constraints that exist in the congressional environment that limit the kinds of reforms we can expect? The first, and one of the more important constraints, is the fact that Congress is a collegial, or egalitarian body. That limits the capacity for vertical or centralizing power. Congress is not a corporation, and it's not a police department. It cannot, because of its very nature, tolerate a tremendous amount of hierarchy. And that causes problems for the party leaders. It follows that if vertical integration is tough, horizontal procedures are relatively easy to put into operation. There's really a tremendous amount of procedure in the Congress that is devoted to questions like who can introduce a bill. It took the House five to six congresses before the rules finally determined who could introduce a bill, what role committees would have, how committees would themselves restrict the individual member's equality. In short, horizontal procedures in the Congress vastly outnumber vertical procedures.

The second constraint on the Congress's reform capacity is its inability to restrict its workload. Congress doesn't have control over that. I believe this was referred to by Mr. Wolanin as the member's "pinball existence." It is true that Congress, as Professor Rieselbach argues, cannot control the rise of issues, like energy and environment, which cause real problems for congressional legislation. The rise of complex issues, plus the increasing complexity of the society, lead to an increase in the congressional workload, and Congress does not have the ability that a corporation does to say: "We're not going to deal with this area anymore—sell it." The only time in the history of the Congress—and in this case I speak of the House specifically—when power was effectively centralized, was the 1890-1911 era, the so-called "heyday of the Speaker." The rise of a hierarchical leadership was in no small way the result of the increased workload of the Congress. Using a crude measure of workload, the number of bills introduced went from 600 in 1870 to about 19,000 in one session by 1896. Congress resolved this workload crisis by centralizing power in the Speaker and in the majority party. However, the era of hierarchy was short-lived. The revolt against Cannon in 1910-1911 was a revolt against centralized power. Congress's natural tendency to equality came forward and the reformers decentralized power. Another instance of the congressional response to increased workload was the Depression. It seems to me that its response to the Depression was in most instances to delegate power to the executive. The Hundred Days bills were passed by a Congress whose members hadn't even read them. They were being written in the cloakrooms, and the pages run out to the floor. Yet by 1937 Congress had begun to reassert some of its traditional powers by delaying the president's programs.

The third external variable that constrains congressional reforms is the status of "party in the electorate." The status of the party system outside Congress affects the ability of congressional leaders to use procedures to affect legislation. That point was made by Mr. Wolanin when he talked about the importance of a national consensus. I'm not sure that there was ever a period in which there was a national consensus along those lines. I prefer to think of it in terms of a party consensus, where there is a real majority and there is a constituent base for the dominant party in the Congress. Then Congress can legislate. If you trace the pattern of congressional leadership, you would find movement from hierarchy during the Cannon-Reed era, to the present bargaining sort of leadership. And the change in leadership is very closely associated with the decline of the political party and other external events. So when we talk about reforms in Congress, I think it's important to put it in the context of what occurs outside Congress.

Egalitarianism, workload, and the status of the party system all impose limits on the potential effects of reform. The history of reform in Congress has been a waxing and waning of centralizing power in the party leaders, and returning to a committee-based, decentralized system. Understanding the reforms of the 1970s requires an understanding of the limits of reform. Both papers spell out limits, and both deal with the effects of conflicting goals on the ultimate effects of reform. However, the most important question about reform—"Is Congress better, stronger, more flexible?"—remains unanswered. The authors conclude that Congress has been both decentralized and centralized, and that the results are mixed. "Congress is different, but it is not necessarily better."

I believe that a good part of the difficulty political scientists have with assessing the impact of reform is that we are not sure what Congress's job is supposed to be. In the first place, are we talking about a Congress or a legislative body that's Lockean? Is it Walter Bagehot's Congress? What is the legislative body supposed to be? What is it supposed to do? Political scientists talk about the fact that as congressmen spend more time on constituent service, they spend less on policy making. Is that inherently bad? Is it wrong? Is there a value associated with that? What is it? I'm not saying political scientists shouldn't make value judgments, but when I read those sorts of things, I think it clarifies matters if we say what our values are. Then we can say: Why can't Congress do such and such?

I'll quit with this example. When Speaker O'Neill was creating the ad hoc Energy and Welfare Committees in the House, was their creation a sign of weakness or of strength? I know most people who have dealt with that question have talked about is as a sign of the chaos

and deterioration of the Congress. Let me say that after reading my colleague Joe Cooper's paper (1981) I'm not at all sure that's what it is. It may well be a more advanced form of organization.

For example (since I'm from Texas, it's obligatory to make at least one reference to oil companies) if you looked at the organization of major oil companies prior to the 1973 Arab oil embargo, what you saw was a pretty straightforward hierarchical organizational chart. If you looked at those same oil companies today, you'd find something called matrix management. As external pressures on oil companies increased, and those corporations had to deal with environmentalists, consumer groups, state governments, etc., they responded by taking people out of different sectors in the previous organizational chart, and putting them together into what they called a matrix management. It may well be that reforms which created new committees such as the ad hoc committees may be the beginning of a more advanced form of organization. Now I don't know whether that's right or not. I'm suggesting it as a plausible alternative. More importantly, I am suggesting that when we deal with the question of what difference congressional procedures make, two things are important. One, a more centralized Congress is not necessarily better. And second, as people from the academic world view Congress, it seems to me that we really do need to define what we think the job of Congress is supposed to be, and then we're better off in determining whether procedures can or cannot affect that.

Response by Richard P. Conlon
Executive Director, Democratic Study Group

Before discussing the two papers, I would like to take note of the fact that the man we are here to honor today, Speaker of the House Thomas P. O'Neill, Jr., played a key role in some of the most important reforms that were adopted over the past decade. The first instance was the so-called "record teller" reform which made it possible to record votes on amendments for the first time in history. Prior to the adoption of this reform in 1970, all votes on amendments to legislation in the House were taken by voice or by counting, but never recording, the members for and against the amendment. This reform was the subject of a major effort by the Democratic Study Group, and Representative O'Neill agreed to be the main sponsor, thereby making the proposal more acceptable to the so-called regulars in the House. Representative O'Neill played a similar role as the Democratic whip two years later when he offered a DSG resolution in the Democratic Caucus, instructing the Democratic members of the House Foreign Affairs Committee to report legislation terminating United States involvement in the Vietnam War within a certain time. Equally as important as the substance of the resolution was the fact that this resolution reestablished the principle that the Democratic members of House committees were subject to instructions from the Democratic Caucus.

Secondly, I would like to take note of my credentials with respect to today's subject matter. The reform movement in the House over the past twelve years has been led and pushed by the Democratic Study Group. I have been the Executive Director of DSG for that period of time and as such I have been deeply involved in all phases of the effort. I am therefore going to concentrate my remarks on areas where I have firsthand knowledge, the reforms adopted as the result of DSG's efforts.

Professor Rieselbach stated that his views and those of Mr. Wolanin are very similar. I find that difficult to comprehend because the difference between the two papers is dramatic, as is my reaction to them. I find myself in agreement with most of what Mr. Wolanin had to say, despite the fact that he totally ignored the role of DSG in his paper, and in disagreement with most of what Professor Rieselbach had to say, despite the fact that he did acknowledge our role. I thank him for that.

The reason for the big differences in the two papers, I believe, is the result of the difference in vantage points from which the two authors write. Mr. Wolanin's paper reflects the insight and understanding of one who has been working inside the Congress and has had the opportunity to observe up close how Congress works, how the reforms have worked, and what additional changes are needed. Professor Rieselbach, on the other hand, writes from afar, relying on papers written by persons who themselves were only observers or at best had only limited experience and exposure. I am therefore going to direct most of my remarks to Professor Rieselbach's paper since it embodies or reflects most of the misunderstandings, misperceptions, and myths which run rampant through much of what has been written about congressional reform over the past eight years.

For example, Professor Rieselbach repeats the arguments that reforms resulted in many unanticipated and undesirable side effects . . . that they decentralized and fragmented the House . . . that the reformers' motives were to enhance their own individual positions in

the House . . . and that the reform movement itself emanated from and was carried out by the so-called Watergate class of seventy-five young Democrats elected in 1974.

In addition, Professor Rieselbach has come up with some unique innovations of his own. For example, the reforms are somehow inadequate because they were enacted incrementally over a period of years rather than all at once in a single comprehensive package . . . that the reformers weren't always sure what they wanted to accomplish . . . the reforms were spontaneous reactions to irresistible forces rather than a product of thoughtful planning . . . and that the reform effort died out because of lack of interest on the part of the press and the public.

The first point that I want to address myself to is the suggestion made throughout Professor Rieselbach's paper that the reforms should have been enacted as a single comprehensive package—what I call a "Great Leap Forward"—rather then incrementally over the years from 1968 to 1975.

We tried the "Great Leap Forward" approach and, as in Mao's China, it failed. The reform packages proposed by the Bolling Committee, the Obey Commission, the Stevenson Committee, and the Patterson Committee were all attempts to make a great leap forward. And all failed for precisely that reason. They proposed so many changes directly affecting the primary interests of so many members that they created a majority in opposition to them. In short, they maximized the opposition.

The incremental approach, on the other hand, voting on one reform at a time and spreading them out over a number of years, minimized the opposition. As a result, DSG reforms were enacted and the others were not.

The fact that reforms are enacted incrementally does not mean they are unplanned spontaneous reactions. DSG's reform objectives were agreed upon during a series of meetings in November and December of 1968 following the election of Richard Nixon. However, implementation was spread out over a period of years because of the need to develop member support and wait for the right opportunity to push specific proposals. Had DSG's basic reforms been offered as a single comprehensive package at any point, there is no question in my mind that they would have been resoundingly rejected, the same as the Bolling, Obey, and Stevenson packages. They would have been rejected because they would have imposed too much change in too short a time. Thus, I would argue

that as a general rule, reform must be incremental.

Professor Rieselbach also states that "it is hard to know with certainty what reformers sought to accomplish." I can tell you that what they sought to accomplish was exactly what their reforms were designed to accomplish: open meetings, recorded votes, secret ballot votes on committee chairmen, democratic procedures in committees, etc., etc., etc. In the same vein, the reforms are referred to as compromises. That, too, is inaccurate. Each of the various reforms was subjected to prolonged and deliberate discussion and debate in the DSG Executive Committee and at DSG membership meetings before being offered in the caucus to make sure they would work as intended and that they would not have undesirable side effects. As a result, virtually all of the major DSG reforms were approved as initially offered.

Professor Rieselbach contends that the so-called subcommittee bill of rights decentralized and fragmented the House by creating a system of autonomous subcommittees. This is simply inaccurate. In no way are House subcommittees autonomous. House rules state: "Each subcommittee of a committee is a part of that committee, and is subject to the authority and direction of that committee and to its rules so far as applicable." In addition, the Democratic chairman and Democratic members of each subcommittee are subject to the caucus of all Democrats on the committee.

What the subcommittee bill of rights and other reforms did was to remove subcommittees from under the thumb of a single individual, the committee chairman, and instead institute a body of House and caucus rules under which subcommittees must operate. In effect, the subcommittee bill of rights transferred many powers previously exercised by autocratic chairmen to the caucus of all Democrats on each committee.

Moreover, while the subcommittee bill of rights did enhance the power and the prestige of subcommittees and their chairmen, they have far less power and independence than did the prereform committee barons who held power by virtue of seniority alone, were answerable to no one, and for the most part did as they pleased, thumbing their noses at the Speaker, at the majority of their Democratic colleagues, and at their own president in the White House, if it suited their purposes. Today, such arbitrary and obstructive behavior is curbed as a result of the various procedural reforms enacted over the past decade, plus an immensely strengthened Speakership and a viable party caucus and committee caucuses. Committee chairmen and their committees, and subcommittee chairmen and their subcommittees, are given wide latitude, but if they obstruct the will of the majority of Democratic members, there are now means of dealing with such behavior.

Another great myth that has been perpetuated by political scientists and journalists is that the reforms enacted in the early 1970s have resulted in a massive proliferation in subcommittees.

I call this a myth because there has been virtually no change in the overall number of House subcommittees. The twenty-one House standing committees which existed in 1970 had a total of 139 subunits. The twenty-two House standing committees which exist today (1981) have only 143 subunits, ten of which are Budget Committee task forces.

However, now that the record is straight regarding the number of subcommittees, it should be noted that there was a significant increase in the number of members who are subcommittee chairmen as a result of the reform prohibiting members from chairing more than one subcommittee. Prior to this reform, committee chairmen and other senior members held two, three, and four subcommittee chairmanships each.

Another hardy myth contained in Professor Rieselbach's paper is that the naive reformers didn't know what they were doing and as a result brought about all kinds of unintended and undesirable side effects. This is simply not true. The so-called side effects cited by Professor Rieselbach and others *were* foreseen and *were* discussed. It was realized that many of the reforms being proposed were two-edged swords that could cut both ways. However, such undesirable results were deemed to be acceptable trade-offs for the benefits of the various reforms. Moreover, the fact that "committee proceedings and voting are now matters of public record, that lawmakers can no longer hide behind closed doors and unrecorded votes," are not side effects. That is what the reforms were intended to accomplish. Also, I cannot let the line pass that "previously, members could help out undetected, in the quiet of the committee room or on a standing or teller vote on the floor, whereas they can no longer do so with open meetings and recorded votes." I am sure that secrecy on some occasions did permit members to "help out undetected." But the more prevalent situation was that behind the wall of secrecy, members were forced to vote against their districts because the only people who knew how they were voting were the autocratic committee chairmen and their allies who were in the room or on the floor with them and who could use their powers to reward and punish accordingly.

Still another myth is that the reform movement emanated from the so-called Watergate class of seventy-five young Democrats elected in 1974. This made a grand newspaper and television story, but it is simply untrue. Nonetheless, Professor Rieselbach asserts: "These newcomers, numerous and independently-minded, were the catalyst for reform; they both created and channeled the reform movement, and without their presence in Washington, the history of the decade would almost certainly have been different."

That is absolutely wrong. The reforms were not a product of the new members elected in the 1970s, they were the product of new members elected a decade earlier in the 1960s. In fact, for the most part they were a direct result of the experiences of the 1960s members being shut out of meaningful participation in the legislative process and watching autocratic chairmen of their own party use their positions of power to obstruct party policies and programs.

Moreover, most of the major reforms were enacted before the Watergate class was ever elected. Open committee meetings, recording of floor votes, automatic secret balloting on committee chairmen, and the so-called subcommittee bill of rights were all enacted in the early 1970s. The same is true of the War Powers Resolution and the Budget and Impoundment Control Act. Some important reforms were enacted after the new members arrived, and without question they added impetus to the reform movement. But all of the major procedural and institutional reforms were already in place when the newcomers arrived in Washington, and in no way did they either "create" or "channel" the reform movement.

I can understand television, with its apparent need to hype the news, perpetuating the myth that seventy-five new members came to Washington and started a reform revolution. But I cannot understand the constant repetition of this myth in the scholarly writings of political scientists.

Throughout his paper, Professor Rieselbach assigns base motives and purposes for various reforms without any supporting evidence.

For example, he asserts that reformers "quickly seized on the reform mood to impose reforms that enhanced their own individual circumstances." There is no question that some members may have been motivated by a selfish purpose. For the most part, however, the primary motivation for all reforms was to correct the perceived inadequacies or faults in the way the House operated. And the fact that some members benefited from a particular reform is not evidence that the reform was designed solely for that purpose. After all, each reform did require a majority approval in the Democratic Caucus, and in the case of House rule changes, on the House floor.

In assessing the impact of reform, Professor Rieselbach notes that "though wounded, the seniority system survives." The suggestion is that the primary goal of the reform effort was to abolish seniority, and we failed to achieve that goal. It is true that abolition of the seniority system has been a cherished goal of many academic and liberal reformers over the years. But it is a goal that was specifically rejected by DSG. Instead, it was recognized that the seniority system had many positive values along with the negatives, and the goal of reform therefore should be to eliminate the abuses while retaining the basic system for the stability and sense of order it provides.

Thus, subcommittee assignments are now determined under a procedure whereby members of a committee select one assignment at a time in order of seniority. Similarly, senior members are given first opportunity to be elected to the positions of committee and subcommittee chairmen under a procedure which permits consideration of only one nominee at a time. Only if a nominee is voted down may another member be considered. Thus the principle of seniority is preserved by giving senior members first consideration and chairmen are made responsive to their party colleagues without subjecting them to constant and destabilizing challenges from ambitious competitors.

Professor Rieselbach concludes his paper by saying the reformed Congress is clearly different, but it is not necessarily better. I disagree. I think it is better. The changes devised and pushed through by the DSG are working as they were intended to work and Congress today, especially the House, is a more effective, more accountable, more responsible institution than before.

Like the good old days, Congress before the reforms is fondly remembered. But let's not forget what it was really like. Let's not forget that it was a system in which all the key decisions were made by a handful of senior members behind closed doors, a system where major votes were unrecorded, where committee chairmen were unaccountable, and where junior members had little or no voice at all in legislative decision making.

But most important of all, let's not forget why James MacGregor Burns entitled his book *The Deadlock of Democracy*. Let's not forget the committee chairmen who bottled up legislation in their committees. Let's not forget the Rules Committee chairman who refused to even call a committee meeting and went to milk his cows, thereby blocking major legislation initiated by a Democratic president and supported by the Speaker, the majority of Democratic members, and a majority of the American people.

Today, thanks to the reforms, House Democrats have the tools to deal with a chairman or any other member who obstructs the party program. Unfortunately we no longer have much of a program to obstruct. Thank you.

PART VI:
CONGRESS AND
FOREIGN POLICY

CONGRESS AND FOREIGN POLICY

Hon. Robert F. Drinan, S.J.
Member, United States
House of Representatives
1970-1980

For thirty years, from 1944 to 1974, the United States was without doubt the leading world power. Some will argue that American domination during that period was due in part to the fact that the Congress gave almost unquestioned deference in foreign policy matters to the Pentagon, the State Department, and the White House. During all of that period, there is no record of any appropriation denied by the Congress to the executive branch for foreign military objectives.There is likewise virtually no indication of any substantial rejection by the Congress of a policy developed by the State Department. The adage during all of the period was not exactly of presidential omniscience—but, rather, that "politics stops at the water's edge."

The Vietnam War changed all of that. The period from 1974 to 1980 brought about unprecedented challenges by the Congress to the hegemony of the executive branch over foreign policy. At this moment, it is impossible to predict how much if any of the codetermination which the Congress wrested from the executive branch may remain during the 1980s.

It was obviously the Vietnam War which upset the traditional relationship between the Congress and the White House. It was the war which aroused Senator Fulbright in 1974 to reverse his previous position, and to state that the Congress had forgotten the "wisdom of the Founding Fathers who had taught us to mistrust power, to check it and balance it, and never to yield up the means of thwarting it." Senator Fulbright conceded that Congress is "slow, obstreperous, inefficient and behind the times . . . but . . . it poses no threat to the liberties of the American people."

During the past six years, congressional assertiveness over foreign policy has grown. There have been, to be sure, previous swings of the pendulum, but never to this extent. It is simply uncertain at this time whether the Vietnam War shattered the consensus that existed over the past thirty years. It is not at all clear that there is a permanent codetermination by the Congress and the executive branch over the control of foreign policy. Many argue that the Congress actually recovered from some of the abdication

over foreign policy in which the Congress was engaged during the genera-
tion-long cold war. During the past six years, Congress imposed restraints
on the sale of arms and nuclear exports, legislated regulations for trade with
the USSR, made human rights a part of foreign policy, and curbed the
intelligence community. In addition, the Congress terminated the Vietnam
War, and enacted over President Nixon's veto the War Powers Resolution.

De-Funding the Vietnam War

On June 29, 1973, the president of the United States acknowledged the
right of Congress to end American involvement in Indochina. At that
moment, immense power shifted from the imperial president and his State
Department to the House and to the Senate. It was a victory for Congress
even though the war was more or less over. By the end of 1972, the troops in
Vietnam were down to 24,100. But it was the renewed bombing of Cambodia which de-funded the war. It was a confrontation which was won
outright by the Congress and arguably, in the process, the way in which the
United States formulates foreign policy was substantially altered.

The final compromise was to allow the bombing of Cambodia for forty-
five days, up to August 15, 1973. There were, to be sure, impressive
arguments for bombing and for a cessation of bombing of Cambodia, but
there was no argument whatsoever for carrying on a military campaign to a
date set by a statute!

The suspicion which Congress had for the executive branch reached a
new high after eight years of escalation, miscalculation, and deception. The
distress was so deep that Congress simply terminated a war which, by the
Tonkin Gulf Resolution, Congress had implicitly authorized and financed
for many years.

The consequences of this unprecedented action are:

1) The United States had, for the first time in history, lost a war. All of the
shattering consequences to the national psyche for a generation or more to
come must still unravel.

2) The turmoil caused in Cambodia and South Vietnam, with all of the
hundreds of thousands of refugees, must be attributed at least in part to the
Congress. The backlash from those events has not yet run its course. But it
has begun—as, for example, in the book by Prof. Guenther Lewy, *America
in Vietnam*, published in 1978.

The fundamental change in the congressional-executive relations
brought about by the termination of the Vietnam War has led both parties

into uncharted seas and has generated confusion and indecisiveness both in Congress and throughout the country.

War Powers Resolution

The humiliation which the Congress experienced in the prolonged agony of the Vietnam War prompted it to reassert its rights and to recapture the powers conferred on the Congress by the Constitution. Article I, Section 8, makes it clear that Congress, and Congress alone, has the power to declare war and to provide for "the common defense." This realization led to a long struggle which eventually produced, over President Nixon's veto, the War Powers Resolution.

The statute required the president to engage in prior consultation with the Congress, where possible, before he committed American troops abroad. The statute also required presidential reporting within forty-eight hours of any use of military force. The statute allowed the president to continue the use of military force in a foreign nation for ninety days, unless the Congress objected. The resolution does, however, provide that Congress can terminate military action at any time.

I personally had many problems with the War Powers Resolution as it went through Congress. I voted against it in the House and against the Conference Committee. I finally voted to override President Nixon's veto on the assumption that the Conference Committee report was better to have than the existing arrangement. The veto was overridden on October 24, 1973, by the narrow vote of 284 to 134.

Sen. Thomas Eagleton voted to sustain the veto—as did several other liberals—on the basis that the act would bring about a Defense Department full of contingency plans for wars of ninety days duration.

The several instances in which the president has used military force since the War Powers Resolution was passed demonstrate that the inherent power of the president to protect national security has not necessarily been diminished. The president used military force to evacuate American personnel from Danang, to rescue the crew of the *Mayaguez*, to evacuate American civilians during civil strife in Cyprus and Lebanon, and to transport European troops to Zaire. None of these military expeditions extended up to the ninety-day grace period. In no instance did Congress attempt to utilize the concurrent resolution by which it can, under the law, terminate a military operation. Consequently, the War Powers Resolution is still fundamentally untested. It seems, moreover, that there is little meaning to the requirement that the president "consult" Congress where possible.

There is an additional substantial ambiguity as to whether the concurrent resolution by which Congress can terminate a military action is constitutional. Is this a congressional veto of an executive action which can be challenged on constitutional grounds? In December 1980, the Ninth Circuit Court of Appeals in San Francisco declared unconstitutional a House veto of an executive action as a violation of the separation of powers. The House of Representatives in this case attempted to force the Immigration and Naturalization Service to set aside a decree by which it sought to deport an immigrant who had come to this country from Kenya. The Ninth Circuit Court of Appeals said that the action of the Congress, in a one-house veto, was a "prohibited legislative intrusion upon the executive and judicial branches."

This is the first court ruling ever to set aside a legislative veto. The federal court in San Francisco, while not ruling specifically on a two-house veto, made it clear that courts will sustain the president when he is carrying out his duty under the Constitution to "take care that the laws be faithfully executed."

Control Over Arms Sale

A third area in which the Congress has sought to regulate and modify foreign policy occurred during the 1970s in the area of arms sales. Between 1941 and 1970, the concept that the United States should be arsenal of the world went unchallenged. From 1950 to 1975, the United States gave or sold more than $85 billion worth of arms to the countries of the earth! In 1975, arms sales totalled $9.5 billion; the clients were in seventy-one countries.

This escalation of arms sales roused the Congress to enact the Nelson-Bingham Act. This law, enacted in 1974, requires the president, before issuing letters of offer for the sale of arms, to send a detailed set of justifying reasons to both houses of Congress. The Congress can set aside any proposed sale of arms over $25 million. But although the Congress intended by this legislation to be able to reverse, for example, a huge sale of Phantom jets to Saudi Arabia, the fact is that the Congress to date has never struck down any proposed sale of arms. The Congress, after much controversy, allowed in 1977 the sale for $1.2 billion of airborne warning and control systems (AWACS) to Iran. Similary, in 1978 the Congress did not strike down a sale of fifty F-5 aircraft to Saudi Arabia.

It is doubtful that the Nelson-Bingham Act is an effective way for the Congress to control the sale of arms. The time is too short and a resourceful executive can frustrate Congress. For example, on January 19, 1981, the Carter administration cleared for President Reagan a proposal to extend $40 million in United States military aid to Somalia. The Congress was not even organized on January 19, with the result that the thirty days will almost certainly go by without Congress objecting. In another instance along the same line, the Carter administration, at the eleventh hour, proposed a $2 billion arms sale to Saudi Arabia. This sale, which presumably will go through, raised to $35.3 billion the amount of arms-related sales to Saudi Arabia over the last seven years.

Reform of the Intelligence Community

The fourth initiative taken by the Congress relates to congressional attempts to control the Central Intelligence Agency. From the inception of the CIA in 1947, to the late 1970s, the agency was almost without congressional supervision. A few persons on key committees were apparently informed or even consulted about covert activities, but the Congress exploded in anger after disclosure of the abuses of the CIA in Chile in 1974. Sen. Frank Church called the CIA a "rogue elephant."

The Congress established a permanent intelligence committee in both the House and the Senate. Under legislation enacted in 1980, however, it is now necessary for the CIA to go to fewer individuals and units in the Congress than before. It still remains uncertain whether the supervisory function of the Congress over the CIA will ever be realized. The law requires that Congress be informed ahead of time, or at least simultaneously, with any covert activity on the part of the CIA. The Reagan administration will in all probability seek to diminish the restraints on the CIA, using the bad intelligence which presumably the Carter administration received from Iran as a reason to "unleash" the CIA, or at least give it the power it claims to need to obtain accurate intelligence from nations which are hostile to the United States.

The Congress Exalts Human Rights

Beginning in 1973, Congress made it clear to the administration that it desired to use the 100 United States foreign assistance programs as a method to improve the level of human rights in recipient states. In that year, the Foreign Assistance Act was amended with the declaration that "it is the sense of Congress that the president should deny any economic or military assistance to the government of any foreign country which practices the internment or imprisonment of that country's citizens for political purposes." That provision developed subsequently so that the law now commands the president to reduce or terminate "security assistance to any government which engages in a consistent pattern of gross violations of internationally recognized human rights, including torture or cruel, inhuman, or degrading treatment or punishment. . . ." On the basis of these declarations, the Congress has terminated economic aid to Chile, Argentina, Uruguay, Ethiopia, and other nations.

Congress also required the State Department to report annually on the state of human rights, not merely among the nations that receive assistance from America, but in all nations that are members of the United Nations. In addition, the Congress established a new position within the State Department of assistant secretary of state for human rights and humanitarian affairs.

Despite some criticism of the four-year record of the Carter administration in the area of human rights, it is undeniable that a very significant step forward has been made in this area. It is very difficult to point with tangible evidence to a "victory" for the human rights program of the Carter administration, but throughout the world, dissidents, refuseniks, and political refugees universally state that the accent on human rights by the Carter administration has created a new climate in which those who invoke human rights are given an unprecedented sympathy and, in some instances, their liberation. There are, obviously, other influences bringing about a more benign attitude towards political prisoners. One of them is the organization Amnesty International, which was begun in London in 1961 and which in 1977 received the Nobel Peace Prize.

The emphasis on human rights in America's foreign policy was an accent added originally by the Congress—largely through the leadership of Rep. Donald Fraser—but which was agreed to enthusiastically by the Carter administration. It exemplifies what can be done to add to America's foreign policy when the congressional and executive branches of the government are in accord.

The Congress over the past six years has taken initiatives in other areas. It dismantled the Joint Committee on Atomic Energy and asserted codetermination in the area of nuclear export controls. The Congress also intervened in an unprecedented way in what the State Department and the executive branch sought to do in the aftermath of the Greek invasion of Cyprus. This was, of course, the reaction of Greece to the Turkish expeditionary force which invaded Cyprus by sea and air in 1974. A long struggle between the Congress and the State Department ensued. The struggle over this question demonstrated that a fractious, somewhat fragmented, and belligerent Congress would no longer be subservient to what the State Department desired with respect to the foreign policy of the nation.

A similar incident occurred when President Ford asked the Congress for funds and military supplies for two pro-Western factions fighting for control of Angola against a minority Marxist movement, supported by almost 20,000 Cuban troops and $400 million in Soviet military assistance. When the Congress refused to give this power to President Ford, he said that the Congress had "lost their guts." Clearly the parallels between Vietnam and Angola were evident to members of the Congress, who did not want to vote for anything that might resemble another Vietnam.

Underlining the entire struggle between the Congress and the State Department is a now no longer monolithic view in the Congress or the country with respect to communism. Members of Congress are not about to say that they wouldn't care if a Marxist or communist group took over in Angola or elsewhere. But they are clearly in the process of reassessing the fundamental major premise of our traditional foreign policy which is that the "containment of communism" is the heart of foreign policy.

The immensity of the recent attempts by Congress to share in the formulation of United States foreign policy at least approaches the "revolutionary." It stirs up the fear which Jefferson noted to Madison when, shortly before the first inauguration of George Washington, he wrote that the "tyranny of the legislature is really the danger most to be feared." Jefferson went on to note that the "tyranny of the executive power will have its turn, but at a more distant period."

Over the past six years, Congress has presumably concluded that the "tyranny of the executive power" has arrived, and that it must be curbed. Congress beheld the White House as an imperial presidency whose powers must be modified.

Prof. Arthur Schlesinger, in his volume *The Imperial Presidency*, published in 1974, details the accretion of political power during the past several decades. He judges that there has been a quantum leap in that power since the end of World War II, but he states in addition that there had been an even more unprecedented intensification of presidential prerogatives in the first five years of the Nixon administration. This was made possible because recent presidents and even recent Congresses tended to look upon the sharing of power with Congress as a presidential courtesy, not as a matter of constitutional obligation.

The gains which the Congress has made over the past six years in the area of foreign policy may not be permanent. This administration, as well as those which will follow, will almost certainly seek to destroy any congressional partnership with the presidency in the resolution of those sensitive problems that constitute our foreign policy.

At the same time, the unbelievable progress which Congress has made since the end of the Vietnam War in insisting on its legitimate role in foreign affairs will make it very difficult and conceivably impossible for any presidency, however dominant, to bring the nation back to a situation where almost every detail of our relationships with 150 nations is decided almost exclusively by the White House and by the State Department.

THE WAR POWERS RESOLUTION

Robert Scigliano
Department of Political Science
Boston College

Introduction

The subject of my remarks is the recent effort by Congress to regain, or gain, authority over the president in the conduct of foreign affairs. My attention will be focused on the War Powers Resolution of 1973, the most symbolic if not the most important example of this effort.

Congress has in recent years attempted to bring into existence a new order in American foreign policy. Its herald was a resolution adopted by the Senate in 1969 expressing that body's sense that the president could not commit the nation to a foreign policy, whether by war or other means, without the consent of Congress.[1] Although this action was in itself without legislative effect, its spirit was enacted into a number of statutes during the 1970s. In 1973, for example, Congress ordered the president to cease the aerial bombing of communist forces in Cambodia and not to engage in further actions anywhere in Indochina; in 1975 it ordered him to withhold military assistance from Turkey after that nation's invasion of Cyprus; again in 1975 it ordered the termination of covert assistance to pro-Western forces in the Angolan civil war; and in several laws enacted during the 1970s, it judged the rights of nations to receive various forms of American aid by their governments' observance of basic human rights. The Senate also gave vigor to the treaty power in its unusual scrutiny of the Panama Canal treaties and, until it was withdrawn from consideration, the arms limitation treaty with the Soviet Union.[2]

I wish to acknowledge the support for this research by the White Burkett Miller Center for Public Affairs of the University of Virginia.

A more extensive treatment of the war powers, from a somewhat different perspective, may be found in my essay "The War Powers Resolution and the War Powers," in *The Presidency in the Constitutional Order*, eds. Joseph M. Bessette and Jeffery Tulis (Baton Rouge, La.: Louisiana State University Press, 1981), pp. 115-153.

1. National Commitments Resolution, Sen. Res. 85, U.S., Congress, Senate, *Congressional Record*, 91st Cong., 1st sess., June 25, 1969, 115, pt. 13: 17,245.

2. For a discussion of most of these and other actions see Thomas M. Franck and Edward Wiesband, *Foreign Policy by Congress* (New York: Oxford University Press, 1979).

Occupying a central place in the new congressional order is the War Powers Resolution.[3] Although it was generated by the domestic conflict that arose during the Vietnam War, the resolution certainly transcends that war and, unlike other legislative acts of the 1970s, which were more or less specific in purpose, it establishes a framework for every warlike employment of force.

What I propose to do is, first, to explain the War Powers Resolution and then to examine its constitutional doctrine and, somewhat more briefly, its policy with respect to hostilities.

The Resolution

What the War Powers Resolution does, essentially, is to define the constitutional authority of the president to engage in hostilities and to exercise some of the authority which Congress claimed for itself.

The president, it says, may "introduce" the armed forces into hostilities or hostile situations "only" when Congress has declared war or specifically authorized the introduction, or in a "national emergency", which it defines as an attack on American territory or armed forces. Hostilities are not necessarily marked by armed conflict, according to the House committee's gloss on the resolution, but include confrontations where no shots have been fired;[4] and authorization, according to the resolution itself, is not to be inferred from treaties unless implemented by legislation or to be inferred from appropriations unless clearly specified.

In exercising its own authority, Congress ordered the president to *consult* with it "in every possible instance" before he uses the armed forces in hostilities; to *report* to it after he has used them; and to *terminate* their use within sixty days (ninety days, under "unavoidable military necessity") or sooner if Congress so directs by concurrent resolution, that is, by a legislative action not submitted to executive approval.

It will help to sort out things a president may not do without the consent of Congress, according to the War Powers Resolution. He may not engage in war on behalf of allies, as Franklin Roosevelt did on a small scale in the Atlantic before Pearl Harbor and as Harry Truman did on a large scale in Korea. Nor may he order preemptive strikes, as John F. Kennedy thought of doing against Soviet missile sites in Cuba in October 1962, or engage in

---

3. U.S., *Statutes at Large*, Public Law 93-148, 87: 555.

4. U.S., Congress, House, Committee on Foreign Affairs, *War Powers Resolution of 1973*, Report No. 93-287, 93rd Cong., 1st sess., June 15, 1973, p. 7.

other acts of preemptive war, such as the naval blockade of Cuba which Kennedy settled upon. Nor may he dispose the armed forces in preparation against attack if this means placing them in hostile situations. According to the resolution, Lincoln was wrong in thinking, back in April 1861, that he had authority to supply Fort Sumter in the face of South Carolina's threat of hostilities against the fort. Nor, finally, may a president engage in such minor acts of force as the landing of forces on foreign territory during disturbances, as Dwight Eisenhower did in Lebanon in July 1958, and as Lyndon Johnson did in the Dominican Republic in April 1965, even if, as in these cases, it is done at the invitation of local authority.

It is not clear how far the War Powers Resolution allows a president to act when the nation or its armed forces are attacked. He may, the resolution states, introduce the armed forces into hostilities "pursuant to" such attacks. This seems broader than the language in the Senate bill, revised in Conference Committee, which stated that he might introduce them to "repel" such attacks.[5] On the other hand, many members of Congress thought that presidential warmaking was limited under the Constitution to strict self-defense. If they are right, Lincoln exceeded his authority when, as he said, he called forth the "war power of the government" after South Carolina's assault on Fort Sumter.[6]

One major presidential action *not* repudiated by the War Powers Resolution is American entry into war in Vietnam in 1965. The resolution acknowledges that wars need not be formally declared in order to be authorized, and the Southeast Asia Resolution of 1964, which is an act of legislation, states that the United States is "prepared, as the president determines, to take all necessary steps, including the use of armed force, to assist any protocol or member state of the Southeast Asia Collective Defense Treaty [including the Republic of Vietnam] requesting assistance in defense of its freedom."[7] It is ironic that the Vietnam War, criticized as having been undeclared and hence as unauthorized and cited "time and again" in congressional debate as evidence of the need for war powers legislation, should be constitutionally vindicated by the product of that debate.[8]

5. U.S., Congress, Senate, *Congressional Record*, 93rd Cong., 1st sess., July 20, 1973, 119, pt. 20: 25,119.

6. Message to Congress in Special Session, July 4, 1861, in Abraham Lincoln, *Collected Works*, ed. Roy P. Basler (New Brunswick, N.J.: Rutgers University Press, 1953), 4: 426.

7. U.S., *Statutes at Large*, Public Law 88-408, 78: 384.

8. U.S., Congress, House, *Congressional Record*, 93rd Cong., 1st sess., October 10, 1973, 119, pt. 26: 33,556.

One thing more needs to be said about the provisions of the War Powers Resolution. Although they inform the president of his constitutional powers in warmaking (to act unilaterally only in case of attack), they do not prohibit him from exercising others, for Congress placed its description of his powers in the resolution's preamble (technically, the "Purpose and Policy" section of the legislation) where it lacks legal status, rather than in the body of the law. In short, the resolution furnishes the president with an opinion of what it thinks the Constitution requires, allowing him to act on his own opinion of the Constitution. This puzzle was the result of a compromise between the House version of the legislation, which sought to control the president's warmaking after he had acted, and the Senate session, which sought also to control the purposes for which he could engage in hostilities. The Senate got the president's constitutional authority defined but the House kept the definition from having the force of law.[9] And so President Ford, in the view of the War Powers Resolution, acted beyond his constitutional powers in the several rescue missions he ordered in the closing phase of the Vietnam War, as did President Carter in the aborted rescue of American hostages in Iran; but they did not act illegally.

I do not wish to give the impression that the War Powers Resolution leaves the president free to use the armed forces as he thinks best, subject only to its limits on the duration of their use. He must be prepared to justify departures from what the resolution says his constitutional powers are, and he must do so against an understandable disposition on the part of many persons to accept the resolution's definition of his constitutional authority, if not to think of it as legally binding on him as well. Some persons in Congress and outside government have already expressed such views, and we should not be misled as to their force by the general approval that was given to Presidents Ford and Carter in their rescue efforts. All of these actions were quickly executed; only one, the mission against Iran, failed of success; and only one, the rescue of the merchant vessel *Mayaguez* from its Cambodian captors, involved actual combat. But what might have happened if American forces had been drawn into protracted fighting in any of these actions? Would Congress have ignored or excused the fact that the president had assumed powers it had instructed him he did not possess? Or might it have ordered him to cease fighting, perhaps censuring him before

9. See Thomas F. Eagleton, *War and Presidential Power* (New York: Liveright, 1974), pp. 206-225; and William B. Spong, Jr., "The War Powers Resolution Revisited: Historic Accomplishment or Surrender?", *William & Mary Law Review* 16 (1975): 823-859.

the nation, perhaps even finding grounds for impeaching and removing him from office?

And so the constitutional issues raised by the War Powers Resolution are important, no less important perhaps than those raised by Congress's exercise of its own authority in the law. To these issues I now turn.

Constitutional Doctrine

In defining the president's warmaking authority under the Constitution, the War Powers Resolution, as its preamble informs us, seeks "to fulfill the intent of the Framers," and in exercising authority which Congress claimed for itself it seeks to "insure that the collective judgment" of the two branches will be applied to warmaking.

It seems undeniable that, in the intention of the Framers, it belongs "exclusively to Congress to declare whether the nation, from a state of peace, shall go into that of war," as the resolution's supporters liked to quote Jefferson;[10] and it belongs to the president, if he approves, to carry on war. If Congress has the power to declare war, it surely can authorize it by specific legislation. The War Powers Resolution is on solid ground in rejecting the view of those who had argued that the Southeast Asia Resolution granted no authority for the president to engage in hostilities in Vietnam because it was not a "declaration" of war. The difference between a war that is formally declared and one that is legislated corresponds to the difference, well understood in the eighteenth century, between general war and limited war, between war that "destroys the national peace and tranquility" and war that "interrupts it only in some particulars."[11] In fact, most wars which Congress has authorized have been undeclared—from those approved against the Indians, Algeria, and France in the 1790s, to the war against the communist regime in Vietnam in 1964.

Congress's exclusive right to authorize war has often been denied in recent decades. Franklin Roosevelt, in effect, denied it in waging limited naval war in 1941, and many persons, influenced by Roosevelt's example, denied it after him. Harry Truman thought he had full authority as commander-in-chief to commit American forces to the defense of the Republic of Korea, and was concerned that he would be impairing the powers of his office by going to Congress. John F. Kennedy believed he had similar

---

10. Paper in Jefferson Mss, prepared in late May 1793, in Thomas Jefferson, *Works*, ed. Paul L. Ford (New York: G. P. Putnam's Sons, 1904), 7: 354 n.

11. *Case of the Resolution*, 2 U.S. (Dallas) 12 (1781), 20.

authority in the Cuban missile crisis and that it would be merely "useful" for Congress to "express their views" on that crisis. And Lyndon Johnson insisted that in conducting hostilities in Vietnam "we did not think the [Southeast Asia] Resolution was necessary to do what we did and what we are doing."[12] These opinions were shared by many members of Congress, especially by Democrats and, above all, by liberals.

By the time the War Powers Resolution came under consideration, however, it was mainly conservatives who defended presidential warmaking. They had, it must be said, much the worse of the constitutional argument, for they spoke of the ambiguity and flexibility of the Constitution, in the face of language which was plain and unyielding; or of the precedents which sustained presidential initiative in war, to those who challenged the precedents in the name of the Constitution; or of the need to adapt the document's arrangements to modern conditions, to those who bridled at the suggestion that the work of the Framers was obsolete. The resolution's opponents seemed to address the constitutional issues with some embarrassment, as well they might, in view of the insurmountable evidence against them on this question. And its supporters often cited that evidence with the enthusiasm of recent converts, as indeed many of them were, having been until a short time before advocates of a powerful presidency in the manner of Franklin Roosevelt.

It seems undeniable, too, that the president may, without the leave of Congress, "introduce" the armed forces into hostilities when the nation or its forces are attacked. In conceding this right, the War Powers Resolution does not specify how far the president may go. The Constitution indicates that he is not limited to measures of self-defense, at least when an attack is not a minor incident but constitutes an act of war. If Congress's war power is that of declaring "whether the nation, from a state of peace, shall go into that of war" (as I have quoted Jefferson) what is there for Congress to do when the nation finds itself at war through the act of somebody else? The Constitution allows the states to "engage in war" without congressional consent when "actually invaded," and it allows the president to use the militia against invasions and insurrections.[13] Could the Framers have

---

12. See Dean Acheson, *Present at the Creation* (New York: W.W. Norton, 1969), pp. 414-415 (on Truman); presidential press conference, September 13, 1962, in U.S., Congress, Senate, *Congressional Record*, 87th Cong., 2nd sess., September 14, 1962, 108, pt. 14: 19,537, 19,539 (Kennedy); presidential press conference, August 18, 1967, U.S., Congress, Senate, *Congressional Record*, 90th Cong., 1st sess., August 12, 1967, 113, pt. 17: 23,393 (Johnson).

13. U.S., *Constitution*, Article I, Section 10 (2).

meant the president to have less authority to use the army and navy in such circumstances? It seems not, and so Lincoln acted within his powers in taking hostile measures against the South after the capture of Fort Sumter (as the Supreme Court acknowledged in *The Prize Cases*[14]).

Where the War Powers Resolution raises serious constitutional questions is in the authority it denies to the president and in some of the authority it exercises on behalf of Congress. It denies presidential authority indirectly, by allowing the use of the armed forces "only" in those circumstances I have discussed. But Congress's power under the Constitution is to declare war, and not every use of the army and navy in hostilities or hostile situations constitutes war. Foreign war, as an early opinion of the Supreme Court defines it, is a "contention by force between two nations, in external matters, under the authority of their respective governments"; and civil war, it seems to follow, is a contention by force between elements of the same nation.[15] By this standard, there was no war in the interventions by Presidents Eisenhower and Johnson in Lebanon and the Dominican Republic; nor in the several Indochina evacuations carried out under President Ford; nor in the attempted rescue of American hostages in Iran under President Carter. And does not the Constitution give the president as much authority to take preemptive measures against attacks as it gives the states, which may act when "in such imminent danger [of invasion] as will not admit of delay?"[16]

Let me turn to the War Powers Resolution's assertions of legislative power. Where does Congress get its authority to require the president to consult with it "in every possible instance" before he introduces the armed forces into hostilities or hostile situations, and to terminate their use in hostilities upon adoption of a concurrent resolution? I suppose that prudence, if not comity, should induce a president to consult with Congress in many instances before taking action, but how can he be compelled to do so? If the president were required by law to consult with Congress before exercising his constitutional power of pardon, the restriction in all likelihood would be considered an encroachment on his authority. How can a similar restriction be justified in the case of his constitutional warmaking? As for the use of the concurrent resolution, does not the Constitution

---

14. *The Prize Cases*, 67 U.S. (2 Black) 635 (1863).

15. *Bas* v. *Tingy*, 4 U.S. (Dallas) 37, 40 (Justice Washington).

16. See note 13.

require all bills and resolutions, certainly resolutions having legislative effect, to be submitted to the president for his approval or veto? Does not this unilateral legislative device reverse the constitutional relationship, in submitting the president's actions to legislative approval or veto?

The War Powers Resolution seems to rest on broader constitutional ground than the right of Congress to declare war. It seems to assume that the president's authority in military and, more generally, foreign affairs is confined entirely, or nearly so, to his enumerated powers in the Constitution, and that everything else belongs to Congress. This doctrine is not stated in the resolution, though it was frequently avowed in the deliberations that took place on it. As the Senate sponsor of the measure, Jacob Javits, informed his colleagues, "a president is commander-in-chief, period." And as the Senate committee which reported it to the floor asserted, Congress possesses "residual legislative authority over the entire domain of foreign policy—not just the war powers."[17]

The doctrine of residual legislative power underlay Congress's consideration of what the War Powers Resolution calls the president's constitutional powers. Should these powers include retaliating for attacks on the armed forces? No, the Senate said, he might abuse it. Should they include retaliating for attacks on American territory and forestalling attacks either on American territory or armed forces? Yes, said the Senate, for that is necessary to security; but no, said the Conference Committee of the two houses for reasons that are not clear. Finally, should the right of self-defense include the rescue of Americans in danger abroad? Yes, said the Senate; no, said the Conference Committee because, as Senator Javits reported, it was decided that the power of rescue was "neither desirable nor necessary" for the president to have.[18]

Thus the War Powers Resolution concedes to the president the power of defending the nation and its armed forces when they have been attacked. The use of force to forestall attack or to retaliate for attack or to protect Americans and American interests by hostile measures short of war were considered to be powers in the legislative arsenal, to be given or withheld from the president as Congress decides.

---

17. U.S., Congress, Senate, *Congressional Record*, 93rd Cong., 1st sess., October 10, 1973, 119, pt. 26: 33,550; U.S., Congress, Senate, Committee on Foreign Relations, *War Powers*, Report No. 220, 93rd Cong., 1st sess., June 14, 1973, p. 13.

18. U.S., Congress, Senate, *Congressional Record*, 93rd Cong., 1st sess., November 7, 1973, 119, pt. 28: 36,189.

Indeed, the War Powers Resolution seems to regard all powers that the president may exercise in hostilities as coming from Congress rather than, or as much as, from the Constitution. This seems to be the basis of the resolution's requirements that the president consult with Congress before engaging in hostilities and that he terminate hostilities when Congress orders him to do so unilaterally, by concurrent resolution. It is hard to see how Congress could require these things when the president is exercising authority which the Constitution gives him; rather the War Powers Resolution seems to suppose that the president is exercising authority delegated to him by Congress when he acts in the national defense, and so is amenable to congressional control. The War Powers Resolution rests then on a constitutional doctrine that war and foreign affairs generally are legislative in character and, moreover, that residual power over them is given by the Constitution to Congress. The document's "necessary and proper" clause, which is quoted in paraphrase in the resolution, allows Congress to carry its residual powers, along with others invested in it, into execution.

Among the leading Framers, Madison seems to be in closest agreement with this doctrine of constitutional power. It was he who proposed to the Constitutional Convention that it define the powers of the executive to be "to carry into effect the national laws."[19] But Madison never claimed that the powers over war and foreign affairs were legislative in nature, let alone that they were residually possessed by Congress. The most that he said, in his Helvidius essays, is that the powers of *declaring* war and making *treaties* were legislative and not executive in character, and then only "substantially" so; and he never believed that Congress had powers beyond those enumerated for it or incidental to its enumeration. Thus from his opinion concerning the nature of the powers to declare war and to make treaties, Madison derived for Congress the rather modest powers of deciding whether a treaty obligated it to declare war, and of being a necessary partner in the suspension of treaties.[20] Madison's constitutional doctrine of foreign affairs, if it can be called a doctrine, is reticent about a good deal of activity by government in this domain including most of what is assumed for Congress by the War Powers Resolution and other recent legislative efforts in foreign affairs.

---

19. *The Records of the Federal Convention of 1787*, ed. Max Farrand (New Haven, Ct.: Yale University Press, 1937), June 1 (Madison's notes), 1: 67.

20. Madison, Helvidius Nos. 2 and 4, in *Writings*, ed. Gaillard Hunt (New York: G.P. Putnam's Sons, 1906), 6: 151-160, 165; Federalist No. 44, in Alexander Hamilton, James Madison, and John Jay, *The Federalist* (New York: Modern Library, 1937), pp. 292-294.

If Madison was their best authority among the Framers, it seems that congressional supporters of the War Powers Resolution did not have as strong a constitutional case as they thought they did. It also happens that the resolution's opponents had a better argument than they used, offered to them by Hamilton in his Pacificus essays. According to Hamilton, the power of Congress to declare war and the power of the Senate to consent to treaties are exceptions to a general grant of executive power conveyed to the president through the vesting clause of Article II of the Constitution. Hamilton did not specify everything contained in the general grant, though it seems clearly to embrace the general domain of war and foreign affairs. He did say here that it included the right to obligate Congress to declare war on the basis of a president's interpretation of a treaty, and the rights to suspend treaties and recognize foreign governments.[21]

Here was a constitutional doctrine that could have been used by opponents of the War Powers Resolution. It did not support the view taken by some opponents that the president could go to war on his own authority or on the basis of a treaty obligation. But it did support their other view, that the president may engage fully in war once it is declared or started by another nation, that he may forestall attacks and order reprisals for them, and that he may take various hostile measures short of war to protect the citizens or interests of the United States.

Madison and Hamilton did not disagree as to whether the Constitution vested general executive power in the president, but as to the scope of that power. Hamilton drew his understanding of the power, it seems clear, from Montesquieu, who considered war and foreign affairs to be an executive power which each nation exercises in its relations with others.[22] Madison and the Constitutional Convention seemed to reject this view, in defining executive power in the limiting way I have noted, as the execution of the laws; and yet the broader view kept emerging in the Convention's deliberations—for example, in its discussions of the difference between "declare war" and "make war" and of the Senate's right to keep secret journals of its proceedings on appointments and treaties.[23] It emerged also in some of the

---

21. Hamilton, Pacificus No. 1, in *Papers*, ed. Harold C. Syrett et al. (New York: Columbia University Press, 1969), 15: 33-43.

22. Montesquieu, *The Spirit of the Laws*, trans. Thomas Nugent (New York: Hafner Publishing Co., 1949), 1: bk. 11, ch. 6, p. 151.

23. *Records of the Federal Convention*, August 17 (McHenry's notes; see also Madison's notes), 2: 320, 318-319; August 6, 10, and 11 (Madison's notes), 2: 180, 255-256, 259.

earliest actions of the new government: in the "executive calendar" which the Senate established in 1789 to receive treaties; in the legislation creating executive departments, also in that year, in which the secretary of the treasury was assigned his duties by law and the secretaries of foreign affairs and war were told to look to the president for theirs; in Jefferson's opinion to the president in 1790, informing him that the Senate could stipulate neither the ranks nor the destinations of diplomatic officers, inasmuch as "the transaction of business with foreign nations is executive altogether."[24]

A broad understanding of executive power also made its way into the War Powers Resolution. After all of Congress's talk about the only true warmaking power of the president being to "repel attacks," it not only substituted language at the last moment which vaguely defined his power as that of "introducing" the armed forces upon attack, but by inference from the preamble of the resolution, permitted him to do all the things it had said presidents of the past had wrongfully done.

Policy

Let me turn now from constitutional doctrine to issues of policy raised by the War Powers Resolution.

The policy of the resolution, like that of Congress's recent efforts in foreign affairs generally, is what members of Congress often call "partnership" or "codetermination" in the conduct of foreign policy. The resolution refers to it as "collective judgment" and it seeks to introduce it into Congress's relations with the president, as we have seen, by limiting what a president may do and by enabling Congress to control whatever he does after the fact.

From the standpoint of partnership, the War Powers Resolution registers Congress's disapproval of the *manner* in which the United States has engaged in hostilities in the past. Presidents had not been in the habit of seeking congressional consent for them, except when war itself was at stake, and not always then; nor had they often consulted with Congress before ordering hostile actions, at least not in any meaningful way. Not many actions escaped this disapproval, for the precedents, as Senator Javits pointed out, went back "two hundred years."[25] The War Powers Resolution was intended to change all this. It would, moreover, allow

---

24. Thomas Jefferson, *Writings*, ed. Andrew A. Lipscomb and Albert E. Bergh (Washington, D.C.: Thomas Jefferson Memorial Association, 1904), 3: 16.

25. Senate, *Congressional Record*, 93rd Cong., 1st sess., October 10, 1973, p. 33,550.

Congress to review presidential actions on the basis of full written reports, and to terminate them, even when it had authorized them in advance by specific legislation, without having to consult the president or do anything at all.

The War Powers Resolution seems also to register Congress's disapproval of *what* some presidents had done in the past, that is, with the substance of American foreign policy. The Senate committee report on the legislation, for example, speaks disapprovingly of "gunboat diplomacy," and individual members referred to various presidential actions which should never have been taken.[26] Congressional supporters had recent events foremost in mind and, above all, the hostilities just ended in Indochina. "I have come through two-and-a-half years of debate on this issue," a senator remarked as the resolution approached passage, "convinced that we are still trying to prevent another war in Vietnam."[27] In this sense, the slogan "No More Vietnams" accurately describes the resolution. It is as though the majority in Congress mused as follows. If there had been war powers legislation in July 1964, President Johnson could not have sent American destroyers along the North Vietnamese coast in an intelligence-gathering mission; if the North Vietnamese had attacked our naval vessels, he could not have ordered retaliatory air strikes over North Vietnam; if Congress had been asked to approve a Tonkin Gulf-type resolution, it would have realized that it was granting authority that the president did not already have, and any authority it granted him might, as a result, have been narrowly defined; if the president later wished to engage in combat hostilities in Vietnam, as Johnson did in May 1965, and could not be dissuaded in his consultations with Congress, the advance authorization given him in the Tonkin Gulf-type legislation would have had to be renewed after sixty days, and perhaps Congress, if it renewed it at all, would have done so by a series of brief extensions, keeping the president on a short tether until it had a clearer view of the situation it was getting into.

The slogan "No More Vietnams" questions not only the Vietnam War but the policy of containment which underlay it. This policy expresses the readiness of the United States "to take all necessary steps, including the use of armed force" (in the words of the Southeast Asia Resolution) in lending

---

26. Senate, Committee on Foreign Relations, *War Powers*, 93rd Cong., 1st sess., June 14, 1973, p. 23.

27. Sen. Gale W. McGee, Senate, *Congressional Record*, 93rd Cong., 1st sess., November 7, 1973, p. 36,192.

assistance to nations requesting it in defense of their freedom against communism. "No More Vietnams" excludes force, and thereby any meaningful threat of force, as a means of containing communist aggression, at least with respect to third world nations which are distant from America's frontiers. The War Power Resolution does not go this far, since, as I have shown, it does not prevent future Vietnams and, in fact, recognizes the authority under which this nation went into Vietnam. But the spirit of the legislation, reflected in its provisions, does seek to discourage the employment of force in the pursuit of American foreign policy.

In its definition of the president's war powers and in its restraints upon his exercise of them, the War Powers Resolution embodies the hope that war might be, if not leashed, subordinated to the rule of law. The Constitution's framers, who were also engaged in policy making, were likewise hopeful in this respect, though to a much less extent. Departing from Locke and Montesquieu, their teachers on the subject of separation of powers, they placed a check on "the dog of war," as Jefferson stated, "by *transferring* the power to declaring war from the executive to the legislative body."[28] But this was as far as they were willing to go in dividing the war power. It is worth noting that they chose not to define Congress's power as that to "make" war (that is, of "to enter into" and also "conduct" war), since that would have transferred more power to Congress than they wished.

The Framers agreed with Locke that laws are much less able to direct the conduct of foreign affairs (including warmaking) than domestic affairs, and that, as a consequence, much must be left to the discretion of those to whom that conduct is entrusted.[29] They acknowledged, too, all of them so far as I know, that the Constitution itself could not provide for every emergency, and that a president might have to act beyond his delegated powers on extraordinary occasions, perhaps to exercise powers assigned to Congress; and they thought (or at least their great student, Lincoln, thought) that the Constitution had provided for its own limited violation when necessary to save its entirety, through the oath it requires of the president alone, to "preserve, protect, and defend the Constitution of the United States."[30]

When they were not arguing about the Constitution but about proper policy, opponents of the War Powers Resolution, in their emphasis on the

28. Jefferson, *Writings*, 7: 461. Emphasis supplied.

29. Locke, *Two Treatises of Government*, ed. Peter Laslett (New York: Mentor Books, 1965), "Second Treatise," para. 147.

30. Lincoln, Message to Congress, July 4, 1861, *Collected Works*, 4: 430.

need for flexibility in regard to using the armed forces, seemed closer to the spirit of the Framers than supporters of the legislation. Also, the House of Representatives was more concerned with flexibility than the Senate. It will be recalled that the House did not want to define the president's warmaking authority and thereby to limit it, whereas the Senate did. The sponsor of the House bill, Clement J. Zablocki, was unwilling to "shackle the president," as he said, but wished, when the president assumes authority beyond what he truly has, to allow him "to proceed for a limited time."[31] The Senate was compelled by House insistence to give way, and to settle for a definition of presidential authority which itself has no authority.

It is a good thing, in my view, that the House, under the leadership of Representative Zablocki, won out in its contest with the Senate, under the leadership of Senator Javits. There are persons who, as I have noted, interpret the War Powers Resolution as forbidding the president to do what it indicates the Constitution does not allow him to do. I think it would be a mistake, and harmful to the interests of the nation, if their views should gain popular acceptance and if the discretion which the resolution finally leaves in the president's hands should disappear in a narrow exposition of his constitutional powers. There is something suspect about an opinion of those powers which runs counter to so much of American experience. It is not, moreover, an opinion engraved in the Constitution but, to the contrary, seems to me to be less sound constitutionally than the one I have associated with Hamilton. Finally, I am wary of a constitutional interpretation that has the implications of this one. How could the president send the armed forces anywhere, by the War Powers Resolution's definition of his authority, if, say, the Soviet Union should warn him of dangerous consequences? Could he send the navy into the Gulf of Mexico or the army along the nation's frontiers if his action would result in a "hostile situation," which, as the House committee tells us, need not be more than an armed confrontation?

Conclusion

In the War Powers Resolution, Congress sought to regain authority over the use of military force which the Constitution had allocated to it but which some presidents had arrogated to themselves, often with congressional support or acquiescence. But Congress also claimed for itself authority

---

31. U.S., Congress, House, *Congressional Record*, 93rd Cong., 1st sess., May 3, 1973, 119, pt. 11: 14,215; and June 25, 1973, 119, pt. 17: 21,209.

which it was not meant to possess or which is constitutionally doubtful. Our politics has been marked by a tendency to excessive reactions, and yet a healthy foreign policy depends on restraining such movements. Moderation did lay a calming hand on the passage of the resolution, amidst the highly charged feelings that existed in Congress, as I have tried to show, and one must hope that the same spirit will be present in situations to which it might apply in the future.

PART VII:
CONGRESS AND
THE AGENCIES

CONGRESS: A VIEW FROM THE AGENCIES

by Joan Claybrook
Administrator, National Highway Traffic
Safety Administration (1977-1981)

Having worked for a representative and a senator, having served my time as a bureaucrat, and having functioned as a consumer lobbyist and a citizen overseer of government agencies, I view the critical question about the relationship between the Congress and the executive agencies as being: "Does the Congress adequately represent the interests of the citizenry in the operation of the government?" As the branch of government closest to the voters, that is clearly its primary role. But does the Congress fulfill this mandate?

The only correct answer to that question is that sometimes it does and sometimes it doesn't. The Congress is indeed schizophrenic. Congressional behavior depends on who is hurt and who is helped by the particular program; the leadership and skills of the pertinent subcommittee chairmen and other interested members; the mood of the country; the determination and attention of various lobbies, both for business and for consumers; the leadership exercised by the government agency; and the effectiveness of the program. In short, the environment as well as the issue are crucial to determining where the balance of power lies, and how a particular issue is handled by the Congress.

The creative tension between the executive and legislative branches structured by the Constitution under the principle of separation of powers clearly works to restrain the executive agencies from indulging in untoward excesses much of the time. There is no question about the need for restraints and guidance. The executive agencies have enormous power and authority because of their size, because of the broad responsibilities delegated by the Congress and the assumption of implied authority flowing from them, because of the complexities of the programs being administered, because of their inaccessibility to the public, because individual members of Congress can be deterred by political pressures, and because usually it is one or two members of Congress, not the entire institution, who are attempting to oversee the government agency.

This is not to dismiss the power of a long-time committee chairman such as Jamie Whitten of the House Appropriations Committee, or Jack Brooks of the House Government Operations Committee, or others. But even committee chairmen have had their wings clipped in the democratic reforms of the Congress in the early 1970s. They must be elected by their peers, they can chair only one subcommittee, and their committee caucuses insist on making decisions previously reserved to the chair.

Despite this imbalance of resources and knowledge, the Congress has a number of powerful instruments for imposing its will on executive agencies. These include substantive legislation, authorization and appropriation power, general oversight (usually exercised through public hearings), investigations by committee staff or the Government Accounting Office, the congressional veto (a device of dubious constitutionality), as well as confirmation, subpoena, and impeachment powers. To assess the role of the Congress, and particularly of a few members, to assure—or not assure—the representation of the public interest in government decision making, I would like to discuss an issue of life and death—automotive safety—which has touched most of the formal and informal relationships between the two branches of government.

For many years the Congress dealt with highway safety matters casually and with little regard for any scientific analysis of how to prevent death and injury. By the mid-1960s, following publication of Ralph Nader's *Unsafe At Any Speed* and several medical treatises and more popular articles, a number of members of the House and Senate were ready to initiate legislation to require the building of safer cars for the American public.

The original auto safety statute was enacted in 1966; it was the first of a number of consumer protection laws enacted in the late 1960s and early 1970s, and has served as a model for the drafting of other consumer laws. The authors, most of whom retired from the Congress in the last several years, designed a law with many different provisions to assure the protection of the public. The statute creates an agency to engage in research and issue federal motor vehicle safety standards to reduce death and injury on the highway. It relies on the informal procedures of the Administrative Procedure Act which assure the opportunity for public comment on government regulations, but in the informal context, allow the agency to proceed expeditiously and not get bogged down in delaying tactics such as cross-examination and other formal procedures. It requires the agency to provide a full explanation of the rationale underlying its decisions in rule making. Because the auto safety law was enacted at the same time as the Freedom of Information Act, it assures the public access to agency documents, particularly those relevant to rule-making decisions. The public is guaranteed the right to sue the agency if it disagrees with the legal basis for an agency action. The statute gives any interested person the right to petition the agency for action and requires a response within 120 days. It requires manufacturers of motor vehicles to notify owners of safety defects and to recall the vehicles for correction without charge. It requires the agency to design and produce experimental safety vehicles as models to show what kind of safety can be readily built into cars by the manufacturers. It creates an advisory committee, the majority of whose members must represent the public, a most unusual statutory requirement. It authorizes the agency to develop technical information for consumers about the durability and safety of vehicles by model.

Clearly, the intent of this law is to assure the installation of improved safety in cars offered for sale, and to involve the public generally in that process. Over the past fourteen years, members of Congress, primarily the chairmen and subcommittee chairmen who oversee the program, have generally pushed the agency to use this authority effectively to help reduce the fifty thousand deaths and four million injuries from motor vehicle crashes each year, and with some exceptions, the agency has followed that guidance.

However, there has been one particular issue, of overriding importance, where the Congress in the last few years not only has failed to represent the interests and, according to all the reputable public opinion polls, the views of the public, but most recently has attempted to subvert their interests. This story, about automatic restraint systems, such as air bags or automatic belts, is in part the story of how one or two determined members of Congress, with the help of a business lobby, can undermine an agency action by using congressional oversight tools; of how knowledgeable citizens had little influence on members of Congress reluctant to vote for a so-called controversial agency decision; of how congressional political attacks on emerging technologies subject to agency regulations can inhibit business investments, in this case investments which would be of exceptional benefit to the public.

Automatic restraint systems, particularly air bags, if used in all vehicles on the highway, could save more than nine thousand lives each year and mitigate thousands of injuries. There is no equivalent public health measure known today with such potential. In short, like the decision in the

1950s to immunize all school children against polio, automatic restraints could be the technological vaccine of the 1980s.

The first vehicle restraint systems, to keep the occupants from being thrown violently into the hard surfaces of the automobile interior, were belts, originally lap belts and then shoulder belts.

In the middle 1960s, the Eaton Corporation began developing for the Ford Motor Company a new concept called air bags, which are made of nylon and inflated with air instantaneously in a serious frontal crash to cushion the occupant's head, neck, and chest from smashing into the steering column, dashboard, and windshield. By 1970, General Motors (under the leadership of its president, Ed Cole, an engineer) was deeply involved in preparing for production of these innovative systems. By that winter, the auto safety agency issued the first motor vehicle safety standard which would measure injury levels in a dynamic simulated crash and require automatic occupant restraints. Just as the companies were getting ready to begin preparing for production systems in the spring of 1971, Henry Ford objected. The Nixon administration, on Ford's advice, changed the safety standard to require interlocking seat belts instead. After a year in production, the Congress in 1974 ordered the agency to remove the interlock because of public objections, and enacted a congressional veto on any other safety standard concerning occupant restraints other than existing belt systems.

In 1976, Secretary of Transportation William Coleman contracted with the major auto companies to produce several hundred thousand air bag vehicles for a two-year demonstration project in 1980 and 1981 in lieu of reissuing the safety standard. But in June 1977, the new Secretary of Transportation, Brock Adams, issued the standard to take effect in 1982 through 1984, giving the companies the very generous lead time they had requested.

During consideration of the new safety standard, several members of Congress testified before Secretary Adams on the need for it, as did a broad representation of public witnesses, including retired General Motors president Ed Cole. However, the next three years witnessed an attack on the lifesaving air bag system by a few members of Congress which has been damaging as well as incomprehensible.

It has been incomprehensible, even from the American automotive industry's point of view, for a number of reasons. First, the addition of such an effective lifesaving and injury-reducing system would go a long way toward repairing the reputation of an industry long thought to have little regard for the public interest. Second, after the first year or two of production, air bags would be highly profitable—just like automatic transmissions or air conditioners, which are far more complex and costly automotive systems. Third, it is an American technology and would bring credit on the industry for its innovative genius. Fourth, air bags could significantly enhance the sales of American cars, particularly the smaller, inherently less safe cars, in competition with the less solid Japanese imports. Fifth, Ford and General Motors have invested millions of dollars in the development of air bag systems during the last decade and should want to recoup that investment. Sixth, in mass production, the air bag should add no more than $200 to the price (not cost) of the car in the first year or two, and $150 thereafter. On the average, consumers spend $800 on optional equipment when they purchase new cars. Finally, the safety standard did not even mandate installation of air bag systems. It is a performance standard which requires automatic protection of front seat occupants in a 30 m.p.h. crash against serious injury or death, and this can be achieved in most cars with either automatic belts or air bags (the exception being three-passenger front seats where the belts do not provide adequate protection).

The congressional attack began with the congressional veto opportunity. Under the 1974 statute, the two houses of Congress were given sixty legislative days to veto the new safety standard or allow it to take effect. A week after the standard was promulgated in June 1977, Rep. Bud Shuster (R.-Pa.) held a press conference attacking air bags because the inflator device used sodium azide, which he called a dangerous and explosive chemical. His attack was grounded on rhetoric, not fact. The chemical is in a processed pellet form which is incapable of causing an explosion. It is encased in a hermetically sealed container behind the dashboard which is inaccessible and virtually impossible to open. When the air bag inflates, the chemical turns into harmless hydrogen gas. To dispose of the car at the end of its life, the air bag need only be inflated and the chemical disappears, unlike battery acid or gasoline in the tank.

These groundless charges continued throughout the summer. The committee hearings in the fall were generally positive, with broad support voiced by a wide spectrum of interests—from the insurance industry to crash survivors who were the owners of a small group of ten thousand General Motors cars sold with air bags from 1974 to 1976. During the committee vote in the House, Rep. John Dingell, a Democrat from Michigan, emerged as the main adversary. The Senate voted 65 to 31 not to veto, and the House Commerce Committee, in a close vote, agreed not to veto the standard, but Representative Dingell then vowed to "get the air bag" at the next opportunity. (Interestingly, a number of very conservative senators, including Paul Laxalt, Orrin Hatch, and Jake Garn, voted for the standard. As with other space-age technologies, the air bag has been developed by companies located in several western states and has thus been supported by a broad political spectrum in the Congress.)

During consideration of the Department of Transportation appropriations bill in mid-1978, Representative Shuster, assisted by Representative Dingell, proposed an amendment to prohibit use of any appropriations for air bag activities. Several members, particularly Rep. Bob Eckhardt (D.-Tx.), Rep. Silvio Conte (R.-Mass.), and the ranking minority on the Department of Transportation's appropriations subcommittee, moved to limit the prohibition to just "enforcement or implementation" of the standard. Since it would not take effect until 1982, the amendment was considered harmless and was enacted into law.

After this attack, a coalition of supporters for the standard and the air bag was formed by the insurance industry, consumer groups, and labor supporters. A separate group was also formed by the air bag suppliers to defend the standard.

By late spring of 1979, several new developments emerged. General Motors, in testing its air bag design for its large l982 cars, claimed to have found a problem with air bags harming small children under age six who are sitting or leaning up against the dashboard when the air bag inflates. The General Accounting Office, which had begun a review of the standard in l977 out of its Detroit office, in an unusual political action released a draft of its report to Representative Dingell the day the auto safety authorization bill was before the House Rules Committee in preparation for floor consideration. The report did not recommend any change in the standard, but it criticized the agency for not having thoroughly researched the problems with sodium azide and with the out-of-position child. The agency responded that the standard did not require use of sodium azide, that it was preferred by the industry, that any environmental or health criticisms had been resolved, and that the out-of-position child issue, to the extent it existed, was caused by the General Motors design and was not an inherent problem of any air bag system.

The General Accounting Office charges were reproduced and enlarged. Representative Dingell made massive information demands on the agency which required 500 hours to answer in a two-week period. He acquired some film footage from a dismissed and disgruntled former employee of an agency contractor showing an air bag inflator failing, and claimed it proved air bags could catch fire. The inflator was not a production type, but one used only in research, with a removable end piece. It was cheaper for repeated research tests and the failure was caused by overuse. It had no relevance to production systems.

After all this fuss, Representative Dingell offered an amendment identical to the earlier Shuster amendment of the Department of Transportation appropriations bill in September 1979, and it passed by forty votes. Following this vote, General Motors announced it could not produce air bags in time to meet the 1982 standard because it had not solved the out-of-position child problem. However, two months later, General Motors president Pete Estes told the new secretary of transportation in their first meeting that General Motors had solved these problems and would be producing 1982 air bag systems. (The presentation was reminiscent of Krushchev's release of Austria to the free world in his first meeting with Eisenhower.)

In December, Rep. David Stockman, a Republican from Michigan, offered an amendment at the last moment to the agency's authorization bill claiming to give consumers a "choice" of restraint systems. It was misunderstood and accepted by the subcommittee chairman and then adopted on the floor of the House by a large margin. Upon careful reading, it was found to completely undermine the automatic restraint standard by giving consumers a so-called choice of only active belts.

By the end of 1979, the on-again/off-again politics of air bags had discouraged many air bag suppliers. They were concerned that should this behavior continue they might lose their entire investment in development and production of these systems. After the General Motors decision, they were willing to continue in the business and they were bouyed by the announcement by Mercedes that it would install air bags as standard equipment in its 1982 models sold in the United States.

In the spring of 1980, with the downturn in auto sales, the automotive industry began an attack on government regulation, apparently to divert attention away from their mismanagement and financial difficulties. General Motors announced it was not going to offer air bags in 1982 models after all because it was redesigning the large cars in 1983 and didn't want to make that investment for one year. They asked for a delay in the standard, and the coverage of small cars first, so the Japanese would be affected at the same time they were.

In the July 1980 Conference Committee on the agency's authorization bill, Sen. John Warner emerged as the major advocate of air bags. He proposed reversing the standard to affect small cars first, but he also got acceptance of a proposition to require the five largest sellers of cars in the United States to offer air bags for sale for three years between 1982 and 1985. After passing the Senate, the bill failed to pass the House by three votes— even though the domestic auto manufacturers supported this final version. The opposition was lead by Representative Dingell, who has just become the new chairman of the House Commerce Committee.

The passive restraint standard is still in effect. The agency decision still prevails, but the automotive industry will make another try during the next few months in the Congress and through the White House to delay the effective date, and will probably succeed, without any concomitant commitment to manufacture air bags as in the Warner compromise. Despite the agency's superior resources and knowledge, despite the hollowness of the attacks, despite the support of strong and effective members of Congress from both sides of the aisle, despite broad public support for improved motor vehicle safety, this story is an illustration of the power a few persistent members of Congress have to deter and delay and perhaps ultimately undermine an agency decision to save thousands of lives and mitigate untold injuries. It shows the power of the business world when it lobbies to oppose or postpone even a safety standard, and the difficulties facing safety advocates who do not have the resources to compete with business political action groups. It shows the reluctance of some members of Congress to vote for a proven safety device once it is characterized as "controversial." It is an example of a trend in recent years toward the deep involvement of Congress in particular agency decisions as part of their oversight activities.

There are many other power struggles between members of Congress and government agencies where the dominant forces in the Congress serve to represent the interests of citizens rather than manufacturers or business developers. And there are plenty of examples of actions by the executive branch that are antithetical to the broad public interest and I presume we will see many more in the next few years.

But if there should be a tilt in the decision making of a member of Congress, particularly on a public health issue, such as the modest improvement in the safety design of cars, that tilt I believe should be toward the broadest interests of one's constituency, not the narrowest. "Duty," as Alfred North Whitehead reminded us, "arises from the power to alter the course of events." But the competition to influence the Congress has become brutal, as its authority and control over the nation's purse strings have expanded. And with the insertion of vast amounts of corporate money into congressional campaigns, the balance of power in the Congress is gradually but surely being assumed by individuals whose allegiances are tied to those interests rather than the social needs of their voting constituency. We should expect the activities of the Congress over the next few years at least, whether in enacting legislation or overseeing the executive agencies, to exhibit additional evidence of these pressures. And as this happens, it will inevitably influence the behavior and performance of the executive agencies in their love/hate relationship with congressional overseers.

CONGRESS AND THE AGENCIES: FOUR THEMES ON CONGRESSIONAL OVERSIGHT OF POLICY AND ADMINISTRATION

by Joel D. Aberbach
Institute of Public Policy Studies
The University of Michigan

When the organizers of this conference asked me to participate, I was a bit wary because I am in the midst of a project on congressional oversight of policy and administration and still have a bit to go before I reach any firm conclusions. But they urged me to come and talk a bit about the topic and my research, while recognizing that these are still preliminary ideas.

With this caveat as background, what I'd like to do is to develop four broad themes about oversight which are related to my research.

1) The structure of American government and the assumptions behind it make congressional oversight of administration and policy important in maintaining control of the bureaucracy by elected officials, and in maintaining Congress's role as a coequal branch of government — but the structure and assumptions also make oversight problematic.

2) With the emergence of the bureaucratic state, Congress has prodded itself to do more oversight, although it rarely seems satisfied with the results of this prodding, both in terms of the amount of oversight done and its results.

3) From all we can tell, the amount of oversight done by Congress has increased substantially, and the increase is linked to recent changes in the environment outside and inside the Congress.

4) Closely related to the third point, oversight, like almost everything else in Congress, is an intensely political activity. It is linked to the political

Thanks are due to the National Science Foundation (Grant Nos. SES 78-16812, SES 80-23315), the Brookings Institution, and the Rackham Faculty Research Program at The University of Michigan for their support. The opinions and conclusions are those of the author and do not necessarily reflect the views of the sponsoring organizations.

environment of members and staff, and is used by them for a variety of political purposes.

Any of you who have worked in this area know that definitions of oversight litter the landscape, but let me give you mine before beginning: congressional review of the actions of federal departments, agencies, and commissions, and of the programs and policies they administer. This includes review that takes place during program and policy implementation as well as afterwards. Oversight, then, is one critical aspect of congressional control of administration.

Let me start with the first theme, that the structure of American government and the assumptions behind it make congressional oversight of policy and administration important, but problematic. The American system of government is one, to use Neustadt's classic characterization, of "separate institutions sharing powers."[1] The framers of the Constitution, fearing the ill effects of the concentration of power and authority, partitioned them with great care. One major reason for this was a deep-seated suspicion of power. The Convention delegates, to use Robert Dahl's words, "shared a hard-headed, unsentimental view of the ability of human beings to withstand the temptations of power. They took it for granted that individuals are easily corrupted by power.... The best way to prevent the abuse, then, was not to trust in human character but to limit the legal authority allocated to any person and to set one power against another."[2] As Madison said in Federalist No. 51: "Ambition must be made to counteract ambition."[3]

The grand design of the system the Framers devised was one where every actor or institution would be checked by another. Power would be diffused, individuals and institutions would be forced to accommodate each other, and the ambitions of political actors would be harnessed, hopefully for the public good. Burns quotes Richard Hofstedter to the effect that the Madisonian aim was "a harmonious system of mutual frustration."[4]

---

1. Richard E. Neustadt, *Presidential Power: The Politics of Leadership* (New York: John Wiley and Sons, 1976), p. 101.

2. Robert A. Dahl, *Democracy in the United States: Promise and Performance* (Chicago: Rand McNally, 1976), p. 73.

3. Alexander Hamilton, John Jay, and James Madison, *The Federalist* (New York: Random House, The Modern Library, 1937), p. 337.

4. James MacGergor Burns, *The Deadlock of Democracy: Four-Party Politics in America* (Englewood Cliffs, N.J.: Prentice Hall, 1963), p. 22.

Where was the bureaucracy to fit into all this? This is clearly an important question from the contemporary perspective, but it did not take up much time in the work of the Framers. As James Q. Wilson says in his essay, "The Rise of the Bureaucratic State":

> The Founding Fathers had little to say about the nature or function of the executive branch of the new government. The Constitution is virtually silent on the subject, and debates in the Constitutional Convention are almost devoid of reference to an administrative apparatus.[5]

Not much thought was given to the problems of administrative responsibility and accountability in a complex bureaucratic state, because a large administrative apparatus was simply not envisaged at the time.

I give this emphasis to the nature of the American system of separation of powers because it introduces a unique element to the problem of legislative control of the executive. To quote Herbert Simon et al.: "The separation of powers in this country between legislative and executive somewhat beclouds the right of the chief executive to control administration."[6] Neustadt puts it even more strongly in his very stimulating essay, "Politicians and Bureaucrats": "Congress, constitutionally, has at least as much to do with executive administration as does an incumbent in the White House."[7] Ironically, however, the American system, which subjects the administrative agencies to control by the two houses of Congress and their relevant committees as well as by the president and the courts, also gives the agencies and their personnel unique opportunities. Again, to quote Neustadt: "Control by two committees of each house can mean control by none, while serving at the same time to dilute direction from above, from the administration."[8] Multiple masters mean multiple opportunities for bureaucrats who are skilled politicians. And skilled politicians are given a boost to the top of the American bureaucracy where the system rewards leaders who can steer their way through the obstacle course of separate institutions sharing powers.

So we see an ironic interplay of factors. The American version of separa-

---

5. James Q. Wilson, "The Rise of the Bureaucratic State," *The Public Interest* 41 (1975): 77.

6. Herbert A. Simon, Donald W. Smithburg, Victor A. Thompson, *Public Administration* (New York: Alfred A. Knopf, 1950), p. 533.

7. Richard E. Neustadt, "Politicians and Bureaucrats," in *Congress and America's Future*, ed. David B. Truman (Englewood Cliffs, N.J.: Prentice Hall, 1973), p. 119.

8. Ibid., p. 123.

tion of powers, designed to check and tame the powers of governmental officials and institutions, gives the legislature enough freedom from the executive to allow it to play an independent role in the control of administration. The growth of the administrative sector, and the power which accrues in the hands of administrators because of the complexity of policy and administration in the modern state, has made control by representative institutions, including the presidency, increasingly important. But our system of separation of powers increases the political opportunities of bureaucrats and gives them incentives to exploit these opportunities. And control by representative institutions is especially difficult to accomplish when one has a bureaucracy which combines extraordinary political resources and skills with specialized knowledge and technical expertise.

These are the reasons why I say that the structure of American government and the assumptions behind it make congressional oversight both important — to aid in the review and ultimately in the control of administrative officials and to maintain Congress's role as a coequal branch — and problematic. These efforts by Congress to review and control can, in our system especially, be counterproductive from the standpoint of the balance of power between elected and nonelected officials. When there are multiple overseers, those being overseen may end up with the advantage.

The second theme, you recall, was that with the emergence of the bureaucratic state, Congress has prodded itself to do more oversight, although it rarely seems satisfied with the results of this prodding — both in terms of the amount of oversight and its results.

In 1946, following the growth of government during the New Deal and World War II, a provision of the Legislative Reorganization Act prescribed "continuous watchfulness" over the actions of the executive agencies in carrying out the laws. In the 1970 amendments to the Legislative Reorganization Act, Congress required most committees to issue periodic reports on their oversight endeavors. This was an obvious attempt to spur them to action. Data gathered on congressional oversight in 1973 for the Bolling Committee staff and comments by congressmen before the committee indicated that this requirement had not produced the desired effect, and the House amended its rules in an attempt to stimulate more activity and provide some coordination of oversight activities.[9]

---

9. Separate oversight subcommittees were suggested for House committees, and the Government Operations Committee was required to issue a report at the beginning of each session of the Congress laying out the oversight agenda of each committee. The ultimate aim of the report was to improve the coordination of House oversight activities.

The Bolling Committee hearings produced one of the most frank comments on oversight and why some committees do not do it that I have ever seen. Rep. Ray Poage was then the chairman of the House Agriculture Committee and a veteran of the House. In answer to a comment by Rep. David Martin of Nebraska that "many of our committees have been negligent in this area of follow-through on how programs are working," Poage said:

> I think that we have been somewhat slow in that respect. As chairman, I will take the responsibility for it. But I would point out that the alternative is to stir up a political "porridge pot" where you simply have things boiling all the time...to drag out some issue every two years for the campaign....About all we would accomplish, as I see it, is to create hard feelings, a loss of confidence on the part of our farmers that the Department of Agriculture could render them a service, because we can be so critical of the Department of Agriculture that there won't be any farmer in the nation that will have any confidence. Maybe we are too critical at times. Maybe we are not critical enough at other times. But I think that you must bear in mind that if we do overdo this we destroy the effectiveness of the administrative agencies. I think by and large the Department of Agriculture has been doing a pretty fair job.[10]

The hearings also produced an exchange between academics and the congressional panel in which there was a wonderful role reversal, with the academics saying that oversight was infrequently done because there was usually little political payoff from it — a realpolitik explanation — and the congressional panelists asking them to rise above such explanations and offer some suggestions for reform. This exchange occurred between Prof. Richard Fenno and Rep. John Culver. Prof. Fenno's comment was: "When the incentive isn't there, you are simply not going to get oversight." And Representative Culver said:

> I am really at a loss to follow you when you say there is not adequate political incentive. I think there should be. What we need from you are suggestions as to how to strengthen the organizational design and shape and activities of the Congress and its members so that we can build into our system a far more effective program of congressional oversight.
>
> After all, it is our primary responsibility. If there is any disen-

---

10. U.S., Congress, House, Select Committee on Committees, Hearings, *Committee Organization in the House*, 93rd Cong., 1st sess., 1973, 2, pt. 1:66.

11. Ibid., pp. 15-16.

> chantment in the country, it derives from the validity of the
> thought that in this respect, Congress is apathetic.
>   I hope we can get something more from you than the idea that
> there is not enough political incentive.[11]

In later years the Senate, especially, devoted much attention to something called "sunset"—a plan for the periodic reauthorization of all programs, except some key entitlements, which the Senate actually passed in 1978. And in 1979, the Congressional Research Service held a seminar designed to help make the Ninety-Sixth Congress what John Anderson called "the oversight Congress."[12] The introductory remarks by Speaker O'Neill, I think, captured the sentiments in Congress about oversight failures in the past, and the ambivalence about oversight in the future. The Speaker said:

> Oversight has been a word in the lexicon of Congress that it does
> not like to hear. It is going to be a watchword in this Congress.
> Oversight and sunset legislation will characterize the Ninety-Sixth
> Congress. Agencies are easy to create and hard to stop. We have to
> cut back. There are so many programs in this government of ours
> that are obsolete in nature and we have done nothing about them.
> We can accomplish these objectives, being ever mindful of the fact
> that we must take care of the needy, the indigent, senior citizens,
> the poor, and the health of the nation. By effective oversight, we
> can cut back that which is obsolete, and nurture that which should
> be ongoing. In doing so, we will be able to do more for our
> nation.... The reluctance to employ oversight has been on the part
> of the members. We have not lived up to our obligation. As I
> indicated, we like to create and legislate, but we have shied away
> from both the word and deed of oversight.[13]

Recall now my third theme. From all we can tell, the amount of oversight done by Congress has increased substantially, and the increase is linked to recent changes in the environment outside and inside the Congress. As part of my study, I have gathered data on committee activities in the first six months of each odd-numbered year since 1961. The focus is on what I call primary purpose oversight hearings and meetings—that is, those where

---

12. John Anderson, "The 96th Congress: An 'Oversight Congress'," in *Workshop on Congressional Oversight and Investigations*, House Document No. 96-217, 96th Cong., 1st sess., 1978, pp. 75-82.

13. Thomas P. O'Neill, Jr., "The Need to Improve Congressional Oversight Capability," in *Workshop on Congressional Oversight and Investigations*, pp. 2-3.

oversight, not legislation or some other activity, is the focus of the hearing or meeting.[14] Therefore, these data underestimate oversight to a degree.

Let me give you a few preliminary results from this section of my study. First, as the literature suggested, and as many of the panelists on the Bolling Committee mentioned, the amount of oversight was indeed at a fairly low level in the 1960s, but it then began to increase in frequency. The greatest growth came after 1973, and oversight continued to grow in the Carter period. If one could say twenty years ago or even fifteen or ten years ago that oversight was a "neglected function" of Congress, to quote John Bibby, that seems no longer to be the case.[15] While the 1973 jump in oversight may well have been the result of Watergate and the events surrounding it, the pattern is not explainable by Watergate alone, since the rise in oversight began before Watergate and has continued well after. Also, split partisan control of the presidency and Congress is not the answer, because the rise in oversight clearly continued while Carter was in office and the Congress and the presidency were controlled by the same party. In fact, the amount of oversight done by congressional committees in 1977 increased over the level found in 1973 or 1975, post-Watergate years of Republican control of the presidency *and* Democratic control of the Congress.

Let me look at some other feasible explanations of this increase in oversight activity since the 1960s. One might be changes in committee structure. Special oversight subcommittees did become more common during this period, and the greater number of oversight units does account for some of the increase in oversight activity. But most of the increase comes from more oversight done by ordinary authorization units. Therefore this particular reform is not the key to understanding the increase.

Another change in the congressional environment, the increasing number of staff members, seems to play a more significant role. There is a clear relationship between increase in staff size and oversight frequency—indeed, a very strong relationship. One must be cautious about interpreting these data,[16] but it is clear from the case studies of committee decision making which I've also done as part of my study, that staff play a key role in

---

14. For details on the 1969-1975 period and a full explanation of my data-gathering techniques and findings, see Joel D. Aberbach, "Changes in Congressional Oversight," *American Behavioral Scientist* 22 (1979): 493-515.

15. John F. Bibby, "Oversight and the Need for Congressional Reform: Congress's Neglected Function," in *The Republican Papers*, ed. Melvin Laird (Garden City, N.Y.: Anchor, 1968), pp. 477-488.

16. Aberbach, "Changes in Congressional Oversight," especially pp. 506-508, 512-513.

the process, often a determining one. And as their numbers grow larger, more and more of the staff earmarked for oversight activity actually seem to do oversight work. In some instances staff time may even be a slack resource for the committees, and staff members often take the lead in finding things to do. My preliminary assessment is that added staff resources and the phenomenon of staff-generated work are important aspects of the increase in oversight activity and, indeed, of the tremendous increase in hearings and meetings by congressional committees.

Basically quantitative factors of the type just discussed are useful in understanding the changing levels of oversight, but inevitably they lead to a consideration of the qualitative factors which lie behind them: the political incentives of the members and the staff of Congress. And that takes me to my fourth theme, namely that oversight is linked to the political environment of members and staff, and is used by them for a variety of purposes. To understand this better, I have undertaken a variety of case studies: some of the process of committee and subcommittee decision making on oversight, and some focusing on particular oversight events. I'm busy now trying to assimilate this information, and I've certainly reached no firm conclusions. But I'd like to share some of the things people who do the oversight have been saying about why it has increased over time and what its purposes are.

First, many people talk about the importance of presidential abuses under Johnson and Nixon in making people on the Hill more feisty vis-a-vis the executive, especially political executives. I'll get back to that in discussing the fourth point below. Second, much oversight seems to be done in response to complaints of constituents and interest groups unhappy about some aspect of a program that affects them. Since the reach of government has grown over time, and since there are more staffers to process complaints, oversight has increased. I should stress, though—and I'll get back to this in a minute—that though this oversight may be acrimonious at times, it is not necessarily hostile to the programs themselves.

Third, there is a general feeling that oversight has taken on a fad-like quality, seen as rewarding by members because the public feels it wants less government and less legislation in general. By doing oversight, members can keep themselves in the public eye—the opposite of the usual argument that there is no political payoff in oversight—and staff can get themselves the credit they need to preserve and further their careers. It may even be a way to win prestige in the House. Listen to the comments of one top staffer on a subcommittee of the House Interstate and Foreign Commerce Committee:

> I think to an extent now this popularity of oversight—it's almost like pet rocks or hula hoops. Since the populace as a whole is being—the sense of the average member is people want less government, less legislation, less regulations. You know, you've got to do something to try to justify having all these highly paid, relatively highly paid, well-trained professionals up here—okay, like me—to talk to you. So to an extent, everybody now has seized on oversight as a popular thing. Now I think that there's oversight and there's oversight. I think that the popularity of it is because of the feeling that people of the country generally are resisting, will resist, massive new legislative programs, and that they want some kind of a question of efficiency and control over existing programs. Whether that's overall going to be salutary or not depends on what kind of oversight is done here. I mean, my own personal feeling is the kind of oversight that Congress has just gotten through doing on the FTC is not something that ought to be emulated.

After the staffer made these comments, he was asked: "But do you think that any long-term improvements in oversight are going to result from the fact that there has been a certain popularity of focus placed on it that has not previously been there?"

> Sure, sure, I think there's no question about it. I mean that people who are now—in fact, I sat around during the discussion of the Commerce Committee's budget by the House Administration Committee last week. All the subcommittee chairmen were represented, and John Brademas [then chairman of the Subcommitte on Accounts] was asking questions about how much oversight each of the legislative subcommittees—we have an oversight subcommittee as well—intended to do. And nearly all of them talked about substantial need for oversight hearings and for oversight. So I think what's gonna happen is that since everyone now is focusing on it, frankly, those subcommittees with competent chairmen and good members and a good staff will find new and innovative ways to do oversight. Those that don't fall into that category will be largely spinning their wheels and, you know, they won't have made much progress at all.[17]

Fourth, and finally, in this preliminary list of reasons, oversight can be used directly to bolster programs—a goal of most committees and subcom-

---

17. Committee Staff Interview Number 51, Part 2, February 1980. Staffers were interviewed on a "not for attribution" basis.

mittees, at least until this Congress. When Richard Cohen did an article for the *National Journal* in 1979, entitled "Will the 96th Congress Become the Oversight Congress?", he quoted John Brademas (then still chairman of the Education and Labor Subcommittee on Select Education) as telling reporters that the subcommittee would conduct oversight of programs designed to aid the handicapped, because "I'm interested in expanding their appropriations, and increasing the dialogue among all parties involved to make sure the programs work."[18] A more elaborate version of this view was expressed by Representative Brademas when he was interviewed as part of my study.[19] In answering a question on whether congressional influence over the bureaucracy had been increasing relative to the president's, he said:

> Well, that's a very difficult question to answer, because like most observations that could be made of federal activities, it all depends. [What does it depend on?] Well, the variables may well be, who is the chairman of the subcommittee, how active is he, how much does he care about oversight, what kinds of interest groups may be involved, is he someone who regards himself as a champion of the interests that are represented by the legislation before him or is he a foe, what kinds of relationships does he have with key people in the federal executive. So that, for example, the relationship that I may have, as a legislator concerned with the arts, to arts organizations is one in which I am generally a champion of what they want, because those are my policy preferences. That doesn't mean I'm not sometimes a critic. But generally I am an advocate.
>
> You will find that—and I'm not telling you anything you don't know—that people who go on the Agriculture Committee in the House generally come from agriculture districts. People gravitate here, normally, to the committees where they can be champions of the legislation that is written in those committees. So I go on Education not to oppose education, but because I'm a champion of education. People go on the Armed Services Committee both because they tend to be hawkish, let's say, in their outlook on military policy, but also because they may come from Florida or the South, which have traditionally had major military bases.
>
> So that you must not assume that you begin your analysis with a tabula rasa, with an empty blackboard. You've got to have a realistic description of the context within which oversight is car-

---

18. Quoted in Richard E. Cohen, "Will the 96th Congress Become the Oversight Congress?", *National Journal*, January 13, 1979, p. 44.

19. Interview with Rep. John Brademas, June 26, 1979.

ried out. Otherwise you're really not describing the real world. And you may well find—in fact, you will find—that there will develop relationships in which congressional committees will become champions of certain programs. They will work closely with an interest group that is the champion of those programs. And they will work closely with the subordinate, let's say the below-the-cabinet-level or below-the-subcabinet-level officials, of the executive branch, often career people who are champions of the particular interest involved—all over against the policy preferences of the president and his cabinet people.

What I have just told you is a faithful generalization about the relationship between the congressional authorizing committees and, to a lesser extent, now the Appropriations Committee, in respect to education policy between a Democratic-controlled Congress and the White House, especially during the years of the Nixon-Ford administrations. And it cuts across party lines. As I told you in our last interview, it is not strictly a partisan proposition—that a group of us up here would work closely with the various groups representing education, and we would work with allies in the executive branch, but not at the political level, not political appointees, because they were obviously there to carry out what Nixon and Ford wanted, which was inimical to what we wanted.

We have a situation now with the Carter administration where we're both—we're Democrats at both ends of the avenue, so you won't have so much hostility. But because the economic and political climate has changed, there are still some tensions between the two. We were here last night on the Labor-HEW appropriations bill until 1:00 in the morning, and it was very difficult for the champions of education to get more money into the education bill than the Appropriations Committee had put in it. The Appropriations Committee had moved to the right even as had the Carter administration, as measured not by the Republican presidents but as measured by the posture of previous Democratic-controlled Congresses, and by the policy preferences of the education and health interest groups. So it's—in other words, there are variables that move—it isn't as if these are fixed for all time and you have to, I think, take into account that climate, ... that environment, that context.

That last comment about a change in environment or context is a good note on which to end the talk. Let me just say in conclusion that this is a very interesting time to be studying oversight, because the subject is right at the heart of the current attempts by Congress to adjust to changing political reality. Many members and staff talk of the growing skepticism about government programs. They are cognizant of the relative resource scarcity they face as pressure increases to balance the budget. They have a large bureaucracy of their own to keep busy, and a need to look busy. It seems the ideal political moment for even more oversight, although much of it may well be to protect people's favorite programs against centralizing antagonists in Congress, such as the budget committees, and in the executive branch. In other words, oversight will be part of a very complex process of evaluating programs and controlling the actions of the bureaucracy, in which the bureaucrats and their interest-group supporters will often be among the key players.

Response by Paul Weaver
Assistant Managing Editor, *Fortune*

What I have today are some quite broken-up and jumbled comments on a number of things that have been said this morning, so let me just get on with it. I don't promise that they will all hang together, or even all be intelligible, for that matter.

The topic for today's discussion, I think, is a good one and a correct one. I discovered something as a beginning journalist in 1974, writing articles for *Fortune* about the newer regulatory agencies—the Occupational Safety and Health Administration, the Environmental Protection Agency, the Consumer Product Safety Commission, that range of new institutions. I had been a political science professor, specializing in American politics and American government, and in my naivete I thought that, among the people one might canvas to get an overview of the issues and the agencies and the people involved, would be the White House staff, especially the domestic policy staff. At the time I was writing a story on OSHA, and I was calling people in congressional committees and the Chamber of Commerce and the AFL-CIO. I was also trying to track down the people on the White House staff who follow these issues. And I discovered that there was apparently no one who really knew anything about OSHA, or in particular about the vinyl chloride problem, and that if I wanted to get information about this I would have to go elsewhere. Everyone else knew all about it. On the Hill and in the interest groups affected, there were a lot of people with an almost scholarly knowledge of these issues who were delighted to talk to anyone about them. But in the White House: very little information of any kind.

And this, I think, is characteristic, especially of regulatory operations, and most especially of the new regulation in American society. It really is a question of the agencies and Congress. In practical terms, the White House is out of the picture, and does not matter, except as an occasional force hectoring from the sidelines, usually in an ineffective way—except possibly to bring certain kinds of activities to a halt, which I think Joan Claybrook must have found to be the case for a while in her tenure. In other words, I discovered, somewhat to my surprise—because political science had not really prepared me for this— that the agencies very much do what they are told, and what they are told is told to them by Congress, institutionally the dominant power shaping their behavior.

It's also true that Congress wrote the laws which in great detail spell out what the agencies are and are not to do. The newer agencies are distinguished in many ways, but one of the ways is the fact that their statutes are lengthy and specific, and give agencies very little discretion. These statutes are deliberately written this way. It's not an accident that it takes hundreds of pages to spell out the new pension reforms. It's not an accident that the Environmental Protection Agency responds to hundreds of pages of laws, whereas the older agencies often had terribly short and vague laws that allowed them to do practically anything. I would say that, by and large, this congressional dominance of the agencies is not only what the Framers essentially had in mind from the beginning, but is the right relationship. That is to say, the president should not be intensely involved in the administration of regulatory programs.

Nevertheless, having said that, I do think that there's a problem. I do think that there is a way in which the relationship between Congress

and the agencies has gotten out of hand. Two examples of this are the apparent growth of congressional oversight activities, and also the growing enthusiasm for the legislative veto which, even if it isn't unconstitutional, is still a dreadful idea. Nevertheless, you could eliminate the excessive use of oversight. You could do away with any vestige of a legislative veto, and this larger problem would still persist, because in essence it is a problem whose roots are cultural and political. Culturally, the problem with Congress and the agencies—and, by extension, regulatory programs and domestic policies in general—is that, whatever may once have been the case, the case today is that in domestic policy, and also in domestic politics, there is very little left that one could reasonably call a center. The center not only doesn't hold, it may never have existed. But in any case, we live in an age of public policy extremism and/or public policy and political incoherence. There are many things that the American people collectively want and hope for, but they typically don't add up to anything coherent. We have many people pursuing extreme projects or holding extreme views. We have little consensus. And yet we have a large government with lots of laws, lots of interventions in our society, and therefore a situation that creates lots of conflict. That is one reason for what I consider to be the problem with Congress and the agencies.

And there is also a structural reason for this, and that's simply that the representative system and the lawmaking process in Congress have disintegrated almost to the point of nonexistence. We no longer have a two-party system, we no longer really have the political party as a mediating and representative institution. And within Congress we have very little structure left. Everyone is an entrepreneur, everyone is in on the action. There are very few constraints, that I can see at any rate, and almost anything seems to go these days.

Well, the combination of these two cultural and structural situations creates a big government, an active government, but a government that has very little consent among the citizenry, a government that becomes the object of a lot of hostility and becomes the seat of an enormous amount of fighting. And a lot of this fighting, inevitably, becomes fighting over the proper relationship between Congress and the agencies, over whether the agencies are doing their job correctly or not, and whether Congress is doing its job correctly.

I have, in an essay that practically no one has ever seen, described this whole pattern as a pattern of "adversary government." By this I meant a number of things. It was an essay written toward the end of the period when I'd written about all of the new regulatory programs, and I came to the conclusion that if you wanted to understand them, you had to begin with the fact that these were mostly programs created by a Congress that meant to assert itself over and against the authority of the executive branch. So they were programs whose laws were drafted (or redrafted) by Congress with little attention—in some cases, practically no attention, to a degree almost laughable—to the input from expert executive agencies. The extreme example here is the pension reform law of 1974, a 200-plus page document reforming pension laws drafted by Congress with almost no formal consultation with the experts in the executive branch agencies who know something about pensions and government regulation thereof. So adversary government comes from an assertive, resurgent Congress.

Adversary government, as embodied in, say, the Clean Air Act and many other pieces of legislation, is adversary in another way. It tends to take one goal as being the thing, but also the *only* thing, that this piece of legislation and its administrators will be concerned with. In the case of the Clean Air Act, it is clean air that is the goal, and the law spells out in great detail how this goal is to be pursued. And it prohibits the administrators at the EPA from paying any attention to anything else that might be affected by the pursuit of clean air. There are standards the EPA is supposed to issue and enforce that the law says explicitly may not be shaped with reference to the cost that these standards will impose on society. Now that's an unbelievable thing for Congress, for a public law, to say. And yet it is the case that EPA is not allowed to pay attention, overtly, to economic considerations in setting and enforcing primary ambient air quality standards. So that's a kind of adversarial conception of the pursuit of public goods. You go after a goal and you ignore anything that might be affected by the pursuit. And naturally, because you set up an agency and direct it to pursue a goal and to ignore many of the important and predictable consequences of pursuing that goal, you really are forcing the agency to make war on certain kinds of activity in the society, because the single-minded pursuit of clean air will in one way or another, sooner or later, cause the pursuer of that goal

to start making war on the smelting industry, or other industries or activities that don't increase the cleanliness of air. And the agency is not allowed to have any sympathy or feeling or concern, as it were, for the institutions, an industry perhaps, that will be affected by this single-minded pursuit of clean air. So that you get an adversary pattern of government almost literally in the sense that the executive is authorized and mandated to go out and assault bits and pieces of our society.

All of this becomes adversarial government also because that kind of behavior on the government's part mobilizes the parties who have been assaulted, who are good at organizing and good at expressing themselves, and who are good at getting their views listened to by someone in Washington. So these pursuits create further conflict which often leads congressmen to call hearings and to assail the agency for doing exactly what Congress and the laws forced the agency to do. And here's where I'm very sympathetic with Joan Claybrook. Joan and I don't agree on all issues, but I think she's quite right in feeling that there was something opportunistic and almost squalid, but certainly something not constitutionally decorous, in the way in which Bud Shuster and other people in

Congress went after the passive restraint standard. To me, the squalor of the assault came from the fact that the correct way to tell Claybrook's agency not to impose air bags is to reopen the law and to rethink what the law directs her agency to do. The fact is that under her mandate, the agency was perfectly right in authorizing air bags. If you don't like the result of the more or less faithful administration of a law, the correct thing to do—certainly in the case of something as large in bad effects as air bags—is to reshape the mandate. And not to engage in what is not just hypocritical but really incoherent behavior, which is, as Congress has, to maintain on the one hand that the law is a good law, and on the other to insist that Claybrook stop asking car companies to obey it. So I agree with her at that level.

On the other hand, I don't think that the passive restraint mandate is a very good mandate. And I think it's not surprising that she got the kind of interference she did as a result of a decade-long effort, still unsuccessful, to get the auto industry to put onto cars a device that will be very expensive, much more expensive than the agency has ever admitted; that will be of somewhat questionable value; and that in any case is something that you wouldn't want to try unless you'd done some other, cheaper, simpler, more obvious things, such as trying to persuade drivers to use their seat belts. Seat belts, if used, are as effective in stopping deaths and mitigating injuries as air bags, and don't have some of the possible but still unknown disadvantages of air bags. I was surprised, and maybe it was rhetoric on Joan Claybrook's part, to hear her say that she did not understand why sensible, responsible people would oppose the air bag. There really are grounds, and one of them, not the least it seems to me, is a philosophical concern about Big Brotherism in government. The air bag, after all, is a case of government telling people to take risks smaller than the risks they might be willing to take with their own lives. That's Big Brotherism, and there's a philosophical objection to that that's important and meaningful, even if all these technical and complicated cost-benefit issues about the air bag might be resolved to everyone's satisfaction.

Anyhow, it seems to me that the project of pursuing and persisting in the air bag, in the circumstances of the 1970s, helps explain why you get that kind of guerrilla warfare. And Joan didn't tell you all of it. It involved, in successive years, prohibitions from Congress against the agency using its own appropriations for purposes of developing and implementing air bags. And that lasted for a few years even though no one knew whether it was really a valid order or not. But there was that. And then there were hearings on air bags, and opposition from Representatives Dingle and Shuster, and it was terribly complicated. And by the way, in all of this, the public understanding of what was really at stake got a little fuzzy, I think. For example, you may have noticed that Joan began by talking about the passive restraint mandate, and then quickly started talking about air bags. The order is for passive restraints—i.e., restraints that don't depend on people buckling up, that don't depend on an action by the occupant of the car. But there are two different kinds, or generic kinds, of passive restraints. One is the so-called passive belt that wraps itself around you as you get in the car whether you want it to or not. The other is an air bag, something that pops out at you and cushions you from crashing into the car when the car has crashed into something

else. At least in the case of the Ford Motor Company, about 85 to 90 percent of Ford's cars, after the date at which passive restraints have to be put into cars, are going to use passive belts. They are not going to, except in special cases, use air bags. I bet that GM's and Chrysler's plans are about the same. And there are lots of good reasons for this, one of which is that air bags are very expensive. Even that is misleading, in the sense that the air bags would only be used on cars that had three passengers in the front seat, because you can't have a passive belt that works for that middle passenger in the front seat. And it's quite possible that if Ford didn't have the few hundred million dollars in capital spending costs available to start up its air bag program, it might simply have eliminated its cars with space for three passengers in the front seat. I don't say that the company had decided to do that, but it was an obvious strategy for inexpensive compliance with this rule originally intended to increase occupant safety. Question: Is it really a desirable thing in the name of occupant safety to eliminate a certain kind of car that has room for three people in the front seat? Well, you can debate one way or the other, but you wouldn't want to say that it was necessarily a good idea.

And in any case, it's the kind of issue that gets you far afield of matters of air bags.

Well, I've gone on too long. Enough of this. But anyhow, I agree with Joan. There really was something unhappy and inappropriate about the way Congress handled this. But it's what I expect. It's part of the pattern of adversary government, where you have an agency mandated or allowed to do extreme things that have large impacts on people's lives or on the national economy, and then Congress is in a position where it can attack the agency for doing what Congress said, maintaining hypocritically that Congress never intended this, but never revising the laws, the rules, the balancing of competing interests and values, built into the laws that the agencies were applying.

Response by Francis E. Rourke
Department of Political Science, Johns Hopkins University

I'll begin by addressing myself to the broad issue that we're concerned with here, the establishment of a viable and productive relationship between Congress, on the one hand, and executive agencies on the other.

A number of speakers at panels I have gone to in the last twenty-four hours have noted that Congress is a much criticized institution, the universal whipping boy of American political life. One of the principal areas in which Congress has been subject to such criticism is with respect to the way in which it structures and handles its relationship with executive agencies. It's frequently argued that Congress does not do a very good job in handling this relationship. This criticism, as Professor Aberbach's paper brings out, comes from two quite different directions.

There are those who feel that the legislature is too lax in the way in which it oversees the work that agencies are doing, and there are those who believe that it is too intrusive in its behavior, too inclined to try to run agencies in ways that may shift management responsibility from the executive to the legislative branch. Critics point to the current rage for the legislative veto as an example of the effort now being made to put Congress into the actual business of running the everyday activities of executive agencies and subjecting all of their decisions to legislative scrutiny and perhaps revision. The one thing that these criticisms reveal is that we don't have a very clear consensus on what role Congress can reasonably be expected to play in its relationship with executive agencies.

I think we face a similar problem in appraising other governmental institutions as well. In the evaluation of presidents, for example, a great many judgments are made about how good or bad particular presidents are in discharging their responsibilities. And yet it's far from clear what our expectations are with respect to presidential performance, what functions we want a president to perform, and on what basis we can pronounce negative or positive judgments on the way in which he carries out the duties of his office. So the problem that arises with respect to the evaluation of Congress's relationship with executive agencies is that of determining what we can reasonably expect Congress to do. What are the principal elements of a model relationship between these two government entities?

The first thing that I think we can expect of Congress in its relationship with executive agencies is that it formulate legislation, usually with the help of executive officials, that will provide clear and consistent signals to these officials as to what is expected of them. Concurrently, it should provide agencies with the resources— personnel and appropriations, for example—that will enable them to achieve the goals that Congress sets for them. The first element in a model relationship is thus the requirement that Congress provide an agency with a clear definition of its responsibilities.

Second, Congress should review and monitor the performance of executive agencies to make sure that the decisions and activities of these organizations are in conformity with legislative intentions as embodied in authorizing statutes, and to see whether the resources allocated to these agencies are being used wisely and productively.

Finally, as the third element in this model relationship, the process of legislative oversight should be used to identify problems that may

need to be resolved by further legislation, or that may call for a revision of existing statutory guidelines. Looked at from this point of view, congressional oversight becomes an instrument of congressional foresight. The legislature reviews what has been done in the past as a means of determining what ought to be done in the future.

Well, it's easy enough to lay out a model of this kind, but as the previous speakers have already indicated, there are many serious difficulties in adhering to it in actual practice. One thing that both papers tend to bring out—particularly Ms. Claybrook's—is the fact that, in the first phase of this relationship, the formulation of legislation, a product emerges that we can loosely and not very precisely identify as designed to advance the public interest. This public interest may reflect an effort to transcend all the special interests affected by a particular piece of legislation or it may simply be an accommodation among all the conflicting interests represented by these groups. In any case, legislation is formulated and guidelines are devised that are designed to realize some broad conception of what the public good requires in a particular area of policy.

Then, in the second stage of the model that I've described, the oversight phase, when Congress reviews the activities of agencies, the special interests tend to reassert themselves. So that, if the first process represents an effort to define a public interest that transcends or accommodates the particular orientation of specialized groups in American society, the second process, the review and oversight of agency activities, often sees a revival of the conflicts that legislation was designed to resolve. The issues raised when the legislation was originally written are then fought out all over again.

There are other reasons why the model is not an easy one to implement. In the area that Ms. Claybrook described, highway safety, or in the case of water pollution, we're often in the business of formulating legislation in advance of developing technologies to achieve the goals which the legislation identifies as being necessary or desirable in the public interest. When the Clean Air Act was written, for example, the technologies to achieve the goals of the legislation were not available. What Congress did was to turn over to the agency the task of coming up with the appropriate means for achieving certain goals that the legislature thought to be important.

This problem arises with particular force in the field of regulation, where the congressional-adminis-trative relationship has been an especially thorny one in recent years. Much of this difficulty stems from the fact that many of the groups involved in pushing for regulation did so before the techniques necessary to achieve their goals had been devised. As noted already, this has been a major problem with the Environmental Protection Agency and the administration of the Clean Air Act.

The rapidity with which technology changes is also a problem for the model of executive-legislative relations that I have described. The field of communications, for example, is a very technology-intensive field, where innovations like cable television and new advances in telecommunications are constantly outreaching the bounds of existing statutes. It is not possible for Congress to use its lawmaking power to send clear signals about problems that didn't exist when it wrote the original legislation designed to guide agency behavior.

Another difficulty that arises in trying to live up to the model relationship between Congress and the agencies is the problem that Professor Aberbach discussed, the inability or unwillingness of members of Congress to give a very high priority to the task of overseeing the work of executive agencies. But it may be that the conservative tide reflected in the 1980 presidential election, and the emergence of the neoconservative critique of governmental performance, will make legislative oversight of the executive a much more important item on the agenda of Congress in the future than it has been in the past. Certainly an era of undernourishment of the public sector, which we seem to be entering, might stimulate a closer legislative look at the effectiveness of existing programs. Moreover, Professor Aberbach's data suggest that there is much more oversight on the part of Congress today than there has been in the past, so the trend is certainly moving in that direction.

A final difficulty confronting the model relationship between Congress and the executive is the process of socialization that has been described here, which tends to draw together the agencies that are carrying on programs and activities and the members of Congress who are supposed to be taking a critical or adversary look at many of these programs. It's commonly said of presidential appointees to executive agencies that they "go off and marry the natives." This was a complaint frequently heard during the Nixon administration, that rather than representing the president's point of view in his dealings with an agency, presidential appointees

soon began to play the role of representing the agency in its dealings with the White House. They underwent a role reversal that completely destroyed their value to the White House. It's clear that something of the same thing may happen to legislators who interact continuously with an executive agency. They become protagonists of the agency, and to some extent lose their capacity to evaluate its activities objectively.

Now everything I've said up to this point on the subject of legislative-executive relations in the United States is in harmony with the general tendency to be critical of the way in which Congress does its job. However, if you think of Congress as compared to other legislative bodies, and if you compare the legislative-bureaucratic relationship in this country with that which obtains in most other modern democracies, I think you'd have to say that while the relationship has many troublesome aspects, Congress deserves a reasonably high mark on the way in which it deals with the executive branch. The most serious and continuing flaw in the relationship is the fact that Congress writes legislation with a notion of the public good at the heart of it and then exercises oversight of its implementation in a way which tends to aggrandize the power of some of the very groups that fought the legislation in the first place.

By way of conclusion, I suppose it's really incumbent on me to come up with some modest proposals looking toward an improvement in the relationship that I've been discussing. A number of such suggestions have already been made, including an enhancement in the size and skill of congressional staffs. I think this development has to be looked at with a wary eye, since staff aides in Congress can develop the same self-serving interests as bureaucrats in the executive. Many of them seem to regard putting down an executive agency and its performance as a very easy and popular thing to do, and a thing that will reinforce their own standing and interests.

From my own point of view, one promising reform is centralizing the ombudsman, or errand-boy function, as a way of drawing together citizen complaints against bureaucracy. In this way we can get a picture of which agencies are, from the citizens' point of view, doing a good job and which of them are not doing a very good job. At the moment, handling constituency complaints is a highly decentralized operation which every member of Congress runs from his own office for his own benefit, and there might be something to be gained if this task were centralized. Members of Congress would still handle all correspondence and contacts with constituents, but complaints would be investigated and recorded by a central office. In any case, I think we have a long way to go in terms of identifying ways in which the relationship between Congress and the agencies might be improved. But it is important, I think, to bear in mind constantly the questions: What do we want this relationship to be? What are the characteristics of a good relationship? As I said earlier with respect to presidents, we need to be more aware, in our evaluations of officeholders, what it is that we want them to do, and in what order of priority they ought to approach the roles we expect them to play.

PART VIII:
FINANCING
CONGRESSIONAL
ELECTIONS

CONGRESSIONAL CAMPAIGN FINANCE AND THE REVIVAL OF THE REPUBLICAN PARTY

Gary C. Jacobson
Department of Political Science
University of California, San Diego

The 1980 elections ended a generation of frustration for congressional Republicans. They won control of the Senate for the first time since 1952 and made sufficient gains in the House to raise hopes of taking over there, too, in the near future. Whether or not they realize that dream, their party has unquestionably enjoyed a major revival. The revival has many sources, from the broad failures of the Carter administration to the vagaries of Abscam. But one important component is surely the remarkably shrewd strategy pursued by national Republican leaders within the framework of laws regulating congressional campaign finance practices. This paper examines that strategy and the legal and political context in which it was carried out. The analysis will reveal, I think, a great deal about present-day congressional election politics. It will also allow us to consider some of the broader potential consequences of more vigorous national parties. And it will hold some useful lessons for shell-shocked Democrats.

Weak Parties and Entrepreneurial Candidates

Contemporary electoral conditions are scarcely conducive to effective action by political parties. Fewer voters are willing to identify themselves with either party, and even those who do are distinctly less loyal than they were twenty years ago. The public has little faith in the parties as institutions. Candidates have learned to get by without much assistance from party organizations, relying instead on campaign management professionals, the mass media, and their own personal followings. Elections at different levels have become increasingly separated from one another, reducing the sense of shared partisan fate. Politicians operate as individual political entrepreneurs, pursuing personal careers in a political environment where parties are a dwindling presence.[1]

These conditions have placed severe limits on what party leaders can reasonably hope to achieve, at least in the short run. In particular, a strategy that depends on building a loyal partisan following in the electorate is likely to prove futile. And they face other obstacles as well. Primary elections head the familiar list of factors that prevent the parties from exercising control over nominations or campaigns, hence access to office, hence political careers. Parties retain few incentives that can be used to influence either voters or politicians directly.

In addition to suffering the usual afflictions of minority status, congressional Republicans have been the chief victims of the secular trend in American politics that finds one expression in the decline of parties. They had the ill fortune to be in the minority during a time when voters began showing a more decided preference for congressional incumbents. As the party out of power, Republicans were directly hurt by the phenomenon of "vanishing marginals" and the rise in the electoral value of incumbency.[2] But they also suffered in less obvious ways. The objective difficulty of overcoming the advantages of incumbency discourages the shrewder and more ambitious—and therefore more effective—among potential challengers. It also affects the flow of campaign resources in ways detrimental to the minority party.

Campaign resources—mainly money, but including organizational and other forms of assistance—have become crucial as parties and partisanship have atrophied. Candidates who find it prudent or necessary to run individual, candidate-centered campaigns must forgo the economies of scale that a party ticket system provides. The technical innovations—mass media advertising, computerized mailing lists, professional polling, and so forth—that make such campaigns possible are expensive. Incumbent members of Congress have been able to deal with the problem by greatly

---

1. William J. Crotty and Gary C. Jacobson, *American Parties in Decline* (Boston: Little, Brown, 1980), pp. 172-202.

2. David R. Mayhew, "Congressional Elections: The Case of the Vanishing Marginals," *Polity* 6 (1974):298-301; Robert S. Erikson, "Malapportionment, Gerrymandering, and Party Fortunes in Congressional Elections," *American Political Science Review* 66 (1972):1240; Albert D. Cover and David R. Mayhew, "Congressional Dynamics and the Decline of Competitive Congressional Elections," in *Congress Reconsidered*, ed. Lawrence C. Dodd and Bruce I. Oppenheimer (New York: Praeger, 1977), pp. 55-56.

augmenting their official perquisites, resources which can be—and are—used to pursue reelection.[3] They are also in a strong position to raise campaign money from every source.[4] Challengers find themselves at a serious disadvantage in the competition for campaign funds, a circumstance which further inhibits ambitious, career-oriented candidates.

It is important to recognize the close connection between campaign money, candidate recruitment, and the strength of a congressional challenge. Individual candidates dominate contemporary congressional election politics. Voters respond to the candidate, not the party. How well they know and like the pair of candidates running in their state or district has a much stronger influence on their vote than do partisanship or national forces and issues. It is clear from recent voting studies that incumbents usually do so well, and challengers so poorly, because the former are well known and well liked and the latter are obscure and held in low regard.[5] The most immediate benefit of incumbency is evidently weak opposition. This is one reason Senate incumbents have not been nearly so successful as have House incumbents—they normally face much more formidable opponents.[6]

The strength of a challenge depends primarily on the quality of the candidate and the vigor of his campaign. These two things are connected, of course. Better candidates attract campaign contributions because most contributors, regardless of their motives, prefer to support candidates who have some plausible chance of winning.[7] And the promise of campaign money attracts better candidates—that is, those with more experience and political savvy. The more money a challenger raises and spends, the better

---

3. Morris P. Fiorina, *Congress—Keystone of the Washington Establishment* (New Haven, Ct.: Yale University Press, 1977), pp. 56-61.

4. Gary C. Jacobson, *Money in Congressional Elections* (New Haven, Ct.: Yale University Press, 1980), pp. 52-97.

5.Gary C. Jacobson, "Congressional Elections 1978: The Case of the Vanishing Challengers," in *Congressional Elections*, ed. Louis Maisel and Joseph Cooper. *Sage Electoral Studies Yearbook*, 1981.

6. Thomas E. Mann and Raymond E. Wolfinger, "Candidates and Parties in Congressional Elections," *American Political Science Review* 74 (1980): 617-632; Alan I. Abramowitz, "A Comparison of Voting for U.S. Senator and Representative in 1978," *American Political Science Review* 74 (1980): 633-640; Barbara Hinckley, "House Reelections and Senate Defeats: The Role of the Challenger," *British Journal of Political Science* 10(1980): 441-460.

7. Jacobson, *Money in Congressional Elections*, ch. 4.

he is known and liked by voters, and the more votes he is likely to receive.[8] Serious challenges are the result, then, of the convergent expectations of potential candidates and potential supporters. If an incumbent seems invulnerable, he is likely to avoid formidable opposition, which ensures that he is, indeed, invulnerable. A strong element of self-fulfilling prophecy is at work. It readily undermines the minority party because electoral failure tends to compound itself.

The system of electoral politics which emerges from the interacting strategies of individual political entrepreneurs frustrates the minority party in one further way. It makes it difficult to assign collective responsibility for the failures of government to individual members of the majority party. Without the constraint of party discipline, members become adept at taking positions which do not affront attentive people in their districts or elsewhere who might mobilize resources against them. Party leaders control few sanctions and, in particular, have little influence on reelection, so members do not hesitate to act contrary to their wishes as electoral necessity advises. Members pursue reelection as individuals, emphasizing personal characteristics and services to the district, carefully avoiding responsibility for the collective performance of Congress or their party.[9] The opposition party cannot easily assign collective blame because members of the majority are so practiced at disassociating themselves from the collective effects of their individual activities.

Congressional election politics do not, then, allow much scope for party intervention. The prominence national Republican organizations have managed to achieve has been won against the odds—and with the rather unlikely help of campaign finance reform legislation.

Direct Mail Fund Raising

The fate of the parties was, at most, a minor consideration in the politics of campaign finance regulation. The Federal Election Campaign Act and its amendments were, after all, enacted by legislators who were themselves products of a system of electoral politics in which parties were a declining force. Given the common view that "if we depended on the party organiza-

---

8. Ibid., ch. 5.

9. Richard F. Fenno, Jr., *Home Style: House Members in Their Districts* (Boston: Little, Brown, 1978).

tions to get elected, none of us would be here,"[10] it is not surprising that their first inclination was to treat parties as no different from other politically active groups. Hence, for example, the FECA Amendments of 1974 specified that local and national party organizations were subject to the same contributions limits ($5,000 per candidate per campaign) as were nonparty political action committees (PACs).

But it was hard to deny that parties were, in fact, something special in American electoral politics. And some members of Congress did find the continuing decline of parties alarming and sought to assure that campaign finance legislation would at least not hasten it. So the 1974 law included a provision allowing *coordinated* spending by state and national parties in addition to the direct contributions. This, too, was limited by the law, but the limits are higher and more flexible. It was by no means clear at the time the law was passed what the consequences of this provision would be. In retrospect, however, it established the opportunity for national party organizations to make themselves important participants in congressional elections for the first time.

The FECA also enhanced the electoral importance of national parties in ways that were quite unintended. For example, different sets of laws now regulate state and federal campaign finance practices. State and local parties must maintain separate accounts for federal candidates; the federal regulations are complicated and the penalties for violations can be severe. Xandra Kayden observed that "most party officials said that the complexity of the law and the distaste for federal regulation had a chilling effect on local party activity" on behalf of federal candidates.[11] They were not all unhappy to transfer the burden of helping these candidates to the national party organizations.

Technical innovations in fund raising and campaign organization also fostered national party activity. Computerized direct mail fund raising is the most prominent example. The technique of raising political money by direct mail requests sent to a large number of individual contributors was pioneered in the Goldwater campaign of 1964 and developed in the McGovern campaign of 1972. It is most efficient when centralized. Large

---

10. Charles L. Clapp, *The Congressman: His Work as He Sees It* (Washington, D.C.: The Brookings Institution, 1963), p. 397.

11. Xandra Kayden, "The Nationalizing of the Party System," in *Parties, Interest Groups, and Campaign Finance Laws*, ed. Michael J. Malbin (Washington, D.C.: American Enterprise Institute for Public Policy Research, 1980), p. 265.

information-processing capabilities are necessary to maintain the lists of contributors and their contribution records and to get out automated mass mailings. The national parties are logical agencies for performing this task.

National Republican committees moved into direct mail fund raising for this and for several other reasons. One was the absence of an alternative. The Watergate revelations made all large political contributions suspect and left major Republican contributors feeling burned and scarcely inclined to further generosity. Small individual donations were unquestionably proper, and they were easier to solicit. In addition, the Republicans' minority status actually gave them an advantage in raising money by this method. It is no coincidence that direct mail fund raising was developed in the Goldwater and McGovern campaigns. Direct mail appeals are most effective when sharp ideological lines can be drawn. The reason is simple. To contributors of small sums of money, electoral victories are strictly public goods; all who prefer the winner to the loser benefit, regardless of whether or not they bear any of the cost of achieving the victory. This means that there are no incentives for contributing small sums other than the satisfactions provided by the act of giving itself. And these are greater when the political stakes are perceived to be more important, when fundamental values seem to be at stake, when people are angry and their anger can be given political focus.[12]

The remnant of the Republican party surviving the 1974 election was conservative and, to an extraordinary degree for an American party, ideologically cohesive. Its leaders were free to exploit ideological passions to raise funds. They could oppose and attack the policies of the majority without bearing responsibility for providing specific alternatives that might have divided their following.

Republicans also raised money through the mails effectively because they are, indeed, the party of, if not the rich, those of relatively higher social and economic status. The argument is often made that their fund-raising superiority over the Democrats has nothing to do with this since they receive most of the money in contributions averaging $25. But people who give even small amounts of money to candidates are not evenly distributed throughout the population; only about 10 percent of the adult population

---

12. Jacobson, *Money in Congressional Elections*, pp. 68-69.

make any political contributions, and this group is strongly skewed toward the upper income levels.[13]

Largely because of the success of their direct mail fund raising, national Republican committees have outraised and outspent their Democratic counterparts by ever larger margins in each succeeding election. As of September 30, 1980, they had raised $78.8 million, compared to $7.8 million for the Democrats.[14] More than half the money came from direct mail solicitations.

"Find, Train, Field, Support"

Republican fund-raising strategies have been enormously effective. National committees therefore control sufficiently formidable financial resources to make themselves a real force in congressional election politics. This is a necessary but not sufficient condition for fruitful party intervention; the party must also figure out how to use the money effectively. The FECA places major constraints on available tactics, but the Republicans have proven that its provisions, used imaginatively, permit a substantial measure of national party activity in congressional elections.

Direct party contributions are limited to $5,000 per candidate per election for House candidates. This means that any committee can give, at most, $10,000 to a candidate in an election year ($15,000 if there is a runoff primary). But both the national committees and the national congressional campaign committees of each party can contribute this amount, so direct national party contributions can amount to $20,000 in House elections— roughly 10 percent of what it typically costs to mount a serious challenge. In addition, parties may make coordinated expenditures on behalf of House candidates, the amount being adjusted for inflation; for 1980, it was $14,720. In 1980, then, national party committees could put as much as $34,720 into a House race—a considerable amount of money, but less than 20 percent of what it is likely to cost to defeat an incumbent.

Much more can be put into Senate contests. Direct party contributions are limited to a maximum of $17,500 per candidate for all national committees.[15] But the limits on coordinated expenditures are much higher

---

13. Ibid., pp. 64-65.

14. Larry Light, "Republican Groups Dominate in Party Campaign Spending," *Congressional Quarterly Weekly Report* 38 (1980): 3238.

15. The ceiling for Senate candidates was increased to this level in the FECA Amendments of 1976.

and can be effectively doubled by a clever legal device. The 1980 limits on coordinated expenditures in Senate races were two cents times the voting age population of the state, adjusted for inflation since 1974, or $29,440, whichever is greater. Fourteen states had $29,440 ceilings; California, the most populous state, had a coordinated spending ceiling of $485,024. State parties may also spend two cents per voting age resident on behalf of Senate candidates, but few of them have the money to do it. Republican leaders adopted an interpretation of the law that allows national committees to pick up the state party's share if the state party agrees to let the national party act as its agent. They entered into agency agreements with thirty-three of the thirty-four states with Senate elections in 1980, leaving out only Indiana, where the state Republicans did not need the help. The legality of this ploy has been challenged by the Democrats, and the issue is currently before the Supreme Court. But it was allowed for at least the 1980 elections; Republican national party committees could thus spend as much as $987,548 on a Senate candidate (twice $485,024, plus $17,500, in California); the lowest limit was $76,380 overall.[16] This amounts to a much larger proportion of the money needed to finance a full-scale campaign than can be supplied to House candidates.

Coordinated expenditures can be made for almost any campaign activity. The only condition is that the party have some control over how the money is spent. National parties typically foot the bill for conducting polls, producing campaign ads, and buying media time—major expenses in areas where technical expertise is essential. These services are most useful in Senate campaigns, and the law allows the greatest party activity in these contests, so most coordinated spending by both parties takes place in Senate campaigns. It is no coincidence that Republicans were so much more successful in Senate than in House campaigns, though other complementary forces were also obviously involved. I will have more to say about this later.

The Republicans have done much more than merely work the campaign finance system to provide more resources for Republican candidates (although this is by no means unimportant), and it is in these other activities that national party leaders have shown the most sophisticated insights into congressional election politics. Their strategy has explicitly recognized that electoral success depends primarily on recruiting strong candidates. In a

---

16. Light, "Party Campaign Spending," pp. 3234-3236.

world of entrepreneurial politicians, decisions about running for office are influenced most readily by altering incentive structures. The most effective use of party resources lies less in helping candidates in campaigns than in persuading potentially formidable candidates to make the race. And the party may further serve itself by building up the pool of experienced politicians from which to recruit congressional candidates. National Republican leaders have done both.

Republicans could not hope to control Congress without defeating Democratic incumbents. Under present political conditions, this is no easy task, particularly in House elections. People with sufficient experience and political savvy to mount strong candidacies know this; the most ambitious, those holding elective offices or with serious plans for a political career, are well aware of the costs and risks and are therefore likely to be cautious about running. Why waste resources and risk losing a position on the political career ladder in what is at best a longshot gamble?

Experienced politicians are also quite aware of how much money it takes to generate a serious challenge and that the principal suppliers of campaign funds are just as skeptical as they are about the possibilities of defeating incumbent congressmen. And this is another consideration working against the decision to enter the contest. For these reasons, it is often difficult for a party to recruit strong candidates to challenge incumbents. Yet this is the only way that incumbents can ever be defeated.

After 1974, the Republicans were faced with an additional problem. Their pool of experienced talent was seriously depleted. Not only did they suffer a disastrous defeat in the federal elections, they also lost a large number of seats in state legislatures, which are the most important source of experienced and qualified House candidates. Their need, then, was to expand their pool of effective congressional candidates and to provide sufficient incentives to get them to run for Congress against incumbent Democrats. They have worked through a variety of means to do both.

One approach has been to put money into state legislative campaigns. This has served the short-term goal of reviving the party's fortunes after the Watergate devastation. In the longer run, increasing the number of Republicans in state legislatures strengthens the congressional farm team and gives the party more influence over the redistricting that is to follow the 1980 census. This shows remarkably long-range thinking for an organization that, in the United States, traditionally does not look beyond the next election.

Another tactic has been selective involvement in Republican primary campaigns. Its basic purpose is to make sure that the strongest candidate gets the nomination, but it has the auxiliary benefit of encouraging that candidate to make the race. The national leaders have taken pains to avoid aggravating local partisans and support only those primary candidates who have local party backing, the support of their state's House delegation, and who can convince the national leaders that they are qualified and effective candidates.[17]

A third tactic is designed to provide a substitute for the kind of political experience that produces high-quality candidates. Selected Republican office seekers have been brought to Washington and taught the basics of running successful campaigns. Secondhand experience is certainly preferable to none at all. The sessions in Washington probably help the party in other ways as well. National leaders can judge who are likely to become the strongest candidates worthy of the fullest support. And the meetings no doubt serve to raise enthusiasm, inspire dedication, and provide further encouragement for reluctant challengers to join the battle.

The most conspicuous use of national Republican money was a $9 million nationwide television advertising campaign intended to lay collective blame for the nation's woes at the feet of the Democratic party and the Democratic Congress. Ads urging people to "Vote Republican—For a Change" were broadcast between April 1 and election day in 1980. If the depiction of congressional election politics offered in this paper is not too far off the mark, this is not a particularly promising tactic. Individual incumbents are skilled at evading collective responsibility. But it may well have served another purpose. As one observer speculated early in the election year: "What the Republican advertising program may succeed in doing . . . is to motivate a better crop of GOP candidates to run than the party fielded in 1976 and 1978. Once recruited, these Republican candidates may feel less isolated in waging a difficult challenge to a Democratic incumbent if they know there is a larger effort behind them."[18]

The thrust of the Republican strategy—to find, train, field, and support better challengers—is perfectly attuned to the current state of congressional election politics. Money, training, and a variety of technical campaign

---

17. Ibid., p. 3235.

18. Charles W. Hucker, "Battle of Attrition for GOP Comeback Bid," *Congressional Quarterly Weekly Report* 38 (1980): 437.

assistance projects themselves create more formidable candidacies. They also attract superior candidates. Skillful and ambitious politicians are given stronger incentives to challenge an incumbent because the costs are reduced and the chances of winning increased.

This kind of attention to candidates has another important consequence. Candidates designated for special party help more readily attract contributions from other sources. And these are essential, for even with coordinated spending, parties cannot, under present limits, supply nearly enough money to finance a full-scale challenge. The campaign finance system is, remember, driven by convergent expectations. Candidates who are expected to do well attract contributions; contributors, whatever their other motives, prefer to give to candidates who have a chance to win. One measure of the odds is their level of support from other contributors. The party is preeminent among these because of its presumed knowledge of which candidates are the most likely to win. Its attentions are a signal for others to enter. The party is thus in a pivotal position to direct the system of convergent expectations by establishing focal points for coordinating the separate decisions of the diverse groups and individuals controlling campaign resources.

Intersecting Strategies

Republican strategists have not, to be sure, been omniscient. They were hardly perspicacious in their choice of which Democratic incumbents were the easiest targets. In 1976, their strategy was to defeat first-term Democrats who had taken Republican seats in 1974. It flopped. Their plan in 1978 was to concentrate on taking open seats that had been held by Democrats, and this was only marginally more successful. *Faute de mieux*, they went after a number of entrenched senior Democrats in 1980 and this time hit paydirt. Eight Democrats who had served more than nine terms in the House went down to defeat.

These victories may be no more than the consequence of trying one thing after another until something works, but the implicit strategy reflects what Richard Fenno has taught us in his illuminating account of the relationships of congressmen to their districts. Fenno identified two stages of a member's "career in the district." Beginning before the initial election, a career first goes through an expansionist stage, during which the member works to broaden his reliable base of support in the district.[19] Members at this stage typically devote most of their time, energy, imagination, and official resources to cultivating the district. And it pays off. Freshman members, for example, have become extraordinarily difficult to defeat; freshman Republicans actually improved on their 1972 vote in the otherwise disastrous Republican year of 1974; first-term Democrats were nearly impossible to defeat in 1976; none of the Democratic incumbents defeated in 1980 was a freshman, even though many faced quite formidable challenges.

Later, as their activties in Washington become more important to them, power and responsibility absorbing more of their time and interest, members' district careers enter a protectionist phase. They attempt to maintain the support built up over the expansionist phase but are not willing to spend time and effort in the district to add to it. There are, finally, more fascinating and rewarding things to do.[20] At this stage they become more vulnerable to a determined challenge. It may not be apparent immediately—indeed, a consistent pattern of past success may keep it from being tested for a time. But once it is tested, a senior member may be in for a rude shock.

There is no evidence that Republican strategists were thinking in these terms in 1980, but they acted as if they were, and that is enough. Some of the senior Democrats targeted for major challenges were thought to have "lost touch with the district," which may be another way of saying that they were not protecting their constituency support. But most of the targets seem to have been chosen for their leadership roles in Congress. As party leaders and committee chairmen, they could not avoid blame for the failures of government as easily as could more obscure junior members, who are free to "run for Congress by running against Congress."

The results of the 1980 elections illustrate some of the points made in this paper in another way. I have argued that congressional election results are affected most strongly by the quality of the candidates and the vigor of their campaigns. This implies that a party's electoral successes are less a direct consequence of national political tides or presidential coattails than of the intersecting strategies of individual candidates, political parties, PACs, and other campaign contributors. Such strategies are themselves affected by perceptions of national forces and presidential candidates, of course, so

---

19. Fenno, *Home Style*, p. 172.

20. Ibid., pp. 215-224.

these are by no means irrelevant. But their impact is largely indirect. A closer look at the 1980 congressional elections bears out this implication impressively.

Republicans were noticeably more successful challenging Senate than House incumbents in 1980. Nine of nineteen incumbent Democratic senators—47 percent—were defeated by Republicans. Twenty-seven House Democrats were also beaten (two of whom were incumbents in name only, having first won in spring by-elections), but that amounts to only 11 percent of the total. Clearly, Republicans did quite well in both sets of elections, but much better in the Senate races. A major part of the explanation lies in the differences in the kinds of candidates and campaigns that were mounted against sitting Democrats.

Consider the nine successful Republican Senate challengers. Four were current members of the House and a fifth was a House member until two years ago. Two more held statewide office as attorneys general. Another was a state party chairman. The only newcomer was blessed with enormous amounts of money, as were, according to preliminary data, all but one or two of the others.[21]

Most of the ten Democrats who held onto their seats faced much less formidable opposition. One was unopposed, and five faced challengers who were written off early by their own party organizations.[22] In the four instances where comparisons with 1974 are possible, these Democrats actually increased their share of the vote by an average of 3.2 percentage points. The other four managed to win against substantial challenges with an average loss of 10.3 percentage points in their vote from 1974. The shift to Republicans in the Senate elections was not uniform, but rather depended heavily on the strength of the challengers and their campaigns.

The same is true of the House, where, according to the preliminary evidence now available, substantially fewer formidable challenges were put together by Republicans. No explanation of House elections relying on national forces is very helpful when we find that no fewer than 73 of the 185 Democratic incumbents who faced Republican opposition in both 1978 and 1980 actually improved on their 1978 vote. The average gain for Republican challengers between 1978 and 1980 amounted to only 2.4 percentage points.

21. From information in "The Outlook; Senate, House, and Governors," *Congressional Quarterly Weekly Report* 38 (1980): 2986-3086.

22. Ibid.

A careful look at the winning Republican challengers indicates that their success was critically dependent on their quality and on the campaign resources they were able to raise. The data in table 1 make it plain that they did not simply ride a favorable tide. The table lists the percentage of winning Republican challengers according to two variables—whether or not the seat was marginal, and whether or not a strong candidate emerged as the challenger. Marginal seats are defined as those which the Democratic incumbent won in 1978 with less than 60 percent of the two-party vote. Strong candidates are defined as challengers who have previously won elective office or who were reported to have raised at least $75,000 by September 12, 1980, almost two months before the election. [23]

Table 1
Successful Republican Challengers in 1980 House Elections
(in percentages)

| | | Democratic Incumbent | | Total |
		Marginal	*Nonmarginal*	*Total*
Republican Challenger	*Strong candidate*	24.3% (37)[a]	46.2% (26)	33.3% (63)
	Weak candidate	3.8 (26)	2.5 (118)	2.8 (144)

[a]Number of cases from which percentages were calculated.

Note: Marginal seats are those in which the Democratic incumbent won less than 60 percent of the two-party vote in 1978. Strong candidates are those who have held elective office or who raised at least $75,000 by September 12, 1980. The table excludes the two challengers who defeated Democratic incumbents who had recently won spring by-elections.

Clearly, the strength of the challenger's candidacy was the crucial variable. One-third of the strong candidacies were successful. Only 2.8 percent of the others unseated incumbents, and in two of the four cases involved, the incumbent was under indictment in the Abscam scandal. Marginal incumbents did attract more formidable challenges, as would be expected

23. From data in ibid. and U.S. Federal Election Commission, *FEC Reports on Financial Activity, 1979-1980*, Interim Report No. 8, U.S. Senate and House Campaigns (Washington, D.C., October, 1980).

in the congressional election system described earlier. Potential candidates and contributors weigh the odds before deciding to enter a contest. But strong challengers actually did *better* in nonmarginal districts. Even more strikingly, only one of the Republican challengers in a marginal district who was not, by these criteria, a strong candidate was elected, and he was close to the cutoff point with $69,000 raised by September 12.

Neither in the House nor Senate elections was every strong Republican challenge victorious, to be sure. The point is that almost every winning challenge involved a vigorous individual campaign that might easily have triumphed without Reagan's victory or Carter's unpopularity. At the very least, successful Republican challengers put themselves in a position to take full advantage of whatever benefits the presidential campaign and other national forces might confer, and this was a necessary condition of their success.

Republicans did better in the Senate than in the House elections because they fielded better challengers with better-financed campaigns. Early spending by national Republican committees clearly favored Senate challengers, as the data in table 2 make clear. Most of the early spending in House races was for incumbents rather than challengers, and the amounts were typically small. Conservative and single-issue political action committees also focused on Senate challenges. Likely targets were selected from among sitting Democrats well before the election year and even before it was known who the challenger would be. Local campaigns were organized against particular Democrats quite independently of any expectations about the presidential election—though not without faith in a long-term conservative trend nationwide. These activities helped set in motion the process of converging expectations that brought national party attention, high-quality candidates, and contributions from other groups and individuals into many Senate contests. And this was the ultimate source of the Republican takeover of the Senate.

This is not to argue that national events, Carter's standing, or even Reagan's candidacy were irrelevant. They were not. But they were most important in galvanizing the actions of experienced, career-minded candidates and party and PAC elites rather than through any direct influence on voters.[24]

---

24. A fuller statement of this argument can be found in Gary C. Jacobson and Samuel Kernell, *Strategy and Choice in Congressional Elections* (New Haven, Ct.: Yale University Press, forthcoming).

Table 2
Early National Party Expenditures for Republican
Congressional Candidates, 1980

	National Republican Senatorial Committee	National Republic Congressional Committee
Receipts	$10,444,980	$11,952,900
Amount spent on federal candidates	$3,275,887[a]	$1,981,150[b]
Share given to: Incumbents	7.0%	60.9%
Challengers	59.8%	18.8%
Open seats	33.2%	20.3%
Number of candidates	35	267
Average amount spent per candidate	$93,596	$5,255

[a]Through September 30, 1980.

[b]Through August 30, 1980.

Source: *Congressional Quarterly Weekly Report* 38 (1980): 3238.

Can the Democrats Catch Up?

The Republicans have shown how effectively the current system of campaign finance regulation can be used by a national party to pursue the collective goal of increasing its representation in Congress in an era of weak partisanship, vigorous PACs, and independent entrepreneurial candidates. The question immediately arises as to whether this rather indirect mode of collective action will lead to a stronger sense of party responsibility and greater party discipline. If the national party is recognized as playing an important role in helping new members get into Congress, will it also have some influence over what they do once they get there?

I think that it will not. The party's assistance may be perceived as crucial for getting into Congress (for training, money, designation as a recipient of money from other sources), but once an individual is elected, other resources are so readily available that the threat of withdrawal of party support is not much of a deterrent. Not only do incumbents enjoy the many perquisites of office that can be turned to campaign purposes, but they are also favored by individual donors and PACs, especially those seeking access to decision makers.

The experience of organized labor with the Democrats is instructive here. Many of the Democrats who took Republican seats in 1974 did so with the generous help of organized labor. Subsequently, however, not a few of them sorely disappointed their benefactors by opposing labor's position on the legislation most important to labor —the common situs picketing bill and the labor reform bill. They did so because, as representatives of districts that were not exactly Democratic strongholds, they did not want to excite opposition back home. They did not have to worry about labor withdrawing financial support because, as incumbents, they were able to raise money from business and trade PACs, particularly when their stands did not offend business interests. This is one reason why labor has fought, so far unsuccessfully, to restrict PAC involvement in congressional races even though they would be affected more than any other group by the restrictions.

Newly elected Republican members will find themselves in the same enviable position, and so will be free to respond to district sentiment if and when this clashes with party positions. An increase in party discipline would only be possible if contributions and other help from the national parties continued to be essential. And even if this were the case, party leaders have traditionally preferred not to hurt a member's chances of reelection by compelling loyalty when it would cause problems back home. Republican unity will depend much more on ideological agreement than on the electoral activities of the national party organizations.

Democratic congressional leaders, notably Speaker O'Neill, are of course unhappily familiar with such dilemmas. The question for them is whether they can imitate or improve upon the Republicans' successful tactics. The answer is not altogether clear. From one perspective, the possibilities look promising. Democrats still outnumber Republicans in the electorate; direct mail fund raising was pioneered by Democrats, though they have made little use of it to raise money for national party committees. There is no reason why they cannot pick up some money this way, especially now that they are in opposition. It will be easier to excite people about the supposed transgressions of the Reagan administration and its allies in Congress than over the successes of the Democrats. It is worth noting in this regard that one immediate consequence of the Republican victory last November was a dramatic upsurge in the membership of prominent liberal organizations—the American Civil Liberties Union, the National Organization of Women, and the National Association for the Advancement of Colored People all reported sharp increases in contributions and members.[25]

But Democrats face special problems here. The party is not nearly so cohesive, ideologically or sociologically, as the Republican party. There are firmer traditions of intramural squabbling and larger ideological divisions. People who contribute to Democrats have more reason to consider *which* particular Democrat they are supporting, because the differences can be much greater. Labor union members will no doubt continue to give money through the union and labor will oppose any policy that would encourage members to send money directly to the party, as this would further diminish their strength within it. So although the national Democratic committees can, and almost certainly will, adopt the fund-raising techniques of their counterparts, they are not likely to be as successful.

This should be the source of some worry among Democrats. They have not in the past found themselves at a serious fund-raising disadvantage because they have controlled Congress. Enough money is available from people who desire to stay on the good side of powerful committee and subcommittee members that Democrats have consistently received a large share of the funds distributed by business and trade groups. Many of these groups might normally be expected to prefer Republicans—unless Democrats are making the decisions. If Republicans were to win control of the House as well as the Senate, this incentive for giving to Democrats would be gone, and we could expect to see a massive shift of funds to Republicans from these sources. Since corporate and trade PACs are the fastest growing source of campaign money, Democrats have ample reason for concern.

Democrats are still in better shape than Republicans in one important respect. They have a much larger pool of experienced officeholders from which to draw congressional challengers. For example, Democrats still hold 61 percent of the seats in state legislatures. The recent Republican experience suggests that, given present-day congressional election politics, their most effective strategy will lie in using whatever resources they manage to acquire to entice these and other potentially formidable candidates to challenge Republican incumbents.

25. "New Members Flock to Rights Groups," *The San Diego Union*, December 10, 1980.

Purity And Public Financing

Martin F. Nolan
Editorial Page Editor
The Boston Globe

Public financing of congressional elections seems to be an idea whose time has come and gone. Its moment of high moral purpose and strong legislative possibility occurred in the mid-1970s during the post-Watergate era when the very words "campaign contributions" connoted bribery and deceit.

Public financing of presidential elections has since become part of American politics, with mixed blessings and mixed reviews. At a time of increasing skepticism and hostility toward federal bureaucracies, a new one has been established. The Federal Elections Commission may achieve a reputation for being as efficient in cleansing America's political climate as the Interstate Commerce Commission has been in improving the nation's transportation system.

Congressional experience with the FEC has not improved prospects for public financing of congressional campaigns. The FEC, according to the private conversation of its litigants, has clearly become the Occupational Safety and Health Administration of politics. Along with their constituents, congressmen are now wary of the prospect of bureaucrats checking their private lives and government accountants pouring over their ledgers. A Congress elected in large part "to get government off the backs of people" is unlikely to transfer the burden to its own back.

Congress follows the election returns. In the first week of the Ninety-Seventh Congress, Sen. Robert C. Byrd introduced a bill "to provide reforms with respect to campaign contributions." The bill is similar to the one cosponsored in the House last year by Reps. David Obey and Thomas Railsback.

To observers of the public financing bill, Senator Byrd's conversion to their cause seems bemusingly late. Throughout the Ninety-Sixth Congress, he displayed little enthusiasm for the idea. The Obey-Railsback bill won House approval, 217-198, in October of 1979, but never reached the Senate floor. Republican senators threatened a filibuster against the measure, which would have limited the spending of political action committees.

Supporters of the bill wanted Byrd's approval for a sustained cloture drive against such a filibuster, but Byrd was willing only to schedule one such vote to end a filibuster.

In the Ninety-Sixth Congress, Senator Byrd was the majority leader. In the Ninety-Seventh, he is the minority leader. Does his change of heart have something to do with his change of status? Is he more concerned about the PAC advantage enjoyed by the Republicans? Perhaps it is best to let Sen. Bob Packwood, a Republican, answer the question. A computerized list of Republican donors that PACs have helped organize has now reached 300,000, almost ten times larger than that of the Democrats. Referring to this financial fact, Senator Packwood was quoted in the *New York Times* as saying of the 1982 Senate elections, "The raising of money is no longer a problem."

In the House Administration Committee last year, enthusiasm also waned after Obey-Railsback perished in the Senate. The Obey-Railsback bill had applied only to House candidates (in a fruitless attempt to mollify the Senate). The bill would have restricted PACs to $6,000, instead of the $10,000 which they can now give to a candidate. Candidates themselves would be restricted to no more than $70,000 in PAC funds during a two-year period.

"Reform" is a word that should never appear without quotation marks. One man's "reform" is another man's loophole. With that maxim in mind, supporters and opponents of public financing will now have the leisure to study the implications of changing the current system, to see whether PACs should play a new role.

To plan for the future requires examining the political atmosphere of 1974, when public financing of presidential elections first caught the public's fancy. In searching for zero-base public philosophy on the subject, the appropriate theorem might be from St. Paul's letter to Timothy: "The love of money is the root of all evil." The apostle did not say that money itself was evil, only an excessive attitude toward it.

In mid-1970s' America, public moralizing about the "lessons of Watergate" was intense. Money was identified as the root of the problem by several of the defendants, the rationale expressed thusly: "If only CREEP didn't have all that loose cash lying around, the burglaries, break-ins, and black-bag jobs wouldn't even have been attempted." Fund raising was too efficient, this argument ran, so fund raising must be made less efficient or eliminated altogether.

In the late 1970s, when an outbreak of bad behavior plagued Congress, alcohol was fingered as the villain by congressmen well known and obscure. Sexual escapades of various kinds, bribery and extortion, misfeasance and malfeasance were all laid at the door of Demon Rum. If the logic of Watergate still obtained, the lawmakers should have enacted for themselves a Congressional Volstead Act, mandating strict prohibition for the House and Senate. They did not.

In retrospect, the "problem" of Watergate should never have been defined by its perpetrators. It was easy for all the president's men to point to W. Clement Stone's wallet and suggest that too much money converted them into felons.

I suggest the opposite. The perpetrators of Watergate would have turned into criminals on a budget. The zeal of G. Gordon Liddy, the single-mindedness of H.R. Haldeman, the determination of Charles W. Colson did not obtain from a love of money, but a love of power. Lord Acton, rather than St. Paul, explained their motivations better in 1887: "Power tends to corrupt and absolute power corrupts absolutely."

Public financing treated one symptom, not the cause, of corruption in presidential politics. After Watergate, many members of Congress, well intentioned and civic minded, thought they could cure the moral problems of their fellow politicians. Public financing may be adjudged a success, but only in its most narrow definition. In the 1976 and 1980 elections, no employees of one presidential candidate were caught burglarizing the headquarters of another.

The post-Watergate atmosphere is now seen in perspective. Three of the major paladins for "reform" in the mid-1970s were more or less hoist on their own petards in 1980. Sen. Edward M. Kennedy found after the first few primaries a unique condition for a Kennedy campaign: poverty. Rep. John B. Anderson didn't realize how much the federal election laws buttressed the status quo and were biased against independent candidacies until he decided to buck the system. Rep. Morris K. Udall found his Tuscon district flooded with money from special-interest groups, using various PACs to channel anti-Udall money from out of state as efficiently as irrigation ditches. Udall survived, but not as comfortably as one would expect from the chairman of the House Interior Committee. All three of these men preached the urgency of public financing in 1974.

In the post-Watergate era, the instinct to "do something" swept aside many considerations that might have been heeded at a calmer time. The

First Amendment arguments against the new election laws made in *Buckley* v. *Valeo* contained many merits, but civil libertarians were also swept up in a tide of detergents "to make elections clean again."

The impulse toward public financing as a panacea continues. In Massachusetts recently, a special commission investigating the awarding of public building contracts concluded that the system was riddled with waste and fraud. Favoritism, nepotism, and patronage were placed above quality in the contract process, the commission said in a lengthy, well-written report. As a result millions of dollars of Massachusetts taxpayers' money were lost. The commission's cure-all? Spending more public money to finance the election of the legislature. The idea faces tough sledding on Beacon Hill.

Purity and nobility have often masked the intent of congressional fund raising. Is any potential donor fooled by the nonpartisanly pure and transideologically noble titles of the National Committee for an Effective Congress or the Committee for the Survival of a Free Congress? No, because public disclosure has been the major weapon against fraud. Public disclosure needs to be strengthened more than ever as a stopgap before a rational, acceptable system of public financing can be devised.

The experience with PACs suggests the need for changes, as long as no one thinks the dawn of a new era will come because the changes are called "reforms." Is there an unfair incumbent advantage? Perhaps so, although long-entrenched incumbents defeated in the 1980 elections hardly think so.

Do lobbies, through their PACs, "own" certain members of Congress? The answer is probably yes. But these members are, as the unfortunate experience of Abscam suggests, available at bargain rates. Reducing the funds of PACs won't bring purity.

Some congressmen spend hundreds of thousands of dollars getting elected or reelected. Others slide by on a few hundred dollars. Some members of Congress feel they must buy television time. Others think they must avoid it.

Some candidates receive the help of strong, vibrant party organizations, brimming with enthusiasm and discipline. Some candidates arrive in Washington unsure whether they are Republicans or Democrats. Some states and congressional districts feature periodic contests of sharp, high-profile ideological disputes. Other political jurisdictions change quietly in the middle of the night, with no commotion.

It's all very messy, untidy, inequitable, and possibly unfair. It's also called democracy.

Response by Herbert B. Asher
Department of Political Science
Ohio State University

Mr. Nolan's paper is delightfully cynical. It also, I think, provides some useful advice and correctives to those of us, as academics or would-be reformers, who would like to give advice to the Congress about institutional reform. It certainly is true that reforms have unintended consequences. As I gather from the panel on reforming congressional procedures, it was argued that some of the undesirable consequences of the committee and subcommittee reforms of the 1970s were anticipated and that reformers nevertheless consciously chose to go ahead with them. Perhaps. However, I could make up a lengthy list of political scientists who testified before the House Administration Committee and who advocated congressional reform in other settings, who today would recant, who today would say "mea culpa," who today would regret many of the recommendations that they made in the name of reform because of the major, unintended consequences of their proposals. So I think that part of Mr. Nolan's paper is very well taken. Whenever we talk about and propose reforms, there will undoubtedly be unintended consequences which we

will come to regret. There are very few of us who are so prescient as to be able to anticipate the unintended.

However, I think that Mr. Nolan's paper does a major injustice to the multiple motivations that exist for advocating campaign finance reform, be it public financing of congressional campaigns or be it other kinds of modifications in campaign finance practices. It is not simply a matter of ending corruption. And in fact, the concern with campaign finance reform clearly predates 1972 and the Watergate revelations, although Watergate certainly provided an impetus here. There are many people who are involved in the reform process who do not equate fund raising with corruption, who do not see political action committees as evil, and yet who find the current system to be undesirable in a variety of ways.

Let me talk a little bit from the perspective of a political scientist. One thing that political scientists are concerned about is the recruitment of candidates. Does the political system attract good candidates to run for office? Political scientists are also concerned with accessibility to political decision makers. And we're certainly concerned with competition. Congressmen might not want competition in their districts, but I think most political scientists value the notion of political competition in and of itself. These goals—providing accessibility to the political system, attracting good candidates for office, and generating meaningful political competition—are really what motivate the attempt by many political scientists to reform campaign finance practices. Other people may be out there screaming "corruption" or "We've got to get the PAC money out, PAC people are evil" and all of that. But as one of the congressmen yesterday said: Look at who some of the PACs are, look at who some of the special interests are. In many cases, they are the senior citizens, the school children, the handicapped, etc. In short, in many cases, they are groups upon whom we do bestow substantial legitimacy. Hence, political scientists do not view private money in campaigns as inherently evil; instead they are more concerned with the amounts and especially the distribution of that money across competing candidates and parties.

To give you some understanding of why political scientists are concerned about competition and why we want to make changes in cam-

paign financing practices, let me talk a little about the electoral history of the two congressional districts that are included in the Columbus, Ohio, metropolitan area. The Fifteenth District is represented by Republican Chalmers Wylie, who won reelection in 1980 by a margin of 73 percent to 27 percent; Wylie has represented that district since his first election in 1966. The Twelfth District was represented by Republican Samuel Devine, who was *defeated* for reelection in 1980 by a margin of 53 percent to 47 percent; Devine had represented the district since his first election in 1958. Devine's loss was incredible. He was a twenty-two year incumbent and was the third ranking Republican in the House of Representatives. He was one of the very few Republican incumbents to lose in the GOP year of 1980. How is it that Wylie won and Devine lost?

Let me talk first about Wylie's district, the Fifteenth. The district is not nearly that Republican, but it is impossible to get candidates to challenge Representative Wylie seriously. Between 1970 and 1976, Representative Wylie faced the same Democratic opponent four times. One wondered what would lead a person to run for office against Wiley four consecutive times—whether it was masochism or whatever. The challenger did once break the 35 percent mark in the Watergate year of 1974. But after running four consecutive times, this challenger decided he had had enough. So he was succeeded in 1978 by another Democrat who had no difficulty getting the nomination. And one of the major claims made by this candidate was that he was going to spend practically no money in the contest. He was going to spend only $600. Now this candidate was not a crank. This was actually a person who had had a reasonably distinguished career in public service. But the handwriting was on the wall. He was not going to be able to raise the kind of money needed to run a serious campaign. So he tried to make a virtue out of a liability. This challenger decided not to run again, and thus we had a new Democratic challenger in 1980, this time one with very little political experience, who managed to spend one hundred dollars less than the 1978 candidate.

Now what would happen if we had had public financing of congressional campaigns? Well, one thing, there would have been some competition for the Democratic nomination in the Fifteenth District which might have resulted in stronger, more credible challengers (although the various Democratic

challengers between 1970 and 1980 did have some credentials). As a general statement, to the extent the nomination is attractive, there will be more candidates competing for it, and the nomination would be made more attractive if in fact there were some resources (e.g., public financing) that the nominee could count upon in the general election. Now perhaps there would be other kinds of problems. I could see problems of administration; I could see problems of would-be challengers grabbing their $60,000 public subsidy and spending the campaign somewhere in the Caribbean. Administering public financing would involve substantial bureaucratic intervention as Mr. Nolan's paper discusses, and I think congressmen certainly get upset by that.

One could imagine that public financing would result not only in greater competition in the primary, but also a more serious general election campaign in which, at the very least, the incumbent Representative Wylie would probably be forced to defend some of his votes. The current situation allowed the incumbent to totally ignore his challenger, and of course, the challenger, by not spending more than $500, made it very easy for everybody to ignore him. So if one really thinks, perhaps in a somewhat naive sort of way, that congressional elections and campaigns in general should entail some retrospective judgment about the performance of the incumbent, then that will probably require that the challenger obtain some resources such as public financing.

In the other district in the Columbus area, the Democratic challenger, Robert Shamansky, knocked off the eleven-term Republican incumbent in a district that Ronald Reagan carried by almost twenty points over Jimmy Carter. There were many reasons why Devine lost, and many of those have to do with Devine, his record, and his ability as a campaigner. Devine's percent of the two-party vote throughout the 1970s was consistently lower than Wylie's—in the 50 percent range rather than the 60 percent range. And in 1974 and 1976, he came very close to being defeated. His reelection in 1978 by a margin of 55 percent to 45 percent led many observers to assert that Devine had once again secured his seat and was a likely victor in 1980. In fact, *Congressional Quarterly* classified the Twelfth District in 1980 as "safe Republican," one of the few major errors that *CQ* made in predicting the 1980 House elections.

How did *CQ* and others err so?

The Democratic challenger had one thing going for him. He was able to lend his campaign $90,000 in early October to pay for his media budget. Now if all candidates were able to lend themselves $90,000, then public financing would be unnecessary. But if Representative Shamansky had not had the resources to lend himself, where would the money have come from? He certainly was not attracting the kinds of contributions needed to sustain a major campaign effort. The whole situation was very self-fulfilling: Devine was a shoe-in, according to *Congressional Quarterly* and local observers, so why should one contribute to the Democratic challenger? Had Representative Shamansky not had the financial resources to sink $90,000 into his campaign, then only the presence of public financing could have made the Twelfth District race a serious one, one that would at least minimally allow the challenger to gain some visibility and attention.

In summary, there are multiple reasons why political scientists are concerned with campaign finance reforms. There are the questions of competition, accessibility, the ability to run a serious campaign, and these have normative implications for classical democratic theory. Most political scientists do not view campaign contributions as necessarily evil or corrupting. Having said that, I think it certainly is appropriate to comment upon the increased costs of congressional campaigns, and the increased amounts of PAC money that are going into congressional campaigns, and also to talk about the higher proportion of congressional campaign expenditures that is coming from political action committees. Now there is nothing necessarily wrong or illegal about these developments, although to the extent that one party receives a disproportionate share of campaign contributions, or to the extent that certain candidates receive substantial monies from special-interest groups, questions will be raised about the dominance of money and what this money is buying.

It is ironic in reading both the Jacobson and the Nolan papers how shortsighted the Democratic majority in Congress was between 1977 and 1980 in not approving public financing of congressional campaigns and thereby limiting the role of private money. Many observers, I think, anticipated correctly what was going to happen after FEC rulings were issued that allowed corporations to use their monies to facilitate the establishment of political action committees within the corporate sector. And

we're not only talking, of course, about corporate PACs, but also about the philosophical and ideological groups. It was very clear that there was no reason to expect corporate and industry money to continue to go evenly to the Democrats and Republicans. Democratic candidates may have been getting their share of the business money, but that was because the Democrats were the incumbents. But what would happen when the Democratic party was no longer the majority in Congress or when a powerful Democratic incumbent decided not to seek reelection and his seat became an open one? Would the business money still flow to the Democrats? With the need to buy Democratic access no longer there, one could expect an increasingly higher proportion of the corporate money to go to the GOP. Democratic candidates of course have received the overwhelming proportion of the labor money, but any observer could have told them that it was business and not labor that was the major untapped source of campaign funds.

Hence, the Democratic party missed a golden opportunity in the late 1970s to insure equity in campaign financing in the 1980s by its failure to pass a public financing bill during the Carter administration. The financial situation will get worse for the Democrats before it gets better. Here the Jacobson paper becomes must reading for the Democratic party because it lays out how the party might emulate the GOP in order to become competitive in the financing game. It is clear from the Jacobson paper that the GOP has managed to harness the technology of fund raising with the provisions of the campaign finance laws.

The Jacobson paper has a message of optimism for political scientists and other political observers who are concerned about the fate of the political parties in an era in which the marketing specialists have taken over campaigns and in which the political parties are in disfavor with much of the citizenry. It is possible today, as the Republican party demonstrated in 1980, for a political party to play a meaningful role in the recruitment and election of candidates. This does not mean that the victors will necessarily feel beholden to their party and that the era of responsible parties is just around the corner. But it does mean that one of the major functions that political parties traditionally performed may still be a relevant party activity and therefore contribute to the viability of parties. More importantly, to the extent that parties can support their nominees beyond token financial contributions, to that extent the candidates may be freed from overwhelming reliance on PAC and special-interest donations. Given that public financing of congressional campaigns is not likely to become law in the foreseeable future, it becomes increasingly important that the political party become a buffer between its candidates and the special interests. The current campaign finance laws allow (though they do not encourage) such an outcome if the political parties are flexible and imaginative in adapting to the laws.

Response by Michael J. Malbin
Resident Scholar
American Enterprise Institute for Public Policy Research

Let me start out by saying something about Martin Nolan's paper. I have been a critic of various aspects of campaign finance reform since 1974. Nevertheless, I hate to see criticisms based on straw men. The Nixon White House did not define the nature of the 1974 campaign finance law, and the arguments in favor of limiting PACs in last year's Obey-Railsback bill, as well as those in favor of limiting expenditures, are based on more serious sentiments and analyses than we have been given. I happen to disagree with Obey-Railsback and with limits on expenditures. But I also happen to believe that understanding is deepened by stating arguments clearly, so one can see the concerns on which they are based. Professor Asher has done most of this for us in his comments. Essentially, the sponsors of last year's HR 1 (public financing for congressional elections) were worried about (1) excessively expensive campaigns and (2) excessive PAC influence on campaigns. Political scientists also were concerned about recruitment, as Professor Asher has said.

I agree that campaigns have become expensive, although whether they have become too expensive

cannot be answered without further argument and analysis. I also agree that PACs have grown tremendously since 1974 and that recruitment is an important issue. However, before one leaps to the conclusion that these agreed upon points call for the proposed legislative remedies, let me interject a few caveats.

1) Although the amount of PAC money in elections has grown since 1974, and although business PACs represent the biggest part of that growth, the proportional electoral power of business may be no greater now than in the days before campaign finance reform. I will return to this point later.

2) I have been convinced by Professor Jacobson's earlier writing that spending limits tend to favor incumbents because of the incumbents' advantage in name recognition. I also think that public financing without spending limits favors challengers. Putting public financing together with spending limits in one bill probably would help poorly financed challengers who have little chance of winning, while hurting well-financed challengers. Therefore, while public financing may help recruitment, its overall

impact depends upon the precise nature of the financing provided and on the other legal provisions brought along with the financing.

3) Finally, I believe that any limits on spending, or on total PAC receipts per candidate, would mean more power to those groups whose own financing and organizational sophistication put them in a position to use independent expenditures, which are protected by the First Amendment. Anyone can give a contribution, but independent expenditures favor highly organized, and particularly ideological, groups. Let us be clear about this: Institutional reform limiting the power of some groups will increase the relative power of others. Since I happen to be more concerned about the power of ideological groups than economic ones, I therefore oppose anything that would increase their power by decreasing the role of economic interests. I will return to my reasons for this later, but I wanted to be clear about this before moving on.

And move on I want to do because I think the overall perspective suggested by Mr. Nolan's title is useful, namely, that there is often a big gap in public policy between intentions and actual effects. Let me use Professor Jacobson's theme— the role of party—to illustrate. Jacobson is correct when he says that most members of Congress wanted to make sure they did nothing further to weaken the role of parties. That was the reason Congress favored the two major parties in public funding for presidential elections; it was the reason Congress allowed parties to spend money on behalf of congressional or senatorial candidates; and it was also the reason why, in 1976, Congress decided to raise the party contribution limits for senatorial candidates.

In fact, there were even some political professionals around at the time who predicted correctly that the law would help national party organizations. Eddie Mahe, executive director of the Republican National Committee at the time the law went into effect, was one. Mahe's reasoning, I should point out, was not the same as Jacobson's. He based his position not on coordinated expenditures—after all, the party had always been able to do that, it just hadn't done so. Rather, Mahe based his prediction on two factors: first the Republican National Committee's technology, which Jacobson has mentioned; and, second, his view that the law would make campaigns so complicated for candidates that they would have to come running to the party for advice. Once the candidates came, they then would learn about the other things the party could do for them.

Mahe was right, but not as much as he had expected. The reason had to do with an unintended consequence of the law, a Federal Election Commission ruling (which I believe the language of the law did compel) that all but stifled state and local party grass-roots activity in 1976. Alarmed at this, a panel of political scientists appeared before the House Administration Committee in 1979 to ask for a small amount of public funds for congressional elections that would be channelled through and controlled by state party organizations. Congress made short shrift of that suggestion, but it reacted far more favorably to a proposal put forward jointly by John White, chairman of the Democratic National Committee, and Bill Brock, chairman of the Republican National Committee. Adopted in 1979, that proposal allowed state and local party organizations to raise and spend unlimited amounts of money as long as they were spent on volunteer activities (such as canvassing and handing out literature) and as long as the activities supported a slate of candidates rather than just one. Both parties saw this as an opportunity to exceed the spending limit for presidential candidates in a way that would help the party organization

both by tying slates of candidates together, and by making it politically worthwhile for candidates to stimulate volunteer activity. The Republicans succeeded beyond their wildest expectations—spending about $8 million on these activities in 1980 and using more than eight-hundred thousand volunteers. The Democratic effort, by comparison, was almost nonexistent. The Democratic National Committee was not even able to raise the full $4.5 million it was allowed to spend on President Carter's behalf.

What will be the effect of this on government? Jacobson dismisses the likely effect of party money on congressional behavior by noting that once an individual is elected, there is enough nonparty money around to minimize the deterrent effect of a party threat to cut off funds. I believe Jacobson is correct on the difficulty of using a threat to cut off contributions to affect performance. That is why I have always maintained that people make too much of the supposed connections between campaign contributions from corporations or trade associations and subsequent behavior in office. While interest groups clearly are important to policy, I believe that contributions are a minor source of their influence on postelection behavior. Whatever the member does in office, there will always be interest groups with money on both sides of most issues.

But, while I agree with Jacobson on this point, I think he leaves something out that is very important to understanding the role of the party in Congress. We know from previous studies of legislative voting behavior that even today, when members are notoriously independent, the party remains the best single predictor of a member's vote. This party voting has virtually nothing to do with threats. It stems, first, from the fact that like-minded people tend to join the same party and, second, from the fact that members of Congress tend to socialize among and take their cues from their fellow partisans. What I have noticed among Republicans is that the growing importance of party in campaign finance seems to have helped strengthen the habits of friendly cooperation that later foster more cohesion within Congress. Challengers get to know each other in candidate school, while incumbents work together and use their legislative positions to develop common campaign themes on which they, the challengers, and the presidential candidates can agree. Maximum effectiveness under the law requires cooperation, in other words, and I cannot help

but believe that this will make a subtle difference in the long run.

Does that mean we should expect to see a net gain in party cohesion in Congress? Not necessarily, because other recent factors work in the opposite direction. Here I should like to return to the role of PACs.

As I said earlier, far too much has been made in the press of the substantial increases in PAC money since the campaign finance law was passed. It is true that the absolute amounts have gone up, but the increases have not been nearly as dramatic if one looks at PACs as a percentage of the whole. Moreover, if one focuses specifically on business power in proportional rather than absolute terms, there is no reason to believe that business is playing more of a proportional role now than before 1974, when business money came in the form of large individual contributions, double envelopes, or illegal corporate contributions. This year I would guess that PAC money will be up again, from about $35 million in 1978 to about $55 million or so. When looked at in percentage terms, preliminary figures suggest that PAC money will represent about 19 percent of Senate contributions, up dramatically from 13 percent in 1978, and about 27 percent of House contributions, up only slightly from the 1978 figure of 25 percent.

As I indicated, I think the focus on dollar amounts misstates the real importance of the new developments. The importance of business PAC growth is not that it increases business power but that it nationalizes the process, replacing the local wealthy entrepreneur with national organizations. This results in contributors who pay much more attention to behavior in Washington. This in turn creates counterpressures to the party for those members who are open to such influences—not so much because of threats as because more corporations now find it in their interest to pay people to stay in Washington, track legislation, and engage in other forms of lobbying activities.

Some of this nationalization of politics would have happened anyway. After all, the reason we have seen about one national association opening a Washington office every week over the past decade is not because of campaign finance but because what Washington does increasingly affects people's lives.

But the destruction of the individual entrepreneur—the rich fat cat, if you will—has had another important effect. Before the 1974 contribution limits, these were the people who traditionally gave candidates their startup or seed money. Business organizations never gave seed money and do not now, but individuals in business and in the professions did. Since 1974, it has become much harder for unknown candidates who are not themselves rich to get seed money. This, in turn, magnifies the role of the groups that are willing to get involved in a race before the candidate is well known. Who does give the seed money now? Not business, not labor, and not usually the parties. What is left in this vacuum? The ideological and single-issue groups. This is the fastest growing group of PACs, with total receipts of about 25 percent of all PAC receipts in 1980. And unlike the other PACs, their contributions often represent early money, committed by uncompromising people who back like-minded candidates.

What is the effect of this money on the behavior of members once they are in Congress? Again, to return to Jacobson's point, the threat of losing money in the next election generally means little to a member's behavior once in Congress. Many people elected with ideological money quickly show themselves to be more moderate than expected once they are in office. But as with the role of the party, the long-range effects may be more subtle and indirect. They will grow more from the type of candidates recruited, and the way they are socialized later, than from direct threats. People are recruited by the ideological PACs because they show a propensity to be uncompromising. Once in Congress, these same people get together with like-minded people in their own organizations and caucuses.

Thus, the indirect effects of these PACs run exactly opposite to the indirect effects of the growing financial role of the party. The party tends to reinforce centrism, habits of deliberation and compromise, which I consider to be crucial in a well-functioning legislature, while the ideological PACs foster the opposite. It would be rash to predict which set of pressures will prove the stronger, but I hope that the probable hiatus Nolan predicts for the Ninety-Seventh Congress leads people who propose future change to be aware of the way the indirect effects of their proposals may tip the present balance.

PART IX:
SECOND PLENARY
ADDRESS

SPEAKING OF CONGRESS
by Elizabeth Drew

I can't think of a more appropriate endowment than a Chair in the name of Tip O'Neill. He is a practicing politician in the best sense of the word. For those of us journalists in Washington who have to deal with him, of course, he keeps us on our toes and off our feed with his politically inspired blarney. But he's always helpful, always interesting. And more important, he enjoys politics for what it is at its best, which is a method of honorably transacting the nation's business. And he has a good time at it. That really is what the practice of politics ought to be about, and *is* about when it's practiced by a real pro.

Speaking of Congress, which is my assigned subject, I always try to give serious thought to what I'm going to speak about when I go somewhere, and a few years ago I was caught in a bind. I had to go to Richmond to speak to a ladies' group, and I had a dreadful case of the flu. I really didn't have time to work on the speech as much as I would have liked. I talked to one of my friends and advisors in Washington, and I said, "I am so sick, and I have to go give this speech, what am I going to do?" And he said, "That's all right, dear. You just talk about the things you know best." At that time, I had just lived through Watergate, having written about it for the *New Yorker* and for a book. And then he said, "When you run out of that, just talk about Congress, because Lord knows, there's always plenty to say about Congress." And so I flew down to Richmond, and I had lunch with the ladies who were in charge. Apropos of nothing, the lady who was very clearly in charge said, "We had Senator Ervin here last year, and thank God he didn't talk about Watergate; nobody wants to hear about that anymore." So, stomach sinking and brow perspiring all the more, I turned to her and I asked her a question about something that I usually check out before I go somewhere, but in my sorry state I hadn't gotten around to. I said, "Excuse me, ma'am, could you please tell me who is the congressman from this area?" And she drew herself up and she looked me in the eye and she said, "Mah husband." (Laughter) Well, I lived.

So my subject is Congress. You have been talking for two days now about many congressional processes, procedures, and problems. I was sorry I couldn't get here until last night, but I drifted around the seminars this morning. And it became clear to me that you were dealing with, in general, a very important problem, which is that there are no lasting truths about Congress and congressional procedure. Fortunately, that keeps a lot of us in business. But it also shows what a fluid situation it is. Things change. In the foreign policy seminar, it became quite clear—the particular case was the War Powers Resolution—that often Congress, responding to public opinion or responding to a problem, will attempt to make a correction. It will sometimes overcorrect or correct the wrong problem, and then people will have to come along and fix it. But that's all right. That's politics, that's a democracy, that is the push and pull and tugging and hauling that goes on and ought to go on in a healthy and working democratic system. So some things are working principles that last for quite a while about congressional behavior, but all of them have to fit within a certain context. And believe me, the context is changing fast. So I don't know how long some of these principles that we all have assumed to be true are going to remain true.

Right now, the context is that both parties are adjusting to their dramatically new circumstances. In the Senate, the Republicans are still trying to figure out how to run committees, run staffs. They haven't had to do that for twenty-six years. That's a long time. In fact, there are only three senators who were there the last time the Republicans were in control, and all three of them are Democrats. So it's a whole new experience. The Democrats are getting used to being in the minority. No, they're not getting used to it, but they're trying to adjust to it, calling someone Mr. Chairman who they never dreamed would become a committee chairman and for whom they don't really feel half the reverence they are supposed to display upon public occasions. The Democrats, due to the rather dramatic events of November 1980, are also engaged in a permanent floating seminar on what happened, what does it mean, what do we do, how do we repackage ourselves. The hairshirts, I think, are a little bit long and overly restrictive. I don't think it was quite the calamity that a lot of people think, but I'll get into that in a moment.

So far, of course, in Congress, not that much has happened. The Democrats are getting out of the big offices and the Republicans are getting into them, and things like that are going on. And that's very important to them, I assure you. We've had the nomination hearings, as you know. And I guess the big question is whether Alexander Haig will frighten the Soviets half as much as he frightened the Senate Foreign Relations Committee. (Laughter) As you know, we took a real step in combatting Soviet world-wide aggression by not allowing the Soviet ambassador to go into the garage at the State Department. He had to take the public elevator. I assume they will pull out of Afghanistan tomorrow.

The Republicans are very busy putting in their oars on appointments. Some of them have longer oars than others—Jesse Helms's is particularly long. They are quite delighted with the idea that at long last, they can call up an agency downtown and, if there's anybody there yet, they pay attention. So far it hasn't been very important. It's been things like getting constituents tickets to an Inaugural Ball that they couldn't get into because it was too crowded. But we shall see.

The Democrats, of course, are laying back. And the big question is what will happen when the real business of governing gets going, which it will when Reagan comes up with the domestic program—the centerpiece of what he is going to try to do—his economic package of tax and budget cuts. Then all hell will break loose, and we shall begin to know more about how this is going to work. The Democrats have no thought of putting forth their own agenda. Among other things, they don't have one. And for another, very sensible reason: they know who won the election. They know that it was decisive. They figure: Let Reagan have his chance. If it works, they will not have been standing in the way trying to hold up progress on his approach; it is doesn't work, they will try to contain their sorrow and tell people about it at the next election.

Every four years, this one included, of course, we hear a lot about a "honeymoon," but the situation that obtains after any presidential election is at best a shotgun marriage, and has about the same chances of lasting. It is an alliance of convenience which will last as long as it is convenient for the allies. Congress has an animal instinct about the flows of power. That's one of the truths that I think will hold up no matter what happens in the future. Lyndon Johnson understood this very well. You may remember he won a landslide election in 1964, and he continued to get bill after bill out of a very complaisant Congress. But Congress was beginning to resent the power that Johnson was exerting over it, and it was storing up its resentment. And then one night, in the House of Representatives, Johnson lost a very minor bill having to do with the District of Columbia—and I assure you nothing is more minor to Congress than the District of Columbia. When this happened, he turned to his aides and he said, "Now the whale has shed some blood, and the sharks will move in." And he was right. He never had the same power after that that he had had before. But that was just the overt manifestation of something that had been building. So, while all may seem sweetness and light for a little while here, don't be fooled. It's just a little rite of passage that we go through every four years.

Jimmy Carter, of course, had a shorter alliance of convenience. He won narrowly. He ran behind just about every other Democrat. And again this animal instinct about the flow of power was at work. When he made his first retreat, which was pulling back the tax rebate that he had proposed, this sent the signal to people who would be his allies in Congress that he didn't necessarily stand for what he said he stood for for very long, and that if they yelled enough, he would probably turn around. This is not a very good thing for people in Congress to understand about a president, because they will behave accordingly.

Another example of the Carter congressional problem was the water projects incident. President Carter did a fairly bold thing. He called for the ending of several water projects, mainly in the West, which he felt to be unnecessary. Then Congress passed a bill to restore some of the projects that Carter had cut. Some younger members in the House of Representatives worked very hard to help Carter. They knew the bill would pass, because there was just too much political support for these projects, and too much logrolling that went on. But some younger members said it was time to change this old logrolling politics, and they were going to try to get enough votes so that it would be clear that the president, if he vetoed the bill, would not be overridden. One of the congressmen, Mr. Butler Derrick of South Carolina, had one of these projects in his district. But he was brave enough to stand up and say: Enough is enough; let's support the president on this. And these congressmen got enough votes so that the president would have been upheld had he vetoed the bill. Without so much as a phone call to Representative Derrick and his colleagues, President Carter signed the bill. This sent a very important message to members of Congress, I assure you. One time after that I saw Representative Derrick and I introduced him to someone and said, "This is a congressman who went out on a limb for President Carter until he heard this funny sawing sound behind him." (Laughter) And Butler Derrick said to me, "No, Elizabeth, you've got that wrong. I never heard the saw."

It's a fairly simple axiom: As long as Congress thinks that the president is doing well with the public, he'll do well with the Congress. And so, when you start to see these things change, you will know it is because they feel that it isn't working all that well. That's what makes the test on the economic package so terribly interesting, because of the particular politics involved in the set of questions before the Congress. As you know, the president is going to try to fulfill his campaign pledge to reduce taxes 10 percent a year for three years. I'm not sure how badly this administration wants to win that fight, but they have to act as if they want to win it. And along with that, they will ask for very severe cuts in the budget. Now, all kinds of members of Congress are for a balanced budget and for cutting back on federal fat and waste and so on. They're just not for cutting certain projects that affect their constituencies or the political action committees that have made contributions to them. Which may sound slightly schizophrenic, and it is. This is why it is so hard to cut the budget, why it always has been. There's not a penny in there that some very organized, articulate group, well connected with people in the bureaucracy and with subcommittees on the Hill, doesn't feel is essential to the national security and the fabric of society. I could cut the budget fifty billion dollars right now if I didn't have to go through the political process. So could you. We wouldn't necessarily agree on the list, but we could all find lots of things in there that we don't think make sense. Unfortunately, there is so much disagreement on that that these things stay in there. It's no accident that they're there. Not everybody thinks that they're foolish. The interesting thing will be to see whether President Reagan, given the election, given some of the economic realities, will be able to change this pattern of behavior. And this gets to how Congress reads the election returns.

In politics, what happens is not only what happened but what politicians *think* happened. It gets pretty derivative by the time they get around to gauging their behavior. I happen to think that the election was not a great ideological sweep, a great ideological mandate. This is an objective statement with which several people, including two very important Republican pollsters, agree. And one worked for Mr. Reagan and one worked for many, if not most, of the Republican senators who won. However, it really doesn't much matter what I think or even what these pollsters think, except to the extent that they are informing future clients. It's what Congress thinks. Certain things become truisms, and they become accepted facts even if they aren't, and they begin to determine the behavior of Congress, which tends to deal in mood swings. This current mood swing began a few years ago, when California adopted Proposition 13. The question went out: Do you think property taxes ought to be lowered? And lo and behold, people said yes. *Time* and *Newsweek* yelled "Tax Revolt." The pollsters went out and asked people if they would like taxes cut, and you know what the answer was. And politicians began to behave accordingly. That doesn't mean that there aren't some good reasons, depending on the economic situation, for cutting taxes. But there tends to be a simplistic overreaction to some of these things. Most members of Congress, I think, believe that it was a great ideological sweep. The Democrats are frightened. They're particularly concerned about the new right-wing groups who have learned how to organize, collect money, and bring out the intense vote, the people who care very much about certain kinds of issues. Republicans are pleasantly surprised; but they are also a little frightened of these people. They're frightened that, no matter how orthodox their behavior, someone on the Right is going to get them. Even Ronald Reagan's afraid of them.

If Reagan makes some missteps, and if they are seen as that; if it is believed that what he is doing is highly inequitable; if he offends enough groups who have justifiable claims—then all bets are off. But that's the interesting test. Of course he won, and he won decisively, but his mandate was really not as great as Johnson's in 1964 or Nixon's in 1972. It was not as great as Eisenhower's in either 1952 or 1956. Yes, it's true that nine Democratic senators, several of them liberals, lost. It's also true that ten Democratic senators, several of them liberals, won. But this fact didn't fit the thesis of a great ideological sweep, so people just put it aside. It is also a fact that every Democrat who lost in the Senate, except for Herman Talmadge—who, as we all know, had certain problems of his own—ran ahead of Jimmy Carter. Frank Church lost 49 percent to 50 percent in the state of Idaho; Carter carried 25 percent of that vote. It's pretty hard for anybody to overcome that much of a tide. I believe that several—not all, but several—of the Democrats who lost would not have lost had it not been for what was going on at the head of the ticket. Several of the things that were happening at the head of the ticket were not ideological, either. Jimmy Carter didn't know how to explain what it was that he was trying to do. Sometimes it was apparent he didn't know what it was he was trying to do. There were economic circumstances. There were Reagan's particular talents as a media candidate. These things are not ideological. They are facts. They are facts that affected the election. And there are other facts that will affect other elections. The Democrats simply got more votes in the congressional elections than the Republicans did. But none of that much matters. They are scared. A congressional aide said to me that Congress is often one step behind public opinion and twice as enthusiastic. And I think that that's probably an axiom worth keeping in mind. As a matter of fact, the budget balancing fever began with the Democrats some time ago. One of the many budgets that Carter submitted to Congress last year was in balance on paper. Sixty billion dollars later it's not, of course. But this is not a new idea invented by the Republican party.

The question is: Can Reagan succeed where no one else has been able to in this field? I don't rule out that he can. I think it will depend on a number of things. If he moves soon, the shock effect on Congress—if it continues to feel that the public is behind the president—will break through some of the traditions that have led us to the sort of budget and the sort of things that go on that maybe could use a little weeding out. I think this is one place where the Democrats blew it a bit. An awful lot of smart people in the Democratic party have known all along that the budget needed weeding out. Having had a period of getting things on the books, they weren't on the books very long before the Nixon people came along and tried to get them. And then the Democrats got in a defensive position about these programs, and they were so busy defending them that they couldn't put the intellectual work into seeing which ones worked and which ones didn't. Then along came the Carter administration with its own form of intellectual confusion. In any event, the Democrats, I think, might be willing to go along with some of this, and I think that the important thing would be for people not to fight every fight, because then not only will they not win; they will not make any sense, either.

But the Republicans have things in their own districts that they want. When it gets to the tax proposals—I have found very few Republicans on Capitol Hill who are crazy about the Kemp-Roth idea. They've had to use some fairly fanciful arithmetic all through the campaign, and even recently in the testimony before Congress, to explain how it is that they can cut taxes so deep, even given budget cuts that may be unrealistically severe, and still leave enough money for increases in defense spending. How is that all going to work? "With mirrors," is what John Anderson said in the campaign, and he may have been close to the truth. A lot of Republican economists, including the chairman of the Federal Reserve Board, think it's a rather fanciful idea. So we'll wait and see whether Mr. Arthur Laffer's curve becomes engraved on the marble of the Treasury Building or goes back to a California hot tub whence many think it came in the first place.

But Congress, especially the Democrats in the House of Representatives, will essentially be in a form of reacting, because Congress is a reactive institution. It's very difficult for Congress to initiate important actions. It's not impossible, as has been shown over and over again, but it is difficult. There are too many interests represented and very little that can draw them together in a cohesive pattern. I don't think it's true, however—though it is fashionable to say so—that only the Republicans have new ideas. I think that there are a lot of new ideas in the Democratic party. But the Republicans had a lot of years to wander in the wilderness, so they came up with some ideas. And they've got the microphones now. They will control the agenda, at least for a while.

Other problems, of course, are the institutional changes that have taken place in Congress. If Lyndon Johnson and Sam Rayburn were to come back and try to run things the way they used to, they'd be told to get lost. It doesn't work that way anymore, and it can't work that way anymore. I'm not sure this is something that goes in phases. We'll have to tune in in about fifteen or twenty years—it will take that long to see. There is more and more of a call for leadership again, because it's very hard on the individual members not to have leadership, but they don't really want it. And so there's another form of schizophrenia that goes on there. But, more and more, members of Congress are self-starters. They package themselves—I hate the term, but that's exactly what they do. They raise their own money. Even with the Republican party giving more to its congressional candidates, they are still pretty much on their own. They have to raise a great deal of money, which I think is getting to the point of obscenity. They have to spend a great deal of time doing that. They have to answer to the political action committees. The demands on them by their constituents are all the greater. And party discipline is very, very difficult to enforce under circumstances like that. The Democrats have a majority in the House, but only a fifty-one-vote majority. That means, of course, that you can only lose twenty-six votes in order to break even, and in the last Congress they used to figure they would lose more than that on most votes.

I think that the Congress, and particularly the House of Representatives, for some of the reasons I've stated, has become more a caucus of caucuses than a House of Representatives. You have an eastern caucus, a western caucus, a steel caucus, a coal caucus, a this caucus, a that caucus. This represents the splinterization of our politics that's been going on and getting deeper. And I really don't see a way out, as long as we stick with the financing system that we now have. Now, I heard a polite but strong argument going on in the panel on financing congressional races. Without giving my opinion as to what ought to happen, I'd just say that as long as the current system keeps up, you can forget about having any real party system, and you can also assume that the things that have made it very hard to get coherent policy on such matters as energy or budgetary matters are going to continue, because you have too many people too dependent on the diverse interests in this country.

It used to be that at the end of each session, the leaders would very proudly put out a list called the "legislative box score," and they would talk about all the bills they passed. I think another thing that we can begin to think about is that it's not necessarily true that the more bills Congress passes, the more good it does for the country. The growth of government leads to more legislating, which leads to the growth of government. I think it's gotten out of hand, and it is part and parcel of the whole breakdown that has gone on of the committee system. The old tyrants, who used to run the committees on the seniority basis and on the basis of keeping the young-sters in their place, were unfair, and there were many things wrong with that system. A lot of us yelled and screamed and said we needed a change. We wanted democratization of the committee system, and we've gotten it. But now there's much less control over what comes to the floors, and there's a lot of silly legislating that goes on. The leaders know this. If you talk to thoughtful people in Congress, they know it. No one knows what to do about it. I don't know how we would measure this, but Congress is more reactive to today's headlines. More often, I think, you see members of the Congress on the floor—it's a little harder in the House because of the rules, but certainly in the Senate—jumping up and offering an amendment to cut off aid to this, or cut off some country or some group, because of some outrage they've read about that morning in the *Washington Post*. There's a great deal of that. Of course, some of the new Republicans in the Senate haven't been much heard from yet, but believe you me, they will. And they're a different breed. They haven't grown up in the legislative system. A lot of them have never been in politics before.

Now I think the citizen-legislator is an okay idea, but you began in the last Senate to have a small body within the Republican party in the Senate who really had no use for the old ideas of comity, of making the thing work. And now there are more of them. And I think that, next to Tip O'Neill, Howard Baker will have the second largest headache in Washington before the year is out. It's going to be very hard, I think, to keep that under control. They're being good boys now, they're new, they're finding their way around. They are also going along with the idea that the president should be allowed to deal with his economic program first. But they've got a lot of ideas, and some of them are real corkers, believe me. They're going to be bringing them to the Senate, in particular, before very long, and watch out.

A couple of general points about Congress in terms of what it is like for the human beings who inhabit it. I think it's true that we have to understand that these people are human, with human limitations of character, of spirit, and also with the interestingness of human nature. One thing that is quite clear is that it is less fun to be in politics and to be in Congress than it used to be. There are good reasons for this. I'm not saying we should feel sorry for these people, because I have noticed that their capacity for self-pity is adequate. But most of them are underpaid; I believe they should have pay raises. I think that the extent to which this issue is demagogued—and that's what it is—is a detriment to the national interest because we're asking them to preside over a $600 billion budget, we're asking them to make life and death decisions. We need the best people we can get in there. And it's no accident that a majority of the Senate are millionaires, because it's very hard to be at a certain age, having children to put through school, having to maintain homes in two cities, to lead that kind of a life for very long. I think it's really quite foolish cost saving. The demands on them are growing all the time. Recently, I decided that it would be very interesting to follow one senator, just to see what he did every day. It began as a rather small *New Yorker* piece and grew into a book. I was aware that senators were busy, because of all the times I'd gone to Capitol Hill and found a senator had forgotten our appointment and was off somewhere else, and some aide would be very busy apologizing. The senator would have to go to the floor to vote and he would be six constituents behind and a subcommittee meeting would suddenly be called. It's unbelievable.

So I spent ten days trailing Sen. John Culver of Iowa, and it was beyond anything that I had imagined. Every constituent who comes to town feels he has a right to see his senator or representative, and they try to oblige them, and that takes time. Usually a senator has to be in three subcommittee meetings at the same time. He is probably meeting with people in the executive branch who want something or other done, with some interest group that wants something or other done or undone. Then he was to race over to the floor and try to understand what it is they are voting on. With these changes have come more roll call votes, and with more roll call votes, senators have even more difficulty in understanding what it is they are saying and casting a vote on. It's almost impossible. It's brutal. At the end of the ten days, I turned to Senator Culver and I said, "I don't know about you, Senator, but I'm not running for reelection." He did, and he's no longer with us. I'm not quite sure what the moral of the story is, although I do believe that Culver's was one of the defeats that we can attribute to Jimmy Carter, because it was close enough.

There is an art to being a good legislator, and that's something else that I wanted to show. It's a wonderful art form and it takes a certain kind of savvy and knowledge to know how to make your moves, which moves to make, to pick your issues—believe me, you just can't wander in there and be good at it. To know how to work your colleagues, to engage in what I would call the purposeful conviviality of Capitol Hill, to spend just enough time in the gym to make the right kinds of friendships, to know when to offer an amendment, which amendment to offer, when to speak—more important, when to shut up— and how to get things done. It's a high art. It's terribly interesting to watch these people try to do it.

Which brings me back to where I began, which is that this event is in honor of someone who is a high practitioner of that art. And believe me, we need all the good practitioners we can get, because there's an enormous amount at stake. I still think Congress is the most accessible and responsive branch. In some places they can overdo the responsiveness, but there they are.

I'll close with one of my favorite stories about politics, which is told by one of my favorite practitioners of politics, and that's good old Russell Long, who may no longer be chairman of the Senate Finance Committee but you can't tell him that. He'll be quite busy. In any event, when the question of reform of ethics came up in the Senate, Russell Long told me a story. It was about his uncle, the famous Earl Long, who's my favorite of that whole fascinating tribe. Earl had become governor of Louisiana and he was very close to Russell, whose father, of course, was Huey, who had been killed. And Russell Long was in college in Louisiana and he went to his Uncle Earl one day, and he said, "Uncle Earl, I've got a problem." And Uncle Earl said, "What's that?" Russell said, "I have to take part in a debate and I need your help." Earl said, "What's the question?" Russell said, "The question is: 'Should you use ethics in politics?'" Uncle Earl said, "Well, what side do you have to take?" "I have to take the pro." So Uncle Earl said, "Well, you stand up there, son, and you just say: 'Of course, you should use ethics in politics. You should use everything you can get your hands on.'" (Laughter)

There's a point to that, and the real point—which is where I began and which was one of the reasons for writing the *Senator* book, and one of the reasons for my own particular fascination with the political practitioners— is that this country can't work without the politicians. They hold it together politically. They're our mediators. We have a lot of conflicting interests in this country. Those interests are getting stronger, more organized, wealthier, more determined. This fact is going to have its impact on incumbents. I think a lot of what happened in the 1980 election was motivated by anti-incumbency feelings, and I think that's going to affect presidents and members of Congress in the future. There are more and more demands. And it is only the politicians, in the end, who can mediate among these conflicting demands. Either we have to have a monarchy, if that's our choice, or we have to have anarchy and shoot it out, or we have to have mediation by the politicians. We need them very badly. In honoring Tip O'Neill and in talking, as you have been for these few days, about the democratic process, you are furthering it, and I honor you for that. Thank you.